D1712779

Management Fundamentals

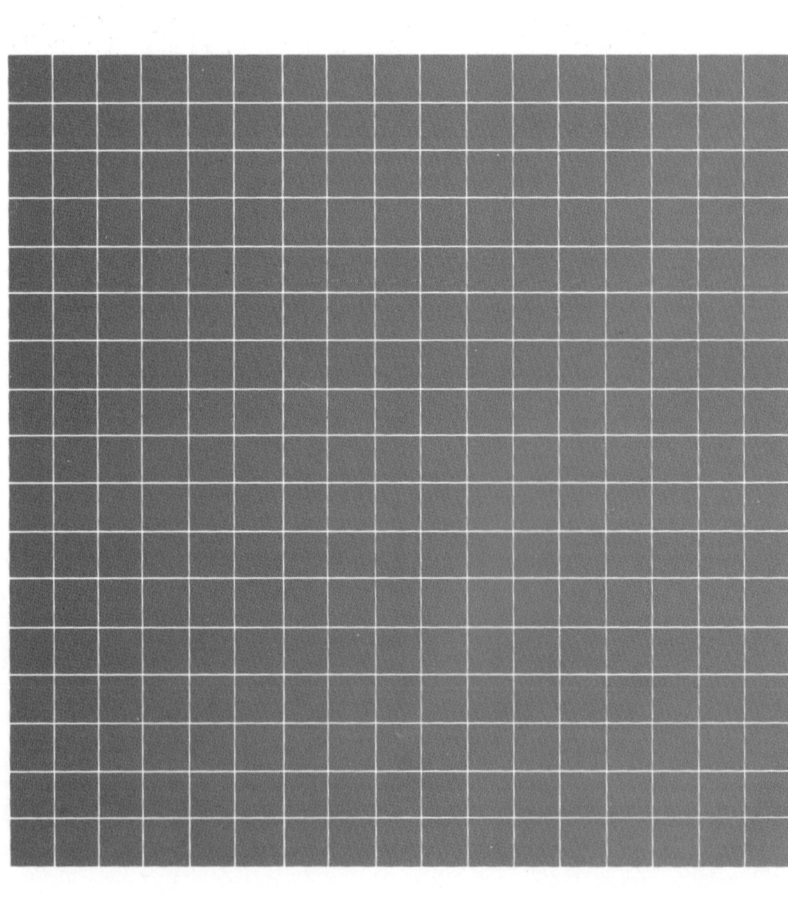

Richard M. Hodgetts
Florida International
University

Management Fundamentals

The Dryden Press
Hinsdale, Illinois

Library of Congress Catalog Card Number: 80-65800
ISBN: 003-058104-4

Printed in the United States of America
012 987654321

Acquisitions Editor/Anita Constant
Developmental Editor/Anne Boynton-Trigg
Project Editor/Bernice Gordon

Art Director/Stephen Rapley
Designer/James Buddenbaum
Production Manager/Peter Coveney
Copy Editor/Wanda Giles
Cartoon Researcher/Jo-Anne Naples

Supplementary cases at the back of the text are adapted from Richard M. Hodgetts and Henry H. Albers, *Incidents on the Basic Concepts of Management* (New York: John Wiley & Sons, 1972). Adapted by permission.

To John F. Mee
Teacher, Author, Mentor, Friend

The Dryden Press Series in Management

Altman and Hodgetts
Readings in Organizational Behavior

Bedeian
Organizations: Theory and Analysis

Byars and Rue
Personnel Management: Concepts and Applications

Duncan
Essentials of Management, 2nd Edition

Gaither
Production and Operations Management: A Problem-Solving and Decision-Making Approach

Gatza, Milutinovich, and Boseman
Decision Making in Administration: Text, Critical Incidents, and Cases

Gellerman
The Management of Human Resources

Glueck
Management, 2nd Edition

Glueck
Management Essentials

Glueck, Jauch, and Coltrin
The Managerial Experience: Cases, Exercises, and Readings, 2nd Edition

Grad, Glans, Holstein, Meyers, and Schmidt
Management Systems: A Guide to the Study and Design of Information Systems, 2nd Edition

Greenlaw
Readings to Accompany Modern Personnel Management

Greenlaw and Biggs
Modern Personnel Management

Hand and Hollingsworth
Practical Readings in Small Business Management

Harbaugh, Byars, and Rue
Readings and Cases in Personnel Management

Higgins
Organizational Policy and Strategic Management: Text and Cases

Hodgetts
The Business Enterprise: Social Challenge, Social Response

Hodgetts
Management Fundamentals

Hodgetts
Management: Theory, Process, and Practice, 2nd Edition

Hodgetts
Modern Human Relations

Hodgetts and Altman
Organizational Behavior

Holley and Jennings
The Labor Relations Process

Hollingsworth and Hand
A Guide to Small Business Management: Text and Cases

Huseman, Lahiff, and Hatfield
Business Communication: Strategies and Skills

Huseman, Lahiff, and Hatfield
Readings in Business Communication

Karmel
Point and Counterpoint in Organizational Behavior

Lindauer
Communicating in Business, 2nd Edition

McFarlan, Nolan, and Norton
Information Systems Administration

Mayerson
Shoptalk: Foundations of Managerial Communication

Miner
The Challenge of Managing

Miner
Theories of Organizational Behavior

Naumes and Paine
Cases for Organizational Strategy and Policy, 2nd Edition

Paine and Naumes
Organizational Strategy and Policy, 2nd Edition

Penrose
Exercises in Business Communication

Robinson
International Business Management, 2nd Edition

Smith
Management Systems: Analysis and Applications

Viola
Organizations in a Changing Society: Administration and Human Values

Preface

Everything today is in a constant state of change. On the international scene we negotiate for precious oil supplies while offering our goods, services, and technology in exchange. At home the government fights inflation and sluggishness in the economy while individual organizations seek to promote their successful product lines and prune or eliminate their unsuccessful ones. Within the organization, managers seek to attain their objectives in the most efficient ways possible. In all these instances—international, national, and organizational—success depends on how well the respective managers can carry out their task of getting things done through others. And this is the primary objective of every manager.

In most cases, people learn to be managers through on-the-job experience. Unfortunately, this is not the ideal way to deveiop managerial skills because it is both time-consuming and unsystematic. The best way to learn management is by first studying the subject and then applying this knowledge on the job.

The purpose of this book is to introduce you to the field of management. In writing it, I have assumed that you are either a newcomer to the field or a beginning manager with little, if any, training in the area. The text coverage begins with consideration of the nature of management. What is management all about? Then the focus of attention is directed toward the manager's job. What do managers do? Finally comes a look at the changing field of management and your place in it.

Is a management career for you? When you have finished reading this book, you will know what management is all about and how managers go about getting things done through others. You will also have an appreciation for both the challenges and opportunities that await you should you choose a career in this field.

Distinguishing Features

In this book I have attempted to present basic management concepts in an interesting, easy-to-read style. In doing so, I have used the following special features which distinguish the book from others in the field.

Organization This text is organized into eight major parts. Part 1 examines the nature of management. In this part, the evolution of management and the modern manager's job is studied. Here you will learn how modern management emerged and how the managers of today carry out their work. Parts 2 through 6 are devoted to an analysis of the management process. In these parts the major functions of management—planning, organizing, staffing, directing, and controlling—will be studied. You will learn what each of these functions consists of and how the modern manager goes about carrying them out. Part 7 deals with management and you. It examines the changing world of management, focusing especially on values, ethics, and social responsibility. Additionally, attention is devoted to management as a career. Part 8 presents supplementary cases. This organizational arrangement is designed to introduce you to where management has been (Part 1), where it is (Parts 2 through 6), and what your role in it can be (Part 7). It also gives you the opportunity to analyze cases in each of the functional areas (Part 8).

A large number of illustrations are used in this book to highlight important concepts and to present them in an easy-to-read way. Additionally, comments have been placed in the margins throughout the book to aid in both understanding and reviewing the material.

At the beginning of each chapter, objectives are set forth. The goals tell what you will be learning in the chapter. At the end of the chapter are review and study questions. These are tied back to the goals so that you can measure your own progress and go back and read any parts that you did not sufficiently understand.

There is also at least one story within the chapter and two short cases at the end of every chapter. The stories are used to illustrate actual examples of ideas discussed in the chapter. The cases are designed to provide you with an opportunity to apply ideas and concepts which have been studied in the chapter, thereby reinforcing your understanding of them.

There are also supplementary cases at the back of the book, written by Dr. Henry Albers and me. They are designed to reinforce the marketing concepts presented in each of the major sections of the book.

Finally, at the end of the text there is a glossary of terms. This is a comprehensive glossary that will provide you with definitions or explanations of the most important topics contained in the book.

Supplements and Teaching Aids The following supplements and teaching aids have been designed to accompany this book:

Student Study Guide—Contains fill-in, true-false, and multiple choice questions, as well as work projects for each chapter. The study guide is designed to review and expand the important concepts in each chapter.

Teachers' Manual—Contains a synopsis of the goals and materials in each chapter, as well as suggestions for teaching the chapter. In addition, there are answers to the review and study questions at the end of each chapter and a large pool of true-false and multiple choice questions for testing purposes.

Acknowledgments Many individuals have played decisive roles in helping me write this book. However, I accept full responsibility for all errors of omission and commission. In particular, I would like to thank Leonardo Rodriguez, Dean of the School of Business and Organizational Sciences of Florida International University, Steven Altman, Associate Vice-President of Academic Affairs at Florida International University, and Dr. Henry Albers of the School of Petroleum and Mines, Dhahran, Saudi Arabia. I would also like to thank those who have read, reviewed, and commented on portions of the text, including Barbara G. Arnold, West Virginia University; Stephen C. Branz,

Triton College; Gary Cameron, Northwest Missouri State University; Frank C. Grella, University of Hartford; David D. Gruennert, Northeast Missouri State University; Joseph Platts, Miami-Dade Community College; John E. Seitz, Oakton Community College; and William F. Wright, Mount Hood Community College.

Thanks also go to John C. Neifert at the W. B. Saunders Company, who initiated this project, and to Anita Constant, Anne Boyton-Trigg, and Bernice Gordon at Dryden Press, who saw it through to completion. Finally, thanks go to Ruth Chapman, Carol Tollefsen, and Irene Young for their assistance in typing the manuscript.

Richard M. Hodgetts
Miami, Florida
April 1980

Contents

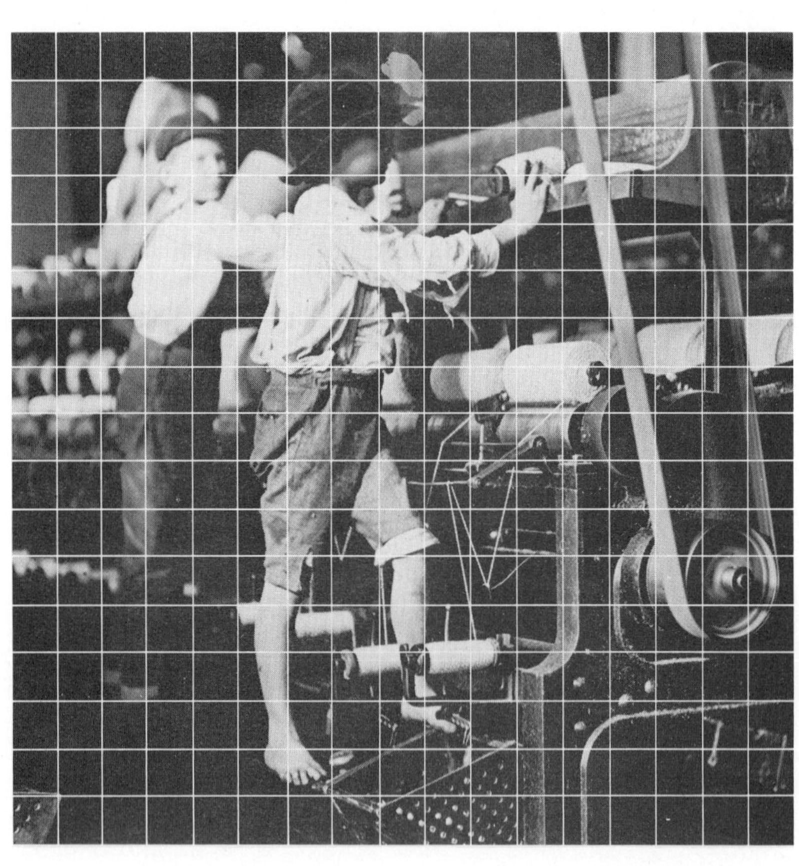

Part One

The Nature of Management

The overall purpose of this book is to introduce you to the field of management. What does the term *management* mean? What do people called managers actually do? How do they carry out their functions? To answer these kinds of questions, this book divides the manager's job into its component parts and then systematically analyzes each of them.

Before that point, however, we need to examine the nature of management. This is the objective of Part 1. Two important aspects warrant our consideration. The first relates to the evolution of management. How did modern management evolve? How did we get to where we are? A grasp of the historical past helps us understand where the field is currently and where it will be going during the 1980s. The second aspect is the nature of the manager's job. What do managers actually do? To answer this question we will study the types of managers found in modern organizations, the skills they use, and the roles they play.

Chapter 1

The Evolution of Management

Objectives of the Chapter

The World Trade Center in New York City is an impressive sight. So are the pyramids near Cairo. But while the former was built in far less time than the latter, the management principles and practices used were basically the same. In fact, many of the procedures and activities employed by modern managers in getting things done were practiced by administrators hundreds of years ago. This is not to say, of course, that things have remained unchanged. Today we know a lot more about effective management than did people a hundred years ago or even twenty-five years ago.

In studying management, however, it is hard to really know where the field is or where it is heading without knowing where it has been. In the first chapter, therefore, we are going to examine the history of management thought beginning with the ancient Egyptians and coming up to the present day.

When you have finished reading this chapter, you should be able to:

1. Define the term *management.*
2. Explain the following statement: The Egyptians and the Romans knew quite a bit about effective management practices.
3. Describe the effect of the Industrial Revolution on the practice of management.
4. Describe the contributions of the scientific managers to the field of management.
5. Discuss the typical functions and principles practiced by many modern managers.
6. Describe the contributions of the early behavioral researchers who conducted the Hawthorne studies.
7. Outline the steps in the scientific method.
8. Define what is meant by the term *situational,* or *contingency, management* and explain why the modern manager likes this approach so much.

What Is Management?

Management is the process of getting things done through people. When one stops to think about this process, it becomes obvious that a manager relies on others to help out in accomplishing objectives.

Many people in modern organizations are very good at what they do. However, they are *not* managers. They find it very difficult to rely on others. They prefer to do things themselves, believing that if you don't do it yourself, it won't get done. An effective manager has to outgrow this belief. The following case illustrates this point.

Barney Wilson was the number one salesperson at the Wilamott Corporation. His sales were almost twice those of any other salesperson. Six months ago Bamey's boss, Mildred Chadron, decided to take early retirement. Mildred and her boss talked about her replacement. The company's policy of promoting from within convinced them that they should promote one of the salespeople. Since Barney was their best salesperson, they made him the offer. To their surprise, he accepted. It was quite a salary cut for him, since he had been working on commission. Nevertheless, he was delighted with the promotion and started his new job three months ago.

Since then things have been going very badly in Barney's department. In particular it has become obvious that although he is good at selling products to customers, Barney does not know how to manage. He delegates very little authority, does not spend enough time talking to the salespeople or office staff about their jobs, and seems to be in a world of his own. His boss summed it up this way: "Barney is used to being on his own. He is a salesman. However, he is not a manager. We made a mistake in assuming that someone who can sell well can also manage well."

Yesterday the boss asked Barney if he would consider going back to his old job. Barney said that he would. "I thought I'd like working with people," he said. "However, I find that I still prefer to do most things myself and not have to rely on others. I think this is a good approach if you want to be an effective salesperson, but it's not very good for being an office manager. I'd like to go back to doing what I'm best at."

Barney is an important asset to the corporation. However, he is not a management type. He has trouble working with and through others.

▪ Management involves working with people.

In this chapter we are going to examine what management is all about by studying its evolution. How did we get to where we are today, and what factors are currently of major importance to management? We will begin our study with management in antiquity and work our way up to modern times. As we do so, we will see that management involves *working with people.* This was as true for the Egyptians as it is for today's managers.

Management in Antiquity

There are many illustrations of effective management practices in early civilizations. Some relate directly to accomplishing a particular project, such as building

"There are plenty of jobs around. People just don't want to work."

a pyramid. Others are more administrative in nature, such as dealing with bureaucratic red tape. The following provides an example of each.

The Egyptians—Master Builders

One of the seven wonders of the world is the Egyptian pyramids, the most famous of which is the Great Pyramid. (See Figure 1.1.) Unfortunately, its technical characteristics are often allowed to overshadow its management significance. From an engineering standpoint, the Great Pyramid is a work of genius. It is almost perfectly square, and it covers an area slightly over thirteen acres. It stands approximately 147 meters high. The sides rise at an angle of 51°52′ and are accurately oriented to the four cardinal points. In all, approximately 2.3 million blocks, each weighing an average of 2.5 tons, were used. Modern engineers have calculated that the inside of the Great Pyramid is so vast that the Cathedral of Florence, the Cathedral of Milan, St. Paul's Cathedral in London, Westminster Abbey, and St. Peter's Cathedral in Rome could all be put inside it.

This is the physical-engineering side of the picture. But how did the Egyptians actually get the blocks to the site and put them in place? They began the process by cutting the stones at nearby quarries, numbering them, and transporting them down-river during the rainy season. From here they dragged the blocks to the site of the Great Pyramid. Then, using a series of weight arms and other labor-saving devices,

Figure 1.1
The Great Pyramid
Source: Photo by Frank Siteman, Stock, Boston.

they moved the blocks from one level of the pyramid to the next and put them into place.

The management expertise required for this project was greater than any humanity had ever before required. For example, there had to be an overall plan for the pyramid's construction, and the number of blocks had to be determined and cut to specifications before being transported downriver. Then the 100,000-man work force had to be assembled, the jobs defined, the lines of authority and responsibility identified, and a work plan drawn up. This was no quick job; the entire project took twenty years. How did the managerial challenges facing the pyramid managers differ from those confronting the modern manager who is responsible for constructing a tall office building or a dam? Certainly there are faster means of communication today, and the manager has better equipment and machinery than did the pyramid managers. However, the basic challenges are the same, and the administrative practices and principles that are used by today's construction managers are vitually identical to those employed by the pyramid managers.

■ The Egyptians used effective management practices.

The Romans—and Bureaucracy

Many of the modern manager's problems are related not as much to building things as to simply managing overall operations. Yet many organizations seem to have giant bureaucracies that stymie even the most effective executive. When bureaucratic inefficiencies are very great, modern administrators commonly try some kind of reorganization.

■ Diocletian reorganized the empire.

This approach to dealing with bureaucracy is not new. In 284 AD the Roman emperor Diocletian found that his empire was simply unmanageable in its existing form. There were far too many people and matters of importance for the emperor to handle personally. He therefore abandoned the old structure and devised a new one with more levels in the hierarchy and less authority given to anyone but himself. Diocletian did this by first breaking the empire into a hundred provinces and grouping the provinces into thirteen dioceses. Then he placed the dioceses into four major geographical divisions. Diocletian kept one of these divisions for himself and appointed three other people to manage the others. In this way he increased the distance between himself and the province governors. He also took military control out of their hands and left them with civil authority only. This reorganization streamlined the empire's bureaucracy and, at least for a time, gave the emperor greater and more effective control over his subjects.

Today, in overly bureaucratic organizations, top managers do the same thing. They redefine objectives, rearrange departments, move people up or down the hierarchy, and increase overall efficiency. Like the Romans, modern managers delegate a lot of authority down the line. But they do so in such a way that no one has too much of it. In this way, the people at the top maintain strong control over operations.

The Industrial Revolution

From the time of the Roman Empire through the Middle Ages and well into the eighteenth century, many civilizations rose and fell. And during all this time much of what people knew about managing organizations was the result of personal experience. However, during the late 1700s and early 1800s the Industrial Revolution occurred. This revolution permanently changed the field of management.

■ Power was now used to drive machinery.

With industrialism, people were able to harness power and use it to drive machinery. This was quite a change in the production process. For example, prior to this time a family with an entrepreneurial spirit could pool its resources, buy a spinning wheel, and begin turning out textiles. These materials would be sold at the local fair for whatever they would bring. With industrialism, however, came power-driven machinery, and the entire production process changed. In particular, the family business operation was seriously threatened for two reasons:

1. The family was unable to produce as much output at as low a price as those who were using power-driven machines.
2. It did not have the money to buy these expensive machines.

Family entrepreneurs were thus pushed out of those industries where high production and low cost were important factors. In their place came capitalists who had the money both to buy the machinery and to build the factories for housing it.

Machines were now placed under one roof, and the employees came to a central location to work. This resulted in the emergence of the factory system.

The Factory System

The factory system was different from anything that preceded it. In particular, management now had to deal with a large number of workers. This presented a major challenge, since most managers did not really know how to manage large groups of workers. In fact, these managers were really interested in one thing only: How could the workers and machines be brought together in such a way as to increase overall output and profits?

▪ The emphasis was on efficiency.

In an effort to answer this question, the early factory managers turned their attention to streamlining operations, eliminating waste, and trying to motivate workers (with money) to increase their output. These managers' major interest was with the technical side of the job. By learning exactly how fast a machine could be run or how quickly a worker could feed material into the machine, they hoped to determine maximum output. Then they wanted to unite the worker and the machine in such a way that both were operating harmoniously, each an extension of the other.

▪ Time and motion study was used.

One of the areas of particular interest to these early managers was *time and motion study,* which has four basic parts. First is an analysis of each job, which involves examining the basic components of the work. Next is the identification of how long it should take to carry out each phase of the job. At this point the time and motion study expert attempts to find shortcuts so that the time or motions involved in doing the work are reduced. At the same time the individual tries to identify the best type of person to do this job. For example, time and motion analysts may ask: How tall should the individual be? How strong? How fast will the person have to work? How much physical endurance will be needed? In this way time and motion studies blend the job and the individual.

▪ People were secondary to work.

As can be seen, the factory system was characterized by an overriding concern for the *management of work.* People played a secondary role, viewed more as factors of production than as human beings. Their primary functions were to increase output, cooperate with management in getting things done, and have faith that the company would reward them properly. These ideas are quite outmoded today. But they were demanded by management and accepted by the workers during the factory system.

•

Scientific Management

Most of the time and motion study experts who dominated the thinking of this time period were mechanical engineers by training. During the great industrial expansion in America, in particular from 1865 to 1925, these people could be found in virtually every factory. And while their first interest was not the management of people, they did open some very important doors to the field of modern management. The most important of these engineers was Frederick W. Taylor.

Frederick W. Taylor

Frederick W. Taylor, pictured in Figure 1.2, is popularly known as the *father of scientific management.* This title is more a result of the fame he acquired through his writing and talks on scientific management than of his actual contributions to the area. In addition to writing two very popular books on the subject of scientific management, Taylor conducted important time and motion study research. His most famous study was the pig-iron experiment conducted at the Bethlehem Steel Company.

The Task Concept. Taylor and his associates noticed that the average laborer at Bethlehem Steel could load 12.5 long tons (2,200 pounds per long ton) of pig iron a day. The worker would pick up the 92-pound ingot, carry it up a ramp, and drop it into an open railroad car. After carefully studying the job, Taylor began devising a way of loading more pig iron. He did this by carefully setting forth how the individual should pick up the pig iron and carry it, the number of steps to be taken in going up and down the ramp, and how fast to move during the entire process. The breaking down of the job into these carefully designed steps was known as the *task concept.* This concept was the most important single element in scientific management. Taylor described it as follows:

■ The task concept was important.

The work of every workman is fully planned out by the management at least one day in advance, and each man receives in most cases complete written instructions, describing in detail the task which he is to accomplish, as well as the means to be used in doing the work. And the work planned in advance this way constitutes a task which is to be solved . . . not by the workman alone, but in almost all cases by the joint effort of the workman and the management. This task specifies not only what is to be done but how it is to be done and the exact time allowed for doing it.[1]

Using the task concept, Taylor and his lieutenants determined that a worker should be able to load 47 long tons of pig iron a day. Choosing one of the workers, to whom he gave the pseudonym *Schmidt,* Taylor carefully instructed him on how to do the job. The next day Schmidt followed these instructions to the letter and managed to load 47.5 long tons!

■ Pay was tied to output.

Incentive Payment Plan. For his efforts, Schmidt's daily pay was raised from $1.15 to $1.85. This rate was determined by a special wage incentive plan devised by Taylor. He believed, as did most scientific managers, that money was the prime motivator in getting people to do things. The more they got, the harder they worked. In Taylor's incentive plan there were two rates of pay: a low rate and a high rate. If the worker did less than what was established as acceptable for the job, he received the low rate. If he reached or surpassed the acceptable level, he received the high rate. As an example, suppose the minimally acceptable rate was 45 tons, the lower rate was 2.6 cents per ton, and the higher rate was 3.9 cents per ton. The pay rate for each of five individuals with differing outputs would then be shown in Table 1.1.

There was a big jump in salary if the person could reach this acceptable level, which was referred to as *standard.* If the worker did less than the standard rate, his pay was quite low. If he reached the standard, however, he was paid the higher rate

Source: Courtesy of the Academy of Management.

Figure 1.2
Frederick W. Taylor
(1856–1915)

Table 1.1
Pay Computation with a Differential Piece Rate

Worker	Number of Tons Loaded	Rate per Ton	Total Daily Wage
A	35	2.6¢	$0.91
B	40	2.6	1.04
C	45	3.9	1.56
D	50	3.9	1.95
E	55	3.9	2.15

for *all* his output. There was thus a bonus built in for attaining the higher rate. Because there were two rates of pay, Taylor referred to his incentive plan as a *differential piece rate.* Other scientific managers may have used different incentive plans, but the plans all had one thing in common. They were designed to motivate the workers to produce more output.

Principles of Scientific Management. In addition to his time and motion studies, Taylor set forth four principles of scientific management, which follow:

▪ Principles of scientific management.

1. Develop a science for each element of a man's work. Find out the best way to do the job.
2. Scientifically select, train, and teach the workers how to do their jobs properly. This is in contrast to letting the individuals train themselves, an often inefficient method.
3. Cooperate with the men in ensuring that all of the work is done in accordance with the scientific principles that have been developed.
4. Divide work responsibility between management and the workers. The former should study the jobs and decide how they should be done. The latter should carry them out.[2]

Note that these principles contained two major new ideas. First, the use of scientific principles in structuring the work was important. Second, management and workers had to cooperate with one another in order to increase overall efficiency. The use of these scientific principles spread to all corners of the industrial world. Even today scientific management principles are employed in determining the best way to operate machinery, carry heavy loads, and do all sorts of other work-related tasks.

Administrative Management

Scientific management brought about great increases in efficiency at the lower levels of the hierarchy. This success eventually resulted in attention being concentrated higher up as well. Organizations found that they needed to do more planning in order to take full advantage of scientific management principles. Also, managers began to realize that while they knew a lot about increasing efficiency at the worker level, they knew very little about how to get greater efficiency at the management level. In particular, they began asking questions such as: What is management? What are the principles of organizing? How can a manager be more effective in a job?

Henri Fayol

The individual who first set out answers to these questions was Henri Fayol, the general manager of a large French mining combine. His book, *Industrial and General Administration*,[3] had such an impact on the field of management that it affected even the teaching of basic management and earned him the title of *father of modern management theory.* The three most important things Fayol did in his book were: (1) discuss the importance of teaching management, (2) describe the functions of a manager, and (3) set forth some useful management principles. Fayol's photograph appears as Figure 1.3.

The Teaching of Management. Fayol pointed out that business people perform a number of activities, or operations. At the lowest level of the hierarchy are technical operations, such as production and manufacturing. At the highest levels of the organization are administrative operations such as planning, organizing, commanding, coordinating, and controlling. As the individual moves up the line, concern for the former must decline and interest in the latter must increase. Figure 1.4 provides an illustration of this idea.

▪ Management can be taught.

How does someone learn how to carry out administrative operations? Until Fayol's time, people learned on the job, but Fayol disagreed with this approach. He felt that administrative practices and principles should *first* be taught in an academic setting. Then the individual could apply these ideas on the job. This philosophy helped lead to the rise of business schools throughout America.

Management Functions. What does a manager do? Until Fayol, no one had ever really sought to identify and analyze a manager's functions. Fayol did so, setting forth five functions:

- Planning. A forecast of future events and, based on the forecast, the construction of an operating program.
- Organizing. The structuring of men, money, machines, and materials in such a way as to efficiently attain the objectives of the plan.
- Commanding. Directing the workers toward the accomplishments of organizational objectives through the use of effective leadership.
- Coordinating. Achieving cooperation and harmony between all levels and units of the organization.
- Controlling. Seeing that everything has been done in accord with the adopted plan.[4]

Are these five functions the major ones performed by *all* managers? Many modern executives think not. They prefer to add such functions as motivating, staffing, training, and communicating, while deemphasizing such functions as commanding and coordinating. The final list really depends on the manager's job. The

Figure 1.3
Henri Fayol
(1841–1925)

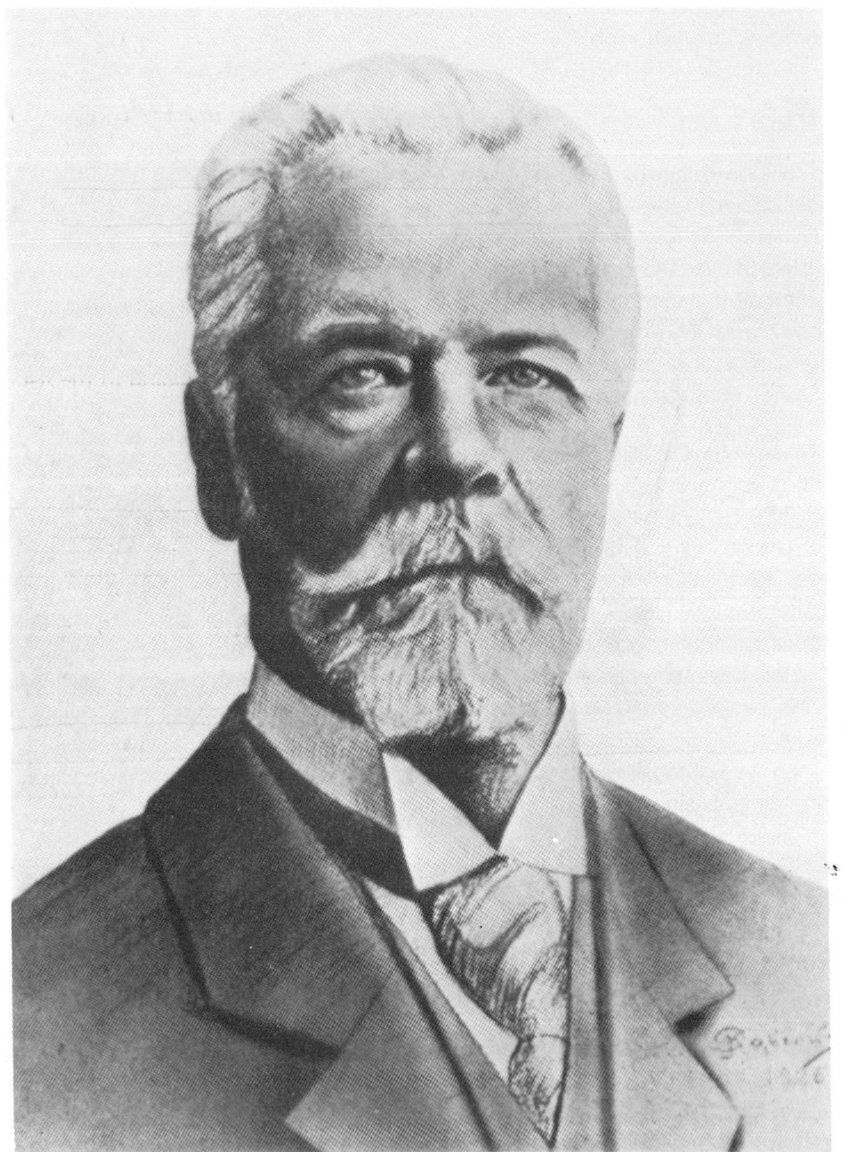

Source: Courtesy of the Academy of Management.

Abilities Required for Satisfactory Job Performance

100%	Technical Ability
0%	Administrative Ability

Lower Level Management → Upper Level Management

Figure 1.4
Abilities Needed by Managers

individual who has to do a lot of training will want to add training to the list. A manager who works for a telephone company will want to add communicating. Likewise, practicing managers will drop the functions they feel are not primary to their job. What was true for Fayol may not entirely hold for them.

Nevertheless, the framework is useful. By identifying the major functions they perform and carefully studying each, modern managers will become more effective in their jobs. Fayol's basic idea is still in use today. In fact, many basic management books, including this one, use a functional approach to teaching management.

■ The functions provide a framework.

Principles of Management. Fayol also set forth the fourteen principles of management which he had the greatest occasion to use. These principles, which are listed below, are not exhaustive; they are only general guidelines for action. They should be modified, adjusted, or—if of no value at a particular time—ignored. In many cases, however, they are still useful to the manager.

■ Principles of management.

1. Division of labor. By using specialization of labor, efficiency can be increased.
2. Authority and responsibility. These always should be equal. No one should have more of one than the other.
3. Discipline. Obedience and proper attitude on the part of the worker are important to organizational efficiency.
4. Unity of command. Everyone should have one and only one boss.
5. Unity of management. There should be one manager and one plan for all operations having the same objective.
6. Subordination of individual interests to the common good. The goals of the organization must take precedence over those of individuals or groups.
7. Remuneration of staff. Compensation should be fair and sufficiently motivational.
8. Centralization. There should be a balance between the amount of authority held by top managers and the amount decentralized to the operating level.
9. The hierarchy. There should be a clear-cut chain of command running from the top of the organization to the bottom.

10. Order. A place should exist for everything, and everything should be in its place.
11. Equity. Workers should be treated fairly and justly.
12. Stability of staff. Organizations should encourage the long-term commitment of their employees.
13. Initiative. Managers need the ability to both conceive and execute a plan of action.
14. Esprit de corps. Morale is vital to organizational success.[5]

Every manager should use these principles whenever they will prove useful. Additionally, each should develop other principles that can supplement this list and further increase the individual's managerial effectiveness. Table 1.2 provides a list of other principles that are typically used by modern managers.

Table 1.2
Typical Principles Used by Modern Managers

- Primacy of planning principle. The first function to carry out is planning; all other functions (organizing, staffing, directing, controlling) follow.
- Unity of objective principle. If an organizational structure is to be effective, it should be designed in such a way that it helps people attain their objectives.
- Scalar principle. The clearer the line of authority or chain of command running from the top of the organization to the bottom, the more effective the organization's decision making and communication systems will be.
- Principle of open competition. The more the organization is committed to having a high quality management team, the more it should encourage open competition among all candidates for management positions.
- Principle of direct supervision. The greater the manager's personal contact with subordinates, the more effective the manager's direction and leadership will be.
- Principle of delegation. Subordinates should be delegated sufficient authority to carry out their jobs.
- Principle of functional definition. The more clearly managers define the authority and responsibility of jobs, the more likely it is that subordinates will be able to perform them effectively.
- Principle of brevity. The shorter a message is, the more likely it will be listened to.
- Principle of clarity. The clearer a message is, the more likely people will understand and remember its content.
- Exception principle. Managers should concentrate their control efforts on things that are extremely good or extremely bad and not worry about things that are going according to expectations. That is, they should concentrate on exceptions.

Behavioral Management

Taylor and the scientific managers helped organize the lower levels of the hierarchy and were able to achieve great increases in worker productivity. Fayol and the administrative management theory people who followed helped managers better understand the jobs they themselves were doing and the principles that could assist them. However, one area of management still had not received much attention. It was the human element in the workplace. Why did people behave as they did?

In an effort to answer this question, all sorts of laws about human behavior were formulated. For example, the scientific managers believed that money was the prime motivator. They also knew that individuals working alone tended to do more than those working in groups. However, they did not know precisely *why* this happened. The administrative theory people, as Fayol's fourteen principles show, had also developed some behavioral guidelines. However, they too lacked a solid understanding of work behavior. Much of what the two groups knew about work behavior was learned on the job. Today, of course, many modern managers obtain their behavioral training in the same way. For example, Table 1.3 illustrates (in a humorous way) some typical rules that are used to explain human behavior in modern organizations. However, in order to really understand human behavior at work and formulate useful rules, a systematic, research-oriented approach has to be employed. One of the individuals who helped light the way to the study of behavior in a work setting was Elton Mayo.

Table 1.3
Laws of Behavior (Which Explain Why Things *Always* Go Wrong)

- Nobody really knows what is going on anywhere within the organization.
- In a hierarchy every employee tends to rise to his or her level of incompetence. Work is accomplished by those employees who have not yet reached their level of incompetence.
- In any human enterprise, work seeks the lowest hierarchical level.
- The inevitable result of improved and enlarged communications between different levels in a hierarchy is a vastly increased area of misunderstanding.
- In a hierarchical organization, the higher the level, the greater the confusion.
- The person who can smile when things go wrong has thought of someone who can be blamed for it.
- If a problem causes many meetings, the meetings eventually become more important than the problem.
- Nothing is impossible for the person who doesn't have to do it.
- As soon as you mention something: (1) if it is good, it goes away; (2) if it is bad, it happens.
- If you want to get along, go along.
- When in doubt, mumble; when in trouble, delegate; when in charge, ponder.
- If a job is fouled up, anything done to improve it only makes it worse.
- If more than one person is responsible for a miscalculation, no one will be at fault.
- Friends come and go, but enemies accumulate.
- Anything that begins well, ends badly; anything that begins badly, ends worse.
- In any collection of data, the figure most obviously correct, beyond all need of checking, is the mistake. Also, no one you ask for help will see it, and everyone who stops by with unsought advice will see it immediately.

Source: Adapted from Arthur Block, *Murphy's Law and Other Reasons Why Things Go Wrong!* (Los Angeles: Price Stern/Sloan Publishers, 1977).

Elton Mayo

Elton Mayo was a faculty member at Harvard University during the late 1920s. He had previously taught at the University of Pennsylvania and had experience

■ Rest breaks were followed by increased output.

conducting research in industry. One of his early experiments took place in a textile mill in Philadelphia. Mayo was called in to find out why labor turnover was so high. He decided to experiment by letting the workers have rest breaks, during which they could sit down and relax. The result: Turnover went down, and output went up. Mayo initially attributed the results to a reduction in fatigue. The workers were tired, and the rest breaks helped them recover their strength. In short, Mayo approached the problem like a scientific manager.

He overlooked the behavioral side of the picture. He failed to realize the workers disliked their jobs because the noise and racket in the factory did not allow them to socialize. The rest breaks did permit this, and the workers liked them. However, the

Figure 1.5 Elton Mayo (1880–1949)

Source: Courtesy of the Baker Library, Harvard University.

study of behavior in the workplace was new in Mayo's time, and scholars missed some things that would be evident to most modern managers. Figure 1.5 is a photograph of Elton Mayo.

Hawthorne Studies. In the late 1920s the most famous industrial behavior study of all time took place. It began at the Western Electric plant near Cicero, Illinois. The company was interested in finding out what degree of illumination would produce the greatest output. By increasing and decreasing the amount of illumination the firm hoped to find an ideal level of lighting. However, it was unable to do so because whether the illumination was moved up or down, output increased. Why? No one seemed to know.

At this point Mayo and some colleagues from Harvard were invited in. During the next five years they conducted numerous behavioral experiments at the plant. One of the things they learned was that the reason the workers produced more and more output during the illumination study was that they liked the attention they were getting. It was not the lighting (a physical factor) but the attention (a psychological factor) that caused increased output.

During the remainder of their investigation and analysis, they uncovered many other behavioral findings, including the following:

■ Behavioral findings from Hawthorne.

1. Workers will often restrict their output. Although they can do more work, they will not. In particular, if management is willing to accept 80 percent of what a good worker can do, this is how much the workers will turn out.
2. The way managers are treated by workers depends on their place in the hierarchy. The higher up the structure a manager is, the more respect the individual will get.
3. Workers tend to form informal groups, or cliques. To be a member of an informal group, one has to obey the rules of that group. Typical rules include:
   a. Do not do too much work.
   b. Do not do too little work.
   c. Never squeal to the management on a fellow worker.
   d. Never act better than the other workers; always be one of the gang.[6]
   e. Do not be noisy or bossy.[7]

After Hawthorne. The initial illumination experiments at Hawthorne lighted the way for the entry of human relationists into industry. Psychologists, sociologists, and other behavioral scientists soon began making their way into the business world. As time went on, these researchers became more and more sophisticated both in studying work behavior and in drawing conclusions about it. Today they rely very heavily on the *scientific method.* The scientific approach to studying behavior is very important because it forces the behavioral scientist to put aside all prejudice and biases. For example, in studying why turnover has suddenly increased, the individual cannot answer the question by asking, "If I were one of these workers, why would I want to quit?" The answer to this question would be too limited. Maybe the scientist would answer, "Because the pay is too low." However, the worker might say, "Because management treats me badly."

The scientific method is important to modern behavioral research because it forces researchers to look for answers outside themselves. It can be seen in the following seven steps:

■ Steps in the scientific method.

1. Identify the problem. What is the objective of the investigation? In this case, assume it is high labor turnover.
2. Obtain preliminary information. Gather as much information as possible about the problem. Find out how many people are quitting and what departments they are coming from.
3. Pose a tentative solution to the problem. State a hypothesis that can be tested and proved either right or wrong. The hypothesis should be likely to solve the problem. In this case, assume that the researcher's hypothesis is that people are quitting because they are upset over low pay.
4. Investigate the problem area. Using available information and any other sources that can shed light on the problem, such as interviews of those workers who are quitting, examine the problem in its entirety.
5. Classify the information. Take all the information that has been gathered and organize it in such a way that it can be used to support or reject the initial hypothesis.
6. State a tentative answer to the problem. At this point, draw a conclusion regarding the right answer to the problem. From the data it should be obvious that the initial hypothesis related to low pay and employee turnover is wrong. The interviews with the workers should give more than enough information to show that the workers do not like the way management is treating them. It is a leadership behavior problem.
7. Test the answer. Now, armed with this answer, give the findings to management. In turn, the top executives can encourage more appropriate leadership behavior by the managers. This should solve the problem.

Today's behavioral scientists are conducting research studies throughout industry. Their findings are available to managers everywhere, who are now learning that the management of people is more than doing what comes naturally. And it all began with Mayo's famous Hawthorne studies.

Situational Management: Where We Are Now

The scientific managers, administrative managers, and behaviorists all contributed important ideas to modern management. On a time continuum, they follow the same order as they have in this chapter. The scientific managers arrived on the scene around 1880, the administrative managers came along around 1920, and the behaviorists began to emerge during the 1930s.

The thinking of each contributed importantly to an understanding of management. Scientific management considerations are very important at the lowest levels of the hierarchy. Managers here are always looking for ways to improve the efficiency of the workers. The administrative management ideas are important at all levels of the management hierarchy, especially the middle and upper levels, where a study of managerial functions and principles can be very helpful. Behavioral knowledge is useful at all levels of the hierarchy. Every manager needs to understand behavior at work. In an effort to bring together the ideas of all three groups, many practicing managers are now finding that a systems approach to the study of management is very helpful.

The Systems Approach

▪ The body is a system.

A *system* is a unit or organized whole that is made up of many different, but interrelated, parts. The human body is a good example of a *human system.* The brain, heart, kidneys, lungs, and other important organs are interrelated. A doctor can specialize in one of these areas, such as the heart. However, the physician (a cardiologist) must understand the effect of the heart on the other parts of the body and vice versa. In treating a person with a heart condition, the cardiologist must take a total systems approach. This same idea is seen whenever one takes medicine. Interrelationships exist throughout all parts of the body.

▪ So is an organization.

Managers are in the same type of situation, except that they deal with an *organizational system* in which each major unit is related to every other major unit. Something that happens in the production department may well affect the finance and marketing departments. For example, if the production department has to stop manufacturing for two weeks in order to tool up for a new product line, this will affect sales. Marketing will find that it cannot meet customer orders, while finance will find that the amount of money it will earn during these two weeks will drop dramatically. Then there is the human side of the organizational system. What happens if the company president gives a 10 percent raise to the people in the marketing department but only an 8 percent raise to those in production? It is likely that the two departments will not cooperate with each other as much as they have in the past, and this will result in lower efficiency.

Thus the organizational system is analogous to that of the human body. Something that happens in one area can affect other areas. But it does not have to be something bad. The president may approve of a particular plan that will involve cooperation from all of the various departments in the organization. This initial management action may result in all sorts of follow-up actions. Figure 1.6 provides an illustration. Note that the decision is carried all the way down the hierarchy and then begins to flow horizontally and upward. Individuals are discussing the plan with people in other departments, talking about how they will carry it out.

Additionally, these decisions will involve matters that require an understanding of tasks (the scientific management approach), people (the behavioral approach), and management (the administrative approach). Which of these three is *most* important to the modern manager? Practitioners find that *all three* are important,

Figure 1.6
The Organization as a System

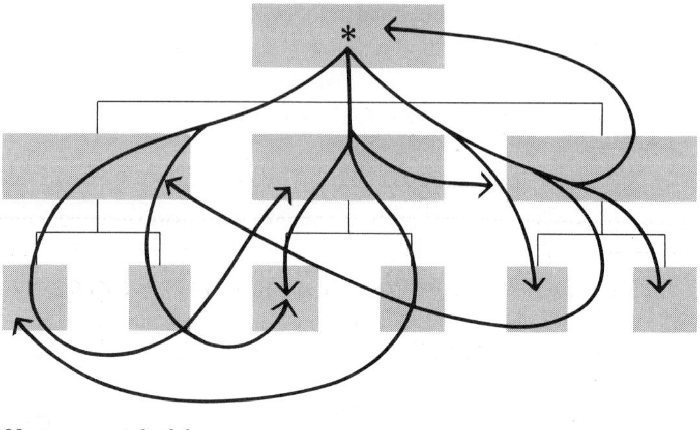
*
* Management decision
⟶ Impact of the decision

Figure 1.7
Major Concerns of the Eclectic Manager

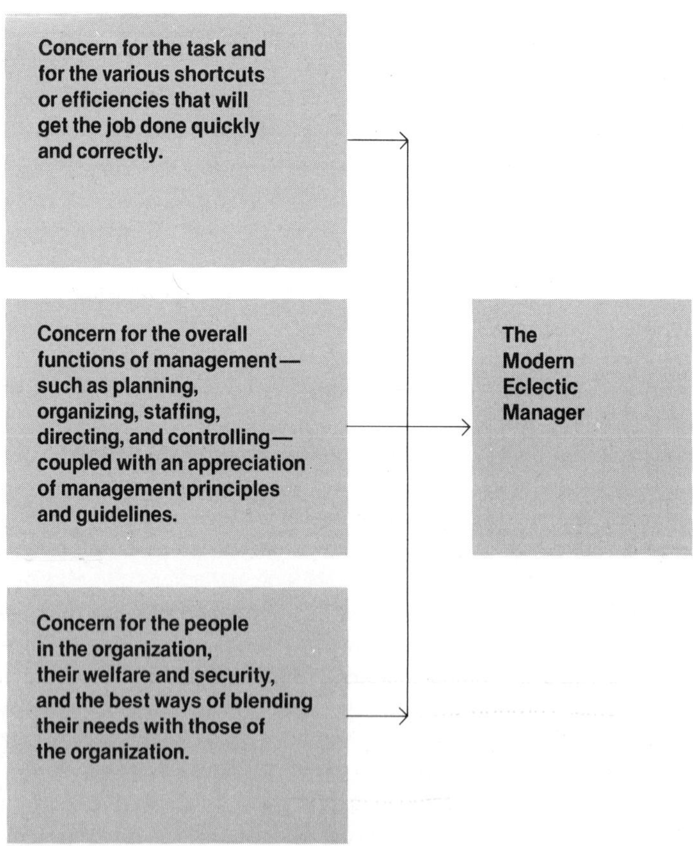
Concern for the task and for the various shortcuts or efficiencies that will get the job done quickly and correctly.
Concern for the overall functions of management— such as planning, organizing, staffing, directing, and controlling— coupled with an appreciation of management principles and guidelines.
Concern for the people in the organization, their welfare and security, and the best ways of blending their needs with those of the organization.
The Modern Eclectic Manager

depending on the situation. Thus the modern manager needs to be what is called an eclectic.

The Eclectic Manager

▪ The modern manager uses what works.

The word *eclectic* means choosing the best of what is available and letting the rest go. Modern managers are eclectic in their concern with using whatever scientific, behavioral, or administrative information will solve tasks at hand. If a job is low level and the manager needs to understand something about cost control, that is the type of information to be found. If the current project requires that the individual know about administrative planning, the manager will investigate this area. Finally, if there is a motivational problem, the manager will turn attention to the behavioral side of enterprise. However, the manager does not need to be an expert in any of these three areas. Nor does the person want to overemphasize any one of them to the exclusion of the others. Figure 1.7 shows some aspects of managerial eclecticism.

▪ The individual is a contingency manager.

Managers must use the skills and training they have in each of these areas and apply them to the specific situations. This calls for *situational,* or *contingency, management,* which simply means that the manager must draw together what has been learned in all the management-related areas of business and apply it to the problem at hand. Some of this information is a result of job experience; the rest comes from formal training. Texts like this give modern students of management information that managers without training would take a lifetime to accumulate.

One of the best ways to start is with an analysis of the manager's job. Exactly what does this person do? This question will be addressed in the next chapter.

Summary

Management is the process of getting things done through people. Many individuals do not have this skill. They like to do things on their own. For this reason, they are ineffective as managers.

While there is currently a great deal of interest directed toward the study of management, its practice is very old. The ancient Egyptians used effective management practices to build pyramids, and the Romans employed management techniques to restructure their bureaucratic organization. The emergence of modern management, however, really began with the Industrial Revolution. The factory system brought the workers together under one roof. This represented a major challenge that most managers of the time did not know how to solve. They were more interested in getting increased efficiency than in studying human behavior problems. Through the use of scientific management principles, they were able to carefully design the work and train the workers so that maximum output was attained.

Then along came those interested in management functions and principles, the most famous of whom was Henri Fayol. Fayol set forth a list of management functions and a series of principles that have inspired the teaching of management ever since.

Meanwhile, in the behavioral area there was Elton Mayo, famous for his work in the Hawthorne studies. Thanks to these studies important insights into work behavior were uncovered.

Today, all three of these areas—scientific management principles, administrative principles, and behavioral guidelines—help the modern manager do a better job than ever before. In particular, the effective individual draws the best ideas from each of these areas, proving that an eclectic approach is indeed the best one. For this reason, the modern manager is often referred to as a situational, or contingency, manager.

Review and Study Questions

1. What is management? Describe it in your own words.
2. Is it possible for someone to be a super salesperson but a poor manager? Explain your answer.
3. How much did the ancient Egyptians really know about management? Could the people who administered the building of the Great Pyramid have helped construct the World Trade Center in New York City? Explain.
4. How can a study of Diocletian's reorganization of the Roman Empire provide useful guidelines for the modern manager in the process of trying to reorganize a giant bureaucracy? Explain.
5. Scientific managers were interested primarily in the management of work. What is meant by this statement?
6. Are Taylor's four principles of scientific management useful to today's manager? In what way? Defend your answer.
7. Technical skills are needed at the lowest levels of the hierarchy and administrative abilities at the upper levels of the hierarchy. What is meant by this statement?
8. What did Fayol mean by each of the following: planning, organizing, commanding, coordinating, controlling? Define each term.
9. Of the lists of management principles presented in this chapter, which five would be of most value to a production-line manager? Which five would be of most value to an executive in an insurance firm? What about a top government official?
10. What types of behavioral findings did the Hawthorne researchers find that could be of value to a modern manager? Explain.
11. What are the steps in the scientific method? Identify and explain each of them.
12. In what way is the organization like a system?
13. Today's manager is an eclectic. What does this statement mean?
14. The modern executive is a situational manager. What does this statement mean? Bring the word *contingency* into your answer.

Key Terms in the Chapter

management
scientific management
task concept
differential piece rate
planning
organizing
commanding
coordinating
controlling
Hawthorne studies
scientific method
system
organizational system
eclectic manager
contingency management
situational management

Notes

1. Frederick Taylor, *The Principles of Scientific Management* (New York: Harper & Bros., 1911), p. 39.
2. Ibid., pp. 36–37.
3. Henri Fayol, *Industrial and General Administration,* trans. J. A. Coubrough (Geneva: International Management Institute, 1929).
4. Ibid., part 2, chapter 2.
5. Ibid., part 2, chapter 1.
6. F. J. Roethlisberger and William J. Dickson, *Management and the Worker* (Cambridge, Mass.: Harvard University Press, 1939), p. 16.
7. George C. Homans, *The Human Group* (New York: Harcourt, Brace & World, 1950), p. 79.

Case: A Payment Option

They could make more money by doing more work—but they didn't.

Jeff Canton owns a medium-sized, nonunionized manufacturing plant. The demand for machine parts in recent months rose so sharply that Jeff decided to introduce a new wage payment plan. Under the old plan, all machinists were paid $8 an hour. The average work day began at 8:00 AM and ended at 5:00 PM. There were two ten-minute rest breaks during the day and one forty-minute lunch break. According to time and motion studies conducted in the industry, the average machinist is able to process 20 pieces an hour, or 160 pieces a day. Each person receives a daily wage of $64 and thus gets $.40 per piece ($64/160).

Jeff introduced his incentive payment plan three weeks ago. Rather than paying everyone $64 a day, he reasoned, why not offer the opportunity to make even more money? This could have a number of important advantages for the firm. First, there was a very large backlog of work. If the machinists would turn out more output, this backlog would be reduced. Second, the average machinist processed only 130 pieces a day, which is less than the amount established as standard by the industry. If this incentive plan were to work, the average machinist would undoubtedly want to produce at least as much as standard and probably more. Third, for every extra piece produced by the machinist there would also be an increase in revenue for the company. After all, the fixed expenses of the firm for such things as administrative salaries, taxes, and insurance would remain the same regardless of how much more work was done. Thus the more the machinists turned out, the greater would be the amount left after all expenses were paid.

Jeff's plan was rather simple. He intended to share any increases in output with the workers. He did not intend to demand that the machinists accept this new incentive plan, however. He merely made it available to those who wanted to participate. Those who did had to remain in the plan for at least sixty days but could go back to their old payment plan after this period. However, anyone wanting to join the new plan could do so at the beginning of any workweek. The plan started on Mondays so that it would be easy to keep track of how much was owed to the worker under its provisions.

Workers who opted for the new incentive plan were to be paid for their overall daily output according to the following formula:

Number of Pieces Processed per Day	Payment per Piece	Daily Wage
100	$.25	$ 25
120	.30	36
140	.35	49
160	.40	64
180	.45	81
200	.50	100

Since Jeff announced the new plan, only four of the fifty-six machinists have opted for it. Each of the four has averaged $72 per day for every day they have been in the plan. However, Jeff has learned that the other workers do not like the plan and are encouraging these four machinists to switch back. Additionally, he believes that no one else is going to go along with the plan. As a result, he is now trying to think up another way to encourage the workers to produce more output and thus help him with his backlog problem.

Questions

1. Is Jeff like the scientific managers? Does he believe that money motivates? Explain.
2. Why are most of the machinists unwilling to accept the new payment plan? Give at least two reasons.
3. Why are the workers who did not accept the new plan giving the other workers a hard time? Based on your answer, what recommendations would you give to Jeff regarding a new incentive plan to help with the backlog problem? Be complete in your answer.

Case: Changing Times

"We never started out to be managers!"

When Elwood and Sam Butler opened their TV repair shop, not many U.S. homes had television sets. However, as they told their uncle Ed when borrowing money from him:

It won't be long before TV will catch on, and all those sets out there are going to need repairs. Given the fact that there are very few repair places around, people will be coming to us and our reputation will grow. In no time at all you'll get back your investment and more.

Uncle Ed was repaid within six months, as the business grew briskly. In fact, within two years the shop was forced to expand. Seven full-time repair people were now working there. This was when Elwood and Sam decided to increase their overall operations. Rather than just repair TVs, they reasoned, why not sell them as well? In this way they could keep people coming back to them all the time. They did so; and a few years later they added radios and home appliances such as washers and dryers.

During this time and the three decades which followed, the Butlers' store grew in both size and volume. But with this growth came an increase in the number of problems the two owners had to face. When they first opened their store, their most important job had been seeing that the television sets were properly fixed. When they added radios and home appliances, the repair side of the job still remained important, although now there were other concerns as well. For example, selling became a major concern. Then, as they grew still larger, they had to hire people for the front office to handle such things as payroll, personnel, advertising, and administrative chores.

The organization has become fairly large. In fact, as far as Elwood and Sam are concerned, it is now too big. As Elwood notes:

Years ago, all we had to do was supervise a few repair people and talk to customers about the types of problem the TVs had and how much they would cost to repair. Now we have to worry about administration of the entire operation. And then there is the human side of the business. I can't tell you how many problems there are here. Motivating the salespeople, letting the repair people know that you appreciate what they are doing, and working with the people in the front office to see that everything flows smoothly. Do you know how much of my time is spent worrying about inventory problems? If we run out of parts, our entire repair business comes to a halt. And then there is the problem of deciding how many TVs and home appliances to reorder every month. I tell you, this used to be an interesting, enjoyable business. Now, every day when I get up I wonder if the operation is too much for me.

Sam echoed these feelings:

We started in this business because we felt we were effective as repair people and knew a little something about selling. But that's not enough today. Now you have to be an executive manager to keep this place going. But what the heck, I don't think Elwood and I intend to run things for more than a few more years. If our sons aren't interested in the operation after they get out of college, we'll probably sell out and retire. We never started out to be managers, just small business entrepreneurs. Boy, have things changed around here since those early days!

Questions

1. When the business was just starting out, what type of ability did Elwood and Sam have: technical or administrative? Defend your answer.
2. As the store continued to grow, how important were technical skills to Elwood and Sam? How important were administrative skills? Explain.
3. Do Elwood and Sam have to be eclectic managers? Explain, being sure to include the definition of the term *eclectic* in your answer.

Chapter 2 The Modern Manager's Job

Objectives of the Chapter
Before we begin to study the field of management, one overriding question needs to be answered: What do managers do? This chapter will show that the answer will vary according to where in the hierarchy the manager is located. Some are concerned with getting workers to do things; others are interested in seeing that supervisors perform their jobs properly; still others are concerned with the long-range direction of the firm. Also, depending on their place in the hierarchy, managers will need different skills. Some will require an abundance of technical skills, while others will need more human or conceptual skills. Finally, regardless of where they are located in the hierarchy, managers perform certain roles. They interact with others, pass on information, and make decisions.

The first objective of this chapter is to study the various types of managers who work in an organization. The second objective is to learn about the different skills that managers need to have. The final objective is to examine the various roles that all of them perform.

When you have finished reading this chapter, you should be able to:

1. Define what is meant by *first-line manager, middle manager,* and *top manager.*
2. Compare and contrast a functional manager with a general manager.
3. Identify and describe technical skills, human skills, and conceptual skills.
4. Explain the importance of technical, human, and conceptual skills at the lower, middle, and upper levels of the hierarchy.
5. Discuss the three major roles that are carried out by all managers.
6. Describe what is meant by the process approach to the study of management and explain why we will be using it in our study of management essentials.

Types of Managers

While managers are individuals who get things done through others, there are a number of different types of managers. Some operate at the lowest levels of the hierarchy and are commonly referred to as first-line managers or supervisors. Others work in the middle of the organization and are called middle managers. The rest work at the top of the organization and are referred to as executives or top managers. Figure 2.1 illustrates this form of organization.

First-Line Managers

▪ First-line managers supervise operating employees.

First-line managers are those who supervise operating employees. In production line settings they are called foremen, while in clerical operations they are usually called supervisors. In contrast to the other types of managers, first-line managers directly supervise the workers.

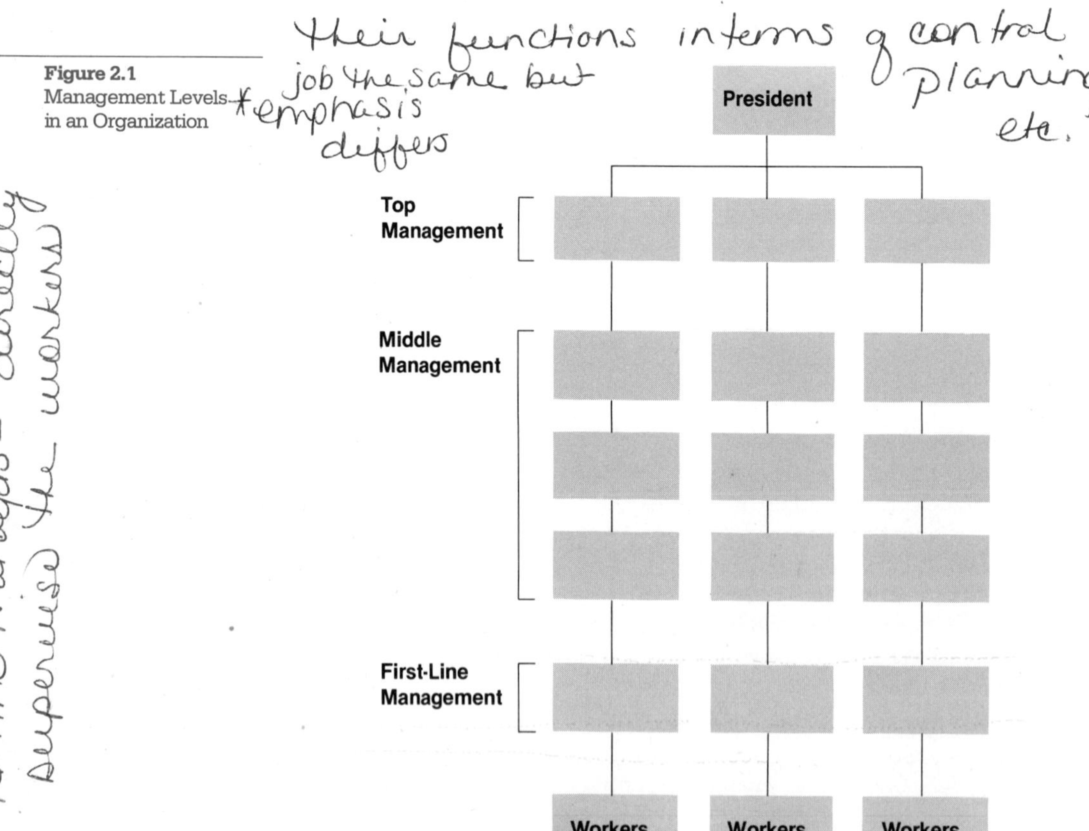

Figure 2.1
Management Levels in an Organization

Middle Managers

Middle managers are located between first-line managers and top managers. However, it is often difficult to determine where middle management begins and ends. In some organizations this has to be done through the use of titles. A person who is a first-line supervisor is, by title, not a middle manager, while someone who has a title of vice-president or general manager is considered to be a top executive. All other managers are in the middle. Even this approach, however, can cause confusion, since in some organizations there are many vice-presidents. Insurance companies are a good example. In this case it is often best to ask where the individual is located on the organization chart. Based on the number of levels in the structure, one can make a judgment as to the middle management range. If there is no organization chart, the two questions to ask are: Does this individual manage other managers? Does this individual report to the president? If the first answer is yes and the second is no, the person is undoubtedly a middle manager.

■ Middle managers are between first-line and top managers.

Top Managers

Top managers make up that small group of executives who determine the organization's major operating decisions. Quite often, especially in medium-sized firms, this group is no more than eight to ten people. Typical titles of top managers include *chief executive officer* (*CEO* for short), *president*, and *senior vice-president.* However, since titles vary from one organization to the other, this approach is not always reliable. The best way of determining whether someone is a top manager is to find out how much authority the person has in setting overall objectives and determining operational policies.

■ Top managers set overall organizational objectives.

Functional and General Managers

While managers can be classified on the basis of their rank in the organization, they can also be described on the basis of the activities they perform. In general, there are two types of managers: functional and general.

■ Functional managers supervise specific activities.

A *functional manager* is responsible for a particular organizational activity such as marketing, production, or finance. (See Figure 2.2.) The vice-president of marketing is a functional manager. The people who report to this individual are all in the marketing area. The vice-president of production is also a functional manager. All key people in the manufacturing end of the operation will report to this individual. The vice-president of finance is another functional manager. This person manages the finance area, directing and supervising key financial executives.

The *general manager*, on the other hand, runs a much more complex unit. A general manager is in charge of a company, an independent operating division, or a subsidiary. For example, all multinational firms have operations in more than one country. If a firm's home office is in New York City and its European division is headquartered in Paris, the president of the firm and the manager in charge of this overseas division are both general managers. The latter individual is responsible

■ General managers supervise operating units.

Figure 2.2
Functional and General Managers

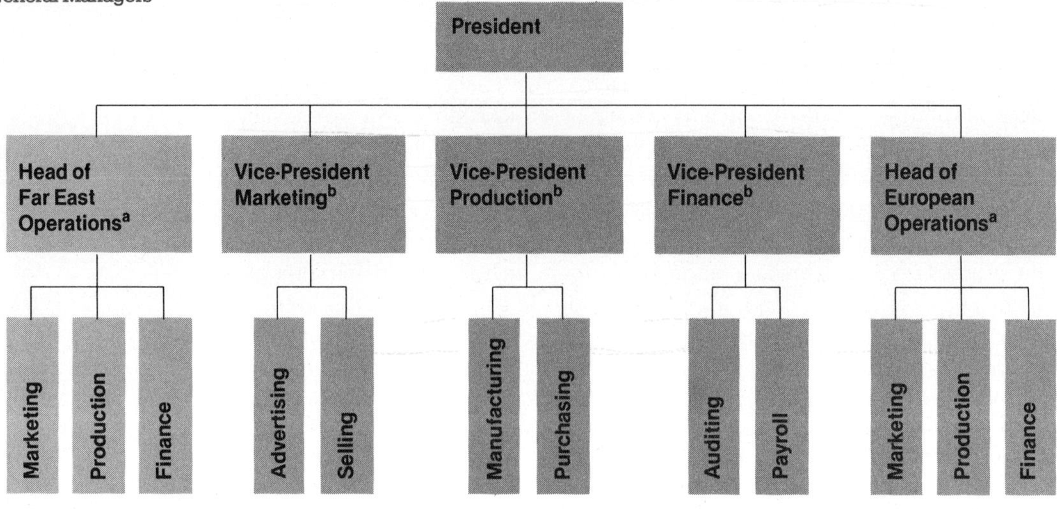

[a]General Manager
[b]Functional Manager

for all activities of the overseas division, including production, marketing, finance, and any other operations vital to the division's success. The same is true of the individual who is head of Far East operations. Figure 2.2 shows a multinational corporation management chart.

In a small company, there will usually be only one general manager, the president. On the other hand, in a large organization with a number of relatively independent divisions, there will be a general manager for each. When comparing the president of a small corporation with, for example, the general manager of a large corporate division, the management student finds a great deal of similarity in terms of what the individuals do. General managers in large firms are quite a bit like presidents of smaller companies.

Management Levels and Management Skills

At each major level of the hierarchy—lower, middle, and upper—different skills are required for success. At the lower levels the manager needs to have more technical skills than any other type. At the middle levels of the hierarchy, the manager needs human skills most of all. Conceptual skills are of greatest importance at the upper levels. Figure 2.3 illustrates this idea.

Technical Skills

Technical skills are useful in understanding and carrying out "doing" activities. There is almost always some physical effort involved in using these skills. Typical

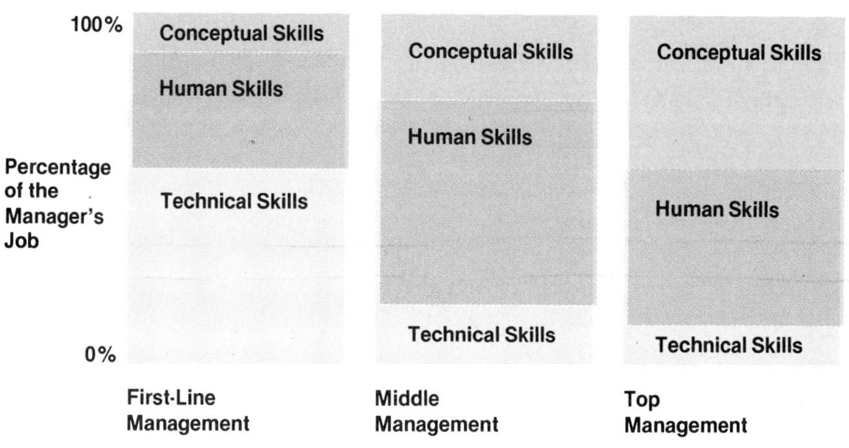

Figure 2.3
Relative Skills Required for Effective Performance at Each of the Three Levels of Management

illustrations of their use include operating a piece of heavy equipment, repairing a machine, and making financial calculations.

These skills are very important at the lowest levels of the management hierarchy because the supervisor or first-level manager needs to know how to do various jobs. Unless the manager has technical skills, the individual will not really understand how and why things operate as they do. This, in turn, will affect the individual's ability to manage. After all, if the manager does not understand what the worker is doing, how can he or she correct or assist the worker? Technical skills are particularly important in supervising new employees who are unfamiliar with the job. While the worker needs these skills in order to learn, the manager needs them in order to teach.

■ Technical skills are especially useful in directing new workers.

Human Skills

Human skills are those that help the manager work effectively as a leading member of a group. They enable the individual to build cooperative effort within the team. In comparison terms, while technical skills are most useful when working with things, human skills are most useful when working with people.

Managers with highly developed human skills are aware of their own attitudes, assumptions, and beliefs about other individuals and groups. They are therefore able to see how the perceptions, viewpoints, and beliefs of the workers differ from their own. Aware of their own beliefs and those of the workers, they are able to blend the two in such a way as to create trust and mutual understanding among all involved. Managers with human skills are particularly effective in communication, motivation, and leadership.

Human skills are needed at every level of the hierarchy. As seen in Figure 2.2, there is less of a change in their importance as one moves up the hierarchy. This is in contrast to technical skills, which decline markedly in importance as one progresses upward, and conceptual skills, which increase dramatically at the highest level of management.

■ Human skills help the manager read people.

Some managers develop human skills without any training. These are people who have always been sensitive and insightful, able to read others very well. Most managers, however, can benefit from some formal behavioral training. Their superiors can be very helpful in this process by coaching them in human relations and by serving as good role models. This informal training can be supplemented with formal training in which the manager learns about human skills and is given the opportunity to apply them to problem situations in a classroom setting.

There are two basic types of human skills. *Intragroup skills* are needed in dealing with problems and issues that occur *within* the group. They are of particular value to supervisors and middle managers. *Intergroup skills* are used in dealing with issues and problems that occur *between* groups. They are especially important in the highest levels of management.

Conceptual Skills

■ Conceptual skills help the manager see the big picture.

Conceptual skills are those that help the manager see the enterprise as a whole. This kind of skill is used in recognizing how the various departments of the organization depend on one another and how a change in any one of them can affect the others. Conceptualizing requires looking at the organization as a *system*. Commenting on this skill, Robert Katz, most famous for his writing on skills of effective administrators, says:

> **Not only does the effective coordination of the various parts of the business depend on the conceptual skill of the administrators involved, but so also does the whole future direction and tone of the organization. The attitudes of a top executive color the whole character of the organization's response and determine the "corporate personality" which distinguishes one company's ways of doing business from another's. These attitudes are a reflection of the administrator's conceptual skill (referred to by some as**

his "creative ability"—the way he perceives and responds to the direction in which the business should grow, company objectives and policies, and stockholders' and employees' interests).[1]

As seen in Figure 2.3, conceptual skills are most important at the upper levels of the hierarchy. How does a manager develop these skills? The manager's boss plays a key role here. By assigning the subordinate a particular job and then encouraging the individual to work it out personally, the top manager can develop in the subordinate a broad problem-solving perspective. The subordinate begins looking at a job from all possible angles. In this type of training, the subordinate who runs into any problems and asks the boss for help does not receive it directly. Instead, the top manager responds with searching questions or opinions while encouraging the subordinate to decide personally what is best.

Another useful approach in developing conceptual skill is to move a management trainee through the organization from one job to another so that the subordinate manager begins to see what happens in each department and how all the departments are interrelated. Some companies also have their up-and-coming managers serve on management boards, making recommendations directly to the firm's board of directors. Another approach is to assign them to help out with interdepartmental problems. In all of these instances, the subordinate manager receives an increasingly broad picture of how an organization operates. And if the firm decides to send the manager to school, it is common to find the individual taking a case analysis course in which the overall operations of a business are examined and an overall plan of action is developed. Again, the concentration is on viewing the enterprise as a whole.

What Managers Do

In recent years there has been a lot of interest about what managers *really* do. Table 2.1 reports some typical erroneous beliefs that people have regarding the manager's job. Research shows that most managers have three particular jobs or roles that they carry out. These are commonly referred to as *interpersonal roles, informational roles,* and *decisional roles.*[2] (See Figure 2.4.)

Interpersonal Roles

Three of the manager's roles, illustrated in Figure 2.4, are direct results of the individual's position of authority. They involve *interpersonal relationships.*

■ Some duties are ceremonial.

The first of these roles is that of a *figurehead.* By virtue of the managerial position, every manager has to perform some ceremonial duties. The individual takes a customer to lunch, greets a visiting dignitary who is touring the plant, attends the wedding of an employee.

■ Others require leadership.

The second is that of a *leader.* By virtue of being in charge of an organizational unit, the manager is responsible for the work of the people in that unit. Therefore

Table 2.1
The Manager's Job: Fiction and Fact

- Fiction: The manager is a thoughtful, systematic planner.
- Fact: Most managers work at a very fast pace. Their activities are often varied and brief. They tend to be most interested in action and dislike having to sit down and think things out. For example, in one study it was found that half of the activities engaged in by chief executives lasted less than nine minutes and only 10 percent lasted more than one hour. In another study it was found that 56 foremen averaged 583 activities in an 8-hour shift. This is an average of one activity every 48 seconds! A lot of the planning done by managers is carried out in their heads and not thought through in some planning meeting.
- Fiction: The effective manager has no regular duties to perform.
- Fact: In addition to handling problems, managers perform a number of regular duties. These include negotiating with people, participating in company ceremonies and rituals (the retirement party, the Christmas party), and serving as a communication link between the external environment and subordinates. One study conducted among presidents of small companies found that they participated in many routine activities because their firms could not afford staff specialists to do this work. Another study found that managers like to see important customers, feeling it is a vital part of their job. Other studies have revealed that managers, because of their status, often receive useful external information that they pass along to their subordinates.
- Fiction: The senior manager needs total information, which a formal management information system (reports, articles, memos, and the like) can best provide.
- Fact: Actually managers prefer getting their information from verbal sources, especially telephone calls and meetings. They do not rely on formal information systems to give them feedback. In fact, research shows that most managers do not really care very much for these forms of information. For example, in one study it was reported that the five chief executives who were being scrutinized responded immediately to only 2 out of 40 routine reports they received during that week. And they read, among them, only 4 items in the 104 periodicals they received. Furthermore, they skimmed most of these periodicals in seconds. What were they interested in? Timely information, such as hearsay, gossip, and speculation. Information they could put to use immediately. Furthermore, by dealing mostly with verbal information, they have something they can store in their minds for later use. They do not end up having to look through long reports or memos to find this information. Finally, it has been suggested that this is also why many managers fail to delegate sufficient authority to their subordinates. They have so much information in their head that it would take too long to tell the subordinate about it. So, rather than fill the individual in on the situation and have him or her take care of it, it is easier to do it personally. As a result, managers often do a lot more work than they should because of the way in which they collect the information that will be needed to carry out specific tasks.

Source: Adapted from Henry Mintzberg, "The Manager's Job: Folklore and Fact," *Harvard Business Review*, July–August 1975, pp. 50–53.

the manager is responsible for hiring, training, counseling, and directing these people. In many cases subordinates look to leaders for some clues as to whether management approves of what the employees are doing. Does management feel this is right or would they like it done differently? How should we write this report for the boss? Does the boss want us to look into buying more efficient machinery, going to a second shift, or giving out overtime?

■ Still others call for a liaison role.

The third interpersonal role of a manager is that of *liaison.* A liaison person is one who goes in between, or acts as an intermediary. In this liaison role the manager interacts with people on the same level of the hierarchy, as well as with others outside the organization. In so doing, the individual often picks up a great deal of information that is useful in running the department and helping the subordinates.

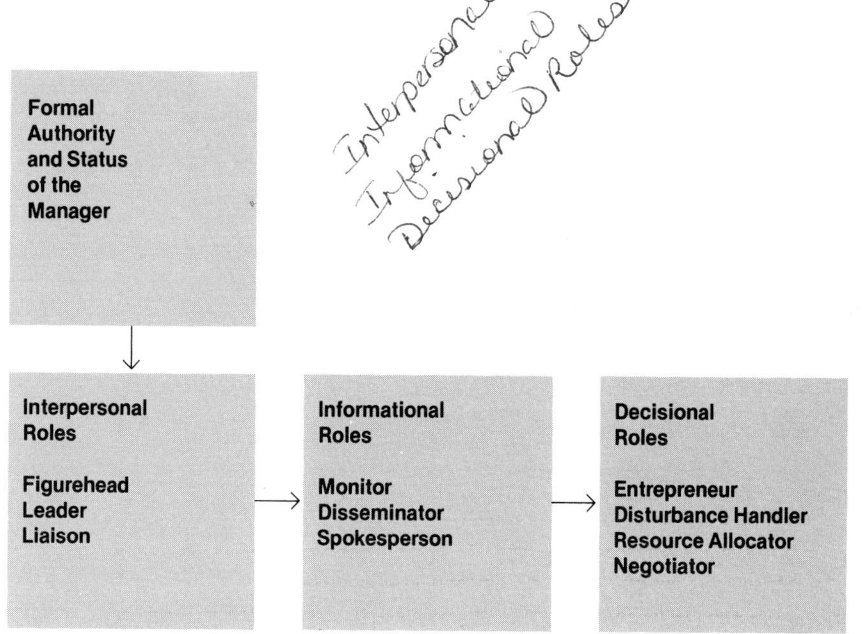

Figure 2.4
The Manager's Major Roles

Source: Adapted from Henry Mintzberg, "The Manager's Job: Folklore and Fact," *Harvard Business Review,* July–August 1975, p. 55.

Because these contacts are so useful in managing, most managers cultivate them and use them extensively.

Informational Roles

By virtue of interpersonal contacts, both with subordinates and throughout the organization, the manager turns out to be the nerve center of the organizational unit. While managers may not know everything, they typically know more than any other member of their staffs, and their *informational roles* are important.

■ The manager monitors information.

In the never-ending quest for information, managers are *monitors.* As such they remain alert for information, continually question liaison contacts and subordinates, and often receive a great deal of unsolicited information. In fact, because managers try to cultivate many information sources, they often obtain a great deal of gossip, hearsay, and speculation. Their contacts provide them with a tremendous amount of information for use in the organization.

■ Communicates it.

Managers are also *disseminators,* since they pass information along to subordinates. Without their manager, these workers would have no access to such information.

■ Serves as a spokesperson.

Finally, managers are *spokespersons.* They send some information to people outside the unit or department. For example, a top manager makes a speech to lobby for an organizational cause, or a supervisor suggests a product modification to a supplier. Additionally, the manager in the role of a spokesperson must inform and satisfy influential people who control the organization. This often involves keeping superiors up to date about what is going on in the unit so that information can be passed up the line to the people who control the organization.

Decisional Roles

In and of itself, information is merely a basic input to the decision-making process. After receiving it, the actual decisions must be made. Decision making is also the manager's job, for only the manager can commit the unit to a new course of action. With the information management has, the manager is in the best position to decide what should be done. In the role of *decision maker,* the manager does four things.

■ The individual acts as an entrepreneur.

First, the individual acts as an *entrepreneur,* or owner-manager, in seeking to improve the unit and adapt it to changing conditions. The manager is always looking for new ideas that will increase the unit's effectiveness.

■ A resolver of conflicts.

Second, the individual is a *disturbance handler.* The manager takes care of problems. If a strike looms or a major customer goes bankrupt, the manager must work to resolve the problems that are going to be created.

■ An allocator of resources.

Third, the manager is a *resource allocator.* The individual has to decide who in the unit will get resources and how much. Some of the resources the manager will give out include not only salary raises and support help in the form of secretarial assistance but the manager's time as well. Also included in the resource allocator role is the responsibility for designing the unit's organization structure. Who will do what? Who will report to whom? Finally, the manager exercises control over the important decisions that are made in the unit. This is commonly done by requiring such decisions to be approved prior to implementation.

■ And a negotiator.

The fourth decisional role of the manager is that of *negotiator.* Research shows that the average manager spends quite a bit of time in negotiations. A company president leads the firm's team in negotiating a new contract. The first-line supervisor argues a grievance problem to its conclusion with the shop steward. These negotiations are part of the manager's job, because only the manager has the authority to commit organizational resources and make the decisions required by these negotiations.

The Manager's Integrated Job

The ten managerial roles just described are not easily separable. They are all part of an integrated whole. The manager cannot perform just one or two of them and let the rest go. On the other hand, it is important to realize that some of these roles receive more managerial attention than others. For example, from his research in this area, Henry Mintzberg reports that

■ Managers perform many different functions.

> **. . . sales managers seem to spend relatively more of their time in the interpersonal roles, presumably a reflection of the extrovert nature of the marketing activity;**
>
> **. . . production managers give relatively more attention to the decisional roles, presumably a reflection of their concern with efficient work flows;**

. . . staff managers spend the most time in the informational roles, since they are experts who manage departments that advise other parts of the organization.[3]

Nevertheless, when examined from a total viewpoint, the interpersonal, informational, and decisional roles of the manager remain *inseparable.*

Studying Management

Depending on the manager's level in the organization, the individual needs to have some combination of technical, human, and conceptual skills. The manager also needs to carry on interpersonal, informational, and decisional roles. How can one individual do all of this well? One way is by going out on the job and learning by doing. However, this is not only a long process but a dangerous one: The individual is likely to pick up some very bad habits. The best way to become an effective manager is first to study management, learning the various functions the manager performs and how they can be carried out effectively. Then a new manager can go out and apply these ideas on the job, modifying them to fit particular situations. The study of management should precede its practice. Table 2.2 gives some reasons for this.

What is the best way to study management? This is not an easy question to answer because there are so many important ideas for students to learn. For example, taking the work of the scientific manager and applying it to present-day challenges, the student should learn about effective decision making and control.

Table 2.2
Teaching Engineers about Management

When a person goes to college to study engineering, the individual usually finds the curriculum full of courses that are technical in nature, to a large degree. And this is exactly the type of training a good engineer needs. After all, how can someone be a good engineer if he or she lacks an understanding of the basic laws of physics or does not know mathematics?

However, there is a problem in training engineers in technical areas only. More and more companies are finding that their engineers have to supervise and manage teams of workers. So they need not only technical skills, but managerial skills, including the ability to communicate, motivate, and lead. In the past, most universities had no course offerings or training in the management area for these people. This, apparently, was something they were supposed to learn on the job.

Today this is changing. Universities like Northwestern, Cleveland State, Stanford, and the University of Pittsburgh, to name but four, are offering courses in engineering management. And to ensure that the courses really do teach the student what he or she needs to know about management, there is a trend toward bringing in industrial advisors to help structure the courses. These advisors know the kinds of problems engineers are going to have on the job, so they can make substantive recommendations regarding course content.

As a result, many engineers are now finding their technical curriculum supplemented with offerings in behavioral management and finance. The result is an engineer who also understands management. And based on the positive feedback from employers, it appears that this new approach is going to be the wave of the future in all engineering schools across the country.

Source: Adapted from "Teaching Engineers to Manage," *Business Week,* November 6, 1978, pp. 197–198.

Included in this material should be some discussion of quantitative approaches to decision making. Additionally, the student needs to learn about administrative practices and principles, including planning, organizing, and controlling. Finally, one needs to know about the human side of enterprise. How do organizations recruit, select, train, and develop their people? Also, how does one communicate, motivate, and lead subordinates? In short, the technical, administrative (conceptual), and behavioral areas all need to be studied. How can this be done? One of the best, and most popular, ways is to use what is called a *process approach.*

The Process Approach

The process approach is the very same one suggested by Henri Fayol when he recommended that managers identify the major functions they perform and then study each in depth. What functions do managers perform? This depends on the individual, the level the person occupies in the hierarchy, and the type of organization. Fayol suggested that the basic functions of management are planning, organizing, commanding, coordinating, and controlling. However, these have been modified by modern writers to include more attention to the technical-quantitative and behavioral areas. In any event, in this book we are going to use a process approach in studying the field.

■ The process approach is comprehensive.

Why is the process approach so effective? The answer is that it is a flexible framework for incorporating just about everything one needs to know about management. For example, if something new comes along in the planning area that can help the manager plan more effectively, this can be included within the planning function. The same is true for all of the other functions that will be studied in this book—organizing, staffing, directing, controlling. As long as the list of functions is sufficiently comprehensive to cover the major areas of management, the student will indeed be acquainted with everything it is necessary to know about the field.

Second, the management process approach views the functions of management as interrelated. This means that they are not performed in a set sequential order such as planning first, organizing second, and staffing third. Rather, the manager performs all of these as the need arises. Practicing managers agree with this process view.

Finally, the management process encourages managers to continually examine their jobs, attempting both to identify effective administrative practices that can be used on the job and to formulate general principles that can help in this process. In this way, the manager does more than just carry out some functions. The individual studies the job and tries to understand how to do it better. In the process, management becomes less of an art and more of a science. The manager, of course, still needs to use intuition, judgment, and gut feeling in deciding how to manage people. However, the individual also uses a series of guidelines and rules that will help get the job done.

Model for This Book

In this book we are going to be using a process approach in studying five management functions. The five are *planning, organizing, staffing, directing,* and *controlling.*

Planning

Planning is the process of formulating objectives and then carrying out the steps necessary to attain them. As such, it has two important parts. The first can be thought of as deciding where to go and the second as getting there. The deciding part is often referred to as *strategy formulation.* Getting there is commonly referred to as *strategy implementation.*

■ Planning establishes direction.

In the planning section of this book we will address both of these areas. We will start in Chapter 3 by looking at where the organization is going, and we will follow in Chapter 4 by examining how decision-making techniques can be used in getting the organization to these objectives.

Organizing

Organizing involves the assignment of duties and the coordination of efforts among all organizational personnel to ensure maximum efficiency in the attainment of objectives. Organizing is a natural follow-up to planning.

■ Organizing provides for coordination of effort.

There are two important areas in organizing. The first involves the assignment of tasks and responsibilities to the personnel. The second involves the organizing of these individuals into logical groups so that they can carry out these tasks. In the study of this process you will learn that there a number of basic factors in organizing. These universal ideals will be the object of study in Chapter 5. There are also contingency organizational design ideas that help organizations meet the specific needs of their environment. These will be the focus in Chapter 6.

Staffing

There is a business cliché which holds that a firm is either growing or declining in size. If a company wants to continue growing, it must hire competent people to replace those who are leaving as well as to handle any increases that are taking place in the firm's business. In this *staffing process* the manager needs to do four distinct things: recruit, select, train, and develop personnel. The recruiting and selecting process will be the focus of Chapter 7, and training and development will be studied in Chapter 8.

■ Staffing involves recruiting, selecting, training, and development.

Directing

Directing involves guiding subordinates toward the attainment of objectives. There are three important aspects to directing: communicating, motivating, and leading.

■ Directing involves managing people to achieve goals.

Communicating is the process of transferring meanings between sender and receiver. Motivating is the process of getting people to direct their efforts toward the attainment of organizational objectives. Leadership is the process of guiding people in the performance of their work. These three areas will be studied in Chapters 9, 10, and 11, respectively.

Controlling

■ Controlling involves checking to see that everything went according to plan.

The *controlling process* involves checking to see that everything was done in accord with the plan. Did things work out the way they were intended? The nature of this control process will be examined in Chapter 12. Then in Chapter 13 the ways in which the manager can control people will be studied.

Summary

All managers get things done through people. However, there are three different types of managers. One type is made up of first-line managers who supervise the operating employees. Often called foremen or supervisors, they directly manage the workers. The second type consists of middle managers, who are located between first-line managers and top managers. These people manage first-line managers and others in the middle ranks of the hierarchy. The third type is made up of top managers, or executives. These individuals make the major operating decisions for the organization. Carrying such titles as president, chief executive officer, or senior vice-president, these top managers set overall objectives and determine operating policy for the firm.

Another way to classify managers is on the basis of what they do. Some managers are functional managers who are responsible for a particular organizational activity such as marketing, production, or finance. Others are general managers who manage a company, an independent operating division, or a subsidiary. The head of a major division of a large corporation and the president of a small company are both illustrations of a general manager.

At each major level of the hierarchy—lower, middle, and upper—different skills are required for success. At the lower levels the manager needs to have more technical skills than any other type. These are useful in understanding and carrying out "doing" activities. While the worker needs these skills in order to learn the job, the lower-level manager needs them in order to teach the new worker how to do the job.

Human skills are those that help the manager work effectively as a member of a group. They enable the individual to develop teamwork among the members of the work group. Human skills are needed at every level of the hierarchy. At the lower and middle levels, intragroup human skills are required, while at the top of the hierarchy, intergroup human skills are most beneficial.

Conceptual skills are those that help the manager see the organization as a whole. This requires a systems approach to viewing the organization. These conceptual skills are of greatest importance at the upper levels of the hierarchy.

In recent years there has been a great deal of interest focused on what managers really do. How do they spend their day? Recent research shows that they perform the three types of roles discussed in this chapter: interpersonal, informational, and decisional.

The last part of the chapter addressed the question of how to study management. It was noted that the most popular approach is the management process. This requires an identification and analysis of the various functions performed by the manager. The ones designated for study in this book are planning, organizing, staffing, directing, and controlling. In the next chapter we will begin our study of the planning function.

Review and Study Questions

1. What do first-line managers do? How do their jobs differ from those of middle managers?
2. How can you tell if someone is a middle manager? Are there any guidelines you can use? What are they?
3. If you were trying to identify top managers based on their titles, what titles would you look for? If you chose to identify them based on their jobs, what would you look for?
4. How does a functional manager differ from a general manager? Which has more authority? Explain.
5. Which of the following is a functional manager and which is a general manager: vice-president of production, vice-president of advertising, president, head of overseas operations, vice-president of finance, and chief executive officer? List and identify each.
6. In your own words, what are technical skills? How can the lower-level manager use them in getting things done?
7. What are human skills? Why are they of such great importance to managers in the middle ranks of the organization?
8. In what way do conceptual skills require the managers to use a systems approach?
9. Why are conceptual skills of greatest importance to upper-level managers? Why not lower-level managers? Explain your reasoning.
10. One of the primary roles of the manager is interpersonal duties. What are the three interpersonal duties that managers perform?
11. Managers also have informational roles. What are these roles?
12. There are four decisional roles performed by managers. What are these roles? Explain.
13. One of the best and most popular ways to study management is the process approach. What does this statement mean? Explain, incorporating into your answer the five functions that will be studied in this book.

Key Terms in the Chapter

first-line manager
middle manager
top manager
functional manager
general manager
technical skills
human skills
conceptual skills
interpersonal roles
informational roles
decisional roles
process approach

Notes

1. Robert L. Katz, "Skills of an Effective Administrator," *Harvard Business Review,* September-October 1974, p. 93.
2. The information in this section comes from Henry Mintzberg, "The Manager's Job: Folklore and Fact," *Harvard Business Review,* July–August 1975, pp. 49–61.
3. Ibid., p. 59.

Case: Developing Management Skills

Can a good engineer be a bad manager and stay happy?

Paul Hannon graduated at the top of his engineering class and immediately went to work for one of the most prestigious firms in the field. During his first four years Paul worked on a series of different engineering projects. The jobs required a great deal of travel, but Paul liked it. Recently, however, he got engaged and has been thinking of settling down. He does not want to be on the road all the time.

Paul has been thinking of putting in for an office job and has discussed this with his boss. Many of the people who work at headquarters are engineers like Paul, but they do not have to travel very much. From time to time they go out to a job site and talk to the project manager, but most of the time they communicate with such people through either memos or telephone conversations.

Paul's boss has indicated that he would be sorry to see Paul leave the field, because most managers who have made it into the upper ranks of management have had between ten and twelve years out there. Nevertheless, he will recommend Paul for a management position back at headquarters if Paul wants it. However, he has asked Paul to think a little more about the transfer. "You've been on a series of projects over the last four years," he told Paul. "During this time you have obtained some management experience, but for the most part you have been engaged in technical work. You are a member of a team, but you don't manage it. If you go to headquarters, you are going to find different types of demands placed on you. You are going to have to work with people in the sense of giving them orders and follow up to be sure the work was done right. This is a lot different from what you are currently doing. I've seen a lot of people come and go in this company. Some of them are great engineers but lousy managers. Others are lousy engineers but great managers. A few are either good or bad at both. I think you're a heck of an engineer but I don't think you'd enjoy managing people. Why not stay in the field and do what you do best? Only instead of traveling nationwide, cut down to a five-state area. This way you'll be in the field during the week but at home on weekends. I can guarantee you this type of arrangement. Think it over and let me know what you decide. I'll back you up regardless." After talking it over with his fiancee, Paul decided to stay in the field and work on projects closer to home. "My future wife wants me to be happy, and I want to be an engineer, not a manager. I think I'll be happiest under this arrangement."

Questions

1. What types of skills would a person like Paul have? Explain.
2. What types of skills would an office manager have to have? Would Paul fit in well as such a manager?

3. Do engineers not have to manage people? Why, then, would the demands on Paul as a manager in the field be any different from those in headquarters? Explain your answer.

Case: What They Say and What They Do

All they seem to do is talk and drink coffee.

Eloise Nuncio is writing a term paper entitled "The Manager's Job" for her basic management class. In an effort to get information for her paper, Eloise telephoned her uncle Richard, who is the president of a large firm. Her uncle suggested that she approach the paper in two ways: (1) talk to some managers in the firm and ask them what they do, and (2) follow a couple of them around for a day and see how they actually do their job. This sounded like a fine idea to Eloise, and she called the executive recommended by her uncle. The latter set up an interview for Eloise with six executives. Two were fairly new in the firm, two had been with the company for over five years, and the other two had been on board for over ten years. Eloise talked to them in a group session for almost two hours. When she was finished, she sketched all her ideas out on a piece of paper and reviewed them with the executives, who agreed that she had captured their ideas. In essence they told her that they spent most of their day planning, organizing, communicating, leading, and controlling. The outline looked just great.

She spent the next day with one of the executives who had been with the firm for five years. She sat in a corner of his office and watched him in action. The executive spent a great amount of time on the telephone. Much of what he discussed seemed to Eloise to be gossip or social talk. A few reports came over his desk, and he skimmed them very quickly and signed them. His secretary placed letters in front of him with the comment, "Sign the ones on the right with your full name and the ones on your left with just your first name." The executive did so without even looking at what he was signing. Twice during the morning and again in the afternoon the executive took coffee breaks during which he spent time trading ideas or suggestions for new product development with other executives. However, the discussion was very general, and Eloise really did not think the man spent enough time getting down to the important aspects of product development. Furthermore, he never took any notes on what was said. It seemed as if he felt he could keep it all in his head.

The next day was a repeat of the first. Things seemed to be done in a haphazard manner. What the executive was doing was nothing similar to what she was told when she had the conference two days earlier.

As a result, Eloise now finds that she has two types of information. The first is very well laid out and presents the manager's job as a series of functions. The second is very general and shows that managers seem to spend most of their time talking to others and handling minor matters. As a result Eloise is confused. She really does not feel she yet knows what managers do.

Questions

1. How accurate is Eloise's initial list?
2. How accurate is the information she has gathered from her two days of watching executives in action? Explain.
3. What should her paper contain? Describe the content.

380
382
383
384

Part Two

The Management Process: Planning

The objective of this part is to study what planning is all about. There are two basic parts to planning: setting objectives and making decisions that help the organization reach these objectives. The first is obtained through the planning process, the second with the use of managerial decision making.

The planning process consists of setting both long- and short-range objectives. The long-range objectives establish direction for the organization. The short-range objectives provide a basis for feedback, useful in determining whether the organization's progress toward its long-range objectives is on target. The planning process systematically weaves together these two types of objectives.

Once the objectives are established, managerial decision-making techniques are employed to achieve them. Yet how does one make a "right" decision? This part will show that a "right," or rational, decision will vary depending on who is making it and under what conditions it is being made.

Chapter 3 The Planning Process

Objectives of the Chapter

While the manager has many functions to perform, planning belongs at the top of the list. Before a manager does anything at all, at least some general direction should be determined. After all, how can one organize workers without knowing what they will be doing? How can one control operations without some initial objectives against which to compare performance? Questions such as these point out the importance of planning, which is really nothing more than a way of answering the question: Where does the organization want to go?

The first objective of this chapter is to study the nature of planning. What is it all about? Then attention will be directed toward the seven steps in the planning process with a discussion of what occurs during each.

The second major objective of this chapter is to examine how strategy is actually formulated. Who determines the organization's strategy and how do they go about doing so? Attention will also be directed to how organizations change their strategy-making approaches.

The last objective of the chapter is to answer the question: Does planning really help? In doing so, we will examine both the advantages and limitations of planning.

When you have finished studying the material in this chapter, you should be able to:

1. Define the term *planning.*
2. Describe the three premises on which strategic plans are based.
3. Set forth the seven steps in the planning process.
4. Compare and contrast strategic and operational planning.
5. Identify the three styles or modes of strategy making used in modern organizations.
6. Compare and contrast these strategy-making modes.

The Nature of Planning

Planning is the process of: (1) setting objectives and (2) determining the steps that have to be accomplished in attaining these objectives. The actual setting of the objectives occurs during the *strategy formulation* stage of planning. The pursuit of these objectives takes place during the *strategy implementation* stage. In practice these two stages often overlap since the organization is working toward certain objectives while determining which new ones should be set for the future.

Top managers are most concerned with the formulating of strategy. Middle and lower-level managers are most concerned with implementing this strategy and following it up by determining how well things have gone. Thus, the top executives set the direction, while the rest of the managers work toward getting there. The former are very long-range in their planning orientation, while the latter are more concerned with the immediate future. Figure 3.1 provides an illustration of this idea.

A Model of Planning

■ Strategic planning is external.

In putting everything into an overall framework, it is helpful to think in terms of strategic (long-range) and operational (short-range) planning. *Strategic planning* is external in its orientation. This means that a strategic plan is constructed by

Figure 3.1
The Planning Process from a Hierarchical and Time-Span Perspective

A Good Executive Thinks Ahead:
A Suggestion for Apportioning Your Thinking Time

	Today	1 Week Ahead	1 Month Ahead	3 to 6 Months Ahead	1 Year Ahead	2 Years Ahead	3 to 4 Years Ahead	5 to 10 Years Ahead
President	1%	2%	5%	17%	15%	25%	30%	5%
Vice President	2%	4%	10%	29%	20%	20%	13%	2%
Works Manager	4%	8%	15%	38%	20%	10%	5%	
Superintendent	6%	10%	20%	43%	10%	9%	2%	
Department Manager	10%	10%	25%	39%	10%	5%	1%	
Section Supervisor	15%	20%	25%	37%	3%			
Group Supervisor	38%	40%	15%	5%	2%			

Source: Ralph M. Besse, "Company Planning Must Be Planned!" Reprinted with the special permission of *Dun's Review*, April 1957, p. 48. Copyright, 1957, Dun & Bradstreet Publications Corporation.

looking at the external environment, trying to anticipate what changes will be taking place out there, and devising a plan for either responding to or controlling these events. For example, in an industry which is heavily oriented to research and development (R&D), the management must continually concern itself with technical breakthroughs that will occur. What is the competition up to? What new patents are they likely to secure during the next couple of years? How will these patents affect our product line? Will we have to drop some of our lines because they will be inferior to the competitive products? Can we develop anything new that will put our competition in a weak position? Questions such as these must be answered in formulating the strategic plan.

Other questions are related to the market itself. What types of goods and services will the customer want over the next three to five years? Where will the individual buy these goods and services? How will the customer pay for them? The queries directed at the marketing area seek to provide the company with important answers regarding the product and the customer.

Finally, in the strategic plan the company must be concerned with financing its operations. How much money will we need for our operations over the next five years? How will we raise the money? How should this money be invested? Can we afford outside financing or should we sell stocks or bonds?

■ Operational planning is internal.

Operational planning, on the other hand, is more *internal* in orientation. In the operational plan the company seeks to be efficient. It tries to develop ways to use its resources profitably. Cost reductions are studied, ways to get more output from machines and workers are examined, methods for improving morale are reviewed. The operational plan is the one people think of most often when the topic of planning is mentioned.

As seen in Figure 3.2, the strategic plan sets the overall goals for the organization, while the operational plan is more concerned with short-run, day-to-day activities. The strategic plan provides the basis for the operational plan. Strategic goals are converted into operational targets.

Figure 3.2
A Planning Model

Strategic Plan	→	Operational Plan
Examination of the external environment		Examination of the internal environment
Concern with the market and the customer		Concern with the operational aspects of the business
Interest in financing long-term operations	→	Interest in efficiency over the short run
Desire to be competitive and grow		Desire to control costs and increase output
Formulation of long-term objectives		Formulation of short-term objectives

Planning Premises

How is a strategic plan actually put together? Before we look at the various steps involved, it is important to examine what are called *planning premises.* These are *assumptions* or inputs that *influence* the strategic plan. There are three in all: (1) the firm's basic mission, (2) the personal values of the top managers, and (3) the company's strengths and weaknesses.

▪ Premises are assumptions that influence the plan.

Basic Mission. In constructing a strategic plan an organization must ask itself two questions: What business are we in? What business should we be in? If a firm concludes that it is in the transportation business, and this is the right one for it, this will help in setting overall objectives. If another company determines that it is in the plastics business, and this is the right one for it, this will help in formulating overall direction. Why? Because the answers to these questions help identify the types of objectives each company should pursue. And by periodically evaluating the business they are in, and should be in, companies can change with the times. For example, consider the past and present businesses of the firms in Table 3.1.

▪ What business is the organization in?

Personal Values of the Top Managers. Another important input into the strategic plan is the personal values of the top managers. Are these managers conservative? If so, the organization's objectives will be conservative. If these managers are the same individuals who founded the firm, the company is likely to be very much interested in new product development. If the owner-managers are no longer in control and the organization is run by professional managers, the firm is more likely to be as interested in the marketing and financial aspects of the business as it is in the production side of things.

▪ Personal values influence plans.

The values of the top managers influence the organization's direction. Often, what is good for the top managers is good for the company. One cannot overemphasize the effect of decisions by the top managers on the firm's overall plan.

Table 3.1
Past and Present Basic Missions

Firm	Past Basic Mission	Current Basic Mission
General Motors	To be in the automobile business	To be in the transportation business
Gulf Oil	To be in the oil business	To be in the business of providing energy
United Artists	To be in the movie-making business	To be in the entertainment business
IBM	To be in the typewriter-calculator business	To be in the information-processing business
New York Life Insurance	To provide life insurance to customers	To provide personal insurance needs of all kinds to customers

■ Always lead from strength.

Firm's Strengths and Weaknesses. Finally, in setting strategic objectives the company needs to lead from its strengths. What does it do well? If we are talking about the Polaroid Corporation, the firm will be interested in leading from its research and development strength. If the company is General Motors, it will push its auto design and styling strengths. If it is the Chrysler Corporation, it will build a strategy around its engineering strength. If it is IBM, it will build a strategy around its high-quality product and its fine service.

These three planning premises affect the strategic plan in that they help determine the *types* of long-range objectives the firm will establish. With these three influences in mind, let us look at the way in which a business actually plans for the future.

Steps in Planning

There are seven steps in planning:

1. Analyze the external environment.
2. Analyze the internal environment.
3. Determine competitive advantages.
4. Identify a target market.
5. Set objectives.
6. Purchase and allocate the resources necessary to implement the plan.
7. Control operations.

Although they are not always carried out in the same order, the following sections examine them in logical sequence.

Analyzing the External Environment

The first step in planning is to analyze the external environment. How does the market look? What is the competition doing? What new opportunities are there in this market?

The answers to these questions require some form of *forecasting.* One of the simplest forecasting methods is *extrapolation.* This approach assumes that the future will be a continuation of the past. If the firm has had the following sales:

1978	$1.7 million
1979	1.9 million
1980	2.1 million
1981	2.3 million

it is assumed that sales in 1982 will be $2.5 million. The problem with this approach is that it does not allow for any dramatic changes. For example, what if there is a recession? Or what if the competition comes out with a new product which is protected by a patent?

A more realistic approach is one based on *externally generated economic information.* The federal government provides a great deal of information about industry trends, lead indicators, and lag indicators. A *lead indicator* is one which signals an upcoming change in the economy. Table 3.2 provides a list of lead indicators for the economy at large. If these start going up, the economy is likely to follow, and business will be in for some good economic times. *Lag indicators,* meanwhile, start to change after the economy has begun moving in one direction or the other. For example, after the economy starts up we can expect to find business expenditures for plant and equipment rising, the unemployment rate going down, and bank interest rates on short-term loans dropping. On the other hand, after the economy starts coming down, we can expect to find these indicators moving in the opposite direction, with plant and equipment expenditures dropping, unemployment going up, and bank interest rates on short-term loans starting to rise. By keeping its eye on lead and lag indicators, a business can anticipate changes not only in the economy at large but in its own industry in particular.

■ Get externally generated economic information.

Another important method of forecasting is *competitive analysis.* What new goods and services has the competition come up with recently, and what is likely to occur during the next couple of years? This question is particularly important to firms in industries where R&D is important. One must always anticipate technical breakthroughs by the competition. Otherwise what looks like a great opportunity may end up being a tremendous threat. For example, in the early 1970s digital watches entered the market. Because of the high R&D investment required to develop them, many firms felt that prices would remain high and they could safely enter the market. However, Texas Instruments Inc. (TI) proved that it not only had the R&D capability to develop these watches but the manufacturing capability to turn them out at a very low price ($10–$30 range). Many firms that entered this

■ Make a competitive analysis.

Table 3.2
Economic Indicators

Lead Indicators	Lag Indicators
Average weekly hours worked	Business expenditures for plant and equipment
New businesses being started	Unemployment rate
New building permits	Bank interest rates on short-term loans
New orders for durable goods	Amount of inventory on hand in manufacturing firms
Corporate profits after taxes	Industrial loans outstanding
Consumer installment credit	Personal loans outstanding

market lost money. They simply did not anticipate the major technical and production breakthroughs that TI would engineer. And today TI is finding itself losing ground to Japanese manufacturers.

After the general economy and the competition are examined, the company needs to ask: What share of this market will we capture? This is where the *sales forecast* comes into play. One of the best ways of forecasting sales is to gather information from consumers, salespeople, and company executives and then construct the forecast. By finding out what the consumer likes, the business obtains some important user information. However, people do not always do what they say they will. Therefore, by asking the salesforce about the market, the firm can modify consumer responses. Salespeople are excellent sources of information because they often know why people buy certain goods and services. They can help interpret the consumer responses. Finally, the company executives can refine the forecast even further. These individuals can modify the forecast to reflect projected market conditions, production capabilities, and the financial state of the firm. The result is a sales forecast.

Analyzing the Internal Environment

■ Cash is important.

Next the firm needs to examine its internal environment. Three internal factors warrant close attention. The first is *cash.* How much money does the company have for developing a strategy? Cash gives a firm flexibility. The more money the business has to spend, the more elaborate a strategy it can formulate.

■ So are the physical assets.

The second factor is *physical assets.* The firm's current inventory, machinery, equipment, and plant are the things it must use to fashion a strategy. If the company has a lot of printing presses, for example, it should build a strategy around the use of these presses. If it has a large inventory on hand, it should formulate a strategy that will help sell this inventory. The physical assets of the firm help determine what the company can do.

■ And personnel competencies.

The third factor is *personnel competencies.* The people who work for the business have certain competencies or capabilities. There are certain things they do well. In a newspaper, it is the skill with which the reporters and editors gather and report the news. In a production plant, it is the management's ability to set up and the line's ability to manufacture units at the lowest possible cost. As do the physical assets of the firm, the people who work for the firm help determine its strategy. To a large degree, in fact, the objectives of an organization are set by the people who manage the firm. If they make wise decisions the firm will prosper and grow. If they make poor decisions the firm will suffer.

Determining Competitive Advantages

■ Get the most profit with the least investment.

After the firm has analyzed its external and internal environment, it should know what it can do well. Often referred to as the *first law of strategy,* this means *lead from strength.*

However, companies must be careful in implementing this law. If a firm is able to produce a large number of units at a low price, it might appear that a strategy of

REACTOR CONTROL ROOM
PUSH
DANGER
STAYSKAL '79 CHICAGO TRIBUNE
"'CHANCE OF HUMAN ERROR! CHANCE OF HUMAN ERROR!' THAT'S ALL I HEAR AND I'M SICK OF IT... HELP ME WITH THIS DOOR, WILL YOU, IT SEEMS TO BE STUCK!"

price competition should be used. On the other hand, if the competition has newer and more efficient machines, it may be impossible to compete strictly on the basis of price. The company's biggest strength is not enough to meet the competition. What should it do?

This is where rule number two comes in: *Choose a strategy that allows you to develop the most meaningful competitive advantage with the smallest amount of resources.* In this case the company should develop this meaningful competitive advantage by doing something that the competition either cannot or will not do. For example, the firm should see if it can develop a marketing campaign that will convince the customer that its products are better, despite the slightly higher price. Such a strategy should also help acquaint potential customers with the product, thereby increasing the chance for sales. Finally, the business should conduct some marketing research to see if the customers want any modifications in the current product. Also, it should consider whether the product requires servicing. If so, the firm may sell its products for more than the competition but also provide a servicing arrangement. Many customers who buy goods like television sets, refrigerators, electric ovens, freezers, and automobiles buy as much on the basis of brand name as price. For example, many people like to buy at Sears, Roebuck because of its "satisfaction or your money back" philosophy. If the customers are not pleased, they can return the product. Does Sears sell the best quality television set for the money? Maybe not, but for every $100 spent by consumers in this country, $1 is spent at Sears. People will buy a Sears brand name or product.

Identifying a Target Market

After a firm determines how to achieve a competitive advantage, it needs to firm up its aim on the target market. How much money will the people buying this product make every year? Where do they usually buy this product? How much do they expect to pay? What type of sales assistance will be required in selling to them?

Answers to questions like these help the firm focus in on potential customers. In marketing terms, this is called *identifying the market niche.* The market niche is identified by concentrating on the *4 Ps of marketing:*

▪ The 4 Ps of marketing.

- Product. What should the product look like? What should it be able to do?
- Place. Where should the product be made available to the customer: supermarket, hardware store, drugstore, newsstand? Where will the good have to be placed in order to be sold?
- Price. How much should be charged for the good? Is the firm pursuing the upper portion of the market via high price? Or is it seeking strong market penetration via low price? Or is the price basically fixed, because everyone is accustomed to paying the same regardless of where they buy it?
- Promotion. How will the good be promoted? Will an advertising campaign be used? Will personal selling be required? How will product demand be stimulated?

Once these questions are answered, the firm has established its direction. Now it is a matter of setting objectives and attaining them. Table 3.3 illustrates these processes.

Setting Objectives

▪ Determine sales growth.

Two types of objectives need to be set: strategic and operational. *Strategic objectives relate the organization to its external environment.* These objectives provide the firm with a basis for comparing how well it is doing in relation to everyone else in the industry. One strategic objective is *sales growth.* Given the data in Table 3.4, how well is Company A doing?

The data in Table 3.4 show that Company A not only is increasing its sales at a faster rate than the overall industry but also is gaining on its major competitor. Note that the competitor's sales growth for each of the last four years has increased at a decreasing rate. The competition is going up more and more slowly. Company A has been going up faster. It is currently increasing its sales at an annual rate of 28 percent, compared to 17 percent for the competition. Sales growth is an important strategic objective because it helps the firm set a target that can be accomplished only at the expense of the competition. Remember, if Company A keeps increasing its sales, that increase must come at someone's expense. The expense must be shared by Company A and the industry at large.

▪ Set a market share target.

Another strategic objective is *market share.* This is closely related to sales growth, but there is a difference. If the industry's sales are increasing at a rate of 15 percent annually, and Company A's sales are increasing at a rate of 10 percent annually, the firm may feel it is doing quite well. However, by examining market share—company sales divided by industry sales—it is possible to determine the percentage of the market being captured. In this example, Company A would be losing ground.

Small companies do not worry too much about market share, but big ones do. General Motors is particularly concerned about its share of the automotive market. By the late 1970s GM was holding 55 percent of the American auto makers' market

Table 3.3
Sears's New Strategy: About Face!

Sears, Roebuck advertises itself as "the place where America shops." Recently, however, the company has found it necessary to change its strategy—or find that America is shopping elsewhere.

What has caused this change in Sears's strategy? To answer this one has to go back to the early 1970s, when the company started offering higher-priced goods. Sears realized that many families now had two incomes; both members of the family were working. How would they spend this extra money? Sears believed they would want to buy higher quality, more expensive merchandise. Following up on this strategy, Sears began building a fashion-apparel image for itself. It opened separate shops to sell Johnny Miller sportswear, and began to stock high-priced women's wear.

The problem, however, was that the strategy confused the customers. They did not come to Sears to buy high-priced merchandise. They were interested in good quality at a low price. If they were going to buy a high-quality suit or dress, they were not going to purchase it at Sears. The result? Sears began to lose customers. So while its sales kept increasing, the competition was doing even better. By the late 1970s almost 67 percent of Sears's volume was coming from markets where it was losing its share of customers. K mart and J. C. Penney hurried in to fill the gap and take away customers. K mart sought to win Sears's budget customers, while Penney attempted to lure away its apparel customers. Sears retaliated by putting in budget shops to win back customers. However, it did not work. People were still confused as to what type of store Sears was. A competitor claimed that people now came to Sears only when something was on sale.

At the present time Sears has backed off and reversed its strategy. It is no longer trying to be everything to everybody. First, it is reducing its product lines from 60,000 to around 35,000. Second, the company is going back to stocking more middle-of-the-road staple goods that are geared more to being functional than fashionable. Third, Sears is cutting its advertising and promotional markdowns, which really did not help in the past. Fourth, it is centralizing more control over field operations so that headquarters makes the major decisions and the stores carry them out. Prior to this time the stores had much more authority over their own operations. Finally, Sears is taking steps to reduce and control its inventory and to thin its corporate staff.

Will Sears succeed with this new strategy? Only time will tell. But one thing is certain—the company is taking steps to identify its target market. It still wants to be the place "where America shops."

Source: Based on "Sears' Strategic About-Face," *Business Week,* January 8, 1979, pp. 80–83.

Table 3.4
Sales Growth

Year	Company A	Company A's Major Competition	The Industry Overall
1979	+22%	+26%	+11%
1980	+24	+24	+16
1981	+26	+20	+14
1982	+28	+17	+13

against 45 percent for Ford, Chrysler, and American Motors combined. As seen through its recent large expenditures for auto research and development and styling, this is a percentage the company would like to maintain. In some industries, like automobile manufacturing, companies will sometimes give up profit in order to capture market share. They believe they can increase their profits later on, when the person returns to buy another new car from them.

■ Establish an ROI objective.

A third strategic objective is *return on investment*—profit divided by assets. Return on investment, or ROI, tells the company how well it is doing with the amount of money it has invested. Smaller firms will obviously be unable to match the larger ones in terms of overall profit. However, they may be able to obtain a higher ROI than their larger competitors. In any event, ROI tells a firm how well it is managing its investments.

■ Operational objectives are efficiency oriented.

While strategic objectives compare the firm to the competition, *operational objectives* are designed to secure internal efficiency. Common operational objectives include *increased output, lower costs, higher quality in the product, low tardiness and absenteeism,* and *high profit.* All these objectives can be accomplished, at least partially, through efficiency measures. For example, by ensuring that machines are in good running order and that their operators know what they are supposed to be doing, a firm is likely to increase output and lower costs. The company should also be able to achieve higher quality and higher profits. Meanwhile, if the business has trained its managers well, morale should be high, and people should like working for the organization. This will lead to low absenteeism and turnover.

Most small businesses spend the greatest amount of their time pursuing operational objectives. They are concerned with short-run success. As long as the company is efficient, it does not worry too much about where it will be in five or ten years. However, as the company begins to grow in size, it is important to become more oriented to the long run. No firm can get very large without taking the competition into account. This is where strategic planning enters the picture. Therefore when it comes to objectives, it is common to find most firms most interested in operational objectives when they are small but developing a growing concern for strategic objectives as they begin to get larger.

Purchasing and Allocating the Resources Necessary to Implement the Plan

■ Allocate the necessary resources.

Now that the company knows its objectives, it has to determine how to reach them. Are there any new machines that have to be purchased? Do more people have to be hired? Are all departments clear about what they are supposed to do? These are *action-oriented* questions. The strategy formulation stage has ended and the strategy implementation stage has begun.

When most people think of planning, they think of this particular stage. They are accustomed to moving toward the objective. However, as has been illustrated, it is first necessary to *plan the plan.* In fact, the more time a company spends planning, the less time implementing the plan takes. This is because more of the bugs have been worked out. Everyone now knows what to do. Figure 3.3 provides an illustration of this idea. Note in the figure that the more time a company spends planning, the less time it will take to implement the plan. *Furthermore, for every day spent on planning, more than one day will be reduced from the implementation time.* While this is, to be sure, a general rule regarding planning and implementation, practicing managers report that it is an accurate one.[1]

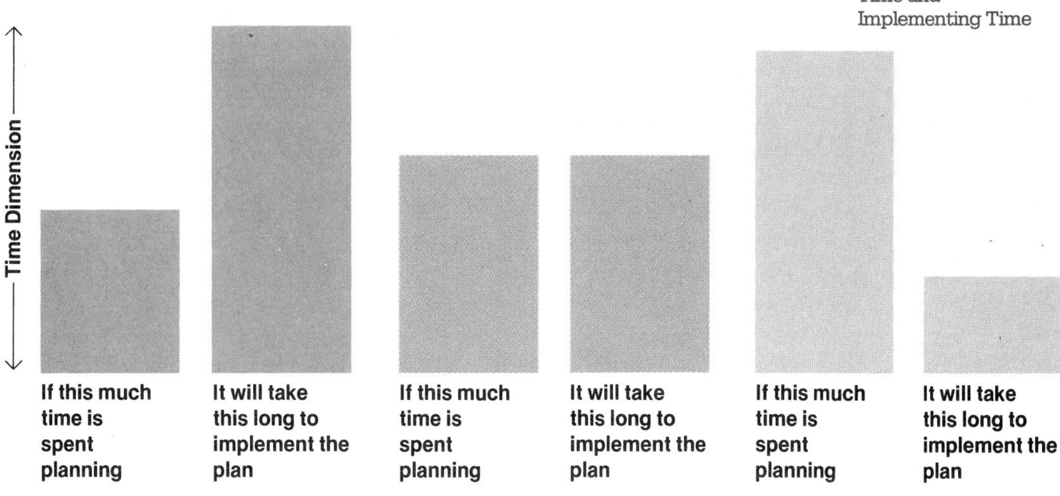
Time Dimension
If this much time is spent planning
It will take this long to implement the plan
If this much time is spent planning
It will take this long to implement the plan
If this much time is spent planning
It will take this long to implement the plan

Figure 3.3
The Relationship between Planning Time and Implementing Time

Controlling Operations

▪ Control significant deviations only.

Once the plan is up and going, the company needs to concern itself with overall control. The best way to control operations is by comparing results against objectives. Are things happening as planned? As will be seen when control is discussed later in the book, the firm should *not* at this point be concerned with minor problems. If profit was targeted at $1 million but turned out to be only $975,000, this may not be a sufficiently significant deviation to warrant attention. However, if the firm wanted to capture 13 percent of the market but captured only 7 percent, that is a significant difference. Where is the line that separates those things that are significant enough to examine from those that are minor and do not warrant attention? The question has to be answered by the top management. However, the point to remember is that not every problem warrants attention. If it is going to cost $1 to find out why five cents was lost, the control is too expensive. *Stick to the important problems which, if corrected, will result in significantly improved profit or efficiency.*

Finally, when something does go wrong, the reason has to be found in one of the six planning steps examined in this section. The firm may have incorrectly analyzed the external or internal environments, wrongly determined its competitive advantages, identified the wrong target market, set unrealistic objectives, and/or implemented the plan incorrectly. At any rate, the important thing to remember is that sometimes a plan will fail and it will be no one's fault. From time to time even the best plans prove unworkable. There is an old saying that if you build a better mousetrap, the world will beat a path to your door. But this is not necessarily true. People have built better mousetraps and not sold them. The story in Table 3.5 provides a classic illustration.

Table 3.5
The Best Laid Plans of Mice and Men

Dick Woolworth of the Woodstream Corporation had an interesting idea. What the world needed, he believed, was a better mousetrap. His company already manufactured traps for catching all kinds of animals, from grizzly bears to elephants. It would not be too difficult to build one for catching mice.

This trap, however, was different. Specially designed so that people could tell the difference between it and the old standard mousetrap, it was made of plastic and looked like a sardine can with an arched doorway at floor level through which mice could enter. Once inside, the mouse would be killed by what amounted to an upside-down guillotine, which snapped up from below.

The product was priced ten cents higher than any other competitive trap, but was also more economical for one particular reason: Instead of throwing out the trap with the mouse, one could reset this trap and use it over and over again. Convinced that they had designed and built a better mousetrap, the Woodstream people sent these traps out to hardware dealers all across the country. What happened? Nothing! No one would buy them. Why not? Because, the company learned to its dismay, no one wanted to have to pick the dead mouse out of the trap, throw the rodent away, reset the trap, and put it in place. Housewives, in particular, were used to throwing out the mouse with the trap.

As a result, the ventured failed. In an effort to get rid of a large percentage of its inventory, the company offered to sell a million of the traps to the city of New York for $144,000. It wired its offer to the governor, but he did not even give the company a nibble. The result: The company gave up on the product. What looked like a great idea on paper proved unworkable in the real world. Another example that the world will not always beat a path to the door of someone who has a better mousetrap.

Source: Adapted from Stephen J. Fansweet, "Dick Woolworth Builds a Better Mousetrap—and Falls on His Face," *Wall Street Journal,* September 24, 1970, p. 1.

Strategy Modes

While the planning process has been explained, there is one overriding question most students of management still ask. Exactly how do firms formulate their strategy? Are they very systematic or do they tend to be quite disorganized? In answer to this basic query, research shows that there are three ways in which strategy making can take place: (1) the entrepreneurial mode, (2) the adaptive mode, and (3) the planning mode. We will examine each.[2]

The Entrepreneurial Mode

An *entrepreneur* is an individual who has founded and developed an enterprise. Quite often this person is the genius behind the company's success. Edward Land is the creative genius responsible for the success of the Polaroid Corporation. Ray Kroc made McDonald's what it is today. And Katherine Graham has brought the *Washington Post* to its current place of prominence in the newspaper world. While these people may not perfectly fit into what we will identify as the *entrepreneurial mode,* people like them do work in this style.

The typical picture of the entrepreneur is one of a rough, pragmatic individual who has been driven since early childhood by a powerful need to achieve and be independent. Research reveals that entrepreneurs have often faced some disruption during their lifetimes and that instead of retreating from the problem, they plunged on into what looked like even greater insecurity.

What characteristics does the person who fits this entrepreneurial mode have?

First, the individual is most concerned with an active search for new opportunities. Rather than sitting around trying to solve problems, as most people would, they plunge on looking for new things to do. They are very active people.

■ Entrepreneurs are action oriented.

Second, power tends to be centralized in their hands. The entrepreneur personally keeps this power and commits the organization to major courses of action.

■ Keep their power centralized.

Third, when there is uncertainty about where the organization should be going, the entrepreneur leaps forward, making bold decisions. The individual seems to seek out and thrive on conditions of uncertainty. These decisions are often referred to as bold strokes or courageous moves that succeed despite all odds and all advice.

■ Thrive on conditions of uncertainty.

Fourth, the most important goal of the entrepreneurial organization is growth. The entrepreneur is motivated by a need for achievement. This results in the manager's decision to grow, sometimes at any price.

■ And want growth.

On an overall basis, the organization that is operated in the entrepreneurial mode believes that the environment can be controlled and manipulated to its own point of view. The entrepreneur sees the environment as a force to confront and control.

The Adaptive Mode

The *adaptive mode* is that used by the policy maker who accepts the environment as beyond the control of the organization. This individual believes that things are going to remain pretty much the way they are, and if there are any changes, there is nothing the organization can do about them. The manager is also faced with a lack of clear objectives. As a result, the individual plans for the short run only, because the long run is too difficult to predict. The adaptive decision maker also feels that the environment is very complex and that no one knows for sure that will happen. So why plan for the next five years, when it is unclear what will happen over the next twelve months?

One of the major characteristics that distinguish the adaptive mode of strategy making is that the organization has no clear-cut goals. In fact, there are so many powerful groups in the organization—unions, managers, owners, lobby groups—that it is virtually impossible to establish a plan that allows the organization to completely satisfy the objectives of all these groups. Some of them can achieve their goals only at the expense of others. Therefore, the decision maker tries to make decisions that will keep everyone moderately happy, without totally pleasing any one in particular.

■ There are no clear-cut goals.

A second characteristic of the adaptive mode is that the manager makes decisions that are reactive rather than proactive. Rather than trying to make things happen (proactive), the organization responds to problems after they have occurred (reactive). When possible, the organization tries to eliminate all risk. For example, the individual tries to establish agreements with others so as to ensure an adequate supply of materials, and negotiates long-term purchasing contracts and any other type of agreements which will ensure that the firm's market is protected.

■ Adaptive decisions tend to be reactive.

■ Planning is short-run in nature.

A third characteristic of the adaptive organization is that it makes its decisions in small incremental steps. Because the environment is complex, the organization feels that it needs feedback from earlier decisions before pushing on and making further decisions. It will not make major decisions for fear of venturing too far into the unknown. Its planning process consists of a series of short-range plans.

■ Not all decisions are in harmony.

A fourth characteristic is that decisions are not always in harmony. Sometimes what one manager does conflicts with what another does. The demands on the organization are so diverse that no one manager has the mental capacity to deal with all of them. As a result, it is easier and less expensive to make decisions that resolve a particular problem and then to let it go than it is to ask whether a decision will cause a problem somewhere else in the organization. A manager may give a subordinate an extra $500 in order to keep the individual from leaving. This may raise problems for other managers, who are now faced with subordinates threatening to quit unless they too get $500 raises. It is important to remember, however, that while strategy making may be fragmented, it is also flexible. The decision maker is free to adapt to the needs of the moment. Many modern organizations are represented by the adaptive mode of strategy making.

The Planning Mode

■ Planning mode gives major attention to formal planning.

The *planning mode* is characterized by major attention to formal planning. One of its essential features is the use of an analyst or planner who works alongside the manager. The planner assumes major responsibility for much of the strategy-making process.

■ Systematic analysis of the environment.

A second feature of the planning mode is systematic analysis, both in searching for new opportunities and in solving existing problems. Proposals are examined in terms of feasibility and profit. The planner is most concerned in dealing with projects that involve risk. Carefully examining each project, the planner calculates the likelihood of success and then recommends projects with the best chance of succeeding.

■ Integration of decisions and strategies.

A third feature is the integration of decisions and strategies. The organization makes decisions that complement each other. As a result, this planning mode is oriented toward a systematic, comprehensive analysis.

Which Mode Is Best?

When is one of these modes preferable to the other two? In answering this question, it is helpful to identify some of the characteristics and conditions of the three modes. (See Table 3.6.) An illustration of the paths of the three modes is also useful. (See Figure 3.4.)

Note that the entrepreneurial mode calls for strategy-making authority resting with one powerful person. Also, the environment has to be responsive to the entrepreneur's moves and the organization must be growth oriented. When are these conditions likely? When the organization is small or young. Then it is dominated by an owner who often has little to lose by acting boldly. In fact, it may be the organization's only hope for survival.

Table 3.6
Characteristics and Conditions of the Three Strategy Modes

Characteristics	Entrepreneurial Mode	Adaptive Mode	Planning Mode
Goals of the organization	Growth	Unsure	Efficiency and growth
Who sets the strategy	Entrepreneur	Done through bargaining with the various groups	Management
Time-horizon in planning	Long run	Short run	Long run
Motive for decisions	Proactive	Reactive	Proactive/reactive
Type of environment they like to work in	Uncertainty	Certainty	Risk
Conditions for Use			
Source of power	Entrepreneur	Divided	Management
Organizational environment	Yielding	Complex, dynamic	Predictable, stable
Status of the organization	Young, small or having strong leadership	Established	Large

Figure 3.4
Paths of Strategic Modes

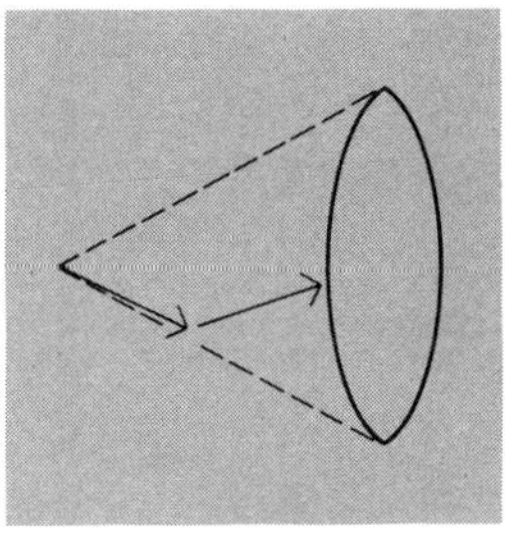

Entrepreneurial Mode: Characterized by Bold Decision Making

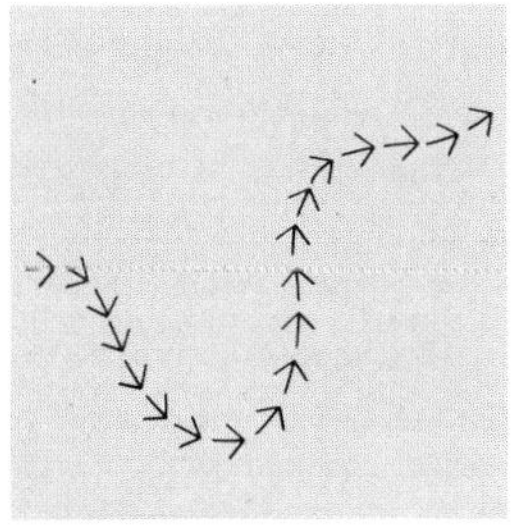

Adaptive Mode: Characterized by Short-Range, Changing Plans

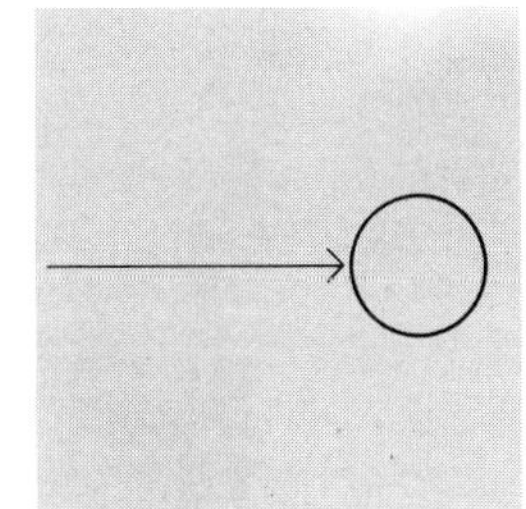

Planning Mode: Characterized by Formal, Directional Planning

The adaptive mode suggests that the organization faces a complex, changing environment. This is usually a large organization with many powerful groups within it. Universities, large hospitals, and large corporations often fit into this mode.

The planning mode should be used by organizations that are large enough to afford formal planning. Also, the environment has to be stable or at least predictable. Otherwise, the planner will have great difficulty in determining a course of action for the organization.

■ Organizations change their strategy modes.

Does an organization always stay with one mode? No, it changes around. For example, as a company grows, it often moves from an entrepreneurial to an adaptive mode. Additionally, departments within the organization will often use different modes. One study, for example, found that in a large hotel, housekeeping and the front office, where operations were routinized, used a planning mode. In marketing, where imagination and bold action were important, the entrepreneurial mode was employed. Finally, in the personnel department, which faced a complicated labor market, the adaptive mode was used.

Thus there are numerous ways to formulate strategy. The manager must choose the one which best meets the needs of the situation.

Summary

Planning is the process of setting objectives and determining the steps that have to be accomplished to attain those objectives. During the strategy formulation stage the objectives are set, while during the strategy implementation stage the objectives are pursued.

The long-range, or strategic, plan is the one in which overall organizational objectives are formulated. This plan is external in its orientation. Primary attention is given to such factors as market conditions, the competition, the product line, and how the overall operations will be financed.

The short-range, or operational, plan is the one in which day-to-day operations are carried out, and short-run targets are established. This plan is internal in its orientation, with primary attention given to such factors as costs, production output, profit, morale, tardiness, and absenteeism.

The three premises on which a strategic plan are based are: (1) the firm's basic mission, (2) the personal values of the top managers, and (3) the company's strengths and weaknesses. These will influence the strategic objectives that the organization sets.

The actual steps in planning are seven in all. They are: (1) analysis of the external environment, (2) analysis of the internal environment, (3) determination of competitive advantages, (4) identification of a target market, (5) setting objectives, (6) purchasing and allocating those resources necessary to implement the plan, and (7) controlling operations. If a plan does not succeed in attaining its objectives, the reason can be found somewhere within these seven steps.

The last part of the chapter examined strategy modes. In all, there are three types of strategy-making modes: entrepreneurial, adaptive, and planning.

The entrepreneurial mode is often used by the owner-manager of a business. This individual has founded the organization and is usually the driving genius behind its success. This person is most concerned with finding new opportunities, as opposed to problem solving. Power tends to be centralized in this person's hands, and the individual takes bold steps forward in the face of uncertainty. The most important goal of the entrepreneur is growth.

The adaptive mode is used by the policy maker who accepts the current situation as a given. The person believes that things cannot be changed very much, and if they can they are outside the control of the organization. The individual is a short-run planner, has no real clear-cut goals, and tends to react to the environment instead of trying to control it. Also, the manager is more concerned with pacifying certain groups than in finding out whether these decisions are in accord with those being made elsewhere in the organization.

The planning mode is characterized by major attention to formal planning. The planning mode uses systematic analysis, both in searching for new opportunities and in solving existing problems. A third feature of the planning mode is the integration of decisions and strategies. The organization makes decisions that complement each other.

Which mode is best will depend on the situation. In young, small firms the entrepreneurial mode is common. In complex, changing environments, the adaptive mode is often employed. The planning mode tends to be used by organizations that are large enough to afford formal planning. However, there are characteristics of all three in virtually every organization.

Review and Study Questions

1. Define the term *planning* in your own words.
2. How does strategic planning differ from operational planning? Compare and contrast the two with the use of at least five different characteristics.
3. What is meant by a firm's basic mission? Explain by citing two examples of basic missions.
4. There are three planning premises on which the strategic plan rests. What are they? Describe each of them.
5. What is the first step in the planning process? What is the second step? Explain what happens in each.
6. How do most companies forecast the environment? Cite some examples.
7. What are the three most important internal factors that warrant attention when analyzing the internal environment? Explain each.
8. The first law of strategy is: Lead from strength. What does this law mean?
9. Another rule of strategy is: Choose a strategy that allows you to develop the most meaningful competitive advantage with the smallest amount of resources. What does this rule mean? Explain it in your own words.
10. How does a company go about selecting a target market? Explain.

11. In what way do strategic objectives differ from operational objectives? Cite some examples of each in your answer.
12. For every day spent on planning, more than one day will be reduced from implementation time. What does this statement mean?
13. In the control process, one of the general rules is: Stick to the important problems which, if corrected, will result in significantly improved profit or efficiency. Explain this rule in your own words.
14. How is strategy making carried out in the entrepreneurial mode? Include in your answer some of the characteristics of this mode.
15. How is strategy making carried out in the adaptive mode? In giving your answer, be sure to cite at least two major characteristics of this mode.
16. How is strategy making carried out in the planning mode? Explain.
17. Which of the three mentioned modes is most effective? Defend your answer.

Key Terms in the Chapter

planning
strategy formulation
strategy implementation
strategic planning
operational planning
basic mission
extrapolation
lead indicators
lag indicators
lead from strength
strategic objective
operational objective
entrepreneurial mode
adaptive mode
planning mode

Notes

1. For more on how planning saves time, see R. Alec Mackenzie, *The Time Trap* (New York: McGraw-Hill, 1972), pp. 41–42.
2. The data in this section can be found in Henry Mintzberg, "Strategy-Making in Three Modes," *California Management Review,* Winter 1973, pp. 44–53.

Case: Ted's Planning Process

My uncle has ninety-day plans for $20 million!

Ted Atwood is the owner-manager of a small manufacturing firm. He has had this business for almost ten years and during this time the firm has grown continuously. During the last five years his sales were:

1978	$ 850,000
1979	1,000,000
1980	1,250,000
1981	1,610,000
1982	2,300,000

This year Ted believes that sales will top $2,800,000.

Last week his nephew, Bob, came by to visit Ted. Bob has a bachelor's degree in business administration from State University, where he was a general business major. He is currently a member of a planning department for one of the largest corporations in the country.

Bob asked his uncle how well things were going. In answer, Ted gave him a copy of a comparative balance sheet and income statement, showing all the financial data for the last five years. "Wow!" said Ted. "You've really been increasing your sales by leaps and bounds. You're going to be over $15 million by the end of the 1980s if you keep growing at this rate." Ted explained that he was forecasting almost $20 million by that time. "Of course, this is all in my head," he hastened to explain. "I don't have any formal plan for getting there."

Bob then asked about Ted's current plan. To his surprise, he found that Ted did very little planning, and all of it was ninety-day planning. Primary attention was given to controlling inventory so that there was always an adequate amount on hand and watching the cash flow so that there was always enough money around to pay bills. Aside from this Ted had a big board on his wall, on which work orders were scheduled. As orders were received they were placed on the board. Currently there was enough work to keep the company going for over three months. More orders were pouring in every day.

What surprised Bob was the simplicity of the entire planning process. Everything seemed to be oriented to operational planning. Ted spent no time forecasting the external environment and seeing what the competition was doing. He learned about the competition from the salespeople and tried to anticipate any price changes that might be taking place in the environment. However, he did little in the way of marketing, except having his staff of six salespeople continually circle the six-state area where he sold his goods, looking for new customers. Most of the firm's sales were a result of reorders, although 20 percent of current orders had come from new customers.

"Uncle Ted," Bob said, "you're going to have a real problem if anything ever happens to any of your old customers. You aren't really picking up any new ones. Nor are you planning any further ahead than the next ninety days. Don't you think that will eventually get you into trouble?" Ted said he thought not. "I plan just as much as I have to. I don't need any long-range fancy plan. All I need to do is keep my eye on the next ninety days. Everything else takes care of itself."

Questions

1. What types of objectives would an entrepreneur like Ted be most interested in? List and explain some.
2. Does Ted need a long-range strategic plan? Defend your answer.
3. If Ted did decide to draw up a long-run strategic plan, how should he go about doing so? Be complete in your answer.

Case: Mary's Strategy

"All you really need is imagination," she said.

The company Mary Morton founded six years ago has grown quite a bit. Last year sales were over $27 million, compared with $400,000 during the first year of operation.

In running her company, Mary prefers to make most of the decisions herself. She says that it is her money at stake, and so she wants to be the one who loses it should a loss occur. During the past two years this is exactly what has happened. After a very successful start and the development of nineteen consumer products that sold extremely well in the local, and in some cases national, market, Mary has had three flops in a row. Each occurred with a consumer appliance that simply was not accepted by the market. In one case Mary knew that one of the biggest consumer appliance manufacturers had already developed something that was very similar to what she had on the drawing board. Nevertheless, she refused to step aside.

"I've beaten the big boys before," she said, "and I think I can do it again." But she was wrong, and her product flopped badly. It was not only rated as inferior in terms of performance by a consumer group that tested both her product and one being offered by a competitor, but it was priced too high. Sales were so low that the company had to stop producing it within ninety days of its introduction.

However, this kind of event does not worry Mary very much. She feels that on some products the company will win and on some it will lose. The important thing is to make enough money off the winners to pay for the losers.

Last month Mary had to go to the bank to get additional financing for her company. In view of her recent setbacks, her banker discussed the value of bringing in a new partner or selling stock in the firm to interested parties. However, Mary does not want people telling her how to run her own firm. She believes that she knows what will sell in the market. "All you really need is imagination," she says, and she feels she is in the process of proving it. Last week she okayed plans for a new product that will go into production by the end of next month. It is another consumer product, and, as before, there are rumors that one of her competitors had a similar product in the design stage about two years ago but scrapped plans to proceed with the manufacturing when that firm learned that there was not enough demand to warrant production. Mary believes that the market has changed in the last two years, although she admits that her company has not done any marketing research to prove this claim. Nevertheless, Mary believes that the market is ready for this type of product.

One of Mary's key assistants disagrees with her decision. Also, he believes that the firm does not pay enough attention to the external environment. "Mary believes that if she wants to sell a product, she can. She thinks that the market responds to her rather than vice versa. However, if we don't start doing some formal planning, we're going to go broke. She has made three bad moves in the past two years. I don't know how many more bad moves we can afford."

Questions

1. Which of the three strategy-making modes is most typical of Mary? Explain.
2. What type of strategy-making mode does Mary's key assistant want her to adopt? What would be its benefits to Mary's company?
3. Which of the three modes of strategy making do you think would be best? Defend your answer.

Chapter 4 Managerial Decision Making

Objectives of the Chapter

After a plan is drawn up, it needs to be put into action. This is where decision making comes in, although, as we have noted earlier, this function is not restricted solely to planning. Decision making is important in all of the management functions. The overall objective of this chapter is to study the decision-making process.

Initial attention will be directed toward the nature of decision making and the three conditions under which all decisions are made. Then the actual decision-making process will be studied, with attention given to each of the specific steps in this process. Next, the focus will become more specific as some of the popular quantitative decision-making methods are examined. Particular attention will be given to decision trees.

The last part of the chapter is devoted to a study of creativity in decision making and the behavioral aspects of the decision-making process. Decisions are not always made by following predetermined rote procedures. Sometimes creativity is required. And then there is the ever-present behavioral side of decision making, which sometimes causes people to opt for choices that are more beneficial to them than to the organization at large. Thus we will be studying all facets of decision making, including the steps in the process, the quantitative aids, and the behavioral aspects that affect the final choice.

When you have finished studying the material in this chapter, you should be able to:

1. Define the term *decision making.*
2. Describe the three conditions under which decisions are made: certainty, risk, and uncertainty.
3. Outline the seven steps in the decision-making process.
4. Explain how quantitative decision-making methods can be of value to the manager.
5. Describe how decision tree analysis is conducted.
6. Compare and contrast the creative thinking process with the decision-making process, describing fully the five steps in creative thinking.
7. Describe some of the behavioral factors which affect decision making, including simplifying, assigning probabilities, and rationalizing.

The Nature of Decision Making

■ Decision making involves choosing among alternatives.

Decision making is the process of choosing among alternatives. In this process the manager is confronted with two or more courses of action and has to decide which is the best. Before examining how this decision-making process works, two points merit attention.

■ Rationality is determined by the decision maker.

The first relates to the *rationality* of the decision-making process. Are all decisions rational? The answer is that they are if they make sense to the individual who makes them. For example, Alternative A will return a profit of $1 million to the firm and Alternative B will return a profit of $1.1 million. Will the company always opt for Alternative B? No, the firm may choose Alternative A because it involves dealing with a firm with which it has had good working relations in the past, while Alternative B involves working with a company with which there have been poor relations in previous dealings. Thus, one cannot examine decision making solely from a dollars and cents standpoint. Sometimes people use criteria other than profit (in this case friendship) in choosing from among alternatives. Rationality is determined by the person making the decision, as Table 4.1 shows.

Table 4.1
Is This Rational?

In Bozeman, Montana, the home of Harry Petroff caught fire. The family had just moved into its new house the previous week and was unfamiliar with the rules and regulations of the community, something that was to have a dramatic effect on the outcome of this event.

Upon seeing the fire, the family immediately called the fire department. Fire fighters rushed to the home and began putting out the blaze. Before very long they just about had the fire under control. This is when Mr. Petroff learned some very bad news. In this locale the only people who are guaranteed fire protection are those who have joined the rural fire association. Upon learning that Mr. Petroff was not a member, the fire fighters were ordered to turn off their hoses. They then stood around and watched while the fire once again began spreading throughout the house.

When the fire was finally out, all that remained were a few tools and sporting goods stored in the garage. Everything else was destroyed. Mr. Petroff explained that his house was already ablaze when he first learned that he had to be a member of the association to get fire protection. On the other side, the fire chief explained that only members of the fire association are entitled to fire protection.

Source: Based on *Miami Herald,* February 27, 1979, p. 5–B.

■ Probability assignments may be wrong.

Second, even when a decision is based strictly on quantitative results, there is always the chance that the decision maker will assign the *wrong probability or payoff* to the alternatives. For example, Alternative A has a 70 percent chance of occurring and will yield to the firm $7 million, and Alternative B has a 30 percent chance of occurring and will provide the firm with a $4 million profit. However, the manager may assign the payoffs and probabilities in reverse order, opting for Alternative B instead of Alternative A. In short, decision making is not a pure science. A great deal of art is involved. In this chapter both the art and science of the decision-making process will be studied. We will begin by looking at the conditions under which decisions are made.

Decision-Making Conditions

Some decisions are easy for the manager to make. The individual knows the outcome before the decision is actually made. Other decisions are more difficult because the manager does not know for sure what the final outcome will be. The individual could give an educated guess about the outcome but cannot say with certainty. Finally, there are some situations where the manager is at a loss to make any prediction about the outcome. The individual has no experience in the area and does not know anyone who does. The manager is totally uncertain about the outcome.

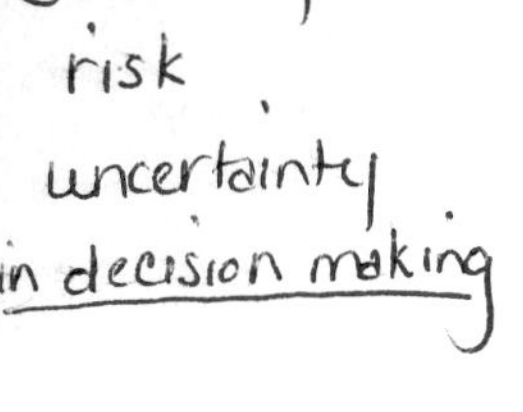

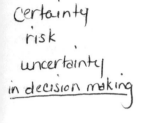

The three conditions described above are known as *certainty, risk,* and *uncertainty.* They can be represented as in Figure 4.1. When possible, the manager would like to operate on the left-hand side of this continuum. However, this is not always possible. For this reason, it is important to understand all three conditions and how decisions are made under each.

Figure 4.1 Decision-Making Conditions

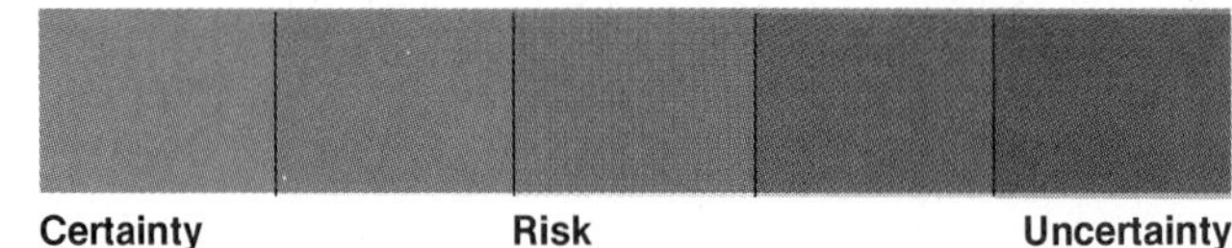

Certainty

▪ Under certainty, the outcome is known.

Certainty is a condition under which the manager knows the outcome of the decision. Some people feel that no result can ever be known with certainty until it happens. However, that is really stretching the point. If a business has extra cash from operations and deposits it in a savings account at the local bank, the interest on the deposit can be viewed as a sure thing. At an interest rate of 6 percent, a 90-day deposit of $10,000 will return $150 in interest. Of course, the bank could go bankrupt, but for all practical purposes the manager will regard this as unworthy of consideration. The deposit is a decision under certainty.

Another illustration is found in the case of a business that has enough parts in inventory to make either 5,000 units of Product A or 4,500 units of Product B. Since all of the necessary parts are on hand, the manager can choose between the two products and know the outcome of the decision. There is no doubt that the manager's decision can be carried out. Thus the outcome is known with certainty.

Risk

▪ Under risk, the outcome is not known with certainty.

Risk is the condition that exists when a manager does not know the outcome with certainty. However, the individual does have some information about the outcome. For example, if a fair coin were flipped into the air and allowed to land on the ground, would the head or the tail be facing upward? No one can say with certainty. However, since there are only two possible outcomes, a head or a tail, and each has an equal chance of occurring, we can assign a probability of 0.5 to a head and 0.5 to a tail.

The same kind of approach is used by the manager in assigning probabilities to business-related outcomes. First the individual gathers all possible information about the various outcomes. Then the manager assigns probabilities to the outcomes. Finally, using the outcomes and probabilities of their occurrence, the manager decides on a course of action. For an example, consider the following situation: There are three possible investment opportunities available to a company. If it invests $1 million in Product Line A and the product proves to be successful, the firm will make $10 million. If the company opts for Product Line B and that line is successful, the company will make $15 million. Finally, if the firm invests in Product Line C and it is a success, the company will make $20 million. After conducting a careful analysis of the situation, the firm estimates the likelihood of Product A being successful at 60 percent. For Lines B and C the success likelihoods are 50 percent and 35 percent respectively. We can state it as in Table 4.2.

Table 4.2
Probability and Potential Profit

Product Line	Probability of Success	Potential Profit
A	0.60	$10 million
B	0.50	15 million
C	0.35	20 million

Which product line should the company invest in? The answer depends on the payoff, or *expected value.* This value is determined by multiplying the potential payoff by the probability of its occurrence. Table 4.3 shows the calculation for the three product lines.

Table 4.3
Computation of Expected Value

Product Line	Probability of Success		Potential Profit	Expected Value
A	0.6	×	$10 million	$6 million
B	0.5	×	15 million	7.5 million
C	0.35	×	20 million	7 million

In this case Product Line B is the best bet. Keep in mind that this line does not have the greatest potential profit. That is offered by Product Line C. Nor does Product Line B have the greatest likelihood of success; Product Line A has that. However, Product Line B has the best *combination* of payoff and success probability as reflected in the expected value.

Note in Table 4.3 that the manager knew the outcomes and success probabilities of the various investments. And by using just this information the individual was able to compute the expected profit. The manager could be wrong about the payoff, the probability of success, or both. However, when working under conditions of risk the best a manager can do is to analyze the situation, estimate the various outcomes and probabilities associated with each, and opt for the one offering the greatest expected profit.

Uncertainty

■ Under uncertainty, probabilities cannot be developed by the manager.

Uncertainty exists when a manager feels unable to develop a probability estimate regarding the likelihood of success. There is simply not enough information available. Some managers contend that there is no such thing as uncertainty. There are always some past experiences that provide useful information. Nevertheless, when the manager feels that the available information is not helpful, the individual is operating under uncertainty. How does the manager make decisions in cases of uncertainty? By using mathematical techniques that have been developed for decision making under uncertainty. Most of these techniques are far too sophisticated to warrant consideration here. One, however, is rather simple. It is called the *LaPlace criterion.* When the manager uses this approach, *equal* probabilities are assigned to all of the conditional payoffs. Applying the LaPlace criterion to the example used in Table 4.3 gives the results shown in Table 4.4.

Table 4.4
Applying the LaPlace Criterion

Product Line	Conditional Payoff	Probability of Success	Expected Value
A	$10 million	0.5	$5 million
B	15 million	0.5	7.5 million
C	20 million	0.5	10 million

In Table 4.4, Product Line C is chosen for investment. Note that in contrast to the decision making under risk situation, now the probabilities of success for all three product lines are set at 0.5. The logic behind the use of LaPlace is quite simple: Since the manager feels that the situation is one of uncertainty, any one of the three alternatives is as likely to occur as any of the others. Hence a success probability of 0.5 is assigned to each.

The Decision-Making Process

When making decisions, the manager carries out seven steps. These are outlined in Figure 4.2. We will now examine each of these procedures.

Identifying and Defining the Problem

■ First, define the problem.

Decision making starts with a *definition of the problem.* A problem can occur for one of two reasons. First, it can be a result of something having gone wrong—for example, people showing up late for work. In this case the symptom is employee tardiness and the problem is what is causing this tardiness; a possible reason

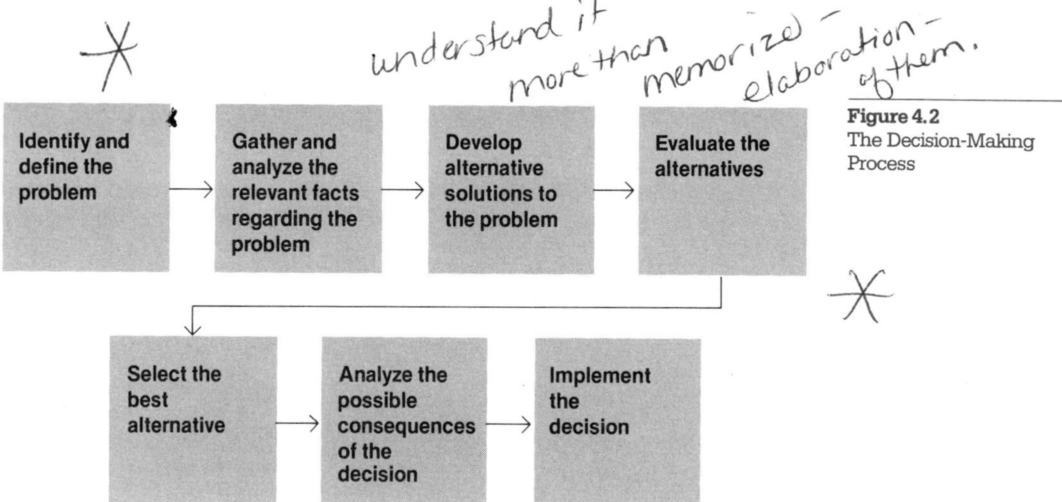

Figure 4.2
The Decision-Making Process

might be dissatisfaction with new work rules. Or the problem could be the result of something in the firm that needs to be done; an example would be the development of a new product to compete with one that had just been introduced by the competition. In either case, the problem sets the stage for decision making because it directs the actions that are to follow. By asking how it can resolve a particular problem, the company can begin formulating a plan of action. And the better the firm understands the problem, the more likely it is that the problem can be solved quickly and completely. Remember, a well-defined problem is partly solved in the defining process because clear definition makes the rest of the decision-making steps easier to implement. Also keep in mind that the manager needs to understand the difference between a symptom and a problem. A symptom is an effect; a problem is a cause. It is the latter which warrants the manager's attention.

Gathering and Analyzing the Relevant Facts Regarding the Problem

▪ Second, gather relevant information.

During the fact-gathering process, the manager asks: What do I need to know about this problem in order to solve it? The answer should direct the individual not only to the types of information that will be needed but to the people who will be able to provide it. For example, how does the manager deal with the situation of tardiness? One way is to examine the time cards to see if there is any pattern to the tardiness. Are people coming in late some days of the week but not others? Is there tardiness throughout the organization, or is it confined to certain departments or units? From here the manager can start working on how to gather the information about *why* the tardiness exists. One way is to talk to the workers who are coming in late and ask their reasons. Another is to ask the supervisors why their workers are late. Answers to these questions will provide the manager with some initial input regarding the tardiness.

▪ And analyze it.

Next, information has to be analyzed. The answers given by the workers may be different from those given by the managers. What accounts for the discrepancy?

The workers may say they are unhappy with their working conditions. The supervisor may say the workers are lazy. If the manager is unsure whom to believe, it is time to get more information. Some ways of doing so are to talk to the supervisor's boss, the union steward, and anyone else who has seen problems like this before and can provide insights into what is happening. Included in this last category would be such people as the head of the personnel department and the director of training and development.

Developing Alternative Solutions to the Problem

▪ Third, develop alternative solutions.

From the information that has been gathered and analyzed, the manager now has to develop alternative solutions. What are some of the most likely answers to the problem? Why are the workers *really* showing up late? The manager may feel that the most likely reason is that the supervisors' changes in some of the work procedures have caused the workers and the union to be angry, and the employees are showing up late as a result.

A second reason might be that the supervisors were well within their rights to make the unpopular changes, which are permitted by the contract. In this case the manager has a disciplinary problem rather than a human relations problem.

Or there may simply be a lack of communication on each side. The workers think they are being taken advantage of, while the supervisors believe the workers are defying legitimate authority.

Evaluating the Alternatives

▪ Fourth, evaluate them.

Now the manager has to look over all the alternatives and try to weigh them. Which is most likely to solve the problem? Which of the alternatives is, at best, only a holding action that will not really bring about satisfactory resolution of the issue?

In answering such questions, the manager must be sure to balance the needs of the employees with those of the organization. Sometimes a manager is better off giving in a little to one side or the other because it creates greater harmony than taking a hard and fast position that is severely punitive to one side. Having thought the situation over very carefully, the manager should rank the alternatives from best to worst.

Selecting the Best Alternative

▪ Fifth, choose the best one.

The next step is an obvious one: The manager should choose the best alternative. In our example, this is the one that will be most effective in reducing tardiness. In this case it might be to get the workers and the supervisors to sit down together to discuss the problem and then see if it cannot be ironed out without disciplinary action. This approach is not punitive, it provides everyone an opportunity to air gripes, and it can still keep the group focused on the overriding objective: to eliminate the tardiness problem. Table 4.5 shows one way of introducing unconventional alternatives.

"Actually, we haven't quite decided whether your proposal will fly."

Source: From the *Wall Street Journal*, October 3, 1979. Reprinted by permission of Cartoon Features Syndicate.

Table 4.5
Would You Vote for a Rhino?

In the latest national Canadian election, the campaign was enlivened by the Rhinoceros Party, which fielded 63 candidates. The platform of the party was rather simple. First, it called for the daily payment of 60 cents to every Canadian, which was to be used for draft beer. This, said the Rhinos, will get the unemployed off the streets and into the taverns, where they belong.

The other part of their platform was designed to solve the country's transportation problems. The Rhinos proposed that Canadian drivers switch to the left side of the road. A gradual changeover plan would be used in accomplishing this objective. For example, during the first year, only trucks would be driven on the left side of the road while everyone else drove on the right. During the ensuing years, all cars would eventually be driven on the left side.

All of the Rhino candidates were required to deposit $200 in order to list their names on the ballot. If the party received less than 15 percent of the vote in their respective constituencies, the candidates would lose their deposits. Such an investment did not seem to worry the candidates, who appeared convinced that Canadians were prepared to vote for their programs.

Source: "Rhinoceros Party Planks Deal with Knotty Issues," *Wall Street Journal*, May 11, 1979, p. 48.

Analyzing the Possible Consequences of the Decision

■ Sixth, analyze its consequences.

Once the manager has selected the best alternative, the individual should try to anticipate what problems will occur when the decision is implemented. Will the supervisor believe that the manager is giving in to the workers? Will the workers see the decision as a sign of weakness on the part of the manager? To some degree the decision maker should have already considered these consequences. However, now is the time to review them once more and be prepared to deal with them.

"Why did you choose this alternative?" is the question most likely to be asked by the supervisors. The manager should have an answer ready. Furthermore, this response must convince the supervisors that the decision does not sell out their position and that it is the best one possible in the situation. This requires the manager to explain the decision in terms that are beneficial to the supervisors. For example: "This decision will help you because it will reduce tardiness and there is really nothing lost by you in the process. All we have done is alleviate a situation that would have gotten a lot worse if this action had not been taken."

Implementing the Decision

▪ Seventh, implement it.

Now a manager has to put the decision into action. This involves not only announcing the decision but following through and explaining the action. Furthermore, it is often helpful for the manager to explain not only why the decision was made but how it will prevent similar problems from occurring in the future. Remember, managers need to make decisions for both tomorrow and today. They should be futuristic in their orientation. Table 4.6 provides a view of a corporation that has been highly successful in reading future decision conditions.

Table 4.6
Conglomerate Decision Making

Decision making takes place in every organization. However, the conglomerates provide some of the most interesting illustrations of decision making in action because so many of them grow through acquisition, and if they make a mistake and buy the wrong firm they are likely to find themselves in big trouble. Warner-Lambert (W-L), one of these conglomerates, has been very careful in its acquisition decisions and, as a result, is currently in excellent financial shape. One reason for this success is W-L's string of successful acquisitions, including American Optical (glasses and opticals), Parke-Davis (pharmaceuticals), Schick (shaving equipment and supplies), and Entenmann's (bakery products). While these firms cost W-L over $700 million, the conglomerate is currently grossing over $1.7 billion annually from them.

How does the firm decide whether or not to purchase a particular company? Some of its guidelines include: (1) find firms that use the same basic distribution channels as W-L but that are not of interest to federal regulators (in this way the company avoids government hassle), (2) refine the new company's products and use advertising to increase its market share, and (3) buy overseas firms that will help solidify W-L markets there. Following such guidelines for example, in 1964 W-L bought Hall Brothers, the British maker of cough drops. Since then W-L has taken this product worldwide, and Hall Brothers now holds 52 percent of the U.S. cough drop market and contributes thirty times as much revenue to the firm as it did when originally purchased. And this is only one of many success stories at W-L, where effective decision making seems to be a daily occurrence.

Source: Based on "Turning Warner-Lambert into a Marketing Conglomerate," *Business Week,* March 5, 1979, pp. 60–66.

Quantitative Decision-Making Methods

Many of the decisions confronting the manager are easy to make. However, some are difficult and demand a high degree of quantitative analysis. Quite often it is impossible to resolve them without the use of quantitative decision-making methods. The overall term that has been given to this area is operations research. *Operations research* (OR) uses the scientific method of solving problems by applying mathematical formulas or equations. While the use of these sophisticated mathematical techniques is not in the scope of this text, it is valuable to examine the types of problems that are often solved using operations research techniques. Two of the most common OR techniques are those used for inventory control and allocation problems.

▪ Computers are important OR tools.

Computers and Decision Making. Before looking at these two methods, however, it should be noted that most OR techniques are used in conjunction with computers. The latest high-speed computers can take input information, process it, and provide answers within seconds. In fact, advances in the computer field are so far-reaching today that there are now home computers which can help the average family keep track of its finances, pay its bills, and solve other household-related problems.

Business computers are much more sophisticated and expensive than the home variety, but if properly used they can be well worth the cost. In fact, as more and more work is turned over to the computer, the cost per computation declines markedly. Most important for business purposes, complex quantitative problems can be solved and the answers provided to the appropriate manager for immediate action. Thus, managers need not be mathematical geniuses to use OR. They simply need to understand the problem requiring a solution and be able to implement the answer. One of the most common kinds of OR problems is that of inventory control.

Inventory Control Problems

▪ Inventories can be properly balanced.

Many firms carry inventory. Wholesale and retail stores are prime examples. These companies do not want to have too much inventory on hand, for the cost of carrying the inventory can be quite high. They must consider insurance costs, warehousing expenses, and the money that is tied up in inventory. On the other hand, if there is not enough inventory on hand, customers will go elsewhere and sales will be lost. Thus the store would like to carry a sufficient amount to ensure that it can meet customer orders without having too high an inventory expense. How can this be done?

The answer is found through the use of what is called the *economic order quantity (EOQ) formula.* This formula tells the firm how much inventory to reorder each time. The company may still run out of inventory on some occasions, while on others the warehouse may be teeming with stock. But overall the formula can provide the company with a balanced approach to inventory control. In particular, businesses like the EOQ formula because it helps them realistically determine how much to reorder. The old guesstimating every time the stock of a particular product line is low is no longer the best they can do. Some companies use the EOQ formula for each of their major product lines. In this way the formula not only helps balance inventory and demand but also saves the manager from having to calculate how much to reorder each time.

For those who enjoy mathematics, the EOQ formula is located in Note 1 at the end of this chapter. However, the logic can be explained in nonmathematical terms. What the EOQ formula does is to balance the cost of carrying inventory with the expenses associated with having to reorder each time. If the firm orders only once a year, its reorder costs will be minimized. However, there will be a large amount of inventory in the warehouse, and that is a cost the firm must bear. Likewise, a lot of money is tied up in merchandise, and the cost of insurance against such perils as theft and fire will be high. On the other hand, if the firm reorders only a small number of units each time, it will face the risk of running out of inventory. Likewise, its order costs for placing the order, ensuring delivery, and checking to see that the order has been properly filled will be high. These two types of costs, *carrying costs* and *order costs,* must be balanced in such a way as to minimize *overall cost.* The EOQ formula does this by identifying the ideal number of units to reorder each time.

Figure 4.3
Determining the EOQ Point

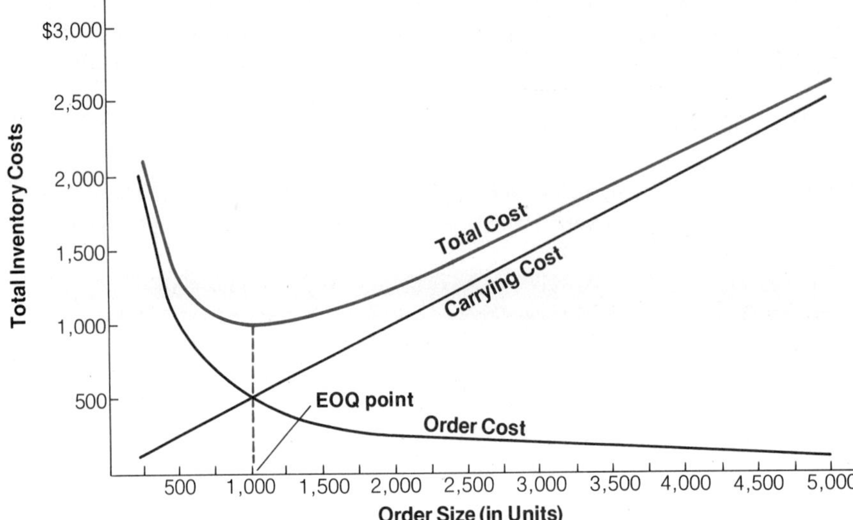

Figure 4.3 provides a graphic illustration of this ideal point. Notice in the figure that there is an inverse relationship between order costs and carrying costs. As order costs go down the firm receives more items per shipment, so its carrying costs go up. Computing the ideal point by trial and error can be quite a chore. However, by plugging the necessary data into the EOQ formula, the manager can arrive at the best solution in a matter of minutes. The manager does not often personally compute the answer. In fact, data will in many cases be plugged into a computer which will handle everything automatically. Thus when the number of units on hand drops to a predetermined level, the computer will determine how many units to reorder and in some cases will even print the order and have it ready for mailing. From the manager's standpoint, the important thing to remember is that a potentially difficult problem is solved with the use of a modern quantitative decision-making tool.[1]

Allocation Problems

▪ Resources can be allocated.

Sometimes a company will be confronted with a mind-boggling allocation problem. For example, consider the case of the firm that is capable of making two products: A and B. It can sell everything it makes, so the question that must be answered is: How many units of each product should it make this week? On hand, it has enough material to produce 1,400 units of Product A or 2,100 units of Product B. It also has enough paint to paint 1,200 total units. Furthermore, there is sufficient labor to assemble 1,000 units of Product A or 1,500 units of Product B. Product A, the more sophisticated model, must be tested before shipment and the firm has the capability of testing 800 units during the upcoming week. Finally, for every unit of Product A the company sells it will make a $4 profit, and for every unit of Product B it sells there is a $3 profit. Given this information, how many units of Product A and Product B should the company produce during the upcoming week?

Based on the information provided, it is actually possible to arrive at what we call an ideal solution. However, managers cannot make these calculations right off the top of their heads. They are not able to put all the constraints together and arrive at the best answer. Here is where operations research comes in. Using an OR technique known as *linear programming,* the analyst can find the best solution to the problem. In this case, the firm needs to manufacture 600 units of Product A and 600 of Product B. There is no better combination. When faced with an allocation problem such as this, the decision maker is really unable to grapple with the situation unless OR is employed.

Like EOQ determination, linear programming—and many of the OR techniques—tends to be outside the capability of most managers. They need to rely on mathematical specialists within the firm to make these calculations. However, this does not mean that managers never use mathematical analysis. They usually employ some of the simpler and more easily understandable decision-making techniques. One of them is the decision tree.

Decision Trees

One of the most popular methods of quantitative decision making used by modern managers is the *decision tree.* This technique is popular because it permits the manager both to think through a decision-making problem and to apply payoffs and probabilities to the various alternatives. Rather than having to say, "I think Alternative 1 is superior to Alternative 2," the manager can examine the two alternatives objectively, with the result being one alternative *proved* superior to the other.

Consider the following situation. A major corporation has sufficient money to buy one of three firms. The first, Company A, produces a consumer product that is fairly high priced. As a result, if the economy is very strong the return on investment from this company will be 20 percent. However, if there is only an average economy, the return will drop to 10 percent. And if the economy is weak the return on investment will drop even further, to 2 percent. Additionally, the likelihood of a strong economy is 20 percent, while an average economy is 50 percent likely, and a weak economy has a 30 percent likelihood. Given this information, should the corporation buy Company A? Before arriving at a decision, two things need to be done. First, the manager must build a decision tree for the investment in Company A. It is shown in Figure 4.4.

Decision Point	Alternative	Chance Point	Probability	Event	Conditional Return on Investment

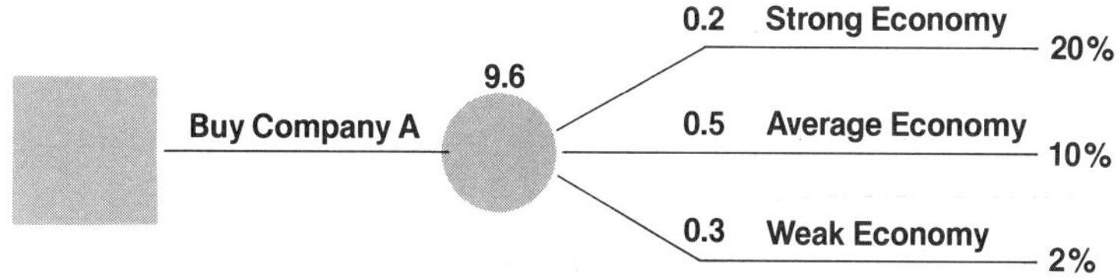

Figure 4.4
Decision Tree for the Purchase of Company A

■ **Expected value** = Conditional return × Probability.

Figure 4.4 should be read from *right to left.* Beginning at the far right are the respective *conditional returns on investment* that can be expected from each of the three states of the economy. These states are often referred to as *events.* If the particular event—such as a strong economy—occurs, then the return on investment associated with this event (20 percent) will be obtained. Next is the *probability* of the occurrence of a particular event, such as the 20 percent chance of a strong economy. Then there is the *chance point,* which indicates that some particular events are going to follow. In this case those were the different states of the economy. Over the chance point is the number 9.6. The 9.6 is the *expected value* from buying Company A. The expected return is computed by multiplying each of the conditional returns on investment by the probability of their occurrence and adding the results. In the case of Company A it is computed as in Table 4.7.

Table 4.7
Computation of Expected Return

Conditional Return on Investment	Probability of Occurrence	Expected Value
20	0.2	4.0
10	0.5	5.0
2	0.3	0.6
		9.6

Continuing to roll back the decision tree, we come to the alternative, which in this case is to buy Company A. Finally there is the decision point, always represented by a square, as opposed to a chance point, which is represented by a circle.

Using this format, it is possible to expand the illustration to include all three companies: A, B, and C. The events and probabilities remain the same for all regardless of which firm the corporation purchases, for the economy will not be altered by such a decision. All that is needed are the various conditional returns on investment associated with Companies B and C. For Company B they are 8, 16, and 6. This indicates that Company B would be a good investment if the economy operates at an average rate but would not do that well if the economy were either strong or weak. Meanwhile, for Company C the returns on investment are 1, 9, and 25 percent. In this case, Company C will perform very well in a poor economy, will not do well in an average economy, and will do very poorly in a strong economy. With all this information, the manager is now in a position to analyze the decision tree and answer the question of whether A, B, or C is the best investment. Figure 4.5 illustrates the decision tree.

Note that the expected values for Companies A, B, and C are 9.6, 11.4, and 12.2, respectively. Thus the firm's best investment is Company C.

The same basic methodology applies to all decision trees. For example, consider the case of the company that has a tremendous amount of backlog business. After examining the situation, management has determined that three alternatives are available:

1. Increase output by purchasing new machines to replace the current ones.
2. Increase output by fixing the current machines.

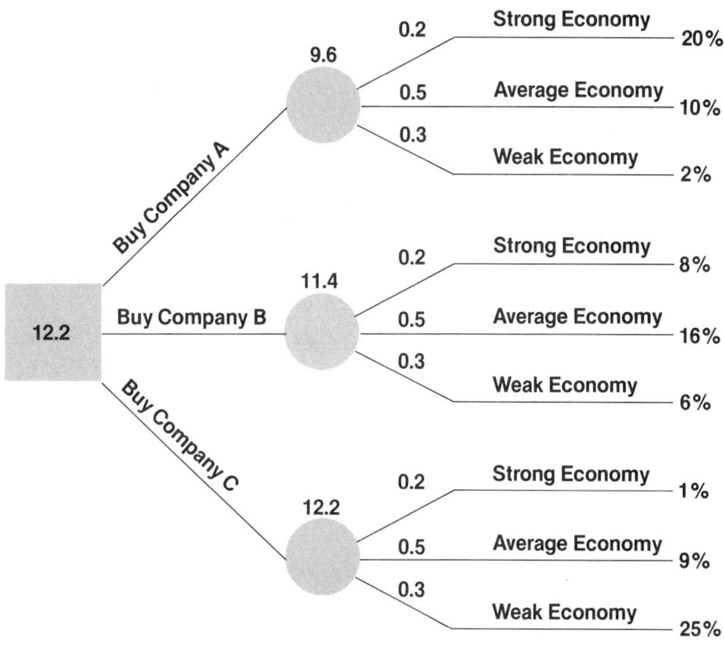

Figure 4.5
Decision Tree for the Purchase of Companies A, B, and C

3. Do as much work as possible with the old machines and subcontract the rest to other firms.

Figure 4.6 provides a decision tree which spells out all the particulars of the situation. Notice in this case that instead of return on investment, the final payoff is presented in profit terms.

Which decision would be best for the firm? It should fix the old machines, because the expected value associated with this alternative is higher than that of the other two. However, note that there is an added dimension in the problem. There are costs associated with buying new machines ($3,000,000) or fixing them ($300,000). Thus, after the initial expected value is determined by multiplying the conditional profit by the probability, the manager must subtract the cost of implementing the alternative. In the case of buying the new machines, the expected value is $7.8 million minus the $3 million purchase price, which leaves a net expected value of $4.8 million. In the case of fixing the machines, the expected value is $6 million minus the $300,000 for fixing the machines, which results in a net expected profit of $5.7 million. Finally, the expected profit associated with having the work subcontracted is $4.25 million. Since there is no direct investment on the firm's part for this subcontracting, this $4.25 million is also the net expected value. Thus in this case the firm should fix the machines rather than buy new ones or have the work subcontracted.

Figure 4.6
Decision Tree Analysis

Decision Point	Alternative	Chance Point		Event	Conditional Profit
5.7	4.8 Buy New Machines ($3,000,000)	7.8	0.2	Strong Economy	$10,000,000
			0.5	Average Economy	8,000,000
			0.3	Weak Economy	6,000,000
	5.7 Fix Old Machines ($300,000)	6.0	0.2	Strong Economy	7,500,000
			0.5	Average Economy	6,000,000
			0.3	Weak Economy	5,000,000
	4.25 Have the Work Subcontracted	4.25	0.2	Strong Economy	5,500,000
			0.5	Average Economy	4,500,000
			0.3	Weak Economy	3,000,000

■ Many managers like decision tree analysis.

Many managers like to use decision tree analysis in decision making because it helps them set out all the details of the situation and attach probabilities to the various events. Then, having constructed the tree, they can determine the expected values by simply rolling the tree back from right to left, making the expected value calculations as they go.

Creativity and Decision Making

While decision making follows the seven steps outlined earlier, sometimes a decision needs to be especially creative. Designing a new advertising program, formulating a new product idea, and thinking up a new personnel incentive program all require some creativity. The five steps in this creative thinking process are: (1) personal need, (2) preparation, (3) incubation, (4) illumination, and (5) verification. Contrasting these steps with those in decision making reveals the following:

Creative Thinking	Decision Making
1. Personal need	1. Define the problem.
2. Preparation	2. Gather and analyze the relevant facts.

3. Incubation	3. Develop alternatives. 4. Evaluate the alternatives.
4. Illumination	5. Select the best alternative. 6. Analyze the possible consequences.
5. Verification	7. Implement the decision.

Creative thinking is closely related to the decision-making process, and to fully understand how decisions are made it is important to have a fundamental grasp of the creative thinking process.

Personal Need

Personal need refers to the inner drive of the individual to be creative. There has to be some motivation to initiate something original. In business settings many people are called on to be creative. As just mentioned, product design people often have to come up with a new type of product. Advertising people have to create ads that will capture audience attention and lead to the desired action. Once an individual is confronted with this need to be creative, the entire process begins. As with the definition of the problem in decision making, personal need is the initial step to creativity.

▪ There must be initial motivation.

Preparation

Preparation is the first work stage of the creative thinking process. During this stage the individual gets ready to be creative. Some people believe that creativity is like a bolt out of the blue. Actually, creative people report that they spend a good amount of time preparing to be creative. During the preparation stage, the individual is saturated with information. The person takes these data and tries to establish a new and meaningful relationship in deriving an original solution to a problem.

▪ The individual must get ready to be creative.

Incubation

The *incubation* stage is marked by the unconscious mind working on the problem. The data the individual has gathered about the problem and the problem itself sit in the person's mind, while he or she goes on to other things. Unconscious thinking about the problem is active.

▪ The unconscious mind works on the problem.

Of course, sometimes nothing will happen during the incubation period. No answer is forthcoming. This is why it is wise to set a time period for resolving the problem. If no solution comes to mind within this predetermined period of time, the individual should go back to the preparation stage and review the notes and other materials related to the problem.

Illumination

Illumination is that stage of creative thinking when the solution to the problem is discovered. Sometimes the individual may gradually work out the solution, illumi-

▪ A solution is discovered.

nation taking place in a series of steps. When the last step is complete, the solution is obvious. In other cases the answer suddenly hits the person. The more complex the problem, however, the more likely it is that the answer will come in bits and pieces. The individual may simply not be able to piece together the entire solution in one big step. It is too involved. When the answer comes in segments, the individual often jots down the partial solutions on a piece of paper so that every detail can be remembered. Then when all the pieces of the puzzle are in order, the person can analyze them and grasp the overall solution.

Verification

■ And is modified, if necessary.

The last step in creative thinking is the *verification* stage. Will the solution work? This is the second of what are often called the *work stages of creative thinking.* In most cases the solution will not work exactly the way it first appeared. There will need to be some adapting, polishing, or minor modifications. In the case of the inventor, this means working out the bugs through a trial and error approach. For the scientist in the lab it means testing the new formula to see that it does indeed do what it is supposed to do. For the business person it means reviewing the overall solution and, in some cases, talking to colleagues to see if they can find any way to improve it. In most cases there will be a need for at least some minor changes.

Creative Thinking within Groups

Sometimes creative decisions should be made by groups. This is especially true when the scope of the problem is too great to be handled by one person. In advertising, for example, it is common to find a team of people thinking up new ideas for use in the next ad campaign. Even the advertising copy itself is often written by two or three people, each bouncing ideas off the others before arriving at final copy. The same approach is often used in new product development. A number of people will design and develop the product, each sharing ideas with the others. Two basic psychological phenomena are common to group participation in creative thinking:

1. There can be an effort to produce as many ideas as possible with no attempt to restrict or restrain what people say. Free association of ideas is what counts, and a group generates more ideas than an individual.
2. There is a chance to shape the opinions and ideas of the group and, in turn, be shaped by them. This further stimulates each individual to contribute to the group effort.

One of the best known and most popular approaches to creative thinking within groups is that of *brainstorming,* formally developed by Alex F. Osborn over thirty years ago. The technique was initially described as an aid in producing ideas for an advertising agency. However, today it is used in many situations where there is a need to develop a large number of new solutions to a specific problem. Free wheeling is used, with people saying whatever comes into their minds and trying to be as creative as possible. Drawing on their own ideas and those that have already been presented, participants are encouraged to adapt, substitute, rearrange, reverse, modify, and/or combine whatever has already been said.

Brainstorming can produce a large number of ideas in a short period of time. However, some guidelines ought to be used when employing it:

1. Hold the session to about forty to sixty minutes in length.
2. Do not reveal the problem before the session begins.
3. State the problem clearly and not too broadly.
4. Use a conference table that allows the people to see and communicate easily with each other.
5. If the matter being discussed is a physical product, bring along a sample to use as a point of reference.

These guidelines have been found to generate many creative suggestions.

The important lesson to be learned from techniques like brainstorming is that the average manager, under the proper circumstances, is able to create new ideas. The free association used in groups, for example, is an excellent technique for generating ideas and creating group motivation. The result is a host of ideas superior to what would have been obtained by the individual working alone. However, even in those instances where the person does work alone, the creative thinking process can bring about improved decisions.

■ Brainstorming can produce creative ideas.

Behavior and Decision Making

Until now we have discussed the process of decision making and some techniques that can be used in choosing among alternatives. However, we have not touched on one of the most important aspects of decision making, namely, the behavioral side of the process. Why do people make the decisions they do? It has been implied that the decision making process is a systematic one, with a careful analysis of the problem and alternative solutions followed by the choice of the best alternative. However, this is not always what happens. Many people make decisions based at least partly on personal interests and goals rather than on what is best for the organization.

Other behavioral factors affecting decision making include simplicity, the assignment of probabilities, and rationalization. The following examines each of these.

Simplicity

In the decision-making process the manager should gather all available information about the problem under study. The data should then be analyzed and a list of problem-solving alternatives developed. However, in most cases the process is not carried out this way. Several reasons can be cited.

First, unless the problem is fairly simple, few managers want to take the time necessary to gather all of the information possible about the problem under study.

■ Simplicity is desired.

They are going to work with partial information, stopping when they feel they have enough data to use in developing alternatives.

■ Only a handful of alternatives are considered.

Second, their list of problem-solving alternatives will usually not be very long. Managers will often come up with three or four alternatives that are most likely to solve the problem. They will give the choices a priority, and they will then evaluate them. Only if they do not work will most managers construct another list.

■ Time is a constraint.

Finally, there is the time constraint. In some cases the manager must make a decision within a short period of time. This will limit the individual's ability to gather and analyze the data. In other instances time will not be of the essence, but the individual will stop gathering any more information and make the decision because he or she wants to be done with the problem.

In pulling together all these factors, it is obvious that decision making is often done on a *simple* basis. The manager works with the information that is most easily obtained and, using common logic, decides how to proceed. Some of the decision-making steps outlined earlier are either bypassed or given minimum attention.

Assignment of Probabilities

As was seen earlier in the chapter, there are times when managers will use *probability assignment* to help them make decisions. On what basis do individuals assign probabilities? There are two. One is to study the problem and then, using all the available information, make a judgment regarding the likelihood of the event. This is a very rational, logical approach. However, in some cases the manager does not have time to make such a systematic analysis, and so probability assignment is made off the top of the head. The problem with this approach is that it is usually inaccurate. Most people tend to underrate the occurrence of common events and overrate the likelihood of rare events. For example, look at Figure 4.7. Notice in the figure that there are two jars. In the jar on the left are seventy red and thirty blue marbles. The jar on the right has seventy blue and thirty red marbles in it. Assume that these marbles have been mixed up in their respective jars. Then a blindfolded individual has been admitted to the room and has drawn twelve marbles from one of the two jars: eight red and four blue. What is the likelihood that these marbles were drawn from the jar that contained seventy red and thirty blue marbles? Write your answer down on a piece of paper, with zero indicating that they were drawn from the other jar, 50 percent indicating that there is an even probability that they were drawn from either jar, and 80 percent indicating that there is a high likelihood that they were drawn from the jar with more red than blue marbles, etc.

■ People have trouble with probability assignment.

What probability did you assign? Remember that most people underrate the likelihood of common events and overrate the probability of rare events. In this case, there is a very good chance that the twelve marbles were drawn from the jar containing seventy red and thirty blue marbles. In fact, statisticians assess the probability as 0.97, indicating that it is most likely that they came from this jar. How well did you do? Most people give an answer between 50 and 60 percent. The point

Figure 4.7
What Is the Probability?

to be remembered is that when managers make off-the-cuff probability assignments, they usually make mistakes.

Rationalization

■ They also rationalize decisions.

Quite often people making decisions are likely to ask themselves what other people will think of their decisions. People often want to be able to defend their choice of alternatives. This leads to *rationalization.* Research shows that in their daily lives people often do things that can be defended. For example, if they are about to buy a new car, they often ask their friends and relatives about cars and, guided somewhat by these answers, finally settle on a choice. The ultimate choice may not always be exactly what they want, but it is one they can live with more comfortably because they know that those around them approve of the decision.

When examining the organizational decision-making process, it is similarly important to remember that managers are influenced by others. As a result, there are some situations when managers will chose an alternative they can defend rather than one they feel is best for the organization. In these cases behavioral factors outweigh all other considerations.

Summary

Decision making is the process of choosing among alternatives. Decisions are made under one of three conditions: certainty, risk, and uncertainty. Certainty exists when the manager knows the outcome of the decision prior to its being made. Risk is present when the outcome is not known with certainty, although the individual does have some information regarding what is likely to happen. In these cases it is helpful to use probability assignments. Uncertainty exists when the manager feels, on the basis of current information, that it is not possible to develop a probability estimate for the likelihood of success. There is simply not enough information available in such cases. The uncertainty is often reduced by the decision maker who uses some type of mathematical technique, such as the LaPlace criterion.

The decision-making process involves seven steps. They are: (1) identifying and defining the problem, (2) gathering and analyzing the relevant facts regarding the problem, (3) developing alternative solutions to the problem, (4) evaluating the alternatives, (5) selecting the best alternative, (6) analyzing the possible consequences of the decision, and (7) implementing the decision. In this process it is common to find the manager using quantitative methods whenever they will facilitate decision making. These methods are particularly useful for complex problems. Inventory control and allocation problems are common examples. Of a less quantitative nature are decision trees, which are popular with modern managers because of the ease with which alternative courses of action can be analyzed and evaluated.

The latter part of the chapter examined the importance of creativity in decision making. The creative thinking process has five steps: (1) personal need, (2) preparation, (3) incubation, (4) illumination, and (5) verification. This process can be very important when searching for solutions to advertising and new product development problems.

Finally, the chapter examined the importance of studying human decision-making behavior. Personal values influence decision making. So do simplifying, assigning probabilities, and rationalizing. In summary, then, decision making is both an art and a science.

Review and Study Questions

1. In your own words, explain what is meant by the term *decision making.*
2. Are all decisions rational? Explain.
3. How do managers know when they are operating under conditions of certainty? Give an example.
4. If a manager is operating under risk conditions, how does the individual go about evaluating the various alternatives? Be complete in your answer.
5. When does uncertainty exist? How can a manager make a decision when operating under uncertainty? Give an example.
6. What is the first step in the decision-making process? Explain.

7. A manager must choose between the production of three new products: A, B, and C. Only one can be chosen. Employing all seven steps of the decision-making process in your answer, how would the manager go about making the choice? Explain.
8. When can quantitative decision-making methods be of value to the manager? Incorporate into your answer a discussion of inventory control and allocation problem solutions.
9. Of what value is decision tree analysis to the manager? Explain, being sure to describe how decision trees are constructed. Include in your answer the following terms: *conditional payoff or return, event, probability, chance point, alternative,* and *decision point.*
10. How does the creative decision-making process work? Describe it in your own words.
11. In what way do the following behavioral influences affect decision making: simplifying, assigning probabilities, and rationalizing? Explain.

Key Terms in the Chapter

decision making
certainty
risk
expected value
uncertainty
operations research
decision trees
personal need
preparation
incubation
illumination
verification
rationalization

Note

1. The EOQ formula is:

$$\sqrt{\frac{2(\text{Expected annual demand})\ (\text{Reorder cost})}{(\text{Value per item})\ (\text{Estimate for taxes insurance, and other expenses})}}$$

Assuming that the firm is trying to balance its inventory for \$20 radios, with an expected annual demand of 5,000 units, a reorder cost of \$100, and an estimate for taxes, insurance, and other expenses of 5 percent, the calculation would be as follows:

$$EOQ = \sqrt{\frac{2(5{,}000)\ (\$100)}{(20)(0.05)}}$$

$$EOQ = \sqrt{\frac{\$1{,}000{,}000}{\$1}}$$

$$EOQ = \sqrt{1{,}000{,}000}$$

EOQ = 1,000 units to be reordered each time.

Case: A Time for a Decision

We want the best incentive plan possible.

Regina Reynolds has a problem. As a new sales manager for her company's northeast region she is currently charged with increasing sales by 15 percent during the next year. Since the market is very competitive, this will not be easy. However, the company has agreed to let her introduce a sales incentive plan. This is a new idea in the company. Previously, every salesperson in the firm was paid a fixed salary. If Regina's incentive plan works out, the company intends to use it throughout the organization. So it is now up to her to formulate the best incentive plan possible.

Regina has not decided what type of incentive plan would be best. However, she has obtained some information about competitive plans and learned that most use a fixed salary approach. Her firm's biggest competitor, though, offers an escalating type of incentive. Based on monthly sales goals, there are incentive overrides. Here is the way they work:

Percentage of Monthly Sales Quota	Salary
Less than 100	Current fixed salary
100	102% of fixed salary
101–105	105% of fixed salary
106–110	110% of fixed salary
111–120	120% of fixed salary
120–130	130% of fixed salary
More than 130	150% of fixed salary

A second competitor is using a straight-line incentive. If the salesperson sells 117 percent of the monthly quota, the individual will get 117 percent of his or her fixed monthly salary. A third uses what it calls a feast or famine approach. If less than 100 percent of the monthly quota is sold, the individual's fixed salary is actually reduced. For every 1 percent below sales quota, salary drops by 2 percent. Thus reaching only 90 percent of the monthly sales quota will result in a salary equal to only 80 percent of the individual's usual monthly salary. On the other hand, salespersons who sell 110 percent of the monthly quota receive 120 percent of the monthly salary.

This is as far as Regina has gotten. She has to make a decision on a plan within the next month, so there is still some time for further analysis and thought. However, she believes she is off to a good start.

Questions

1. What is the next step Regina should take? Explain.
2. Now identify the remaining steps, explaining each of them.
3. Is this an example of decision making under certainty, risk, or uncertainty? Can quantitative analysis help in this process? Explain.

Case: Decision Making and Creativity

After the creation comes the implementation.

The Eckert Advertising Agency is always looking for new clients. Last month the agency managed to land the account of a large local bank. Most of the bank's prior advertising had made heavy use of billboards and radio time. The effect had not been very positive, resulting in the bank's current decision to change ad agencies.

The bank wants a new, creative approach. The president feels that the institution has an image of being old and stodgy. He wants a television ad campaign that will convince people that the bank is interested in moving forward. One part of the campaign is to focus on the bank's personnel, their warmth, and their concern for customer needs. The other part of the campaign is to concentrate on the services the bank can provide.

Tim Eckert, president of the agency, is personally taking charge of the account. He has called all his people together and asked them to think about ideas that can be incorporated into this ad campaign. Three different approaches were derived from their efforts. Each was considered interesting, creative, and likely to help develop the new image desired by the bank.

The bank president and top officers reviewed the proposed approaches and liked them all. However, working with one of the marketing people in the bank, Tim was able to get the following information:

Ad Campaign	Likelihood of Success	Increased Deposits Brought about by Campaign
1	0.80	$15 million
2	0.85	14 million
3	0.75	13 million

Based on these data, Tim feels that it will be possible to identify the ad campaign with the best chance of success. The creativity stage of decision making is over. Now it is time to implement the decision.

Questions

1. What are the creative decision-making steps that Tim's people used in formulating the three ad campaigns? Describe them.
2. Based on the data in this case, which ad campaign should Tim implement? Explain your answer.
3. In his business, which type of decision making is of most value to Tim: quantitative or nonquantitative? Support your answer.

interconnect the dots c̄
4 straight lines
s̄ removing pen.

Part Three

The Management Process: Organizing

The purpose of this part is to study the organizing process. This process can be examined in two phases. The first is often referred to as *classical* or *fundamental organizing concepts.* These are the basic building blocks used in designing organization structures. Then there are organizing concepts that are developed specially for an organization. The latter are called *contingency design ideas,* and they help custom-make the structure to fit the organization's specific needs. Together, these principles of organizing are used to combine people and work in such a way as to ensure maximum organizational efficiency.

Chapter 5 Fundamental Organizing Concepts

Objectives of the Chapter

Every enterprise needs to organize its resources. In doing so, firms use some fundamental building blocks. Often referred to as universal concepts, they provide an initial point of departure. Organizations may use the building blocks in different ways, but somewhere in the structure these design concepts can be found. The objectives of this chapter are to study the four basic building blocks used in designing organizations.

When you are finished studying this material, you should be able to:

1. Define the term *organizing.*
2. Explain the importance of job descriptions in the organizing process.
3. Describe some of the most important forms of departmentalization, including functional, product, territorial, and mixed.
4. Discuss the primary advantages and disadvantages of the committee organizational form.
5. Define the term *span of control* and explain how this span influences organizational design.
6. Compare and contrast the three types of authority used by managers.
7. Explain the importance of decentralization and delegation of authority to the modern manager.

The Nature of Organizing

In the two previous chapters, planning and decision making were examined. The organization first sets objectives and then pursues them. This is where organizing enters the picture. *Organizing* is the process of assigning duties to the personnel and coordinating employee efforts so as to ensure maximum efficiency in the fulfillment of these duties. Thus, first comes planning and then organizing—in management terms, from strategy to structure.

In designing their structures, modern organizations rely heavily, although not exclusively, on *universal design concepts.* These ideas provide what can be thought of as building blocks. These blocks, of which there are four, help ensure adequate attention to task and authority-responsibility considerations.

All organizations make use of four universal design ideas. Starting at the individual level and working up to the organization at large, the four are: (1) job descriptions, (2) departmentalization and the use of committees, (3) span of control, and (4) authority-responsibility relationships. First, individuals have to be given jobs. Then they have to be grouped or departmentalized in some way, such as putting all the accountants in the accounting department or forming committees to deal with operating problems. Next, there must be some determination of how many people the manager will supervise; for this will directly affect the number of levels in the hierarchy. Finally, everyone has to be given some authority and responsibility, and there must be some determination of who will coordinate efforts with whom. When these four steps have been taken, the basic structure of the organization will be complete. In the remainder of this chapter an examination of these four building blocks will be undertaken.

Job Descriptions

The value of job descriptions was illustrated in Chapter 1 when it was noted that the most important aspect of scientific management was the task concept. Remember the way Frederick Taylor laid out Schmidt's job so that the latter knew exactly what he was to do, when, and in what manner? Today many jobs are defined in less detail, but there are at least some general guidelines regarding what the individual is supposed to be doing.

At the lower levels of the hierarchy it is more common to find jobs spelled out in greater detail than at the upper levels. For example, a machinist will know exactly what the job requires, while the vice-president of advertising will have a general idea but will not usually have a job description in writing.

■ Job descriptions can help in organizing.

Do job descriptions really help? It depends on the job. If it is complex or requires a great deal of coordination with other people, it is a good idea to have the job described in writing. Likewise, if the individual doing the job were to leave and a new person would be unsure of what the job entailed, it would be a good idea to have a written job description. If the job is basically simple, many organizations will have, at best, a very brief description. If it is involved, the description will often be much more detailed. In either event, there are books such as the *Dictionary of Occupational Titles,* published by the U.S. Department of Labor, which can provide general guidelines for writing such descriptions. The important thing to remember is that job definitions, written or verbal, are basic to effective organizing.

Departmentalization and Committees

Departmentalization is the grouping of employees into units for the purpose of attaining common objectives. There are three very popular forms of departmentalization: functional, product, and geographic. However, most organizations use a hybrid, or mixed, form of departmentalization. We will examine each of the forms and also consider the role and value of committees.

Functional Departmentalization

▪ Some firms organize by function.

Functional departmentalization is an organizational arrangement under which people are placed in common units based on the jobs they perform. For example, the employees who carry out manufacturing functions are placed in the production department; those who are in advertising or selling are put into the marketing department; and those who are accountants go into the finance department. Figure 5.1 provides an illustration of a functional departmentalization arrangement. Note in the figure that under this arrangement, the heads of the *major* functional departments report directly to the president. In turn, there are *derivative*

Figure 5.1
Functional Departmentalization

President

Vice-President Marketing
Vice-President Research and Development
Vice-President Production
Vice-President Personnel
Vice-President Finance

Advertising
Selling
Manufacturing
Purchasing
Accounting
Credit

Major Departments
Derivative Departments

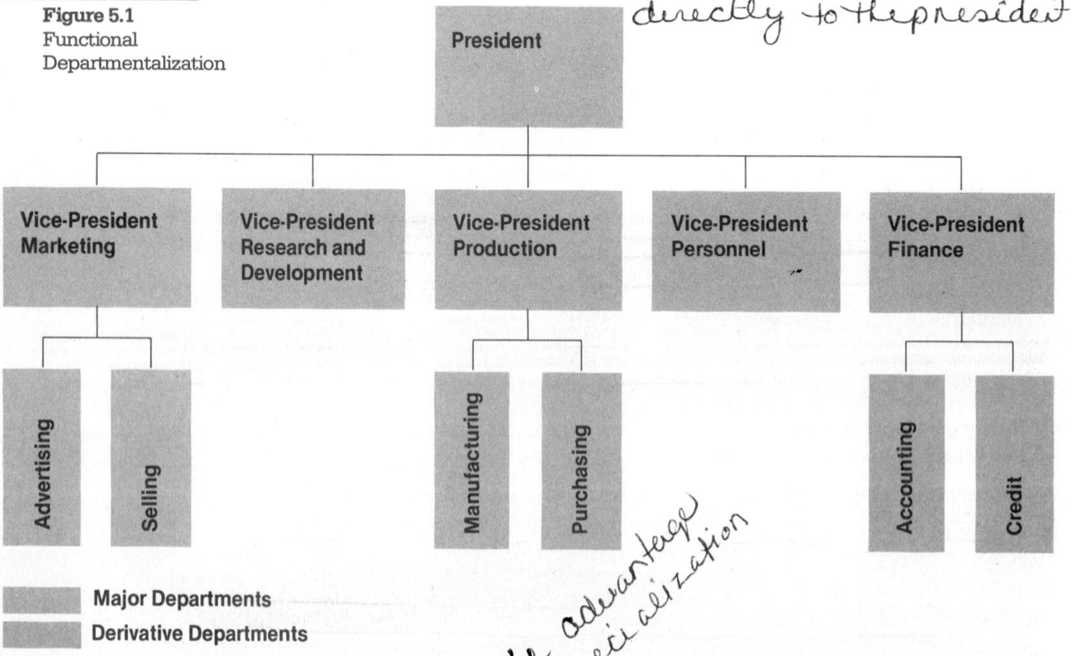

functional departments that report to the functional department heads. Everything is organized on the basis of job function.

Today functional departmentalization is the most widely used form of departmentalization, especially in small organizations. The primary reason for its popularity is that it helps the organization concentrate on its primary activities, providing a basis for specialization. In a manufacturing firm, for example, the primary, or *organic,* functions are marketing, production, and finance. As seen in Figure 5.1, these are right at the top of the structure along with other important functions.

Product Departmentalization

■ Others by product.

Product departmentalization has been increasing in importance in recent years. This is especially true among multi-line, large-scale enterprises which have found that as they grow larger, a reorganization along product lines has become necessary. Currently, such firms as Ford, General Motors, and Du Pont all use this form of departmentalization.

An example of departmentalization by product line is provided in Figure 5.2. The company has taken its consumer goods–recreational product line and divided it into four product divisions. Each is responsible for its respective product line. In this way the company has created a series of *profit centers*. The firms can then measure the annual profitability of each division in determining whether to make a further investment in the product line, leave it alone, or sell it away because it is not sufficiently profitable.

Where product departmentalization is used each division, in a manner of speaking, operates as a small company within the overall corporation. Although not shown in Figure 5.2, each division often has its own manufacturing and marketing departments as well as a small finance department for handling financial matters. Thus when comparing product departmentalization with functional departmentalization, the management student can see that the former actually incorporates the latter. The major difference is that instead of having one production department producing all the goods and one marketing department advertising and selling them, these functions are broken up and spread throughout the divisions. Keep in mind, however, that most firms also maintain centralized finance and

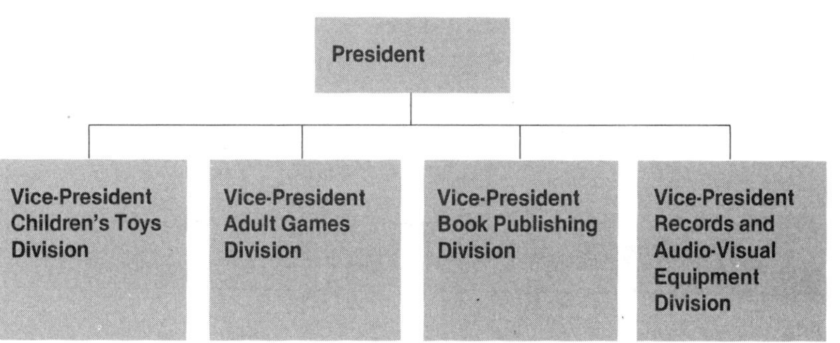

Figure 5.2
Product Departmentalization

marketing departments to coordinate these functions across divisional lines. However, the profit center concept still remains, and this is the major advantage of the product departmentalization arrangement.

Territorial Departmentalization

■ Others by territory.

As they increase in size, some organizations find themselves becoming physically dispersed. Retail firms are an example. J. C. Penney, Montgomery Ward, and Sears, Roebuck have stores all across the country. On a more local basis, law enforcement agencies are organized territorially. In major cities precincts are charged with maintaining law and order within their assigned geographic locales. Figure 5.3 provides an illustration of a *territorial departmentalization* arrangement.

Figure 5.3 Territorial Departmentalization

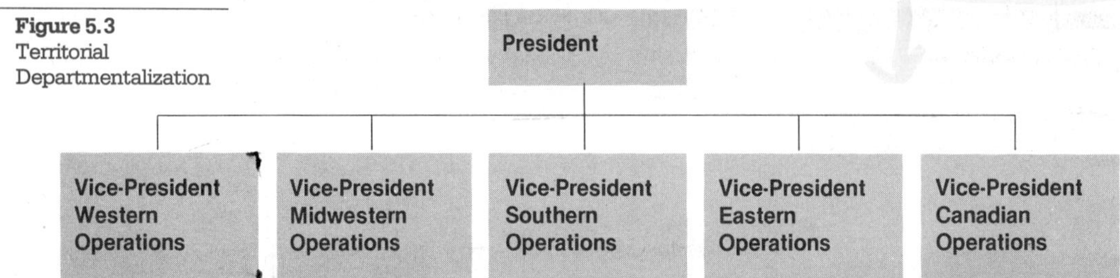

If Figure 5.3 represented a manufacturing firm and were extended to include all the various departments in the structure, it would be seen that each geographic area had its own sales force and, in many cases, its own production operations. Additionally, there would be an accounting department to take care of the financial matters. Meanwhile, back at the top of the structure would be major departments that reported to the president—finance, marketing, personnel, and purchasing. These would be centralized so that they could provide assistance to all the territorial operations.

The main advantage of a territorial organizational arrangement is that of local operation. For example, by producing the goods closer to the supply of raw materials the firm can manufacture the product at a lower cost per unit. Additionally, if a firm sets up a local sales department, the employees can get to know both their customers and their markets much better.

Mixed Departmentalization

■ But most use mixed departmentalization.

While most firms rely heavily on one of the three previously mentioned forms of departmentalization, very few use a pure form of departmentalization. Most employ what might be labeled functional with a little product departmentalization, or, product departmentalization with a little functional and territorial added in. The reason is quite simple. Most organizations start off with a functional structure. But as they get larger it becomes necessary to incorporate product and/or territorial elements into the design. At this point the arrangement is known as *mixed departmentalization*.

Department stores are an excellent example. Consider the operation when the owner has only one store. How is it organized? The most typical arrangement is by product line or customer. There is a menswear department, a toy department, a cosmetics department, and so on. However, the store will also have an accounting department for handling payroll and financial matters and an advertising department to handle the ad campaigns. Some functional departmentalization is already being used. Finally, as the store proves successful and starts to expand to other geographic locales, territorial departmentalization also occurs. Figure 5.4 provides an example.

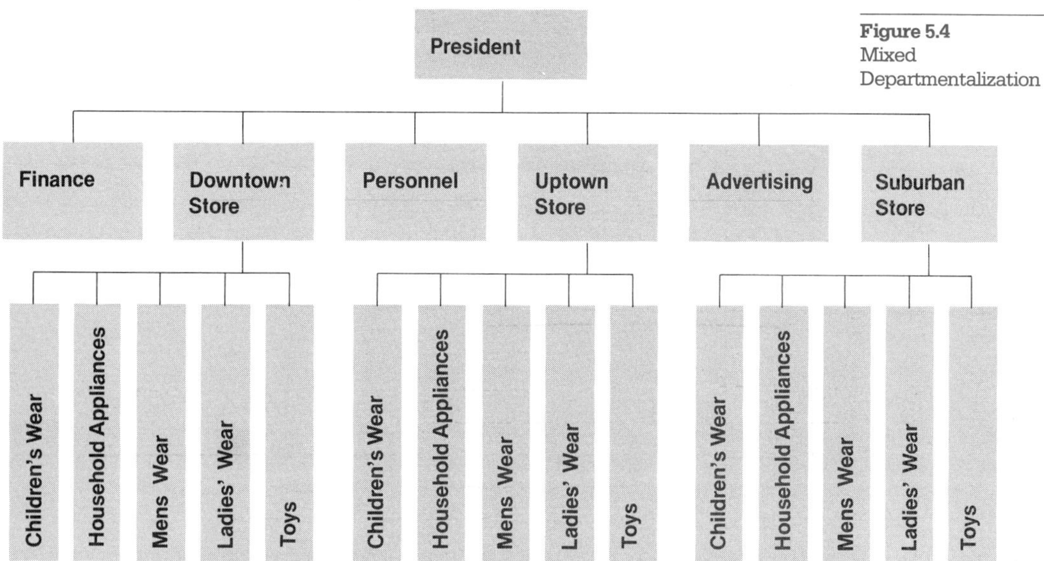

Figure 5.4
Mixed Departmentalization

When examining departmentalization arrangements, it is important to remember that unless the organization is very small, it undoubtedly uses a mixed form of departmentalization. The basic ideas employed in the actual design, however, are those that have been discussed in this section.

Committees

Another common organizational form is that of the *committee.* Businesses use committees for such undertakings as analyzing problem situations, conducting research, and providing recommendations for action. Many are *ad hoc committees,* which means that they are formed for a particular purpose and then disbanded when it is accomplished. Some are *standing committees,* in which case they exist indefinitely. While most are advisory in nature, some have the authority to order implementation of their recommendations. These are called *plural executive committees,* the most common example being the board of directors.

▪ Some committees are ad hoc, others are standing.

ad hoc
standing
plural exectutive
(10)

Advantages of Committees. Committees offer some very important advantages. Four of these are high quality decisions, managerial training, improved coordination, and the enhanced likelihood of decision acceptance.

High Quality Decisions. The adage "two heads are better than one" applies well to committees. If a committee's membership is carefully chosen, there can be a breadth of knowledge and a range of perspectives that are far beyond the ability and scope of any individual manager. As a result, when considering a proposal or analyzing a problem, a committee is likely to come up with a much better decision than one manager working alone.

Managerial Training. Some companies like to put their young managers on committees because this gives the individuals an opportunity to participate in problem solving and to obtain insights into organizational problems. Additionally, the managers obtain experience in decision making.

Improved Coordination. Committees can be very helpful in coordinating plans and transmitting information. In the implementation of a major plan, for example, a number of departments may be involved. A committee approach to the implementation can help each see where each department fits into the overall plan. Additionally, the approach can be useful in obtaining agreement from each regarding what it is going to do and by when. In short, there can be better coordination of overall efforts because of a committee approach.

Enhanced Likelihood of Decision Acceptance. When there are problems, especially those that cut across department boundaries, a committee can be very useful. By putting people from each of the departments that are affected as well as others from different areas of the organization on the committee, management enhances the likelihood that whatever decision is made will have the backing of all the members. Thus committees can help an organization deal with interdepartmental problems.

Disadvantages of Committees. Unfortunately, not all committees perform as well as could be hoped. Table 5.1 provides a list of some of the behavioral rules that are often used to describe committee behavior. Other commonly cited disadvantages include a waste of time and money, individual domination, compromise, and lack of responsibility.

High Expense. Committee meetings can cost a lot of money. For example, if there are nine people in the group and they meet for two hours a week for ten weeks, this is twenty hours per person. Assuming that the average member makes $20,000 a year, the cost of the committee is $192.30 per person or $1,730 for the entire group. Was the decision they made worth this amount of money? As noted in Table 5.1, the time spent on agenda items tends to vary inversely with the amount of money involved. If the committee were examining a problem that did not involve much money, the cost to the firm was probably exorbitant.

Individual Domination. Sometimes one person dominates the committee. This can be the chairperson, who steers the meeting and decides what topics are to be discussed and how long will be spent on each. Other times the domination is done by a powerful

Table 5.1
Some Laws That Explain and Govern Committee Behavior

- The efficiency of a committee meeting is inversely related to the number of people on the committee and the amount of time that is spent on deliberations.
- The length of a committee meeting will rise with the square of the number of people who are present.
- The time spent on any agenda item will be in inverse proportion to the amount of money involved. Decisions involving millions of dollars will be made in a matter of minutes, while nickel and dime items are debated endlessly.
- The less you like to serve on committees, the more likely it is that you will be pressed into doing so.
- If a problem causes many meetings, these meetings will eventually become more important than the initial problem.
- Never show up early for a committee meeting, or people will think you are either a newcomer to the organization or a total fool.
- During the committee meeting never speak first. Allow others the opportunity to lead off and put their feet in their mouths.
- When you speak, either ask a question (since this will endear you to the other party, who now has the opportunity to take the floor) or make a factual statement backed up with all of the statistics you can muster (remember, it is not as important to be accurate with your statistics as it is to have them).
- During the committee meeting, if you cannot convince the other members with a logical argument, then spend your time trying to confuse them.
- Never say anything that will make someone else look foolish unless you are sure that this person's career is already on the downslide.
- At the earliest opportune moment, move for adjournment. This is what everyone has been waiting for all along.

Source: Some of the ideas in this table can be found in Arthur Block, *Murphy's Law and Other Reasons Why Things Go Wrong* (Los Angeles: Prince/Stern/Sloan Publishers, 1977).

member of the committee—for example, a finance department head who is a senior level executive while the chairperson is not. In any event, rather than getting everyone's ideas, the dominant individual pushes personal opinions and beliefs to get the committee to go along. Such behavior, of course, defeats the purpose of the committee.

Compromise. Sometimes there are two strong factions on the committee. The first would like Alternative A while the second prefers Alternative B. The two fight each other to a standstill, at which point a compromise, Alternative C, is offered. This alternative is not totally acceptable to either party but both groups can live with it, and so it is accepted. The problem is often that one or both of the initial alternatives are better than Alternative C. By compromising, the firm gets less than it could if the committee members put aside their personal biases and objectively examined the alternatives.

Lack of Responsibility. Critics of committees like to point out that in committees everyone is collectively responsible but no one individual is responsible. When the group makes a mistake, everyone has the opportunity to hide behind the fact that it was a group decision. "I really wanted the group to opt for Alternative A, but they voted me down and chose Alternative C. So if you are looking to assess blame you have to put it on those guys who were fighting for Alternative B. They're the real reason we took a financial bath on Alternative C."

The individual defending a personal decision may be right. However, it is so difficult to assign responsibility for any committee decisions that it is best not to try. What the organization should do is spend its time learning how to use committees effectively.

Using Committees Effectively

There are a number of guidelines that can help committees function effectively. For example, in regard to formal procedures, the following are important:

■ Guidelines for using committees effectively.

1. Clearly define the committee's goals. If possible, put them in writing.
2. Make sure the committee's authority is spelled out. Is it an advisory committee or a plural executive?
3. Determine the optimum size of the group. How many members will be too few? How many will be too many?
4. Select a chairperson on the basis of ability to run an efficient meeting.
5. Appoint a permanent secretary to handle communication.
6. Make sure the agenda and all supporting material for the meeting are passed out ahead of time so everyone can come prepared to work on the issues.
7. Start the meeting on time and end it on time.

The chairperson should be concerned with providing direction and maintaining the right atmosphere. From time to time this individual should step in, summarize what has been said, and offer suggestions for further discussion. For example: "Now that we have uncovered what appear to be the symptoms of the problem, let's see if we can focus on its cause." Additionally, the leader should have an understanding of when to stay on the sidelines and allow things to move along at their own clip.

Finally, there are some useful guidelines that committee members should follow. Six of the most beneficial follow:

■ Guidelines for committee members.

1. State your ideas as clearly and logically as you can, but do not argue for your position.
2. Listen to, and think about, reactions from other members before you push your point.
3. Accept solutions based on logic rather than simply going along for the sake of harmony.
4. Refuse to go along with techniques that bypass logic for the sake of conflict reduction. This includes flipping a coin or averaging the vote.
5. If someone in the group finally agrees to go along on some point, do not feel you owe this person a favor and yield to him or her on some other point.
6. Work to root out the differences of opinion, and try to get everyone involved in the discussion.[1]

Suggestions such as these can be very helpful in using committees effectively. Remember, most organizations have committees; so it is important that the manager have a basic understanding of how they work, what some of their pitfalls are, and how one can overcome these shortcomings while taking advantage of their benefits.

Span of Control

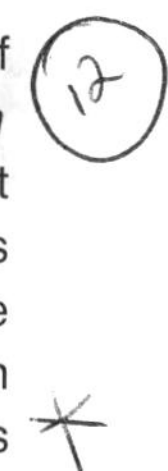

Once employees are organized into departments or groups, there is the matter of how many people each manager should control. This is called the manager's *span of control.* Classical theorists like Henri Fayol and the administrative management people believed that the ideal number should be between three and six. While this is open to dispute, one thing is certain. The span of control will affect the organizational design. For example Figure 5.5 is an organization chart with a span of control of three. This is a *narrow span.* Notice that there are forty people in this chart, and the firm has three levels under the president. This is in contrast to Figure 5.6, which shows a span of control of six. There are forty-three people in this chart,

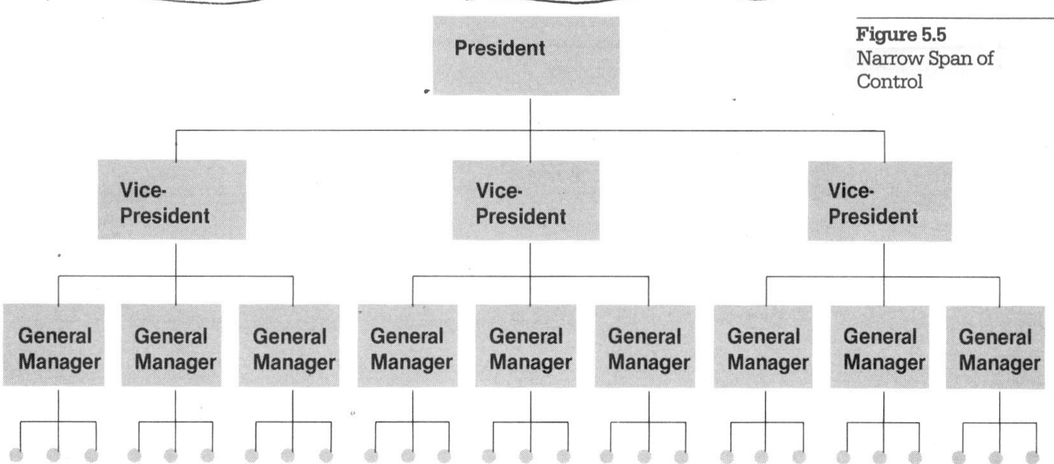

Figure 5.5
Narrow Span of Control

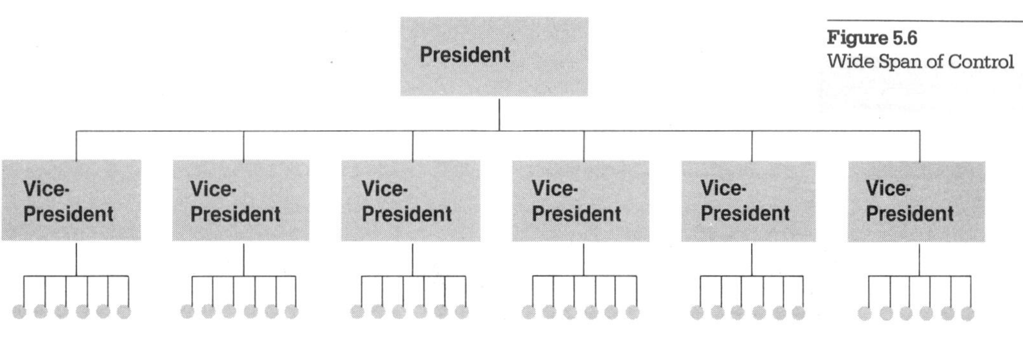

Figure 5.6
Wide Span of Control

but only two levels are under the president. The *wide span* has enabled the organization to incorporate more people into fewer levels.

Tall and Flat Structures

Classical structures, with their narrow spans of control, tend to be very *tall*. With these structures, the manager is able to exercise tight control. Having only a few subordinates to supervise, the individual can be aware of everything the work force is doing. Conversely, wide spans of control create *flat* structures in which the manager commonly employs loose control. There is not enough time to closely supervise six, eight, or ten subordinates.

For a long time debate raged about which span of control was most effective: narrow or wide. Supporters of narrow spans pointed to their popular use in industry. Supporters of wide spans pointed to specific examples such as Sears, Roebuck, which found that with wide spans its managers were encouraged to hire competent people, train them, and then turn them loose. This approach led to both high morale and high quality performance.[2] Furthermore, supporters of wide spans point to such well-known management authorities as Peter Drucker, who has noted that "a basic rule of organization is to build the least possible number of management levels and forge the shortest possible chain of command."[3]

▪ Research does not support the superiority of either narrow or wide spans.

However, research does not substantiate the superiority of either span.[4] It all depends on the situation, although there are major factors that tend to influence the span. For example, subordinates who have little job experience need greater supervision than those who know the jobs well. A narrow span would normally work better with the first group and a wider span with the second. Likewise, if the organization is small, it is typical to find a wide span of control being used. Things are handled informally, and there is a teamwork approach to things. Conversely, in large firms jobs are well defined and the span of control tends to be smaller. Even then, however, it is dangerous to say that small firms use a wide span of control and large firms prefer narrow spans. There are many more factors involved than mere size. Table 5.2 provides a look at some of the major factors that determine span of control.

Authority-Responsibility Relationships

At the same time the organization structure is being designed and jobs defined, there exists the need for determining the authority and responsibility that the staff members will have. While this is taken care of indirectly in the construction of the job definitions, the area is so important that it warrants specific consideration here.

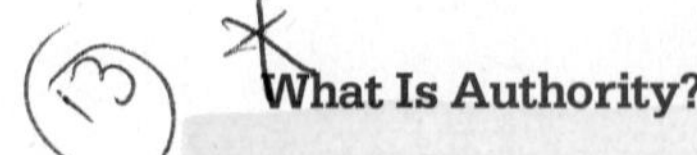

What Is Authority?

▪ Authority is the right to command.

Authority is the right to command. With it, the manager can get things done; without it, the individual is ineffective. And in broad terms, this right to command

Narrow Span	Wide Span
Subordinates do not have much job experience and often need assistance in getting the work done.	Subordinates have a great deal of job experience and do not require much, if any, assistance in getting the work done.
Subordinates have no assistants to help them.	Subordinates have assistants of their own.
Subordinates are supervised exclusively by their superior	Subordinates are supervised in part by others.
Subordinates are all carrying out many different functions.	Subordinates are all carrying out similar functions.
The organization is very large.	The organization is very small.
The work is nonroutine.	The work is routine.
Worker errors will prove to be costly mistakes	Worker errors will not prove to be costly mistakes.
There is a need for coordination among the subordinates	There is no need for coordination among the subordinates.
The manager personally likes to use close control with the subordinates.	The manager prefers loose control to close control.
The manager is located high up in the organization.	The manager is located at the middle or lower levels of the hierarchy.

Table 5.2
Some Major Factors That Determine Span of Control

can be examined from two perspectives: formal and informal. Formal authority comes with the position. For example, whoever is vice-president of finance has the authority that attaches to that position. Informal authority is a result of the individual's ability to influence or persuade others to cooperate in getting things done. This is often a result of the manager's personality and ability to interact with others.

In getting things done, most managers first use informal authority. They suggest or ask for assistance: "Barney, how about giving Sally a hand?" There is really no need to bark orders at people. In most cases, people are willing to go along with the request. If Barney is not willing, then the manager can fall back on formal authority and order Barney to comply.

Types of Authority

While all managers have formal authority, they do not all have the same kind. There are three types of formal authority: line, staff, and functional. Each is an essential part of the basic framework of organization structure and is of central importance to an understanding of the organizing process.

■ Line authority is direct authority.

Line Authority. *Line authority* is the most fundamental type of authority. Often defined as *direct authority,* it encompasses the right to give orders and to have decisions

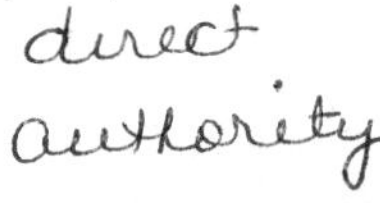

Figure 5.7
Line Authority

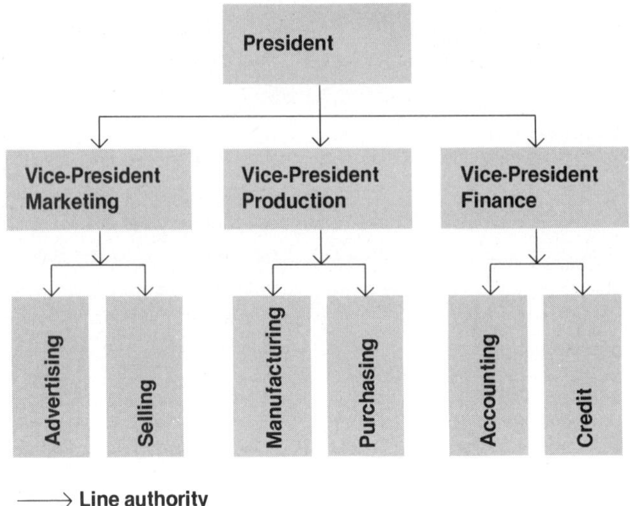

implemented. All superiors have line authority over their subordinates, and this establishes a chain of command from the top to the bottom of the organization. Figure 5.7 provides an example. The president gives orders to the vice-presidents who, in turn, give orders to their subordinates.

- Staff authority is auxiliary authority.

Staff Authority. *Staff authority* is auxiliary authority. It is supportive in nature. When individuals have staff authority, they are charged with assisting, advising, recommending, and/or facilitating organizational activities. In a business setting it is common to find the company lawyer having staff authority. The individual counsels the president and provides legal advice on company matters ranging from advertising claims that can be made by the firm to the way in which someone should be fired after being caught stealing company property. Figure 5.8 provides an illustration of a line-staff organization.

Figure 5.8
Line-Staff
Organization

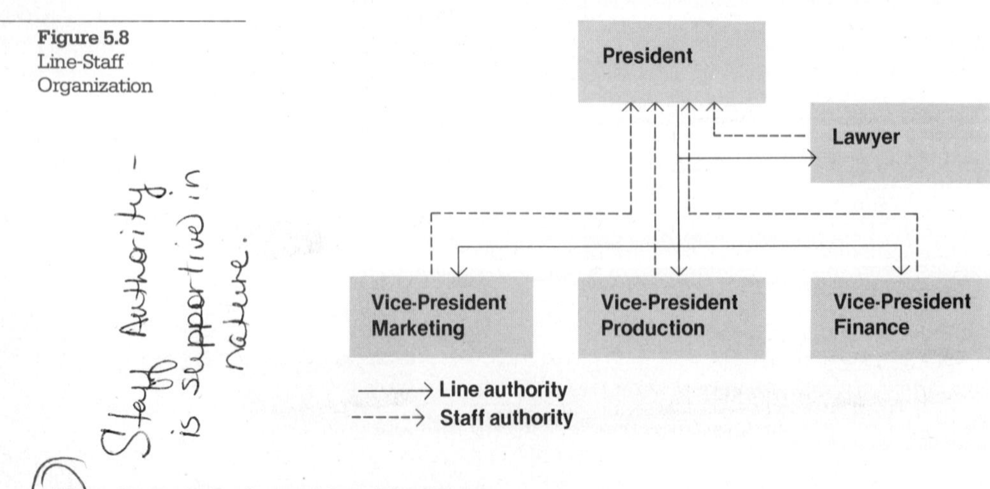

Line-Staff Conflict. Many organizations have found that there are problems among those managers who have line authority and those who have staff authority. The former are charged with giving orders and getting things done. The latter are responsible for providing assistance.

Line managers are often nuts and bolts people. They are trained on the line and are most concerned with getting the work done. The staff people are often younger, better educated, and full of ideas about how to improve efficiency. However, they sometimes lack practical experience. Line managers are responsible for any decisions they make, and so they tend to be skeptical about staff advice. Staff people, in turn, often see the line managers as reluctant to take good advice. How can these conflicts be resolved? Some of the most helpful measures include the following:

▪ Ways of overcoming line-staff conflict.

1. Line people should be made to realize that the staff people are there to help them get things done. The line people should be encouraged to draw on expertise.
2. Staff people have to realize that their jobs entail advising and recommending, not giving orders. They have to follow the adage: Sell not tell.
3. Line managers have to keep staff people informed about the types of problems they need help on. A good staff specialist is only going to perform well when what is expected is clear.
4. Staff people should follow the principle of *completed staff work.* This principle holds that all solutions or recommendations should be presented to the line manager in such a way that the latter can either approve or disapprove the action. All details have been worked out prior to the staff presentation.

These suggestions can ensure better use of staff people and overcome many of the common line-staff problems found in modern organizations.

▪ Functional authority extends into other departments.

Functional Authority. Authority in a department other than one's own is *functional authority,* which is illustrated in Figure 5.9. This authority is often given to an individual or department in regard to specific processes being carried on by individuals in other units. For example, the legal department often has functional authority to examine advertising copy and require any changes it feels are necessary in order to avoid the use of misleading statements or claims that cannot be backed up with proof. Likewise, the major functional departments often have functional authority over the heads of the various product divisions.

Sometimes the assignment of functional authority can cause problems. In particular, there is the issue of undermining managers' authority in their own departments, as well as the issue of power grabbing. In eliminating or reducing such problems, several guidelines have proven useful:

▪ Guidelines focusing functional authority.

1. Functional authority should be given only to those who can provide a specific expertise or who need it to improve organizational efficiency.
2. This authority should be limited to telling people *how* they are to do something

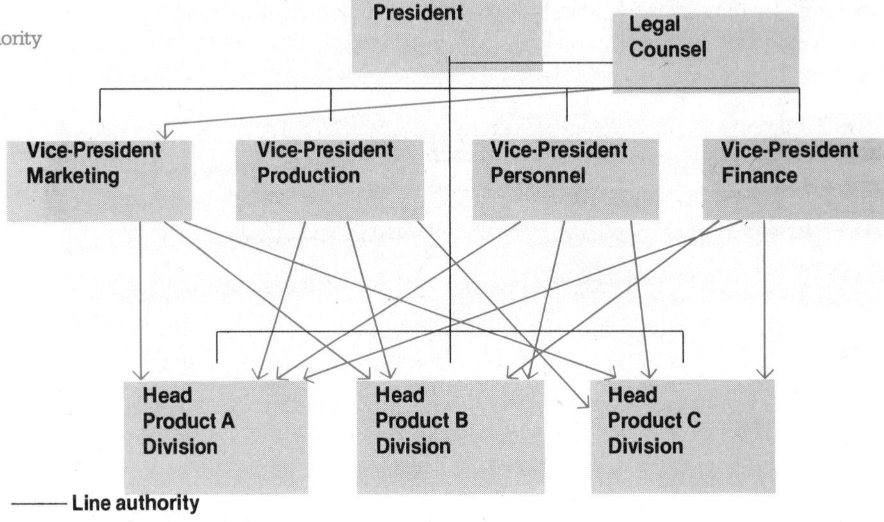

Figure 5.9
Functional Authority

(provide us the financial data in this format) and by *when* it is to be provided. This authority seldom involves *where, what,* or *who;* for this would seriously undermine department managers' authority.

3. Functional authority should be spelled out in writing so that everyone knows who has the authority and what areas it covers.
4. No one should have functional authority in another department without the manager of that department having been informed of this decision.
5. When this authority is used, the manager of the department should be kept informed so that the person knows what is being requested of his or her personnel. Otherwise, the manager's role in the department is seriously undermined.

Decentralization and Delegation of Authority

Decentralization is a system of management in which a great deal of decision-making authority rests at the lower levels of the hierarchy. Conversely, in organizations that are highly centralized most decisions are made at the upper levels. Many companies have found it beneficial to decentralize. However, there are factors that will influence the *degree* of decentralization. The following are some of the major ones:

■ Factors influencing decentralization.

- Cost. If a decision involves a great deal of money, it is common to find the decision being made at the upper levels of the hierarchy. Minor expenditures ($500 or less in large firms) are often made further down the hierarchy.
- Company size. As a firm gets larger, more and more decentralization typically occurs. The people at the top cannot maintain their tight grip any longer, assuming that they would want to do so.

- Philosophy of top management. Some firms are highly centralized or decentralized because this is the way management wants it. In companies run by their founders, it is common to find much more centralization than in similar firms where the owner-manager is no longer in charge and professional managers handle the operations.
- Philosophy of the personnel. If the workers and subordinate managers want more authority, the firm is likely to be more decentralized than if these groups indicate that they do not want to make important decisions.
- Functional area. In many cases, the activities of the particular department help dictate whether there will be decentralization. For example, in the finance department there tends to be more centralization than in production, where authority is decentralized to the operating level. Likewise, the salespeople often have more operating authority than those in the advertising department. Most firms want to centralize advertising so that there is uniformity regarding the type of image projected to the general public.

By taking factors such as these into consideration, it is possible to determine why some firms are more decentralized than others. Keep one thing in mind, however. Many management students believe that decentralization is better than centralization. This is fallacious. What is better depends on the situation. Some industries, like mining and smelting, are much more centralized than others, like auto manufacturing and retail sales, because in the former greater efficiency can be attained through such a philosophy. Table 5.3 describes a situation in which management has apparently risked a lot to gain a lot through decentralization.

Table 5.3
Decentralizing for Innovativeness

The battery market is a very competitive one. Firms like Eveready, Gould Inc., and P. R. Mallory & Company are very aggressive. As a result, the time lapse between development of a new type of battery and its reaching the market is decreasing. Those competitors who are unable to keep up are left far behind.

David C. Dawson, president of ESB Ray-O-Vac Corporation, is determined to keep his firm in the thick of this competitive business. That is why he recently reorganized the corporation and divided Ray-O-Vac into four clearly defined and autonomous operating firms. Responsibility for performance is being placed on the shoulders of the managers running these autonomous divisions, and research and product development is now being conducted at this level. This is a big change from when it was handled at the corporate technology center where the parent company is located.

Will this new reorganization, in which decentralization plays such a key role, result in that spark of innovation that will enable the corporation to once again claim its position in the battery business? Right now it is too early to say. However, one thing is certain. President Dawson believes that decentralization can recharge the firm's innovative spirit, and he is determined to test this thesis. By letting each division act as an independent firm, he feels he can create that driving spirit that will put the company right back in the middle of this industry battle.

Source: Based on "ESB Ray-O-Vac: Decentralizing to Recharge Its Innovative Spirit," *Business Week,* March 12, 1979, pp. 116–117.

- Delegation defined.

Delegation is the process the manager uses in distributing work to the subordinates. In all, there are three steps: (1) assigning duties to the subordinates, (2) granting them the authority to carry out these duties, and (3) creating an obligation whereby the subordinate assumes responsibility to the superior to complete the task satisfactorily.

Like decentralization, delegation depends on a number of factors for success. In particular, the philosophies of the manager and the subordinates play key roles. Some managers prefer to hold onto a great deal of authority and delegate very little, while other managers are just the opposite. Some workers like to have a lot of authority while others shun it because they are afraid they will make a mistake and get into trouble with the boss. How can delegation be made to work best? Some of the most helpful steps follow:

■ Steps for improving delegation.

1. Managers need to realize that they cannot do everything. Decide what can be done only by them and try to delegate the rest.
2. Managers should delegate in explicit terms. Tell the subordinates exactly what is to be done.

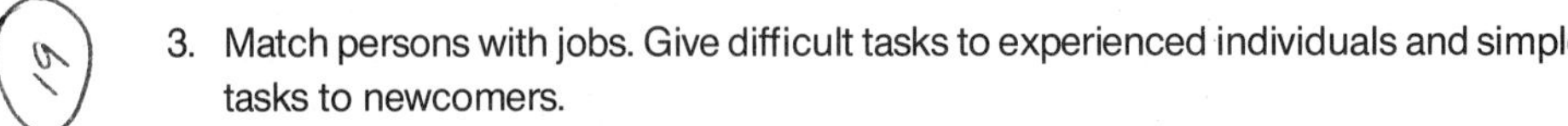

3. Match persons with jobs. Give difficult tasks to experienced individuals and simple tasks to newcomers.
4. If there is a recurring job-related problem, have an established procedure so that people can come back to the manager and discuss it.
5. When an individual has a problem, offer some assistance. Show or tell the person how to do the job right. Offer some help.

"I hereby empower you, Ambrose T. Wilkins, to water my plants. And let's hear no more talk about how I never delegate authority."

6. Use broad, not narrow, controls. Look over the individual's shoulder only when it is absolutely necessary.
7. When the job is done, specifically praise the employee for good work. If there were some problems, then talk about how these can be avoided in the future.

Summary

Organizing is the process of assigning duties to employees and coordinating their efforts to that they achieve maximum efficiency in their work. In organizing a structure, there are four basic building blocks; job descriptions, departmentalization and the use of committees, span of control, and authority-responsibility relationships.

Job descriptions spell out what the individual is to do. They provide the basic foundation for all organizing efforts.

Departmentalization involves grouping employees into units for the purpose of attaining common objectives. Some of the most common forms include functional departmentalization, product departmentalization, and territorial departmentalization. However, there are very few examples of pure forms of departmentalization. In most cases, enterprises use a combination of each of the three. This results in mixed departmentalization.

Another important organizational form is the committee. While the advantages of committees should be weighed against the disadvantages, if they are carefully organized and skillfully managed, committees can be very important organizational tools.

Span of control is a term which refers to the number of individuals who report to a given superior. A narrow span will result in a tall structure, while a wide span will bring about a flat structure. Depending on the situation, either can be beneficial to the organization. In determining the optimum span, it is important to study the major factors that influence the span. A list of some of these factors was provided in the chapter.

Authority is the right to command. There are three basic types of authority. Line authority is direct authority. Staff authority is auxiliary authority. Functional authority is authority in a department other than one's own. In using staff authority, the manager must remain alert to line-staff conflicts. But if the manager uses the guidelines set forth in this chapter when assigning functional authority, organizational efficiency can be increased.

Decentralization is a system of management in which a great deal of decision-making authority rests at the lower levels of the hierarchy. Not all organizations are highly decentralized. Some perform better under centralization. Some factors that influence the degree of centralization and decentralization are cost, company size, philosophy of the top management, and functional area.

Delegation is the process the manager uses in distributing work to the subordinates. Many times delegation can be used as a motivational tool. Employees work well when they are given increased responsibility. In delegating authority, certain helpful steps should be followed. These too were explained in the chapter.

Review and Study Questions

1. In your own words, explain what is meant by the term *organizing.*
2. How can job descriptions help an organization design its structure and organize its resources?
3. What is meant by the term *departmentalization?*
4. Which form of departmentalization is most commonly used: functional or product? Be sure to describe both types of departmentalization in your answer.
5. What is meant by the term *derivative departments?* Give an illustration.
6. What is the major benefit of functional departmentalization? What is the major benefit of product departmentalization? Describe each.
7. Who do some firms change their structure from a functional departmentalization arrangement to a territorial departmentalization arrangement?
8. Most organizations employ what can be called *mixed departmentalization.* What does this statement mean?
9. What are some of the major advantages of committees? What are some of the major disadvantages of committees?
10. How does a plural executive committee differ from an advisory committee? How does an ad hoc committee differ from a standing committee?
11. What are some useful guidelines that committee members should follow in ensuring that the committee functions properly?
12. What does the term *span of control* mean? In what way does this span influence whether an organization will be tall or flat?
13. In your own words, what is meant by the term *authority?* Where does authority come from? Defend your answer.
14. How does line authority differ from staff authority?
15. Cite four ways of minimizing or eliminating line-staff conflict.
16. How does functional authority work? Give an example.
17. What are three useful guidelines to follow in using functional authority? Explain each.
18. What factors influence whether an organization will be basically centralized or decentralized? List and explain at least four.
19. How does delegation of authority work? What are some of the helpful steps the manager should use when delegating authority? Explain.

Key Terms in the Chapter

organizing
job description
departmentalization
functional departmentalization
derivative functional department
organic function
product departmentalization
territorial departmentalization
ad hoc committee
plural executive committee
span of control
narrow span
wide span
tall structure
flat structure
authority
line authority
staff authority
functional authority
decentralization
delegation

Notes

1. Jay Hall, "Decisions, Decisions, Decisions," *"Psychology Today,* November 1971, p. 86.
2. James C. Worthy, "Organization Structure and Employee Morale," *American Sociological Review,* April 1950, pp. 169–179; and "Factors Influencing Employee Morale," *Harvard Business Review,* January 1950, pp. 61–73.
3. Peter F. Drucker, *Management: Tasks, Responsibilities, Practices* (New York: Harper & Row, 1974). p. 546.
4. Rocco Carzo, Jr., and John N. Yanouzas, "Effects of Flat and Tall Organization Structure," *Administrative Science Quarterly,* June 1969, pp. 178–191.

Case: The Mohrling Structure

How do you connect screwdrivers to turbines and make money as efficiently as possible?

The Mohrling Corporation manufactures and sells industrial equipment. Its organization chart is shown below. This equipment ranges from very expensive, sophisticated machinery down to moderately expensive, relatively unsophisticated apparatus. The expensive machinery is sold by the Product A Division. Its sales are the highest in the company, as are its profits. Unsophisticated apparatus is sold by the Product C Division. Its sales are the second highest, but its profits are the lowest in all three divisions. Equipment with prices and sophistication falling between Products A and C is sold by the Product B Division. Its sales are lower than the other two divisions, but its profits rank just behind those of Division A. The International Division sells all three product lines. However, it was formed only nine months ago; so it is too early to tell how successful the division will be.

Mohrling Corporation

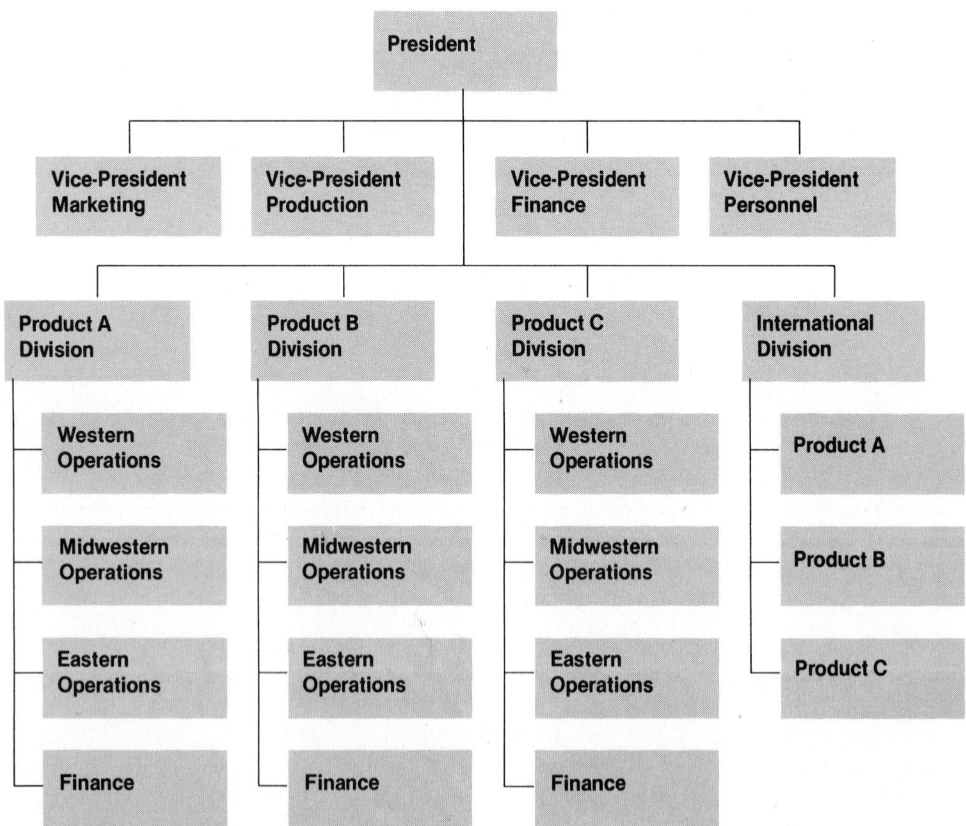

The three domestic divisions—A, B, and C—are really marketing outlets that sell their respective lines throughout the country. All equipment sold is manufactured at a central locale just outside Chicago. The equipment is sent directly to the buyer from this factory. The marketing department handles all product advertising and provides marketing assistance to each of the divisions. The central finance department controls overall finances and exercises functional authority over the divisional finance departments. The personnel department keeps employee records on all of the organization's workers.

This organization structure was developed only nine months ago. However, the president reports that both sales and profits are higher than ever. He attributes much of this to the reorganization. "It's increased our overall efficiency," he recently told the board of directors.

Questions

1. What type of departmentalization structure does the Mohrling Corporation employ? Explain.
2. What type of authority does the marketing department have in the product divisions? What type of authority does the finance department have in these divisions?
3. How decentralized do you think this organization is? Support your answer.

Case: A Financial Bath

It's everybody else's fault, and we all have to work together.

Things are not going well at the Campton Corporation. Last month the president made his decision, and production of the company's small pocket calculator was halted. An audit by the finance department now reveals that the company suffered a loss of over $17 million on the venture.

The idea for making a small pocket calculator originated about eight years ago. Campton had a sophisticated research and development department, and the marketing people in R&D suggested that there was a demand for such a calculator. After looking into the matter, the head of R&D told the president that it would take five or six years, but Campton could develop such a product. A marketing analysis revealed a great demand for such a product, and the president gave the go-ahead. The firm pumped over $10 million into the venture.

About two years ago the firm had a developed product. It would sell for about $35 and could add, subtract, multiply, divide, perform a few other calculations, and store information in its memory. The R&D people told the president that they could get the cost down to $25 if they could spend another year on research. The president agreed.

About this time, however, Texas Instruments came on the market with a low-priced, handheld calculator. Campton was shocked and the president immediately formed an advisory committee of staff specialists to research industry trends and report back on the feasibility of the project. The committee recommended that the company cut its losses immediately by halting all further R&D on Campton's calculator. However, the heads of marketing and production disagreed. Both argued that the firm could recoup its investment and make money if it would push ahead, produce the calculator at low cost and advertise it effectively. The president, after a great deal of thought, agreed.

The final product came off the assembly line seven months ago and was met with a fanfare of advertising activity. The calculators were sent out to wholesalers and retailers all over the country. However, sales never materalized. Most buyers were unable to distinguish between Campton's product and TI's product. Moreover, the Campton model sold for $25. TI had some models that sold for more and some that sold for less, thereby providing competition at virtually all levels of demand. Campton could not compete.

Last week there was a postmortem analysis in the Campton board room. The advisory people on the committee began to yell and shout at the line people in production and marketing, saying that they were the ones to blame. "We should have cut our losses," they asserted. The line people replied that advisory people never have to worry about taking responsibility for bad advice and can always demand credit for good advice. The head of marketing jumped in: "We made the mistake and we're responsible. However, we read your report about how the market wasn't there and how we would lose out to TI. And we found the report full of errors. So we rejected it as wrong. And it was. The real reason we failed wasn't even covered in your report. You guys have some nerve pointing the finger at us. Your participation was no more praiseworthy than ours."

The president suggested that both groups calm down. "Let's not fight about what went wrong," he said. "Let's see how we can prevent problems like this from occurring again. We've got to work together. The big problem we now face is how to counter our previous failure with a successful product. For this we need both line and staff help." Everyone agreed to pitch in and give it their best effort.

Questions

1. What type of authority did the committee have? Explain.
2. What type of authority did the heads of marketing and production have? Explain.
3. If you were a consultant to this company, what would you recommend in getting both groups to work together effectively? Explain.

Chapter 6

Contingency Organization Design

Objectives of the Chapter

Modern organizations are discovering that while the ideas presented in the last chapter are useful, these design concepts sometimes have to be modified to fit the needs of particular enterprises. In order to operate efficiently, their structure must be able to meet the demands of *both* the internal and external environment. Some companies can rely exclusively on the classic building blocks in doing so; others require more flexible designs. This has led to the emergence of what is called *contingency organization design.* What is currently known about contingency organization design, and what effect is it having on modern organization structures? The objectives of this chapter are to answer these questions. This will be done by first examining some of the contingency organization design research. What is happening in the area of contingency design? After reviewing some of the major research, an examination will be made of modern organization structures. What do these designs look like and how do they work? Some answers will be provided. Then the subject of span of control will be reviewed and a contingency approach to its use will be discussed. Finally, attention will be focused on job design.

When you have finished studying the material in this chapter, you should be able to:

1 Define the term *contingency organization design.*

2 Compare and contrast mechanistic and organic structures.

3 Discuss the effect of technology on organization structures.

4 Identify six of the major variables in organization design.

5 Explain what a matrix structure is and how it works.

6 Discuss what a free-form structure is and how it works.

7 Relate how a weighting system can help a firm identify ideal spans of control.

8 Define the term *job design* and explain how job rotation, job enlargement, and job enrichment work.

Contingency Organization Design Research

Over the last twenty-five years there has been a great deal of research directed at understanding organization design. In particular, researchers have sought to answer the question of why some firms use a semi-bureaucratic structure while others employ a very flexible fly-by-the-seat-of-the-pants design. Three major studies have provided a foundation for understanding overall organizational design: (1) the Burns and Stalker research, (2) the Woodward studies, and (3) Lawrence and Lorsch's research.

Burns and Stalker's Research

Tom Burns and G. M. Stalker were interested in investigating how changes in the technological and market environments influenced management processes in industrial firms.[1] In their study of twenty companies, they realized that different types of organization structures were being used. They therefore arranged the firms along a continuum that described the environment in which the firms operated. At one end they put the firm that was in the most stable environment. This rayon mill had a highly structured organization, carefully defined roles and job tasks, and standing plans for handling day-to-day matters. On the other end of the continuum, in the most dynamic environment, was an electronics development manufacturer. This company had no organization chart, used no job descriptions, and placed a great deal of emphasis on teamwork and interpersonal interaction in ensuring goal attainment. Between these two extremes, Burns and Stalker grouped the remainder of the twenty companies.

■ Environment influences the organization structure.

Burns and Stalker found that as one moved from a very stable environment to a less predictable one, the organization structure changed. Bureaucratic rules and procedures worked well in the stable environment, but were not used by organizations in dynamic, turbulent environments. The researchers labeled the structures used by those in a stable environment as *mechanistic* and those in the dynamic environment as *organic.* Figure 6.1 shows a continuum like Burns and Stalker's.

Figure 6.1
A Mechanistic-Organic Continuum

Mechanistic **Organic**

When organization design is discussed today, it is common to find people using the terms *mechanistic* and *organic* in describing the type of structure employed by a particular enterprise. Table 6.1 provides a comparison of some of the key dimensions of these two types of structures. A close analysis of this table shows why many modern firms are finding it necessary to abandon their mechanistic design and move toward more organic ones. Their environments are becoming too volatile and competitive to be served adequately by mechanistic structures.

Table 6.1
A Partial Comparison of Mechanistic and Organic Structures

Key Dimension	Mechanistic Structure	Organic Structure
General nature of the environment	Calm	Turbulent
Predictability of the environment	Certain	Uncertain
Technology	Stable	Dynamic
Overall values of the people	Efficiency, predictability, security	Effectiveness adaptability, risk taking
Involvement in goal setting	Hierarchical from the top down	Participatory, bottom up as well as top down
Time perspective of the managers	Short-term	Long-term
Decision making	Programmed and autocratic	Nonprogrammed and participatory
Authority of the managers	Based on one's position	Based on one's knowledge
Job definitions	Fixed and specific	Flexible, based on the situation
Interpersonal relations	Formal	Informal
Planning process	Fixed and repetitive	Flexible and changing
Control process	Impersonal, use of rules and regulations	Interpersonal, use of suggestions and persuasion

Source: Adapted from Fremont E. Kast and James E. Rosenzweig, *Contingency Views of Organization and Management* (Chicago: Science Research Associates, 1973), pp. 315–318.

The Woodward Studies

Another important research study related to organization design was carried out by Joan Woodward.[2] She investigated 100 British firms for the purpose of determining whether any differences between successful and unsuccessful companies appeared when the firms were examined along the lines of structure, management, and operating processes. After conducting a great deal of nonproductive analysis, she and her associates decided to investigate whether any relationship between technology and organization structure existed. In order to do so, they divided all of the firms into one of three basic groups:

1. Unit and small-batch production. This is used by firms producing one-of-a-kind items, prototypes, custom-built cars, or a small number of units produced to customer specifications.

2. Large-batch and mass production. This is used by firms producing large numbers of goods, usually with the use of assembly lines. Mass-produced autos are a classic example.
3. Process production. This is used by firms that produce a continuous flow of the same product—as in the production of gases, liquids, and crystalline substances.

This classification system ranged from the oldest and simplest form of production (unit and small-batch) to the most modern and sophisticated (process production). When this technological classification was used, the researchers found a strong relationship between organizational structure and success within each group. Successful unit production firms had organizational characteristics in common. The same was true for both successful large-batch firms and successful process production firms. Table 6.2 provides some of the comparisons.

Table 6.2
Organizational Characteristics of Firms in Woodward's Study

Characteristics	Unit and Small-Batch Production	Large-Batch and Mass Production	Process Production
Number of employees controlled by the first-line supervisor	Small	Large	Small
Relationship between work group and supervisor	Informal	Formal	Informal
Basic types of workers employed	Skilled	Semiskilled and unskilled	Skilled
Definition of duties	Often vague	Clear-cut	Often vague
Degree of delegation of authority	High	Low	High
Use of participative management	High	Low	High
Type of organization structure	Flexible	Rigid	Flexible

■ So does technology

Woodward and her associates found that there was a tendency for organic management systems to predominate in the unit and small-batch production and process production firms, while large-batch and mass production companies relied most heavily on mechanistic structures. Those with the most and least sophisticated technology employed flexible structures, while those using an intermediate degree of technology relied more on classic organization principles such as those described in the previous chapter. Continuing the research, Woodward was able to further substantiate her findings. As a result, she proved that technology is a *causal* factor in organization design. It has an impact on the structure.

Lawrence and Lorsch's Research

Burns, Stalker, and Woodward have provided important insights into how organizations at large are designed. Paul Lawrence and Jay Lorsch have helped explain why specific departments within a structure will be designed differently. For example, regardless of the overall structure, why does one department have more of a mechanistic design while another is more organic?[3] Conducting their investigation among six firms in the plastics industry and two each in the food and container industries, they sought to determine how these organizations dealt with economic and market conditions, not only on an overall basis but by major department.

In the container firms they found three major departments: marketing, research, and production. These departments had little difficulty in determining the type of products that should be developed, produced, and sold. All could usually get very quick feedback regarding the success of their performance. As a result, all made heavy use of mechanistic structures. Coordination was attained through the use of policies, rules, and procedures; and decisions followed the established chain of command.

However, the situation in the plastics firms was different. While the production and marketing departments faced routine tasks and were organized mechanistically, the research department faced a great deal of uncertainty. Workers were usually unable to accurately predict the best type of product to develop, and they had to wait longer to get feedback on the success of their job performance than did their counterparts in production and marketing. As a result, the research department had a more organic type of structure, as shown in Table 6.3. Meanwhile, the firms in the food industry operated between the two extremes found in the container and plastics industries.

■ Even within organizations there are different types of organization designs.

Table 6.3
Lawrence and Lorsch's Research Findings

	Two Container Firms	Six Plastics Firms
Production department	Predictable tasks; mechanistic structure	Predictable tasks; mechanistic structure
Research department	Predictable tasks; mechanistic structure	Unpredictable tasks; organic structure
Marketing department	Predictable tasks; mechanistic structure	Fairly predictable tasks; basically mechanistic structure

The research results from Lawrence and Lorsch's study support and extend the general pattern found by Burns, Stalker, and Woodward. Depending on the environment, whether external or internal, a mechanistic structure will be best in a stable setting, while an organic design will be superior in a dynamic setting.

Determining the Right Organization Design

Research such as that just reviewed reveals that there are a series of key variables which affect organization design. John Child (see Table 6.4) has suggested still others. While some are more important than others, drawing on all that is currently known about contingency organization design, six variables appear to be of major importance:

■ Variables affecting organization design.

1. Environment. Is it stable or dynamic?
2. Size of the organization. Is it small or very diverse?
3. Type of personnel. Under what type of structure would the people like to work?
4. Technology. Is it unit or small-batch, mass production, or process production?
5. Dependence on the external environment. How responsive does the organization have to be to this outside environment?
6. Perceived complexity of the environment. How stable or dynamic does the management think the environment is?

To rank these six variables in terms of importance, the first three are considered strong predictor variables in determining organization design. Technology is a moderately strong predictor. The last two have proved to be only somewhat strong.

Modern Organization Designs

■ Characteristics of a bureaucracy.

Modern organization designs, as has just been noted, can vary anywhere along the mechanistic-organic continuum. Which will be best for the firm? This will depend on the situation. Mechanistic structures are very commonplace. They tend to be basically bureaucratic and (1) make heavy use of classic organization ideas such as division of labor, (2) have a hierarchy of offices with each lower one being controlled and supervised by the one immediately above it, (3) use a consistent system of abstract rules and standards, which assures uniformity in the performance of duties and the coordination of various tasks, (4) have a spirit of formalistic impersonality in which people carry out the duties of their office, and (5) have employment based on technical qualifications and protected from arbitrary dismissal.[4]

However, many modern organizations are finding that they cannot rely solely on these structural ideas. Their environment is too dynamic. These firms are turning to more organic designs. One of these types is the matrix structure.

The Matrix Structure

The matrix structure has been widely used in the aerospace industry, as well as in multi-line corporations that want to design and develop new products. The idea behind the matrix organization is quite simple. The enterprise establishes a project

Table 6.4
Organization Structure and Performance: Some Key Research Findings

Many factors appear to influence organizational performance. Five of the structural ones relate to environment, the size of the organization, the diversity of its operations, technology, and the type of personnel who work in the organization. Based on his research in the area, John Child has reported the following organization structure and performance findings:

1. Environment. When the environment in which an organization operates is subject to change, successful enterprises will readily adapt. They will remain flexible, coordinate their activities, and share information among themselves. They will use organic structures. Meanwhile, if the environment is basically stable, successful firms will rely more heavily on formal, mechanistic designs. This finding supports the work of Burns, Stalker, Lawrence, and Lorsch.

2. Size. As organizations increase in size, they will tend to become more bureaucratic. Despite what critics say about bureaucracies, profitable, fast-growing firms with 2,000 or more employees tend to increase their degree of formalization as they grow. Conversely, small firms of around 100 employees tend to perform better with very little formal organization.

3. Diversity of Operations. As organizations increase their operations and become more diversified, they will achieve higher levels of performance if they group their basic activities into divisions. This allows them to create decentralized, semi-autonomous operating units which can better deal with the increasing size and diversity of the organization.

4. Technology. Organizations have to design their structures to suit their technologies. If they do, they will achieve higher levels of performance. The importance of this was illustrated by the research of Joan Woodward, who reported that technology is a causal factor in organization design.

5. Type of Personnel. Organizations have to design structures that are consistent with the expectations of the personnel. If the people want a decentralized structure, the organization will achieve higher levels of performance if they design such a structure. The same is true in the case of desired centralized structures. The rule is always the same: Give the employees what they want!

Source: John Child, "What Determines Organization: The Universal vs. the It-All-Depends," *Organizational Dynamics,* Summer 1974, pp. 10–18.

objective, assigns it a project manager and a small team, and then tells the group to accomplish it. For example, in the aerospace industry it is common to find a project manager being assigned the job of developing a new type of aircraft and seeing the job through to completion. This manager's job is to work with the rest of the organization in completing the project.

Figure 6.2 provides an illustration of a matrix organization. Note in the figure that there are currently three project managers heading project teams. Meanwhile, directly under the general manager are seven line departments. These departments support the various project managers. Here is how it works. First, the project manager contacts the head of each of these seven departments and tells the individual what the project is all about. The manager then asks the department head to support the project by providing assistance. The head of research and development is asked to provide some people to help conduct research and development. The quality control department is asked for some people to provide quality control assistance. The test and assurance group is asked to set up tests that will check out the aircraft to ensure that it is being built properly.

Notice that the project manager *asks* the department heads to cooperate in getting the project accomplished. This is because the manager does *not* have line

Figure 6.2
Matrix Organization

General Manager

Research and Development | Quality Control | Test and Assurance | Contract Administration | Purchasing | Manufacturing | Engineering

Project Manager A: Research and Development Group | Quality Control Group | Test and Assurance Group | Contract Administration Group | Purchasing Group | Manufacturing Group | Engineering Group

Project Manager B: Research and Development Group | Quality Control Group | Test and Assurance Group | Contract Administration Group | Purchasing Group | Manufacturing Group | Engineering Group

Project Manager C: Research and Development Group | Quality Control Group | Test and Assurance Group | Contract Administration Group | Purchasing Group | Manufacturing Group | Engineering Group

——— Line authority
– – – – Project authority

■ Project personnel have two bosses.

authority to order these department heads to help. Of course, if they do not cooperate, the project manager can always go back to their common boss, the general manager, and complain. However, this is very seldom necessary. The heads of the various departments understand what is being asked of them and they know that the company expects them to assist the various project managers. Each will therefore assign the necessary people to the project. And while they are working on the project, these people will have *two* bosses. First, they will be under their departmental boss, who has line authority over them. Second, they will be responsible to the project manager, who gives them orders on project-related matters. Keep in mind, however, that the project manager cannot fire them or take any punitive action against them. The manager can only report them to their department head for being uncooperative. When this happens, their regular boss will then decide what to do about the matter.

■ Project authority flows across the structure.

Since the department heads maintain control over the people they lend to the project, they maintain line authority. Meanwhile, the project manager has what is called *project authority* over the group. This is the authority to give project-related orders.

Several important characteristics distinguish the matrix structure from a typical line-staff organization. First, there are two types of authority: line and project. The line authority flows *down* from superior to subordinate, while the project authority flows *across* the structure. Project authority flows across because the project manager's authority is really that of coordinating efforts (a horizontal function) rather than one of giving orders.

Second, each of the departmental people who work on the project have two bosses: their regular department head and the project manager. There is thus a *violation* of the unity of command principle—one and only one boss.

Third, while authority and responsibility in bureaucracies are supposed to be equal, in a project organization the project manager always has *less* authority than responsibility. The individual is charged with getting the project accomplished but has only project authority. This results in the manager having to *supplement* his or her authority. Some of the most common ways they do so include: (1) using their personalities and persuasive abilities to secure support from the department heads, (2) showing the department heads that they are competent and therefore entitled to support on the project, and (3) making use of reciprocal favors, for example, an understanding that if you help me on this project, I'll owe you one later on.

Finally, a matrix structure is only a *temporary* one. Once the project is over the individuals who were helping out all return to their functional department and the project manager goes on to another project. The project group is phased out. This is in contrast to the typical department which remains in existence indefinitely.

■ The structure is a temporary one.

Other Forms of Adhocracy

While the matrix structure is one form of adaptive, organic design, there are many others. All of them have one thing in common; they are *adhocratic* in nature. This means that they are formed for a particular purpose and are changed as necessary. Rather than trying to solve major problems with the old structure, new departments or divisions are created to deal with the problems. If these do not work, they are disbanded and others formed in their place. Today, in many enterprises, bureaucratic designs are being replaced by adhocratic ones.

"My own observation as a consultant," says D. R. Daniel, an official of McKinsey & Company, a large management consulting firm, "is that one major restructuring every two years is probably a conservative estimate of the current rate of organizational change among the largest industrial corporations. Our firm has conducted over 200 organization studies for domestic corporate clients in the past year, and organization problems are an even larger part of our practice outside the United States." "What's more," he adds, "there are no signs of a leveling off. If anything, the frequency of organizational upheavals is increasing."[5]

Furthermore, task forces and other ad hoc groups are becoming more and more prevalent throughout government, the scientific community, education, and other major institutions in our society. One reason for the deterioration of bureaucracies is the need for adapting to the changing environment. A second is the rise of the specialist who can handle specific problems. By putting together ad hoc teams of these people, modern organizations are finding that they can solve heretofore difficult problems. However, the team does *not* operate on old hierarchical principles. Quite often, authority is based not on job title (group leader, for example) but on competence (who knows the most about the problem under analysis).

Additionally, great emphasis is being given to coordination of efforts. Previously, managers gave orders to their subordinates, and there was a vertical flow of authority down the structure. Now, experts coordinate with other experts, and there is give-and-take in problem solving. The adhocrat is the person who is willing to cooperate with peers in getting things done.

Free-form structures are highly flexible.

Many people refer to these newly designed forms as *free-form structures.* A free-form organization structure is one designed in such a way that the major units operate both flexibly and independently. Organization charts and chains of command are not emphasized. Meanwhile attention is given to the use of the profit-center concept, which is often used in product departmentalization and team approaches to problem solving. Some divisions and departments are permanent; others are temporary, being phased out after they have served their purpose. The overall objectives of the free-form structure are to take advantage of opportunity, change as needed, grow, and expand. The main ingredients of such a structure are centralized control and decentralized operations, the profit-center concept, and a stress on risk taking consistent with reward.

In summing up this discussion of free-form structures, it should be pointed out that if a bureaucratic type of structure works best, the firm should use it. If not, the company should restructure and adopt a more flexible, organic design. In short, *use what works*!

Span of Control Determinants

Span of control can also be approached from a contingency standpoint. What determines whether an individual should have a wide or narrow span? In the previous chapter some of these factors have been discussed. Moreover, the Lockheed Corporation has devised a way of determining an ideal span by giving weights to various span of control factors. Figure 6.3 provides an illustration of the weighting chart used in this process. The factors that are employed are:

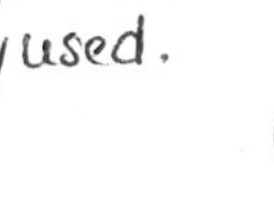

Span of control determinants.

1. Similarity of functions. If all the subordinates are doing the same thing, a manager can handle more of them than if the workers are all performing different tasks.
2. Geographic closeness. If everyone is located close together, it is easier to control large numbers of workers than if they are geographically dispersed.
3. Complexity of functions. If the work is simple and repetitive, the manager can control more subordinates than if the work is varied and complex.
4. Direction and control. If minimum amounts of time are needed in directing and controlling the subordinates, the manager can supervise more subordinates than if they require constant, close supervision.
5. Coordination. If the individuals work alone and very little coordination is required among them, it is easier to manage a large number than if a lot of coordination is needed.
6. Planning. If the manager does not need to spend much time planning the work of the individuals, more of them can be supervised than if a great deal of planning is required and the work is complex.

Using the Weighting System

Figure 6.3 shows a series of continua for each of the six span of control factors used by Lockheed. Some control factors are more important than others. For

Main ingredients of a free form structure

- Centralized control
- decentralized operations
- profit center concept
- Stress on risk taking, consistent c̄ reward.

Figure 6.3
Lockheed's Span of Control Weighting System

1	2	3	4	5
1	2	3	4	5
2	4	6	8	10
3	6	9	12	15
2	4	6	8	10
2	4	6	8	10

different, located in many dispersed geographic areas, and in need of constant, close supervision.

In Figure 6.3 the weighting system has been used for two managers. The first is a lower-level supervisor managing workers who are performing similar functions. They are all located in one area, their work is routine and calls for limited supervision with any required coordination by the workers spelled out, and the planning involved in supervising the individuals is minimal. These factors have all been circled in the figure and the total of all six factors is nineteen. (Check the chart and verify that the six numbers that have been circled do indeed add up to nineteen.)

The other individual is a top executive. This person is supervising managers who are performing very different functions. The individuals are located in one plant location but in separate buildings there; their jobs are complex and varied; there is a need for frequent, continuing supervision on the part of the top executive; close coordination is required; and considerable effort is needed for planning, since only broad policies are available. The weights attached to these factors have been boxed in and they total forty-three. (Check the chart and verify that the boxed-in numbers do indeed add up to forty-three.)

Based on the final number, a span of control can be developed. In the case of the lower-level manager, nineteen is a very low total, suggesting that the individual can employ a wide span of control. Lockheed recommends a range of nine to twelve. Conversely, in the case of the top executive who has a high score of forty-three, the span of control, according to Lockheed, should range between three and five.

Firms that want to identify effective span of control ranges need to develop systems similar to the one discussed here. The approach requires only three steps:

▪ How to use a weighting system.

1. Identify the important span of control factors that influence the job—similarity of functions, geographic closeness, and the like.
2. Develop a continuum for each of the factors and assign a weight to each degree—a 1 for identical jobs, a 2 if the jobs are essentially alike, and so on.
3. Evaluate each management job using this weighting system.

Keep in mind that in some cases it may be necessary to develop a series of weighting systems since the span of control factors to be used in evaluating one type of job may not fit very well when used with another type of job. However, the basic idea will be the same.

Job Design

Overall structures and span of control are important contingency organization design areas. However, another is perhaps even more important—design of the work itself. How can the organization ensure that jobs are properly designed? There are two ways:

1. See that the job is structured in such a way that the worker can carry it out with a minimum of problems.

2. Design the job so that it is interesting, challenging, and personally rewarding.

Of course, some jobs are dull and repetitive and there is not much the organization can do about them. Assembly-line work is an example. It is highly structured and not very satisfying. However, unless the entire line is redesigned, the way the work is done today is the way it will be done ten years from now. Other jobs are interesting and challenging. For example, people in advertising departments, like copy writers, designers, and artists, report that they truly enjoy their work. What differentiates boring jobs from exciting ones? One way of answering this question is to use a series of typical job characteristics and see how structured or challenging the work is. The following eight characteristics provide a basis for examining any job:

■ Job characteristics.

1. Variety. Is the job narrow and routine, or does it involve a lot of different, interesting tasks?
2. Wholeness. Does the job consist of doing one thing and then passing the work to someone else, or does it involve carrying out a whole series of activities so that the worker personally completes all, or a large part, of the job?
3. Human interaction. Does the work isolate the individual, or is there the opportunity for socializing with fellow workers?
4. Freedom. Is there a set pattern for doing the work, or does the individual have discretion in deciding how to carry out tasks?
5. Physical fatigue. Is the work physically tiring, or does it require minimal physical effort?
6. Job environment. Is the work carried out in a noisy, hot, dirty environment, or are the surroundings pleasant?
7. Work locale. Is the individual confined to one particular workplace during the day, or can an employee get up and go elsewhere in the course of work?
8. Work time. Does the individual have to be in the office at a certain time and stay there until quitting time, or does the person have a more flexible time schedule?

Boring and unrewarding jobs fit into the first half of these eight descriptions. Those that are best described by the last half of each description are interesting and exciting. How can jobs be redesigned so as to contain some of the desirable aspects of these latter characteristics? The answer is found in what are called *redesign techniques,* an exercise for which can be found in Table 6.5.

Job Redesign Techniques

There are a number of ways of redesigning jobs to make them more enjoyable. Three of the most common methods are job rotation, job enlargement, and job enrichment. The following examines each.

Job Rotation. Many jobs are boring because the individual performs one or two simple tasks and quickly learns to master them. There is no challenge or feeling of

Table 6.5
Boring and Stressful

Some jobs are highly stressful, but there is little that can be done about them. The individual simply has to accept these conditions. Others are basically boring. This is where job redesign can help—assuming, of course, that the organization is willing to do so. The following presents a list of ten jobs, five of which are boring and five of which are high stress. Look the list over. Identify the five boring jobs and rank them from first to last. Do this in five minutes and if there is any time left, rank the high stress ones from first to last.

1. Industrial laborers in factories and forges
2. Typists
3. Inspectors on blue-collar assembly-line operations
4. Bank guards
5. Clinical laboratory technicians
6. Car-watchers in tunnels
7. Highway toll collectors
8. Health technology technicians
9. Miners and mine workers (not necessarily working underground)
10. Assembly-line workers

When you finish, check your answers with those given below. Most people can identify the boring ones but have trouble ranking them in correct order. The same is true for the stressful ones. How well did you do?

Answers: The five boring occupations in correct order are Numbers 10, 7, 6, 2, 4; the five high stress ones in proper order are Numbers 3, 8, 5, 9, 1.

accomplishment. In an effort to overcome this problem, some firms use *job rotation,* whereby the worker is rotated among jobs. For example, consider the case of three workers who are putting together a consumer good. The first assembles the product, the second tests it, and the third packages it. The job can be diagramed as in Figure 6.4

Figure 6.4
Job Rotation

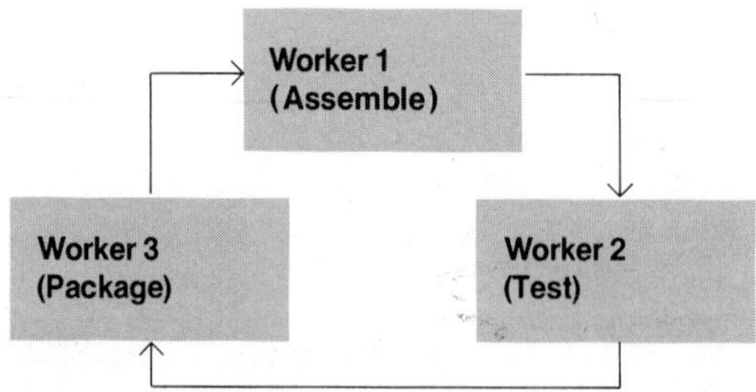

■ Job rotation involves trading jobs.

With job rotation, the workers trade jobs so that the assembler becomes the tester, the tester becomes the packager, and the packager becomes the assembler. The three will do these jobs for a while and then again trade, so that each eventually becomes capable of performing all three operations.

Job rotation is not a sophisticated technique; it is easy to implement. Furthermore, some workers like jobs that permit them to daydream and/or socialize with fellow workers, and job rotation allows this. The work pattern changes, but the difficulty of the new job is not great. Thus, job rotation sometimes offers a simple solution to the elimination of boring work. In particular, it increases the variety of tasks.

Job Enlargement. *Job enlargement* involves an increase in the total number of tasks the worker carries out. Under this arrangement the individual performs a series of jobs. Applied to the example in Figure 6.4, job enlargement would have each worker doing all three tasks: assembling, testing, and packaging, This is a move away from job specialization or work simplification, which is used in bureaucratic structures.

▪ Job enlargement increases the total number of worker tasks.

Job enlargement has some important benefits to offer. First, it increases both job variety and wholeness. The worker is given a number of different tasks to perform, and the work has more variety than before. Additionally, if individual workers do not do the entire job, they now complete a more substantial part of it. Second, the time required for jobs often decreases. For example, if a worker specializes in one task, the task may take a minute to do. If there are three tasks to the entire job, it will take three minutes *plus* the amount of time necessary for passing the work from one individual to the next. If one person does the entire job, it may take slightly over a minute per task, but no time is needed for passing the work along. The result is often an *overall decline* in time and an increase in output.

Research studies reveal that job enlargement appears to increase job satisfaction and work quality. For this reason, many organizations have used it in job redesign.

Job Enrichment. The most popular redesign technique is *job enrichment.* This technique attempts to build into the job psychological motivators such as variety, increased responsibility, and chances for accomplishment. In recent years many job enrichment programs have been reported. Perhaps the most famous are those of the Swedish automakers, Saab and Volvo. In America, meanwhile, success with job enrichment programs has been reported by such firms as AT&T, Travelers Insurance, and Corning Glass.

▪ Job enrichment builds in psychological motivators.

"I see Dressler, Strole & Cutting have implemented their mandatory-retirement program."

Source: *New Yorker*, August 9, 1969, p. 41. Drawing by Lorenz;

When job enrichment is used, the employee is given more authority over the *planning* and *controlling* aspects of work. In planning, for example, the worker is given authority to organize and schedule tasks and solve problems that arise in doing so. In controlling, the individual carries out such functions as inspecting, testing, repairing, evaluating, and recording the output. The result is often an increase in worker motivation, followed by a rise in output.

Summary

While organizations use the basic building blocks discussed in the previous chapter, many of them modify their use via a contingency approach. In particular, the more dynamic the environment, the more likely that the organization will adapt its mechanistic structure and become more organic. The research of Burns, Stalker, and Woodward has proven this. Meanwhile, work by Lawrence and Lorsch shows that this mechanistic–organic continuum is as true for specific departments as it is for the organization at large. If departments face stable environments they will be organized mechanistically; if they face dynamic environments they will be organized organically. Some of the major variables which influence organization design include the environment, size of the organization, type of personnel, technology, dependence on the external environment, and perceived complexity of the environment. The first three of these are considered to be strong predictors of organization design, while the latter two are somewhat strong. Technology falls between them in terms of importance.

What do modern organization structures look like? One of the most common is the matrix structure, with its use of the project manager and project authority. Others are more free-form in scope. The latter have a series of common characteristics including de-emphasis of organization charts and chains of command, attention to the profit-center concept, use of ad hoc groups and departments, authority based on knowledge rather than position, decentralized operations and centralized control, and an emphasis on organization growth, expansion, and flexibility.

Span of control can also be approached from a contingency standpoint. By identifying key span of control factors and weighting each appropriately, it is possible to determine ideal control ranges.

Finally, in discussing organization design it is important to examine job design. Low-level jobs, in particular, can be boring and routine. Some ways of redesigning them include job rotation, job enlargement, and job enrichment.

Review and Study Questions

1. In your own words, what is meant by the term *contingency organization design?*
2. What did Tom Burns and G. M. Stalker learn from their research about the types of organization structures used by industrial firms? Explain.

3. How does a mechanistic structure differ from an organic one? Compare and contrast the two types of structure.
4. According to Joan Woodward, what types of firms are most likely to use mechanistic designs? Organic designs? Explain.
5. In what way did Paul R. Lawrence and Jay W. Lorsch extend the research findings of Burns, Stalker, and Woodward?
6. Are there any variables that determine what we call the *right organization design*? Include at least three of these variables in your answer.
7. How does a matrix structure work? Explain, incorporating into your answer the role and authority of the project manager.
8. What are some of the characteristics that distinguish a line-staff organization from a matrix structure?
9. Exactly what is meant by the term *free-form structure*? Who uses these designs?
10. In what way can a weighting system help a firm identify ideal spans of control for its managers?
11. What is meant by the term *job design*? Put it in your own words.
12. How does job rotation work? Explain.
13. How does job enlargement work? What benefits does it offer?
14. In what way does job enrichment differ from job enlargement? Explain.

Key Terms in the Chapter

contingency organization design
mechanistic structure
organic structure
matrix structure
project authority
adhocracy
free-form structure
job design
job rotation
job enlargement
job enrichment

Notes

1. Tom Burns and G. M. Stalker. *The Management of Innovation* (London: Tavistock, 1961).
2. Joan Woodward, *Industrial Organization: Theory and Practice* (London: Oxford University Press, 1965).
3. Paul R. Lawrence and Jay W. Lorsch, *Organization and Environment* (Homewood, Ill.: Richard D. Irwin, 1967).
4. Peter M. Blau, *Bureaucracy in Modern Society* (New York: Random House, 1956), pp. 28–33.
5. Alvin Toffler, *Future Shock* (New York: Bantam, 1970), p. 129.

Case: Business as Usual

RDA—a billion-dollar nonsystem that mom and pop started years ago.

Many organizational experts are quick to point out that as a company gets larger it will tend to become more of a bureaucracy. However, some firms have defied the experts and grown in spite of what appear to be errors in organizational design. Reader's Digest Association, Inc. (RDA), is a classic example.

Founded by DeWitt Wallace and his wife Lila in 1922, the magazine has grown tremendously. By 1929 circulation was 228,000 and by 1939 it was approaching 3 million. Today circulation is 18.3 million in the U. S. (exceeded only by TV Guide) and 11.7 million abroad. When *Digest* sales are coupled with those from the company's book publishing, educational materials, records, cassettes, and tapes, the firm grosses approximately $1 billion a year and has net earnings of at least $100 million.

Suprisingly, its organization structure has not changed very much. Things are basically centralized and run from the top. The founders no longer hold top management positions, but they help run things from the sidelines. The current president, John O'Hara, says it best with his statement, "We march to a different drummer." Of course, things are changing somewhat. For example, there is now more emphasis on personnel development, a specialist has been hired to teach supervisors how to manage, and there are more frequent staff meetings and action-oriented committees. In short, there is more systematized operation and business organization than before. However, all operations report directly to Mr. O'Hara and many things are still done the old way. Despite efforts at tighter procedures and tougher cost controls, things are still very informal at *Reader's Digest.* As the president put it, "We've no master plan for growth. All Mr. Wallace ever wanted was one fine magazine. Everything else was a spinoff from that." Today, as a privately held corporation with no outside stockholders to please or investors to impress, RDA continues to be what it has always been—a highly successful, internationally known, informally managed corporation. And it is unlikely that this will change. As one RDA executive explained, in reference to a leading management consulting firm that was hired to review operations and recommend changes in procedures and organizations, "They were baffled by the way our nonsystem worked. It defied everything that the consultants stood for. They left with a nice fee and their tail between their legs." It is unlikely that if they returned today the scenario would be any different.

Questions

1. What type of organization design does *Reader's Digest* use: mechanistic or organic?
2. Under what conditions would RDA's structure change? Incorporate into your answer a discussion of the six variables discussed in this chapter that help determine the right organization design.

3. Would a free-form structure ever work well for RDA? Explain.

Source: Based on "*Reader's Digest:* Modernizing the Beat of a Different Drummer," *Business Week,* March 5, 1979, pp. 98–100.

Case: Giving It a Try

There's a lot to be gained and very little to be lost . . . isn't there?

Charlson Industries is a manufacturing firm that produces components used in electrical equipment. Most of these components have been specially designed by Charlson, but they do not require a very high degree of R&D skill. In fact, Charlson has never seen itself as an R&D firm; rather it is a manufacturer of components.

Recently, however, the president has been thinking about becoming more research and development oriented. He believes that if the company were to begin investing more money in R&D, it could develop more sophisticated components and increase its market share. The problem with this strategy is that there are already three large firms that dominate the R&D side of the business, and Charlson would have to compete with them. Also, there is a large initial investment needed to get into this area.

The president has talked to the financial vice-president and has been told that the firm can afford the risk involved. Additionally, the new components will not be mass-produced; they will be assembled by hand. Each worker will put together the entire unit. And while the process will be slower and the cost of the unit will be higher, so will the selling price, so that profit will increase dramatically.

After serious deliberation with the other top managers, the president has decided to go ahead, increase the R&D budget, and bring in five more research specialists. He believes that within two years the firm will be known for its research and development as well as its manufacturing of components. Meanwhile, if things do not go well and the venture is unsuccessful, the company will simply de-emphasize its R&D concentration and go back to doing what it was doing before. The president put it this way, "There's a lot to be gained and very little to be lost from this venture. So why not give it a try?"

Questions

1. Under this new strategy, will the overall organization structure change? What about the structure in the R&D department? Explain your answer, bringing into your discussion the research findings of Tom Burns, G. M. Stalker, Joan Woodward, Paul Lawrence, and Jay Lorsch.
2. If the firm's investment does not pay off and it goes back to the old way of doing things, will this influence the organizational structure? Defend your answer.
3. Will the workers like the new component assembly better than the old one? Why or why not? Explain your answer.

Part Four

The Management Process: Staffing

Every organization is in a constant state of flux. Some are increasing their sales and seeking to hire more people. Others are suffering financial setbacks and are laying off or firing some of their employees. At the same time, within all organizations people are retiring, being promoted, and quitting. The overall result is a movement of people into and out of the organization. How does a business firm balance its need for staff with the available supply of such people? This is where staffing comes in.

Staffing consists of four basic activities: recruiting new people, selecting those who are best equipped to do the job, properly training these individuals, and developing their potential to the greatest degree possible. In the two chapters of Part 4 we are going to examine what staffing is all about.

Chapter 7 Recruiting and Selecting

Objectives of the Chapter

The first steps in the staffing process are to recruit and, from the recruitment pool, select those employees already on board or those available through the pool who are most likely to do the best job. The initial objective of this chapter is to study the ways modern organizations go about recruiting employees. Particular attention will be focused on the various sources that can be used in recruiting the necessary labor force.

The second objective of this chapter is to examine the steps used in deciding who will be selected from the initial recruiting pool. How does the organization decide whom to hire and whom to bypass? In answering these questions, we will make an examination of the seven steps in the selection process.

The third objective of this chapter is to explain the value of orientation for new employees and to present some of the major legislative acts that influence the recruiting and selection processes.

When you have finished studying this chapter, you should be able to do the following:

1. Discuss the importance of human resource forecasting and job analysis.
2. Identify and describe the four major recruiting sources: internal sources, external institutional sources, media sources, and competitive sources.
3. Compare the advantages and disadvantages of internal recruiting sources with external recruiting sources.
4. Explain how the selection process works when an organization uses a multiple cutoff technique or a counterbalancing approach.
5. Describe the seven steps in the selection process, noting what occurs during each step.
6. Explain the importance of orientation for new employees.
7. Note some of the major legislative acts that affect recruiting and selection efforts.

The Changing Work Force

Recruiting and selecting are important management functions because the work force of every organizational department or unit is constantly changing. Figure 7.1 provides an illustration of why this occurs.

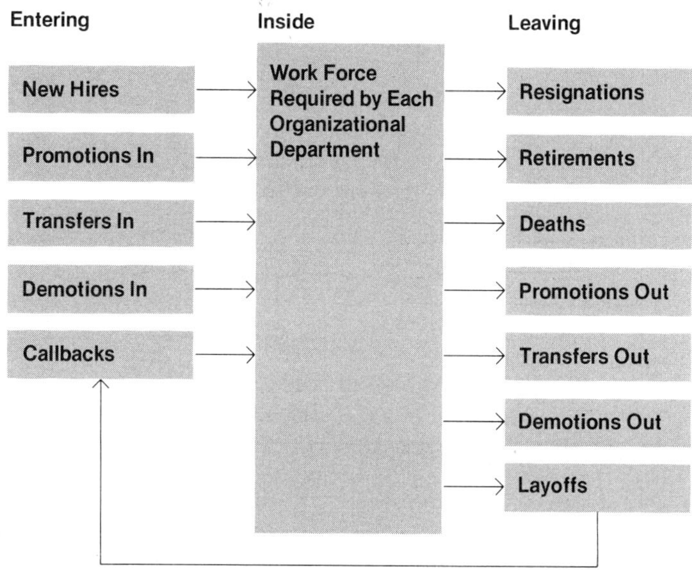

Figure 7.1 Makeup of an Organizational Department's Work Force

Over the period of a year, some people are likely to quit, others retire and, from time to time, an employee will die. All these events will create labor shortages in the department or unit. Additionally, if the organization is large enough, some of the workers will be promoted or transferred to other departments while on occasion a few will be demoted to other units. And if there is an economic crunch, layoffs are likely to occur.

▪ The work force makeup will change.

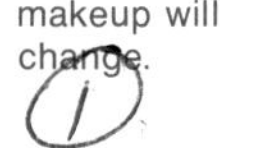

In the short run, most departments try to close ranks and operate with these labor shortages. However, this cannot continue indefinitely. The organizational unit must either reduce the amount of work it is doing or bring in more people. The most common sources of workers are new hires, people being promoted or transferred into the department from other units, and individuals being called back from layoffs.

Human Resource Forecasting

As a reference point, Figure 7.1 shows that every organization needs to adjust personnel inflows and outflows so that the number of people in the organization is equal to the number required to get the work done. This can be accomplished through *human resource forecasting.* Four factors will influence this forecast of the number of employees required by a department or organization: (1) production, (2) technological changes, (3) supply and demand, and (4) career planning.

▪ Four factors influence human resource forecasting.

If the organization believes that there will be an increase in the *demand for its goods and services,* labor will have to be increased. The manager will have to increase the inflows and/or decrease the outflows so that there is an overall net gain in employment.

If there are *technological changes* in the industry, one of two things can happen. The manager may need to retrain the people in the unit to operate new machines or equipment, or the individual may have to let some people go because their jobs have been replaced by the new machines.

Both of the above factors assume that there is an available labor supply. However, if demand increases dramatically, the organization may find there is not a large number of qualified people in the local area, and without careful planning it will be impossible to recruit enough workers to meet demand. Likewise, new technology may require more skilled people who are not to be found locally. In either case, *supply and demand conditions* must be forecast so as to prepare the firm for the eventuality of a labor shortage.

Finally, the organization must take into account that many employees want to better themselves via *career planning.* As a result, these workers are continually looking around for higher paying jobs or jobs that offer more opportunity for advancement. Every organization will lose people to other firms. By forecasting these losses, the company is in a position to replace these individuals.

The problem is most acute at the upper levels of the hierarchy, since it is more difficult to replace managers than subordinates. In handling the problem, some organizations use what is called a *manager replacement chart.* Figure 7.2 provides an example. The plant manager has foremen and supervisors in the department and each has been rated in terms of both promotion potential and performance. By quickly examining the chart, the manager has a good idea of which foreman is most qualified to become the new plant manager, and which supervisor would make the best general foreman.

In the above case, there is no need to go through a recruiting and selecting process. However, in most instances the organization does need to do so. In these cases, the first step is to identify the recruiting sources that will provide the most likely candidates for the job openings. Then the selection process can be carried out.

Job Analysis

Before beginning the selection process, the organization will want to be sure that the right type of person is being hired. This will be done by first conducting a *job analysis,* in which all work activities are outlined in depth. The analysis concentrates on the work activities, machines, tools, equipment, job related knowledge, work performance, physical working conditions, and work experience needed to do the job. Sometimes when this analysis is done, the organization finds that the individual it is seeking needs to have slightly different skills and abilities from the one who previously held the job.

Next, job descriptions and job specifications based on the job analysis can be

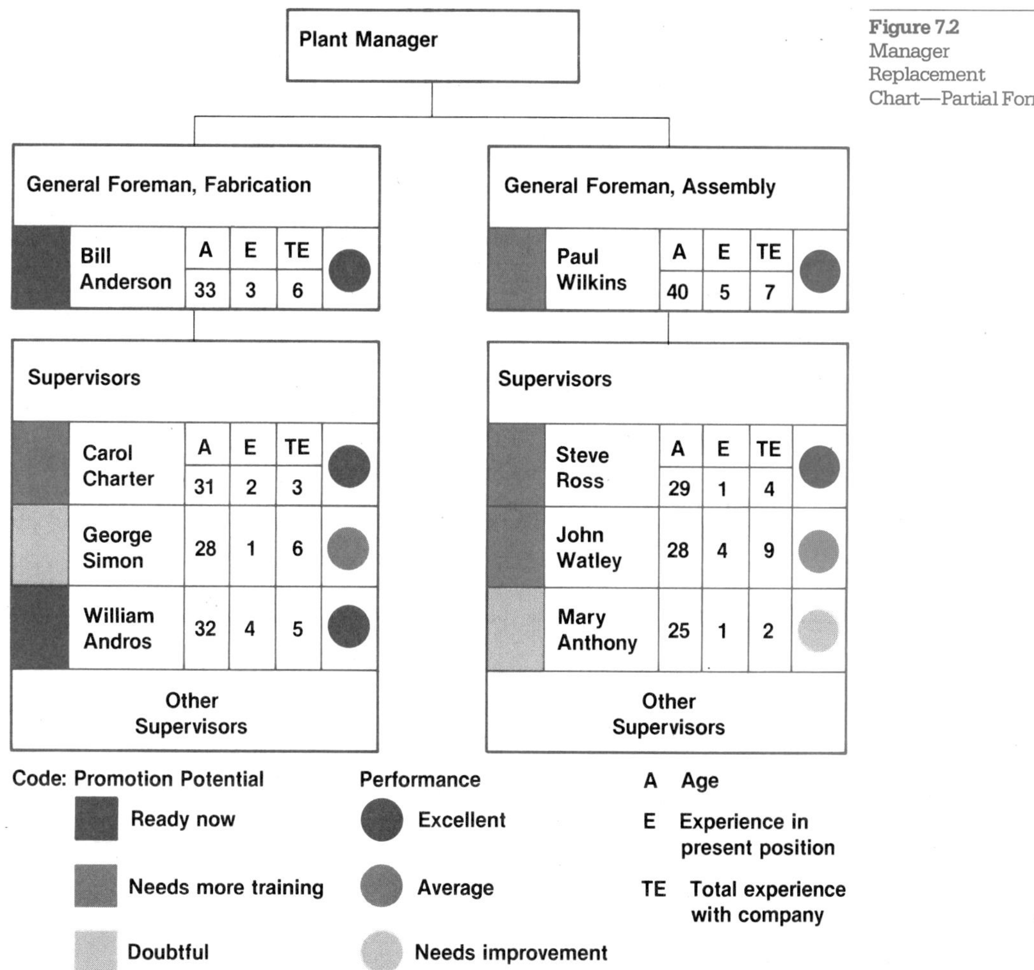

Plant Manager
General Foreman, Fabrication
Bill Anderson
A E TE
33 3 6
General Foreman, Assembly
Paul Wilkins
A E TE
40 5 7
Supervisors
Carol Charter
A E TE
31 2 3
George Simon
28 1 6
William Andros
32 4 5
Other Supervisors
Supervisors
Steve Ross
A E TE
29 1 4
John Watley
28 4 9
Mary Anthony
25 1 2
Other Supervisors
Code: Promotion Potential
Ready now
Needs more training
Doubtful
Performance
Excellent
Average
Needs improvement
A Age
E Experience in present position
TE Total experience with company

Figure 7.2 Manager Replacement Chart—Partial Form

determined. A *job description* provides a general outline of the responsibilities of the employee. What will the person be doing? What does the work involve? What are some examples of the type of work to be performed? All this is included in the job description. A *job specification* relates the general requirements the applicant must have. These include such things as experience, training, education, knowledge, skills, and abilities.

Job descriptions and job specifications are determined from the job analysis. The latter, in turn, serves as a basis for determining the approach to use in recruiting, selecting, orienting, evaluating, and training.

Recruiting Sources

Recruiting is a natural follow-up to human resource planning. Now that the organization knows the number and types of people that will be needed, it has to identify sources for locating and recruiting them. In all, there are four major recruiting sources: (1) internal sources, (2) external institutional sources, (3) media sources, and (4) competitive sources.

Internal Sources

Some of the most common internal sources include current employees, former employees, and individuals who have previously applied for jobs but were not hired. Many organizations like to go inside first, because they feel this is one way of motivating their employees. If they are unsuccessful, they then turn to external sources.

■ Most managers recommend their own replacements.

In the case of management promotions, it is common to use internal sources. One way of doing so is to post the job opening and invite applications. A supplemental way is to have the managers recommend their own replacements. Quite often they will support a subordinate who has the necessary experience and has performed well. After evaluating all the candidates, a decision will be made. Seeking qualified management candidates from within the organization is a wise strategy. Many people will stay with a firm because of the opportunity it affords them for upward mobility. If it were denied, they would seek jobs elsewhere. However, if there are managerial problems and a new top manager is brought in, the individual may bring along his or her own team of people and promotion from within will dry up. After all, the previous management helped bring about the problem, so the new management team would not logically promote from within.

■ Job posting can be used.

At the worker level it is common to find *job posting,* or *bidding,* used to fill vacancies. Employees are notified of job vacancies through notice posting, in-house publications, or open invitations to apply for the job.

If the work force does not provide the necessary people, the organization will then start to look at other internal sources. Some retired employees may be willing to come back to work on a part-time basis or may be able to recommend someone who would be interested in working for the firm. The greatest advantage of hiring former employees is that their performance is known.

Still another personnel source is the organization's applicant files. These files are made up of résumés of people who have applied for jobs before and, for one reason or another, have not been hired. Often these individuals have come in and filed their applications even though there was no job opening at that time. They then asked to be contacted should an opening occur. Therefore, these people constitute a ready source for recruiting.

▪ As well as application files.

External Institutional Sources

▪ Academic recruiting can help.

If internal sources do not produce an acceptable candidate for the job opening, there are *external institutional sources* that can be tapped. These include academic institutions, employment agencies, and temporary help.

Depending on the academic qualifications needed for the job, the organization can recruit at high schools, junior colleges, and four-year colleges or universities. If the jobs are not very demanding or do not pay very well, high schools may be the organization's only alternative. There are many school counselors and other faculty members who are concerned with job opportunities and business careers for their students, and contact with them can open many doors.

At the university level, most recruiting is done through placement offices. Business firms list their openings with these offices, which advertise when and where a company's representative will be on campus. Interested students sign up and interview at the scheduled times. This approach can be very beneficial to both the businesses and the students. In one day, a representative may be able to see ten applicants, while a student can interview with a half dozen firms.

What are recruiters looking for? Research shows that some of the factors they seem to value most highly in college graduates include ambition, motivation, specialized courses—for example, in accounting or engineering—grades, and students' ability to express themselves. The only jobs for which grades are not considered that important are sales jobs, where interpersonal relations, appearance, leadership, and the ability to impress the interviewer favorably seem to be of greater importance.[1]

Another source of human resources is employment agencies. There are state employment agencies in every state, and private employment agencies can be found in most cities. For a fee, paid by either the employee or the employer, the agencies will do some of the preliminary screening and put the organization in touch with applicants.

▪ As can employment agencies.

Finally, there is temporary help. The most easily accessible and immediate personnel source, these agencies usually supply secretarial, clerical, or semi-skilled labor on a day-rate basis. Many organizations use temporary help in meeting seasonal peak demands or replacing workers who are on vacation. Once the personnel shortage is over, these workers are let go.

▪ And temporary help.

Media Sources

▪ Newspapers are an important source.

Media sources are widely used and are familiar to most people who are seeking employment. Some of the most popular are newspapers, magazines, television, and radio. Of these, newspapers seem to get the greatest attention. While a newspaper ad does not give a lot of information about a job, those looking for work often scan the help wanted sections. Sunday is a particularly good day to advertise, and people looking for work wait eagerly for the Sunday papers because the number of ads is far greater than during any other time of the week. Newspapers like the *Wall Street Journal,* however, come out every day of the week, and executives seeking to change jobs scan the ads daily.

Trade and Competitive Sources

■ So are trade publications.

Other sources for recruiting include trade associations, trade publications, and competitors. Trade associations often have newsletters or magazines that contain job ads. For example, in academia there is the *Chronicle of Higher Education.* Anyone looking for a job as a college dean would want to look through this journal, for all such openings are advertised here. They have to be advertised because the law requires that such positions be available to all qualified individuals. The same logic applies to many other occupational groups. By hiring through an industry or trade journal, the company seeking to recruit a manager can advertise in the appropriate journal and be almost certain of reaching potential applicants.

■ And competitive hiring.

Other times, an organization will pick up an applicant after learning that the individual is unhappy with his or her current firm. Contacting the person, either directly or indirectly, can result in a formal application for employment. Of course, the further up the hierarchy the individual is located, the more likely it becomes that the person will not want an application made known. If a current employer learns of an application, it can reflect negatively on the individual if the candidate does not get the job. On the positive side, employees recruited from competitive sources need less training because they already know the industry and the job, and their track records are known.

Internal and External Sources: An Evaluation

■ Both sources are important.

Which source should a recruiting organization use: internal or external? There is no one right answer to this question, since there are pros and cons associated with both sources. Generally speaking, however, many firms favor promotion from within and only go outside if they are unable to fill the vacancy any other way. The problem with this approach is that there is no new blood in the organization, and internal hirings can result in things being done the same old way.

On the other hand, when someone from the outside is brought in, the organization takes the risk of choosing someone who may not fit in very well. Additionally, time is needed to train the individual to perform at an acceptable level. Finally, there is always the problem that hiring from outside will cause morale problems among internal candidates and their friends. Table 7.1 provides some of the major pros and cons associated with internal and external sources of selection.

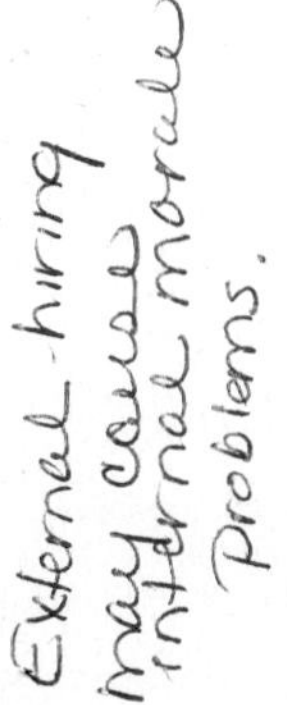

Table 7.1
Internal versus External Recruiting Sources

Internal	
Advantages	**Disadvantages**
1. The morale of the person being promoted is high.	1. There is the danger of inbreeding.
2. It is easier to make an assessment of the applicant's abilities.	2. There can be morale problems among those who have not been promoted.
3. Good performance is rewarded.	3. There can be political infighting for the promotion.
4. A succession for promotion is developed.	4. A strong management development program is needed.
5. It is necessary to hire only at the entry level.	

External	
Advantages	**Disadvantages**
1. New blood is brought into the organization.	1. The person who is selected may not fit in very well.
2. It is an inexpensive way to hire a highly qualified professional.	2. There may be morale problems among those who have not been chosen internally for the job.
3. There is no danger that the individual owes favors to those in the organization who arranged for this promotion.	3. There is often a longer orientation or adjustment period for someone coming in from the outside, since the person has to learn the organizational ropes.
4. Outsiders can bring fresh insight to things.	

Selecting the Right Candidate for the Job

In some cases, recruiting efforts may leave an organization with more candidates than job openings. In other instances, there may be only two applicants and two job openings, and it can turn out that neither individual is capable of doing the job. For such reasons as these, the organization needs to evaluate all applicants. This is done with the use of a selection process.

The Selection Process

The selection process varies among organizations. Some use a very expensive and rigorous method while others are more informal and flexible in their approach. In either case, the organization should be as thorough as possible while still considering the costs associated with selecting the candidates.

Most employee selection programs use a form of *multiple cut-off technique.* Under this arrangement, each applicant has to be judged satisfactory on a series of screening devices such as the application blank, interview, tests, and physical exam. If a candidate is judged unsatisfactory in any one of these, he or she is then eliminated from consideration. In using this approach, many firms like to set the process up so that the job performance areas are examined first. In this way, they can quickly eliminate those who are unable to do the job. Then from here on it is a matter of judgment: Which of these people has the best personality for the job? Which can work best with the department's employees? Which will generally fit in best?

Other organizations feel that it is better to use a *counterbalancing approach.* This involves weighing all of the individual's qualifications and seeing if any deficiencies are counterbalanced by strengths. For example, a person may turn up who does not have a college degree but who does have three years of college and six years of job experience. Does the job experience make up for the lack of a college degree?

Which is best, the multiple cut-off technique or the counterbalancing approach? While each has its advantages and disadvantages, some researchers feel it is best to use the multiple cut-off system in all but borderline cases. Then the counterbalancing approach can be employed. The reason for choosing the multiple cut-off system is that it is fast and it therefore keeps selection costs down.

In carrying out the selection process, most organizations use a series of sequential steps, as shown in Figure 7.3. Following is a typical sequence.

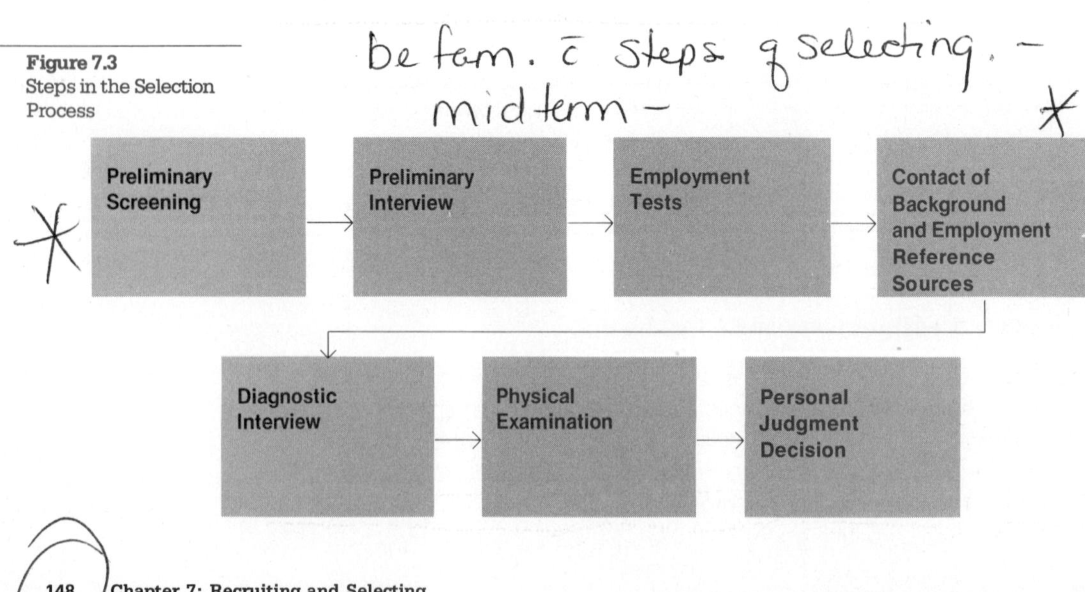

Figure 7.3
Steps in the Selection Process

Step 1: Preliminary Application Screening. The first thing many firms do is have job candidates fill out an application blank. This form contains information related to the individual's personal and job history. While there are many different types of application forms, all of them should provide the firm with information that helps evaluate the person's hiring potential. It is important to remember that the Equal Employment Opportunity Commission, supported by the courts, has found that some application form questions not related to jobs can discriminate against certain groups. Illustrations include the use of non-job-related questions about sex, age, race, religion, education, marital status, arrest records, and credit rating. Where such questions are used, charges of discrimination can be brought against the user firms. The best way to avoid this problem is to ensure that all questions are related to the job itself.[2]

■ The application blank helps in screening.

Step 2: Preliminary Interview. The purpose of this step is to screen out any unsuitable or uninterested applicants who have passed the preliminary screening phase. The purpose of this interview is to explain the job and its requirements and answer any questions the applicant might have. During this time, the interviewer—usually a specialist from the personnel department or the manager for whom the applicant will be working—often takes the opportunity to talk to the individual about the application form, finding more out about the type of work the individual has done in the past, what the person's strengths and weaknesses are, and why the applicant wants the job. Table 7.2 shows some problems that occur during the selection process. They are not all interviewing problems, but the one-on-one interview especially tends to bring out many of them.

■ So does the preliminary interview.

Step 3: Employment Tests. Employment tests are designed to find out how well the individual can do the job. Many organizations, especially large and medium-sized ones, still use these tests, although they have come under attack in recent years and the company must be very careful about how it uses them. In particular, the tests must be designed for both validity and reliability in order to be fair.

Validity is present when the test measures what it is supposed to measure. If a test is given to individuals to determine whether they have the necessary technical skills to be mechanics, the test has to measure mechanical ability in order to be valid. If some of the questions are merely general intelligence test questions, the company should be able to show how these questions relate to the mechanic's job—for example, how they help distinguish the mechanic from the nonmechanic.

Reliability refers to the consistency or reproducibility of the test results. If five mechanics all take the test and all five receive high grades, the test may indeed be reliable. It consistently measures mechanical skills and abilities. However, if only two of the mechanics do well, then something is wrong with the test and it needs to be revised. It is not consistently identifying those with mechanical skills.

Numerous types of tests can be given, but in screening applicants it is advisable

Table 7.2
Watch Out for Those Selection Problems

Most managers think they are pretty effective when it comes to selecting candidates. However, research shows that many of them fall into common selection pitfalls. The following are twelve ways of overcoming these problems.

1. Know what you are looking for. Many managers are really not sure what characteristics the job applicant should have. They basically believe, "I'll know the right person when I see him or her."
2. Don't overlap your coverage of some job dimensions and miss others entirely. It is not uncommon for several managers to spend a considerable amount of time interviewing a candidate, only to find out later that they all asked basically the same half dozen questions. Thus they know a lot about a few areas but do not really have a comprehensive picture of the entire candidate.
3. Don't misinterpret applicant data. Many managers act like amateur psychiatrists in interpreting data. They spend half of their time discussing the applicant's early childhood. The best predictor of future performance is past performance, and this is where they should concentrate their attention.
4. Don't let your judgment be affected by biases and stereotypes. Some managers have biases against such things as long hair, white socks, or women applying for managerial positions. When these problems exist there is little chance that the candidate will get a fair hearing.
5. Don't permit one dimension, favorable or unfavorable, to influence your judgment of the other dimensions. Often known as the "halo effect," a candidate's ability in some area such as verbal facility will easily impress some managers. The person talks well and they like this. In turn they overlook the individual's job-related abilities.
6. Don't jump too quickly to decisions. Some managers are most influenced by first impressions. A firm handshake or a warm smile outweighs a poor past performance record.
7. Don't be overly alert to negative information. Some managers are often more determined to avoid hiring a poor worker than to hire a good worker. They try too hard not to make a mistake, and in the process bypass some competent people.
8. Don't rely too heavily on the interview in making a selection decision. Valid paper and pencil tests should be used to supplement the interview. Too many managers and organizations are afraid of misusing these instruments, so they stay away from them completely.
9. Have the various selection elements organized into a system. Sometimes one candidate's references will be checked, a second will be given a test, and a third will be interviewed. However, there is no uniform procedure used for all candidates.
10. Be sure that applicant data are integrated and discussed in a systematic manner. Managers who meet to make final hiring decisions often use information that is really not relevant. Typical comments include, "I liked that guy's attitude" or "That woman appeared really motivated." Little attempt is made to discuss the really important job dimensions.
11. Don't let your judgment be affected by pressure to fill the position. Research reveals that many managers lower their standards under pressure to fill positions. They tend to rationalize poor information and to overemphasize the impact of training on weak dimensions so as to justify a hiring decision.
12. Don't let your judgments be affected by the other available candidates. Some managers rate people high or low based on what the previous candidates looked like. Thus an average candidate can get a superior rating if the individual follows four below-average candidates.

Source: William C. Byham, "Common Selection Problems Can Be Overcome," *Personnel Administrator,* August 1978, pp. 42–47.

never to rely on just one test. Always use two or more. Some of the most common types of tests used today include the following:

■ Common types of tests.

1. Mental ability tests. One of the oldest and most popular types of tests. People who score high on mental ability tests often have the capacity to use good judgment, think ahead, and make effective decisions in a variety of situations.
2. Aptitude tests. These are designed to measure the individual's capacity to learn a particular job or type of work. They measure the desires and abilities of the applicant and compare them to those of people who successfully perform the type of work in question. Some of the more frequently used types include mechanical and clerical tests.
3. Achievement tests. These measure proficiency in a given area. Achievement tests are of two types: oral-written and work sample. The first measures knowledge of an area, and the second assesses ability to do a sample of actual work.
4. Vocational interest tests. These attempt to determine an individual's preferences among different types of work. It is assumed that if an individual has interests in common with people who are successful in a certain type of work, this individual will like that job.
5. Personality tests. The most controversial and least reliable of all tests, these are of two types: objective and projective. The former are written tests. The latter ask the individual to give his or her interpretation of certain situations. Based on the results, trained testers, sometimes called psychometrists, offer interpretations of the individual's personality.

Are tests still widely used? Indeed they are. However, some are more popular than others, with aptitude tests for clerical and mechanical ability, mental ability tests, and personality tests leading the list.

Step 4: Contact of Background and Employment Reference Sources. This step is often used to obtain a more objective evaluation of the applicant. In doing so, most employers will contact individuals from three reference categories: personal, academic, and past employment.[3] While the degree of thoroughness will vary, it is common to find the organization making a more complete check of its managerial applicants than of those applying for lower-level jobs. In fact, the higher the position in the structure, the more thorough the background and reference check.

■ Previous employers should be contacted.

The most important reference check is the previous employer, for this person is in a position to supply objective, work-related information. In most cases, these contacts are done either through telephone or personal interviews. The amount of information that can be obtained will very much depend on what the other party is willing to divulge. However, some of the most common questions revolve around information the individual has provided on the application blank and relates to performance, salary, promotions, demotions, reasons for leaving the previous job, and whether the organization would be willing to rehire the individual.

Step 5: Diagnostic Interview. The diagnostic interview is usually carried out by the manager in whose department the applicant will work. The purpose of this interview is

to take all the information gathered in the previous stages of the selection process and use it in evaluating the individual's ability to do the job.

This interview can be either structured or unstructured. A *structured interview* follows a determined pattern so that all the people being interviewed are asked the same questions. This allows systematic coverage of those questions which are deemed necessary by the organization and minimizes personal bias of the interviewer.

An *unstructured interview* has no definite checklist or planned strategy. The interviewer sets the direction of the interview, and the candidate follows. Some interviewers like to give the candidate a chance to do some of the structuring, to bring out the most positive information. Such an interviewer might simply say, "All right. Sell me." Typical unstructured interview questions include: Tell me about your last job. Why did you decide to quit? Why would you like to work for us?

While many interviews are part structured and part unstructured, there is always the chance that one candidate will influence the manager because of something the individual says or the way the person says it. In order to reduce personal bias, the interviewer should do the following:

■ How to reduce personal bias.

1. Plan the interview in advance.
2. Establish and maintain rapport with the applicant.
3. Remember that the primary goal is to gather information that will aid in the employment decision and move the interview toward that goal.
4. Record the results so as to insure that all pertinent facts are retrievable.

In addition, there are certain specific things that the interviewer can do and others that the person should not. Table 7.3 illustrates some of these.

How effective are diagnostic interviews? One way of finding out is to have the manager evaluate each of the applicants and then compare the performance of those individuals who were hired with their appraisal at the time of the interview. Such a cross-check can prove beneficial not only to the interviewer but to the organization as well. In particular, it pinpoints the effectiveness of diagnostic interviews.

■ The physical exam is important.

Step 6: Physical Examination. After the applicant has completed these preliminary steps, the individual is often given a physical exam. The purpose of the exam is twofold: (1) to ensure that the person is physically capable of doing the job and (2) to determine the applicant's eligibility for group life, health, and disability insurance. If the job involves manual labor, the person should be physically capable of doing the work. For example, if there is heavy lifting, the individual must have the required strength. If the applicant is seeking a managerial position, a physical exam can sometimes help determine whether the person can endure stress or other management-related problems.

■ Finally comes the hiring decision.

Step 7: Using Personal Judgment to Make a Final Decision. The last step in the selection process is that of choosing the best individual(s) for the job. If these steps have been carried out properly, only the best candidates should still remain. Now it is a

Table 7.3
Do's and Don't's in Recruiting Interviews

Subject	Can Do or Ask	Cannot Do or Ask
Sex	Notice the individual's appearance.	Make sex-related comments or notes unless gender is an occupational qualification.
Marital status	Ask status after hiring (for insurance purposes).	Are you married? Single? Divorced? Engaged? Are you currently living with anyone? Do you see your ex-spouse?
Children	How many children do you have? How old are they? (for insurance purposes).	Do you have any children at home? How old are they? Who cares for them? Do you plan to have more children?
Physical data	Explain manual labor, lifting, and other requirements of the job. Show how it is carried out. Require a physical exam.	How tall are you? How heavy are you?
Criminal record	If a security clearance is necessary, questions related to this can be asked. However, this should be done *prior* to employment.	Have you ever been arrested? Have you ever been convicted? Have you ever spent any time in jail?
Military status	Are you a veteran? Why not?	What branch of the service did you serve in? What type of discharge do you have?
Age	After hiring the person you can ask, "Are you over 18?"	How old are you?
Housing	If you have no phone, how can we reach you?	Do you own your own home? Do you rent? Do you live in an apartment or a house?

Source: Reprinted from the May 26, 1975 issue of *Business Week* by special permission, © 1975 by McGraw-Hill, Inc. All rights reserved.

question of determining which is most suitable for the job. Sometimes the individual who is chosen is unwilling to take the offer unless management will pay more money. Other times the manager will not be particularly impressed with any of the candidates and the process will have to start all over again. However, this last alternative is not a very good one since the organization may have no better success the next time around. After all, if it carried out the recruiting process correctly, it should have already attracted all of the available candidates. What should be done in this case? If the salary for the job cannot be raised, many managers find that redesigning the job so that it is more rewarding and/or talking to the candidate about the future of the job is sufficient motivation to get the individual candidates to change their minds. Table 7.4 shows how organizations make final employment decisions.

Table 7.4
Making the Final Choice

How should an organization make a final employment decision when there are four or five people applying for the job? One of the best ways is to use an applicant selection matrix. Each person who evaluates a candidate gives the person a numerical score on a series of job-related factors. These scores are then added up and the applicant with the highest total gets the job. Exactly how does the selection matrix work? With the matrix opposite as an example, let us examine how the final candidate is selected.

The matrix shows five job applicants. Each has been evaluated on the basis of education, job knowledge, management capability, and personality characteristics. On each of these four factors an applicant can receive a score ranging from 1 to 5. This score is then multiplied by the appropriate weight factor. For example, education has a weight of 0.1, so whatever score the individual gets for education is multiplied by this weight. Applicant A received an average score of 4 and wound up with 0.4 points after the weight factor was employed, while Applicant D had 5 points and wound up with 0.5 points.

The other three major factors have been broken into subfactors, so that, for example, the applicant's average score on knowledge of large computerized production planning systems is multiplied by 0.15 while the average score on ability to delegate effectively is multiplied by 0.1 and interpersonal skills are multiplied by 0.05.

A person with the highest possible rating in each category would end up with 5.00 points. As seen on the matrix, the highest is 4.00 points by Applicant B, who should be offered the job. What if there were a tie? In this case, the job factor scores would be analyzed and the person with the highest score in the most critical area would be offered the job. For example, if Applicants A and B had equal scores, but job knowledge was considered to be the most important factor, A would be given the job. This individual has 1.75 points in job knowledge, as contrasted with B's 1.45 points. However, if management capability had been more important, then B would have gotten the nod (1.55 points to 1.2 points).

Easy to use? Many organizations think so. What they like best is the way it helps quantitatively pinpoint the best applicant.

Source: Adapted from Jack Bucalo, "The Balanced Approach to Successful Screening Interviews," *Personnel Journal,* August 1978, pp. 420–426, 446. Reprinted with permission, *Personnel Journal,* Costa Mesa, CA, copyright August 1978.

Evaluation Scale: Outstanding: 5; Excellent: 4; Good: 3; Average: 2; Marginal: 1. Legend: Must: M; Preferred: P	Education 10%	Job Knowledge 40%			Management Capability 35%			Personality Characteristics 15%		
	College degree and other educational training	Knowledge of large computerized production planning systems	Knowledge of program control systems	Knowledge of different inventory control systems	Ability to plan and control large budget	Ability to supervise a large department (50 employees)	Ability to delegate effectively	Effective written and oral communication	Interpersonal skills	Total
Must/ Preferred	P	M	M	M	M	M	P	P	P	
Weight factor	0.1	0.15	0.15	0.1	0.15	0.1	0.1	0.1	0.05	1.00
Applicant A	0.4	0.6	0.65	0.5	0.6	0.3	0.3	0.4	0.2	3.95
Applicant B	0.4	0.7	0.45	0.3	0.75	0.4	0.4	0.4	0.2	4.00
Applicant C	0.4	0.45	0.45	0.3	0.45	0.3	0.4	0.5	0.2	3.45
Applicant D	0.5	0.5	0.5	0.4	0.6	0.4	0.4	0.35	0.2	3.85
Applicant E	0.3	0.5	0.55	0.3	0.75	0.45	0.4	0.4	0.25	3.90

". . . But I'm sure you'll all agree that what our new general manager lacks in ability and experience, he more than compensates for by being my son."

Orientation

■ Orientation is important for new employees.

Once an individual has been hired, proper orientation should follow. *Orientation* involves introducing the new employee to the other individuals who make up the work group and familiarizing the person with the job. Orientation is important because first impressions often have a lasting impact. A new employee who thinks the job is going to be interesting and challenging is likely to look on the work much differently than on a job that seems likely to be boring and uninteresting.

Many organizations start orientation by giving the person an organization manual that tells the employee all about company policies and procedures and explains fringe benefits. Others start the individual out with some petty task to perform, with the intention of adding more duties later on. Both of these approaches are poor because they do not create the initial positive attitude the employee needs to do the job right. A better approach to follow is to integrate organizational and employee concerns by providing information that tells the individual how things are done in the department while also showing the person how to do the job. This approach creates the basis for interpersonal relations between the new individual and the regular work team. Figure 7.4 illustrates how this can be done by a supervisor who is orienting a new employee.

Figure 7.4
Orientation Checklist

Employee's Name	Discussion completed (please check each individual item)
I. Word of welcome	
II. Explain overall departmental organization and its relationship to other activities of the company	
III. Explain employee's individual contribution to the objectives of the department and his starting assignment in broad terms	
IV. Discuss job content with employee and give him a copy of job description (if available)	
V. Explain departmental training program(s) and salary increase practices and procedures	
VI. Discuss where the employee lives and transportation facilities	
VII. Explain working conditions: a. Hours of work, time sheets b. Use of employee entrance and elevators c. Lunch hours d. Coffee breaks, rest periods e. Personal telephone calls and mail f. Overtime policy and requirements g. Paydays and procedure for being paid h. Lockers i. Other __________	
VIII. Requirements for continuance of employment—explain company standards as to: a. Performance of duties b. Attendance and punctuality c. Handling confidential information d. Behavior e. General appearance f. Wearing of uniforms	
IX. Introduce new staff member to manager(s) and other supervisors Special attention should be paid to the person to whom the new employee will be assigned	

Form continues on following page

X. Release employee to immediate supervisor who will:
   a. Introduce new staff member to fellow workers
   b. Familiarize the employee with his work place
   c. Begin on-the-job training

If not applicable, insert N/A in space provided.

Employee's Signature	Supervisor's Signature
Date	Division

Form examined for filing: ______ Date ______ Personnel Department

Source: From "Orientation of New Employees," by Joan E. Holland and Theodore P. Curtis. In *Handbook of Modern Personnel Administration,* edited by Joseph Famularo, pp. 24–25. Copyright © 1972 by McGraw-Hill Book Company. Used with permission of McGraw-Hill Book Company.

How useful is a proper orientation? Research shows that it is a very important follow-up to the selection process. At Texas Instruments, for example, researchers gave one group of new employees the organizations' conventional two-hour orientation while a second group was given a full day's orientation, beginning in the morning with the regular two-hour session. The group then spent the rest of the day in a room with trainers, becoming acquainted with one another and with the organization. The researchers reported that the group that received the full-day orientation had reduced job-learning time, higher output, and better attendance than the other group.[4] Thus, orientation is indeed an important follow-up to the recruitment process.

Recruiting and Selecting: A Look at the Law

In recruiting and selecting applicants, the organization must be sure that it is acting within legal bounds. There are many legislative acts that set forth what an organization can and cannot do during this process. The following examines some of the major ones that affect recruiting and selection efforts.

Race and Sex Discrimination

Title VII of the Civil Rights Act of 1964, coupled with amendments that have been made to it, prohibits in certain private and all public workplaces discrimination based on race, color, religion, national origin, or sex. Specifically, this act applies to companies with fifteen or more employees, labor unions with fifteen or more members, employment agencies, and state and local governments. Some of the ways Title VII affects recruitment and selection were seen in Table 7.3, where the do's and don't's of interviewing were presented.

The federal government also uses executive orders to control employment discrimination. One of these, Order No. 11,246, applies to government contractors and not only forbids discrimination but orders these contractors to take affirmative action to ensure that discrimination does not exist. This requires the contractors to go out and actively recruit minorities for these jobs and be prepared to document their efforts. Thus, by law, a company with a federal contract must try to hire minorities from the local area.

Age Discrimination

■ People between forty and seventy are protected from discrimination.

The Age Discrimination in Employment Act protects individuals from forty to seventy years of age from discrimination in hiring, retention, compensation, and other conditions of employment. In recent years the upper limit was raised from sixty-five to seventy for people in private enterprise, and mandatory retirement for federal employees was eliminated. It is now illegal to discriminate against older people because of their age. In fact, when evaluating an applicant, one should not write down anything on the official evaluation related to age. For example, "Nice guy, but isn't he too old for this job?" or "Let's try for a younger person" are comments that are construed as discriminatory under the law.

Other Legislation

Other laws protect the applicant from having his or her privacy violated. For example, the Fair Credit Reporting Act requires an organization to tell an applicant who was refused employment on the basis of information received from a credit reporting service the name and address of that reporting service. Additionally, if the applicant was refused a job because of a reference, the individual must be informed of this fact and can request a summary of the information in the reference letter.

Another recruiting law about which the manager should be informed is the Federal Rehabilitation Act of 1973, which extends to disabled people the same protections that are given to racial minorities and women. While this act applies only to contractors and subcontractors, it requires that they take affirmative action in employing and advancing qualified disabled individuals.

In the last twenty years, more and more civil rights and regulatory legislation has been enacted. Given these developments, it appears likely that the future will see a continuation of this trend. Thus in recruiting and selecting applicants, the manager must work within the law. Since law can be quite difficult, many organizations have personnel specialists who keep abreast of such legislation and help establish recruiting and selection guidelines. The manager, in turn, relies on them for assistance in carrying out this process.

Summary

Few organizational work forces ever remain the same for very long. Resignations, retirements, and promotions leave openings that must be filled by promotions, transfers, and new hires. How can the organization ensure that it has an adequate labor pool? One way is through the use of human resource forecasting, in which openings are anticipated and recruitment and selection efforts are undertaken to fill these vacancies.

Recruiting can be done from four major sources. One is internal sources; it involves promoting current employees or hiring back former workers or those who have previously applied for jobs without having been hired. A second is external institutional sources. These include recruiting at academic institutions and through employment and temporary hiring agencies. A third is media sources, such as newspapers, magazines, television, and radio. A fourth is trade and competitive sources. Which of these sources should the organization use: internal or external? There are pros and cons associated with each, as seen in Table 7.1, and the organization should weigh these carefully.

After the recruiting effort is over, there should be a sufficient pool to hire from. The problem now is one of determining which applicants are most qualified to do the job. In deciding, some organizations use a form of multiple cut-off technique while others opt for a counterbalancing approach. In either event, the process begins with a preliminary applicant screening and a preliminary interview. These are followed by employment tests, contact of background and employment service reference sources, a diagnostic interview, physical exam, and, finally, a personal judgment decision on who will get the job.

Once an individual has been hired, proper orientation should follow. Orientation involves introducing the new employee to the individuals who make up the work group, explaining the job, setting out the requirements for continued employment, and answering initial questions the person might have.

In this recruiting and selection process, it is important for the organization to stay within legislative guidelines. A number of important acts must be complied with, including Title VII of the Civil Rights Act of 1964, the Age Discrimination in Employment Act, the Fair Credit Reporting Act, and the Federal Rehabilitation Act. While many managers are not very familiar with such legislation, the organization's personnel specialist can help ensure that the laws are followed.

Review and Study Questions

1. What factors are most likely to account for job openings? What are some of the most common ways of filling these vacancies? Explain.
2. What are the four factors that affect human resource forecasting? Explain each.
3. How does a manager replacement chart work? Is it of any real value in the staffing process?
4. What is meant by each of the following: *job analysis, job description, job specification?*
5. One of the most common sources for recruiting is internal sources. How does an organization fill a management position using internal sources? How does it fill a nonmanagement position using these sources?

6. When might an organization use external institutional sources rather than internal sources in filling job vacancies? Explain.
7. How can media sources help an organization recruit personnel? Explain.
8. In what way can trade and competitive sources help an organization recruit personnel? Explain.
9. What are some of the advantages and disadvantages of using internal recruiting sources? What are some of the advantages and disadvantages of using external recruiting sources? Explain.
10. In the selection process, how does the multiple cut-off technique differ from the counterbalancing approach? Define each term in your answer.
11. In the selection process, what happens during the preliminary application screening? the preliminary interview?
12. What are some of the commonly used employment tests? Why must all be both valid and reliable? In answering this last question, define both *validity* and *reliability.*
13. Which type of employment reference source do many organizations feel is most important: personal, academic, or past employment? Why?
14. How does a diagnostic interview work? Include a discussion of structured and unstructured interviews in your answer.
15. Why do most organizations insist that the applicant take a physical exam? Explain.
16. In making the final employment decision, how should the manager decide when the applicant selection matrix shows two people with identical scores? (Hint: See Table 7.4.)
17. What takes place during the orientation period? Explain.
18. How do each of the following affect the recruiting and selection of job candidates: Title VII of the Civil Rights Act of 1964, the Age Discrimination in Employment Act, the Fair Credit Reporting Act, and the Federal Rehabilitation Act of 1973?

Key Terms in the Chapter

human resource forecasting
manager replacement chart
job analysis
job description
job specification
multiple cut-off technique
counterbalancing approach
validity
reliability
structured interview
unstructured interview
orientation

Notes

1. R. A. Stone, L. R. Drake, and H. R. Kaplan, "Variables Affecting Organizations in College Recruiting," *Personnel Administrator,* September–October 1973, p. 47.

2. U.S. Equal Employment Opportunity Commission. *Affirmative Action and Equal Opportunity—A Guidebook for Employers,* vol. II (Washington, D.C.: Government Printing Office, 1973), pp. 40–44.

3. George M. Beason and John A. Belt, "Verifying Applicants' Backgrounds," *Personnel Journal,* July 1976, p. 347.

4. Earl R. Gomersall and M. Scott Myers, "Breakthrough in On-the-Job Training," *Harvard Business Review,* July–August 1966, pp. 62–72.

Case: Improving the Hiring Process

Which comes first—validity, reliability, or the selection matrix?

During the past five years the Harding Corporation's sales have tripled, and management believes this growth rate can be maintained during the entire decade of the eighties. As a result, the corporation is currently interested in reviewing its recruiting and screening process to ensure that only the most qualified individuals are hired. After all, if sales are going to be growing by leaps and bounds, the organization will need highly capable people to make all operations go according to plan. Carl Williams has been hired to head up the personnel department and direct this overall recruiting and screening effort. He came on board at Harding just last week.

Since his arrival Carl has learned that most hirings for managerial positions follow the same basic procedure. First, the prospective employee is interviewed by a member of the personnel department. A candidate who looks promising is given two tests. One is a mental ability test; the other is a personality test. The former, in the view of the previous head of personnel, helps identify those with analytical ability, while the latter pinpoints whether or not the person will fit in well with other members of the management team. Carl has been thinking about his predecessor's philosophy and is not sure whether these two tests are either valid or reliable. He intends to check into the matter.

Also, Harding has a procedure for choosing between candidates who are judged to be of equal ability. While this does not happen often because of the number of managerial positions to be filled, the organization has developed an applicant selection matrix similar to the one discussed in this chapter. After each candidate is evaluated, the one with the highest score is offered the job. Carl has looked over this selection matrix and feels it is simplistic. More variables need to be added to make the matrix more sophisticated. This will not only improve the selection instrument but reduce the likelihood that two candidates can end up with identical scores.

If the personnel department uses valid and reliable tests, Carl is convinced that the organization's growing need for competent managers can be met. Furthermore, revising the selection matrix will make it easier to choose among two or more qualified applicants. Of course, there are many more things that the department needs to do, but these are the ones Carl intends to tackle first.

Questions

1. What is the difference between *validity* and *reliability*? Use examples in your answer.
2. In addition to mental ability and personality tests, what other tests do organizations use in the selection process? Which of these would be useful to Carl's organization?

3. What is an *applicant selection matrix*? Of what value would it be to Carl's company? If you were giving him recommendations, would you suggest that he devote his initial attention to the issues of validity and reliability or to the selection matrix? Defend your answer.

Case: Filling the Vacancies

How will Harriet hire?

Lufting Incorporated is a medium-sized manufacturing firm located in the Midwest. On the average, the firm hires 250 people a year to fill vacancies caused by resignations, retirements, and dismissals. Every Thursday the personnel department determines how many vacancies there are and what is being done to fill them. If there is a new vacancy, the department determines the role it should play in helping fill it. If it is an old vacancy, the personnel people look into what is currently being done about it and whether further action on their part is warranted.

This week all the vacancies are new. There are five in all. The first is a request from the marketing department for a management trainee. This individual is needed to work in the nonsales area, is to have a college degree and, if possible, some job-related experience. However, if the personnel department cannot locate someone who has had such experience, the marketing department will still consider the person.

The production department needs another machinist. One of the workers quit this week to move to another locale, where he is taking a job with a competitor. There are no people in-house who have the qualifications to fill this position, so the personnel department is going to have to look outside.

The third opening is from the marketing department and calls for a salesperson. This individual will have to be on the road at least three days every week and, in order to reduce the amount of training time, the department would like to have someone with sales experience.

The fourth vacancy is in the secretarial pool. Because of vacations, there is a need to hire a total of four typists. These people will be only temporary and will be let go when the summer is over and the department is back at regular strength. For the moment, however, it is impossible to handle all of the typing without some additional help.

Finally, there is a supervisory opening in the assembly department. In the past, these positions have been filled from within; and the department would like to do it this way again. However, if there are no qualified people in-house, outside sources can be used.

After looking over these five vacancies, Harriet Schelling is in the process of following up on each. The first thing she needs to do is decide the recruiting sources to use. From here she has to take the steps necessary to announce the position and list all the applicants. Her list will then be turned over to someone else in her department who will do the initial screening and then send the applicants to talk to the manager in each respective area. The latter is the person who will make the final hiring decision.

Questions

1. For each of the five vacancies, which major recruiting source would you recommend?
2. How would you recommend the firm go about its recruiting efforts? How should it announce the openings? What form should the announcements take? Where should the announcements be made?
3. As the firm carries out this recruiting effort, will any legislation regulate or influence its actions? Explain.

Chapter 8 Training and Development

Objectives of the Chapter

Once an organization has recruited and selected the necessary personnel, vacancies will have been eliminated. However, the staffing function is not complete. Now these employees have to be trained and developed. The first objective of this chapter is to examine the nature of training and development. The second objective is to study the ways in which training and development needs are determined and to review the design of training and development programs.

Having examined what training and development are all about, attention will be turned to the programs themselves. Some of the most popular kinds of employee and management training programs will be studied.

The last objective of this chapter is to look at the ways in which training and development programs can be evaluated. Particular attention will be focused on what can be evaluated, by whom, and how. Finally, the effectiveness of different training methods will be reviewed.

When you have finished studying the material in this chapter, you should be able to:

1 Define the terms *training* and *development*.
2 Know some work-related clues for determining when training and development are needed.
3 Explain how the training and development cycle works.
4 Tell how the manager can ensure that the climate is right for learning.
5 Explain some of the typical types of training and development used among both employees and managers.
6 Discuss the importance of evaluating the training and some of the ways in which evaluations can be done.

The Nature of Training and Development

The terms *training* and *development* are often used interchangeably, although they do have different meanings. *Training* is the process of systematically changing behavior and/or attitudes of employees in order to increase organizational effectiveness. The programs that are designed for this purpose provide participants the opportunity to acquire job-related knowledge, skills, and attitudes. A large part of training consists of learning new ideas and skills which result in relatively permanent changes in behavior.

Development is the process by which managers obtain the skills, experiences, and attitudes necessary to become or remain successful leaders. Note that development is thought of as action at the managerial level. Thus, it is common to refer to employee training programs and management development programs. In practice, however, there is little attempt to distinguish between training and development. Who can say where one leaves off and the other begins? And why should development be a term reserved for the management level? Therefore, in this chapter the two terms will be used interchangeably. Furthermore, most attention will be devoted to types of training programs managers can use in teaching their subordinates the job-related skills and activities they need to adequately perform their jobs. Some of this training is most typically provided to workers, while other types are most commonly reserved for managers, and still others are given to both. For example, on-the-job training is a typical form of worker training; the case method and in-basket exercises are used in management training; and both groups are given coaching and counseling by their respective superiors.

Determining Training and Development Needs

■ First should come an overall evaluation.

Training and development should begin with an overall evaluation of the organization's needs. At the lower levels it is common to find inexperienced people hired for jobs, with the intention of training them later. At the middle and upper levels, training needs are often a result of promotion. The manager is first given the job; the training and development comes later. At every level of the organization, there are employees who are deficient in work-related skills. They either have not been properly trained in the first place or they have forgotten their training and have begun picking up bad work habits. All of these people constitute the pool of organizational personnel in need of training and development. How does an organization know when such training and development is needed and by whom? One of the simplest ways of picking up these needs is through work-related clues. The following are some of the most common.

- Standards of work performance are not being met.
- There is excessive scrap.
- The number of accidents has increased.
- There is a frequent need for equipment repair.
- The rate of transfer and turnover is high.

- There are too many low ratings on employee evaluation reports.
- Too many people are using different methods to do the same job.
- Employees are excessively fatigued, fumbling, discouraged, and struggling with their jobs.
- There are too many bottlenecks in the operation. Too many deadlines are being missed.

When problems such as these exist, the organization needs to make an evaluation of its training needs. In most cases, training programs are based on requests from supervisors and managers. However, the programs should not be restricted solely to these recommendations. Some supervisors construe every problem as a training problem; some managers want all training restricted to "how to do it" material, with no conceptual or theoretical input. If an organization listened exclusively to this input, there would be an overabundance of wrongly directed programs.

How then should the organization carry out a training and development appraisal? First, there should be *needs assessment* to answer the question: *Exactly what type of training and development programs are needed?* If the organization is small, it is typical to find the managers determining the training needs of their own units and submitting them to a superior for approval. In these instances training is usually done externally by local universities or professional training organizations such as the American Management Association. If the organization is large, it will have its own training department.

Designing the Program

- Followed by an overall training program.

Regardless of who does the training, there should be an identification of *training objectives* and a development of criteria to be used in *evaluating the results.* Figure 8.1 provides an illustration of this *training and development cycle.*

Figure 8.1
The Training and Development Cycle

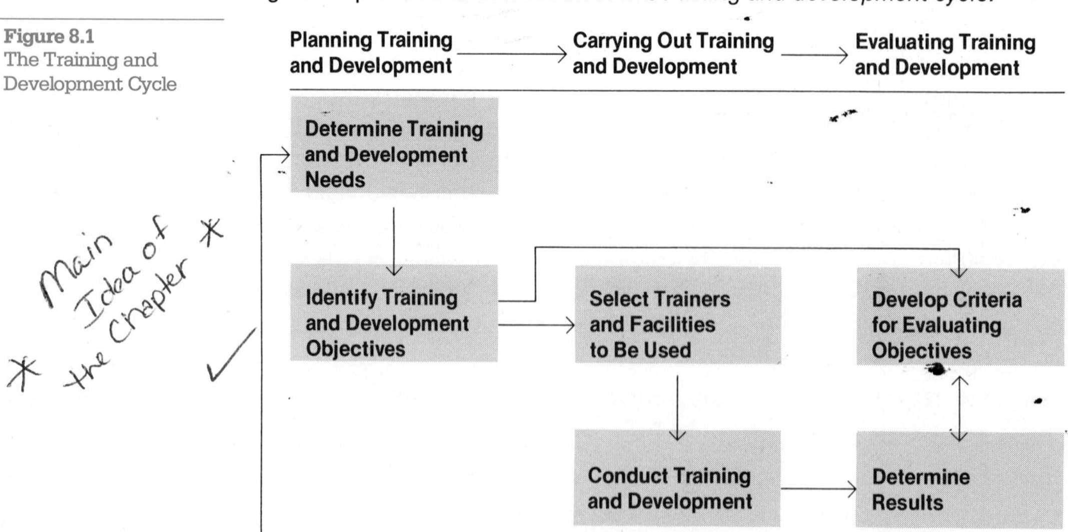

Notice in the figure that there are three phases to training and development. The first involves planning the programs, the second entails carrying out the training, and the third involves controlling or evaluating the outcome. Many organizations overlook the planning and evaluating phases, concentrating their attention solely on the training aspect of the program. This is a mistake, for it does not take into account whether the training is the right type or whether it is effective. To accomplish these objectives, the training designers should emphasize meaningful material, realistic training, and the opening of feedback channels. Table 8.1 shows how to design training programs that respond to perceived needs in the organization.

Use Material That Is Meaningful. Trainees are more likely to understand and remember meaningful material. How can the manager ensure that training material meets this criterion? Some recommended ways follow:

■ How to develop meaningful material.

1. At the beginning of the training, give the trainees an overall picture of the program. Let them know what is going to be happening.
2. Organize the material so that it is presented logically. The trainees should have very little trouble following the presentation.
3. Use familiar examples so that the participants can relate to the material.
4. Use terms and concepts the trainees are familiar with.
5. Feed the material to the participants in small bites. This will make it easier for them to follow the entire program.
6. Where possible, use visual aids to supplement any theoretical material that is being presented.

■ Combine theory and practice.

Make the Training Realistic. The further up the hierarchy the participants are located, the more likely it is that the training will contain some theory. For example, low-level workers have to be trained in such things as how to run machinery or perform mechanical chores. A great deal of their training will be nontheoretical. However, middle managers need training in interpersonal skills—effective communication, motivation, and leadership. This training will consist of *both* theory and practice. The same is true at the upper levels of the hierarchy. Top managers need to know about strategic planning and other general management areas. These subjects cannot be covered without introducing some theoretical ideas.

Regardless of the level of the hierarchy, however, the trainer should make the material as realistic as possible. For example, consider the following theory of learning: If you reward people immediately after they do something right, they are more likely to repeat that behavior than if they are rewarded at some point in the more distant future. Rather than just tell the trainee about this idea in training, the trainer should show the individual how or why it works in practice by incorporating positive feedback into training when possible. Additionally, offering some practical guidelines for implementing the theory makes it more likely that the trainee will follow this guideline on the job.

Table 8.1
Here's What We Need

Training and development programs should begin with a need assessment designed to determine the type and nature of programs that will be of most value to the organization. What are some of the typical problems that modern managers would like to see addressed in these programs? A recent national survey of sales managers asked over 1,000 of them to answer questions such as: What organizational factors are adversely affecting your performance as a sales manager? What factors are adversely affecting the performance of your salespeople? What skills do you personally need to improve? In answer to the question about those factors that adversely affect sales performance, the respondents gave the following replies:

Factors	Percentage Naming This Factor
Don't prospect very well	33.6
Don't know competitive products	26.5
Don't plan their calls	24.8
Are reluctant to make cold calls	28.9
Don't build strategies for working with customers	22.1
Don't match call frequency to account potential	20.4
Spend too much time with old accounts	19.6
Don't understand features and benefits of the products	14.4
Don't make enough top-level contacts	14.2

Obviously, a well designed sales training program would be very useful in helping overcome these particular problems. And the survey did not stop here. The respondents were also asked about the types of skills they felt they needed to improve. The sales managers said the following were the seven most important:

Factor	Percentage Naming This Factor
Managing my time	40.7
Helping my people set objectives	33.6
Motivating my people	28.3
Evaluating potential in inexperienced salespeople	24.8
Tolerating others' weaknesses	23.0
Influencing my boss	22.1
Training experienced people	19.5

One of the findings pointed out by the people who conducted the survey was that the major problems affecting sales performance were all related to planning activities. These planning factors could be worked on within training programs. The same is true for the list of the seven skills that sales managers said they would like to improve. In short, while selling takes place out in the field, the preparation occurs in the office; and this is where an effective training and development program comes in.

Source: Adapted from Ron Zemke, "What Sales Managers Say about Their Training and Development Needs," *Training/HRD*, March 1979, pp. 26–27.

Another way of making training realistic is to train the individuals in conditions that approximate the real ones. If machinists are being trained how to run machines and this training is taking place away from the regular work place, check to see how much noise there is in the regular work environment. If there is a lot, tape it and play it back in the training area. In this way, the person is trained under realistic conditions. Many firms find that if they train their people in quiet, pleasant surroundings, but the work place is noisy, the trainees need extra time to adjust to the regular work environment. They have not worked under conditions like this before.

Still another way of introducing realism into the training is to get everyone involved. In lower-level jobs this is fairly easy. The manager can start by showing the worker how to do the job and then telling the individual, "Okay, now you do it." However, in management training this can be more difficult, because the emphasis is more on getting the participants to understand management-related ideas than on simply doing things. However, it is possible to blend management theory with practice by using role playing, management games, or case analysis techniques. These will be studied later in the chapter.

Allow for Feedback. Another key element in motivating people is the use of feedback. When workers know they are making mistakes, they are likely to correct them; when managers know they are handling a situation improperly, they are likely to change their ways. Conversely, when feedback tells them that they are doing a good job, the event is going to be motivational. The individuals are going to give themselves a psychological pat on the back and keep on doing things right.

How can feedback be provided? On simple jobs that call for running machines or typing manuscript, the feedback is automatic. Individuals can see from their own output whether things are going well or poorly. When they cannot, the trainer can quickly point out any errors that they are making. The machinist may be feeding the machine incorrectly; the typist may be making too many errors per page or be typing too slowly. Of course, the supervisor will improve performance by having a good word to say when things go well. Lower-level workers need both points of view—good and bad—like everyone else.

■ Ensure feedback.

On managerial jobs most of the feedback is going to have to come from the boss. The trainer can ensure that the trainee understands the theory and how to apply it. However, when the trainee makes a mistake, it is often out on the job. Then it becomes the boss's responsibility to call the individual in and explain what is being done wrong. Effective managers do not hesitate to do this, for they know their people's training does not end when the formal training program is over. There must be continuous counseling and coaching on the job.

Some training techniques are more commonly used with workers, while others are more typically employed with managers. The following examines each.

Employee Training

Managers are expected to train their employees so that they can properly carry out their assignments. Some jobs require hardly any training at all. The manager informally shows the worker how to do the work and within a few days the individual masters the task. Any further training is carried out by the worker, who personally develops short cuts or techniques for doing the job better or easier.

Sometimes, however, formal training is required. The four most common techniques are: (1) on-the-job training, (2) vestibule training, (3) off-the-job training, and (4) coaching and counseling.

On-the-Job-Training

■ OJT is the most common method.

The most widely used method of employee training is *on-the-job training* (OJT). The employee is placed in the work situation and shown the job by either the supervisor or an experienced worker designated by the supervisor. Table 8.2 illustrates the steps used in the OJT method when teaching someone how to handle equipment, materials, tools, or other low-level, mechanical jobs. This training is carried out in the supervisor's own department.

Source: *New Yorker*, November 22, 1969, p. 62. Drawing by Donald Reilly; © 1969 The New Yorker Magazine, Inc.

Vestibule Training

■ Vestibule training simulates the work environment.

Vestibule training takes place in an environment that stimulates the actual work place; in fact, it is often located in another area of the building or plant. In this area the trainee learns how to do the job. A common example is that of training individuals to run machinery under the supervision of a trainer. Once the individual learns how to use the equipment properly, he or she is sent to the shop floor.

One of the primary benefits of vestibule training is that there is a trainer who can devote full attention to the trainee, correcting mistakes and offering encouragement in the process. This is in contrast to the regular supervisor, who may be too busy to provide the type of training needed to learn the job properly. Also, the

Table 8.2
The Four-Step Method of On-the-Job Training: Some Hints

Step 1:	Preparation of the Learner

1. Put the learner at ease—relieve the tension.
2. Explain why he is being taught.
3. Create interest, encourage questions, find out what the learner already knows about his job or other jobs.
4. Explain the why of the whole job, and relate it to some job the worker already knows.
5. Place the learner as close to his normal working position as possible.
6. Familiarize him with the equipment, materials, tools, and trade terms.

Step 2:	Presentation of the Operation

1. Explain quantity and quality requirements.
2. Go through the job at the normal work pace.
3. Go through the job at a slow pace several times, explaining each step. Between operations, explain the difficult parts, or those in which errors are likely to be made.
4. Go through the job at a slow pace several times, explaining the key points.
5. Have the learner explain the steps as you go through the job at a slow pace.
6. Have the learner explain the key points as you go through the job at a slow pace.

Step 3:	Performance Tryout

1. Have the learner go through the job several times, slowly, explaining to you each step. Correct his mistakes, and, if necessary, do some of the complicated steps for him the first few times.
2. You, the trainer, run the job at the normal pace.
3. Have the learner do the job, gradually building up skill and speed.
4. As soon as he demonstrates that he can do the job put him on his own, but don't abandon him.

Step 4:	Follow-Up

1. Designate to whom the learner should go for help if he needs it, or if he needs to ask questions.
2. Gradually decrease supervision, checking his work from time to time against quality and quantity standards.
3. Correct faulty work patterns that begin to creep into his work, and do it before they become a habit. Show him why the learned method is superior.
4. Compliment good work; encourage him and keep him encouraged until he is able to meet the quality/quantity standards.

Source: William Berliner and William McLarney, *Management Practice and Training,* 6th ed. (Homewood, Ill.: Richard D. Irwin, 1974), pp. 442–443. © 1974 by Richard D. Irwin, Inc. Reproduced by permission of the publisher.

supervisor is a manager first and a trainer second. With vestibule training, the worker is in the hands of a professional trainer who knows how to explain things properly, picks up mistakes when they occur, and shows the trainee how to avoid them. If the organization has a large number of people who could profit from vestibule training, it will often make the necessary investment and build the facilities. However, if the organization is small many firms forgo vestibule training and rely on the supervisor to handle training with OJT.

Off-the-Job Training

■ Sometimes off-the-job training is less expensive.

Sometimes workers need technical training but the organization cannot afford the time to provide it. In these cases *off-the-job training* is often used. Individuals are sent to vocational schools or institutes where they can learn necessary job-related skills. The range of available technical training is quite large, extending from courses on machinery or electricity to secretarial or typing skills to computer or electronic data processing. Lacking the facilities, equipment, or personnel to train these individuals, the organization finds it less expensive to have others do the training for it.

Coaching and Counseling for Lower-Level Workers

■ Coaching and counseling are important.

While much more widely used among managers than lower-level workers, *coaching and counseling* is also an effective training approach for employees. Remember, the manager's job is to set a good example and be available to answer questions and provide advice to subordinates. Additionally, every successful supervisor knows that promotion involves two things: (1) an opening into which he or she can be promoted, and (2) someone to take the vacated job. Effective coaching and counseling can be used not only to train workers how to do their jobs but to groom one or two of them for the supervisor's own job. In this way, when a promotion is offered, the supervisor has someone available to fill his or her position. Thus coaching and counseling work as a two-way street, good for the organization and good for the supervisor.

Management Training

Just as the supervisor or lower-level manager must train subordinates, so middle and upper-level managers must train theirs. This training, however, is more broadly based than that commonly used with workers. In particular, it involves more theory and less technique. Some of the most common training and development techniques include job rotation, the case method, the in-basket technique, role playing, management games, and coaching and counseling.

Job Rotation

■ Job rotation broadens managerial experience.

One of the most popular in-house management training approaches is *job rotation.* Trainees are rotated through a series of jobs in order to broaden their managerial experience. Organizations that intend to promote people into top management positions often use job rotation so that the individual learns what all key departments are doing. For example, an individual in the finance department may be rotated to the production and marketing departments, spending a little time in each learning what these departments do. Then when the individual moves into a top slot, the new manager is aware of how the activities of all the departments fit together in attaining overall organizational objectives. Without this job rotation, the person coming out of the finance department might support only finance-related activities and feel that the other departments are not that important. Not only does job rotation help the up-and-coming manager get a better view of the overall operation; it also helps develop the person's conceptual skills.

The Case Method

■ The case method allows interaction and discussion.

Another widely used training technique is the *case method.* A case is a written description of a real decision-making situation. Trainees are asked to study the case, determine the problems, analyze them, and choose a course of action. The purpose of the case method is to acquaint the trainees with situations they will be facing on the job. For the manager in the production department, a case related to disciplining late or unruly workers can be used as a vehicle for discussing the right and wrong ways to handle workers who are out of line. For the manager in the marketing department, a case related to a major customer who needs a special order filled within two days can provide the individual with insights on the importance of balancing customer needs with in-house production capability. It also provides a basis for discussing how the individual should approach the manufacturing department to ask for special assistance in processing the order.

The value of the case method is that it permits the trainees to put themselves into job-like problems and solve them. Their solutions can then be analyzed by the trainer and the rest of the class for the purpose of determining whether the individual identified the major problems and solved them correctly. The case method is extremely useful in dealing with issues that cannot be adequately covered through lecture or textbook material alone. Interaction and discussion are needed.

In-Basket Technique

■ This method develops decision-making abilities.

Another method used to develop managerial decision-making abilities is the *in-basket technique.* The training consists of giving the trainee a box of material containing typical items that might be found in his or her mailbox and a telephone list. In addition to the routine business matters are a number of important, pressing issues which need to be dealt with as soon as possible. Illustrations might include a complaint from a major vendor, a memo saying that certain inventory is now out of stock and requesting an immediate decision regarding how much to reorder, and a note from the boss asking the trainee to respond to the attached letter at the earliest convenience.

After looking through all of the in-basket material, the trainee is asked to make decisions on what should be done. The individual has only a limited amount of time for dealing with all these matters. When the time period is over, the trainee is evaluated and critiqued on the number of decisions made in the time allotted, as well as on the quality of the decisions and the priorities that were chosen in making them. Research shows that trainees like this method and that it has value in predicting future managerial effectiveness.[1]

Role Playing

Role playing is very similar to what an actor does on stage. The person is given a part to act out and does so as well as possible. In management training sessions, the trainee is given an assigned role and asked to act it out, reacting to the other players who are participating in the role playing. Unlike the actor, however, the trainee is given only background information on the situation. From here the individual improvises. For example, two managers are asked to role play a situation in which one is to be the boss who must tell the other that after careful deliberation, management has decided to give the next promotion to another person. The other manager is to play the individual who did not get the promotion. The latter, of course, is going to be raising a whole series of questions: Why didn't I get the promotion? My record was extremely good. What does this mean for my career with the firm? The individual playing the decision-bearing manager must try to resolve the issue, possibly by calming the person down and reassuring him or her that it is only a matter of time before another position opens up and the promotion is given.

■ So does role playing.

Placed into role playing situations like this, the participating trainees get a feel for what it is like to be directly involved. Meanwhile, the participants who watch the role playing session can empathize with both people. When it is over, the group and the trainer discuss what went well during the scenario and what was not handled correctly. By pointing out problems and mistakes now ("don't tell him he'll get the next promotion; you don't know that; you might say he is sure to get one eventually; but never promise what you cannot deliver"), the members of the training group can prevent their being made out on the job.

Management Games

Many types of *management games* can be employed for training purposes. Some relate directly to a particular area, such as production scheduling, advertising, materials purchasing, or product development. These games are called *functional games* and are useful for training managers in specific functional areas.

■ And management games.

Other games are broadly based and require either that the individual work alone or with a few colleagues to run an entire company and compete against the other trainees, who are running competitive firms of their own. This type of game is called a *general management simulation* and is used in training top managers. Each team of players is asked to make a series of operating decisions often related to areas such as product price, purchase of materials, production scheduling, hiring of personnel, advertising, R&D expenditures, funds borrowing, and the sale of stocks and bonds. These decisions are then collected by the game administrator and, using either a computer or manual scoring technique, scored according to a predetermined series of formulas. The results are then fed back to the participants, who can see how well they did. The trainees are then asked to make another series of decisions based on these results, each time trying to increase their profit or share of the market. The objective of the game is to show the participants what impact their decisions have on their competitors and vice versa.

If used properly, these games not only provide the managers with top decision-making experience but create a high level of motivation among the participants.

Coaching and Counseling for Managers

While these other techniques are more related to training, *coaching and counseling* help to develop managers. And while the other techniques are often carried out away from the job, coaching and counseling take place on the job, with the superior playing the role of the coach.

■ Coaching and counseling develop management skills.

One of the most important things the boss can do in coaching is to set a good example, for subordinates tend to emulate their superiors. Additionally, the boss must be available to answer questions and explain why things are done in a given way. This helps the subordinate understand the scope and importance of the job.

Some managers set aside time every week to talk to new subordinates. At this time they review what the individual has been doing, the progress that has been made, the types of problems that have arisen, and the action that should now be taken. Such an approach is built around a philosophy of delegating authority and giving the trainee a chance to prove what he or she can do. Remember, effective managers delegate authority and let subordinates carry the ball. Otherwise, the trainees would be continually dependent on the boss for all decision making, and the manager would never get any work done since time would be entirely devoted to helping the subordinates.

While there are various ways of coaching and counseling subordinates, there is one overriding consideration for the manager. The individual needs to establish the right kind of *climate* for learning. This climate is dependent on the manager's willingness to delegate authority to the trainees and develop a feeling of mutual confidence with them. Each must learn to trust the other.

Evaluation of the Training

The last phase of training and development programs is an *evaluation of the results.* Did the individuals learn what was taught to them? Are they applying it on the job? Was the time and money well spent? There is an area where many organizations fall down. They spend all their resources putting together the program but do not take time to evaluate the results. As Figure 8.1 shows, evaluation is the stage that ties together the planning—what was supposed to be done—with the outcome—what was actually accomplished.

What Can Be Evaluated?

Many aspects of training can be evaluated. Some of the major categories are the following:

■ Evaluation categories.

1. Improved attitudes among the participants.
2. Increased quality and/or quantity of work output.

3. Ability to apply the subject matter to organizational problems.
4. Increased learning ability or aptitude in a job-related area.
5. Altered points of view among the participants.
6. Development of strong esprit de corps among the group.
7. Dissemination of knowledge about a particular subject.

These are measurable end points. The person doing the evaluating can determine the extent and degree to which these training objectives can be attained. Keep in mind, of course, that these objectives, or end points, should have been established before the training program. The manager or trainer should have asked: What should the individual be able to do after this training is complete, and how can I determine whether this competence exists?

Who Does the Evaluation?

■ Numerous groups can evaluate.

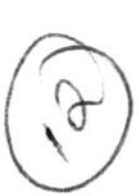

Three groups can carry out the evaluation, depending on the type of program that was offered. These are the management, the trainer, and the trainees. If the training is done by an outside group, it is common to find the management conducting its own evaluation of the training. If the training was done by a supervisor or lower-level manager, both this person and his or her boss will be interested in the results. The further up the organization the training is done, as in the case of the upper-middle managers who train their own subordinates, the more likely it is that the trainers (or managers) will evaluate their own training methods' success. Finally, trainees can sometimes help in the evaluation process, especially if the material was not too difficult to grasp and if they have a full understanding of what they were being taught. For example, machinists and lower-level workers can often provide important feedback regarding the clarity of instruction, the realism of the examples, and the overall value of the program. At the upper levels, however, this is neither feasible nor desirable. The subordinates may need time to think about what they are being taught and may not really be competent to judge the overall training until some future time.

How Is It Done?

■ Evaluation forms can be helpful.

One common way of evaluating training is to ask the participants how useful the training has been. This is not a very effective approach because it puts pressure on the individuals to give it a good rating. A better way is to provide the participants with an evaluation form such as the one in Figure 8.2 and ask them to fill it out and send it back to the individual or department charged with evaluating overall training effectiveness. In addition to check-list items or objective answers, some short answer questions should be included. In this way the trainees can express some ideas in their own way. In particular, many organizations like to ask the participants what they liked most and least about the training and the trainer.

While many evaluation questions can be asked of the participants, some should relate back to the initial objectives of the training. For example, questions about

Figure 8.2
A Training Course Evaluation Form

Date______________________ Name of course______________________

Name of instructor____

Where training was held ____

Please evaluate the instructor and the course. Do not leave out any questions. Do not sign your name.

Inadequate	1
Well below average	2
Average	3
Well above average	4
Excellent	5

Using the above 5-point rating scale, please give your evaluation to the following:

Course
Objectives were made clear. ________
Lectures were relevant to the objectives. ________
Discussions were relevant to the objectives and the course content. ________
Assignments were explained, and their relevance to the objectives was made clear. ________
Constructive comments were made about the assignments. ________

Instructor
Was well prepared. ________
Presented the material in a systematic, organized fashion. ________
Used examples and material that made the course relevant. ________
Was able to maintain interest and direction during the course. ________
Was able to relate to the participants. ________
What did you learn during this training that was most helpful?

What were the major shortcomings or problems associated with the training?

Overall, how useful was the training? Be as detailed as possible in your answer.

the room, the adequacy of the facilities, and the effectiveness of the trainer should be asked. There should also be questions related to what was learned. In an effort to prevent people from making their evaluations too early, some organizations wait a couple of weeks before sending around the evaluation form. Once back on the job, the trainee may be in a much better position to decide what part of the training was useful and what part was of little, if any, value.

Effectiveness of Different Training Methods

In addition to the overall evaluation of training, research has been conducted on different training methods. Which are more effective and which are less effective? In one study, researchers surveyed 200 training directors from large corporations, asking the training directors to fill out a questionnaire and to rank various training methods from 5 (highly effective) to 1 (not effective). Additionally, the directors were asked to rate each method in regard to how effective it was in attaining each of the following training objectives: (1) acquisition of knowledge, (2) changing attitudes among the trainees, (3) increasing the problem-solving skills of the participants, (4) improving interpersonal skills, (5) increasing trainees' acceptance of the training method, and (6) the trainees' retention of knowledge. Table 8.3 shows the results.

Table 8.3
How Training Directors Evaluated Alternative Training Methods[a]

Training Method[b]	Knowledge Acquisition	Changing Attitudes	Problem-Solving Skills	Inter-personal Skills	Participant Acceptance	Knowledge Retention
Case study	2	4	1	4	2	2
Conference (discussion)	2	3	4	3	1	5
Lecture (with questions)	9	8	9	8	8	8
Business games	6	5	2	5	3	6
Movie films	4	6	7	6	5	7
Programmed instruction	1	7	6	7	7	1
Role playing	7	2	3	2	4	4
Sensitivity training (T-group)	8	1	5	1	6	3
Television lecture	5	9	8	9	9	9

[a]Evaluations are all by mean rank.
[b]1 is high, 9 is low.
Source: Adapted from Stephen J. Carroll, Jr., Frank T. Paine, and John J. Ivancevich, "The Relative Effectiveness of Training Methods—Expert Opinion and Research," *Personnel Psychology,* Autumn 1972, p. 498. Reprinted by permission.

▪ Training method effectiveness depends on the situation.

These results show that, depending on the objective, different training methods were effective in some cases but not very effective in others. For example, business games were very useful in teaching problem-solving skills but ranked much lower in both knowledge acquisition and knowledge retention. Likewise, programmed instruction was given a very high rating in knowledge acquisition and knowledge retention, but was very low in all other categories. Sensitivity training, a form of training designed to make participants more aware of their own feelings and those of others, was ranked number one in terms of changing attitudes but near the bottom of the list when it came to knowledge acquisition.

Since certain training methods are more effective than others, depending on the objectives of the training, the manager needs to first determine the purpose of the training. Is it for knowledge acquisition or retention? Or is it to change attitudes or improve problem-solving skills? The answer will help determine the specific type of training that should be used.

Trainees also have responsibilities to their trainers. They must do their part if the training is to work well, as Table 8.4 shows.

Table 8.4
The Trainee's Job

Many managers spend a lot of their time trying to train their subordinates. The same is true for professional trainers, whether they are part of an in-house staff or outside training agency. Both managers and trainers alike should be interested in increasing their training and development effectiveness. Recently, however, attention has been directed at how people can become more effective trainees. How can the people who participate in formal training programs ensure that the trainer does the best possible job? Some trainees would argue that it is not their business to help the trainer do a good job; it is their business to simply pay attention, take notes, and be cooperative. However, by their very statements, they reveal that they can play a positive role. After all, the things they have just mentioned all constitute positive feedback for the trainer. What else can the trainees do? Gerald Marsh and Millard Mott have set forth this list of ten commandments for trainees:

1. Be on time. If you are too early, the trainer may feel uncomfortable setting up with you watching. If you are late, the trainer may be distracted by your entrance.
2. Be eager. Enter with a pleasant expression and, if possible, acknowledge the trainer. Tell the latter that you are looking forward to the session.
3. Be attentive. When the trainer presents material, nod your head and act enthusiastic.
4. Be responsive. When the trainer opens a discussion period with a request for reactions or comments, respond immediately, even if only to say, "What you just talked about really got me thinking."
5. Be trusting. If the trainer says, "Please interrupt me if you have any questions," do just this. This action provides the trainer with feedback and helps ensure a communication exchange between the trainer and the trainees.
6. Follow directions. When the trainer gives directions, follow them to the letter. If you are in a small group, take the initiative by repeating these directions and helping other group members follow them.
7. Volunteer. From time to time the trainer may request a volunteer from the group of trainees. When the person does, help out by volunteering. This cooperation can help ensure the overall success of the training.
8. Be sensitive. Be aware of the trainer's concern for such things as time. If the trainer is hurrying because the hour is late, let the training go on. Conversely, if the trainer has more than enough time, help the person use it effectively by asking questions and getting the trainer to elaborate on some ideas you have heard but would like to have explained in more detail.
9. Recognize the trainer. When talking to the trainer, make it a point to refer to something the person has said earlier in the day. "Like you said a while ago . . ." or "As we discussed earlier and the handouts reinforced. . . ." These things build the trainer's ego and encourage the person to do an even better job.
10. Give feedback. During breaks, talk to the trainer about the topic. After the session, thank the person and, if you feel it was indeed a good session, say, "I'm going to recommend this to my friends."

Source: Adapted from Gerald Marsh and Millard Mott, "Ten Commandments for Trainees," *Training/HRD*, December 1978, pp. 78–79.

Summary

Training is the process of systematically changing behavior and/or attitudes of employees in order to increase organizational effectiveness. Development is the process by which managers obtain the skills, experiences, and attitudes necessary to become and/or remain successful leaders. In this chapter, the terms *training* and *development* were used interchangeably, since it is difficult to determine where one leaves off and the other begins.

The first step in developing a training and development program is to conduct a needs assessment. Exactly what type of training is needed, by whom, and how should it be given? In the design of the program it is important to determine the objectives, how they will be carried out, and the way in which the results will be evaluated.

Another important aspect of training is the environment in which the learning will occur. In particular, the material that is presented should be meaningful and the training should be realistic. Examples of the ways in which these things can be done were presented in the chapter.

There are two basic types of training: employee training and management training. Common employee training techniques include on-the-job training, vestibule training, off-the-job training, and coaching and counseling. Common management development program techniques consist of job rotation, the case method, the in-basket technique, role playing, management games, and coaching and counseling. Each of these was described in the chapter.

The last phase of the training and development program is the evaluation of results. While the methods to be used for this evaluation will differ, the important thing is that the evaluation be tied back to the original objectives. Was the training successful? Did it accomplish its initial goals? By answering this question, the organization ensures a tie-in between planning (what was to be done) and controlling (what was actually accomplished).

Key Terms in the Chapter

training
development
training and development cycle
on-the-job training (OJT)
vestibule training
off-the-job training
coaching and counseling
job rotation
case method
in-basket technique
role playing
functional game
general management simulation

Review and Study Questions

1. What is meant by the term *training?* What is meant by the term *development?* Define these terms in your own words.
2. How does the training and development cycle work? In what way can it help the organization improve the effectiveness of training and development programs?

3. How can the trainer ensure that the material being used is meaningful? How can the training be made realistic? Explain.
4. One of the most common methods of training employees is OJT. How does OJT work? How does it differ from vestibule training?
5. When would an organization use off-the-job training with its lower-level employees?
6. Can coaching and counseling be of any value to supervisors in training and developing their people? Explain.
7. How does job rotation work? the case method? the in-basket technique?
8. How does role playing work? When is it an effective training method?
9. For what type of training would a management game be a suitable training tool? Explain.
10. What is the purpose of coaching and counseling at the managerial level? How can it help train and develop managers?
11. Can training objectives or end points be evaluated? Cite at least three.
12. How can an organization go about evaluating the effectiveness of a training program?
13. Drawing upon Table 8.3 in the text, when would each of the following be an effective training method: case study, role playing, and management games? Explain.

Note

1. Herbert H. Mayer, "The Validity of the In-Basket Test as a Measure of Managerial Performance," *Personnel Psychology,* Autumn 1970, 297–307.

Case: In-House Development

It's easy to match up training programs with the needs of the people—right?

The top management staff of an eastern insurance firm held a meeting recently at which a key training and development decision was made. Instead of relying exclusively on the in-house training and development of managers by their superiors, the firm is going to establish a training department and also will use outside training programs when the in-house department lacks the capability of conducting the desired programs.

Of particular concern to management is the fact that competitive firms are spending a great deal of time and effort on training and developing their people. This was made clear to the company president, George Cole, at a recent meeting of top insurance executives that he attended. One of the key speakers talked about what his firm was doing and what it intended to do over the next decade. George was shocked. His company was doing nothing like this. Oh sure, the company encouraged coaching and counseling of subordinates by superiors, and it gave in-house training at the lower levels for new workers. But the training was not as systematic as the program described by this other company executive. "If they are doing more training and development," reasoned George, "we'd better too."

The individual who has been chosen to head the new training department is Willa Franklin. She has been an assistant training department manager for another insurance firm, so she has a basic understanding of the types of training that are needed by company personnel.

Her first step has been to find out the types of training that management feels it needs. Each department head has been contacted and asked to identify the people who need training and the kind of training desired. Willa has found that a lot of the training can be easily handled by the superior through either OJT methods or coaching and counseling. However, some of it can be done more efficiently with formal training programs. In particular, some supervisors and middle managers have had no formal management training. Additionally, two of the top executives have indicated an interest in learning more about strategic planning.

Willa intends to work closely with management in helping identify training needs. She is also going to develop some special in-house programs and keep her eye out for external programs that will provide the kind of training the top executives have expressed interest in. "I think we can establish a training and development program here that will make the rest of the industry envious," she recently told the president.

Questions

1. What kind of training programs would be useful at the supervisory level? What do these people need to learn, and how can formal training help?
2. What about the middle and upper levels of the organization? Which of the training techniques discussed in this chapter would Willa be most likely to use? Explain.

3. How should these programs be evaluated? What would you recommend? Be specific.

Case: Stopping a Downturn

First you've got to make a needs assessment.

Productivity in the manufacturing department of Hodgman Inc. has been declining over the last twelve months. Some of the most noticeable problems have been the following:

1. The accident rate has increased by 27 percent.
2. Equipment maintenance costs due to improper operating procedures have resulted in excessive repair bills.
3. The current turnover rate is twice the average of the last three years.
4. The scrap rate is up 45 percent in the last six months.
5. Delivery deadlines have been missed on 14 percent of all orders during the last three months.
6. During the last fiscal quarter, 10 percent of all orders have been returned because they did not meet minimum production specifications as set forth in the customer contract.

In an effort to deal with these problems, the training department has interviewed all the plant supervisors and sent every manager in the production department a training needs assessment questionnaire. The training people intend to conduct formal training, based on the interviews and the questionnaires, to give the supervisors and managers some support.

In particular, the head of the manufacturing department wants to see all of his managers, with the help of the training department, start retraining inefficient personnel and provide more guidance and counseling to new employees. Where necessary, off-the-job training will also be used. For the moment, the supervisors are to work with the training people in determining the specific kinds of training that are needed. Using this approach, the head of manufacturing believes that the current productivity problems can be overcome and their recurrence prevented.

Questions

1. In addition to the problems cited in this case, what other signs should a firm look for that would indicate that training and development are needed?
2. How important is a needs assessment preceding training and development problems? Will the questionnaire the training department is going to use be helpful in this assessment? What about the management interviews? Explain.
3. What kinds of training would you expect to be used by both the supervisors and the training department? Explain your answer.

Part Five

The Management Process: Directing

The overall objective of this part of the book is to study the directing function. Directing consists of three activities: communicating, motivating, and leading. These are behavioral functions that many managers have problems with. They may encounter little trouble planning and organizing, and staffing is often handled via a well thought out recruiting and training program. However, when it comes to dealing with people in the work place, many managers have great difficulty. Effective management of people at work is achieved through understanding (a) why communication often breaks down and how the resulting problems can be overcome, (b) some of the most important findings in the field of motivation and how they can be applied to people at work, and (c) what leadership is all about and which types of leadership styles seem to work best in which types of situations.

Chapter 9 The Communication Process

Objectives of the Chapter

Every manager needs to communicate effectively. Yet many admit that they have problems getting subordinates to understand what they are saying or getting them to comply with directives. Why does this happen? Various answers can be given, but all of them can be traced to the communication process itself. The first objective of this chapter is to examine the communication process to find out what goes on when messages are sent from one party to another. The second objective is to study the various types of communication flows used in organizations. Then attention will be focused on communication problems. For example, we shall discuss what causes such problems and what form they take. The final objective of the chapter is to examine the ways in which communication effectiveness can be improved.

When you have finished studying the material in this chapter, you should be able to:

1. Define the term *communication.*
2. Describe the five basic elements in the communication process.
3. Explain the communication flows that exist in the modern organization.
4. Tell how physical and psychological settings can create communication problems.
5. Identify and describe some of the major barriers to effective communication.
6. Explain how these communication barriers can be overcome through an understanding of the steps in the communication process and through empathy and effective listening.

The Nature of Communication

Communication is the process by which meanings are conveyed from sender to receiver. Notice in this definition that it is "meanings" being sent *and* received. Often managers say or write words, but their meanings or interpretations are not received. As a result, the intended receiver does not really understand the manager's message. In this chapter we are going to study the reasons that meanings are sometimes misunderstood and what can be done to minimize or eliminate such problems. The place to start is with an analysis of the way in which communication actually takes place.

▪ Meanings are conveyed.

Communication Process

The communication process has *five* basic elements. These are illustrated in Figure 9.1. Everything begins with a *source,* or sender. This individual has a message for a receiver.

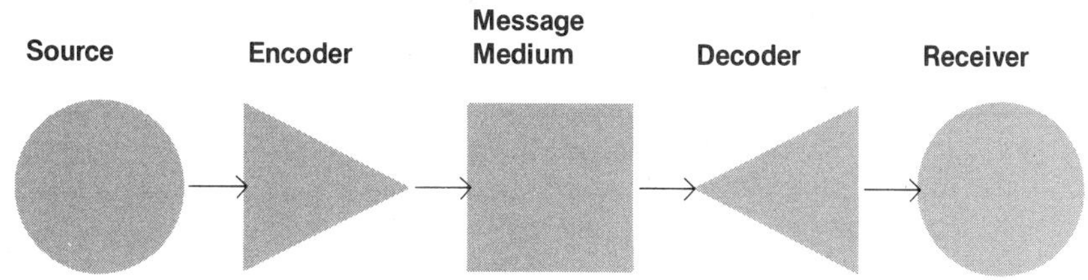

Figure 9.1
The Communication Process

In getting the message to the other party, the source needs to *encode* it by putting it into a form that is understandable to the receiver. Words, gestures, and facial expressions are all examples of encoding. In the encoding process the sender not only thinks through the message but translates it into some code or symbol.

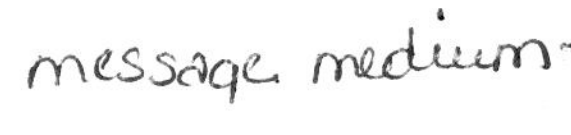

Next, the source must choose a *message medium.* How will the information be sent? The person might use the telephone, send a memo, or talk directly to the other party.

The message is then *decoded,* or interpreted, by the receiver. This is where communication often breaks down. The receiver simply misunderstands the message.

Why does misunderstanding occur? To answer this question, we need to consider the *receiver.* What type of background or training does the individual have? Was the person capable of understanding the message? Did the person receive it in sufficient time to take the appropriate action? Does the receiver like the sender, or are the two at odds?

Answers to these questions can help pinpoint communication problems, and from here corrective action can be initiated. One of the most effective ways of doing so, without bringing in outside parties, is to have the sender and receiver discuss the problem. This type of discussion is known as *feedback* and provides a control loop for analyzing communication breakdown. The following is an example:

Luisa: **George, I called you yesterday and told you that I needed that report immediately. Where is it?**

George: **I put it in the interdepartmental mail just this morning. It should be on your desk by 3:00 P.M.**

Luisa: **We have a meeting starting in fifteen minutes and I want to distribute some of the data from the report to the salespeople who will be here. When I said *immediately,* I meant for you to have someone hand carry it to my secretary right away.**

George: **Gee, I misunderstood what you meant by the word *immediate.* But let's straighten it out quickly. The report is still in our out-box. I'll have my assistant bring it to the Xerox room right now and make copies. Why don't you have your secretary meet him there.**

Luisa: **Good idea. I'll need ten copies of pages 4 to 7.**

George: **Okay. It'll all be taken care of within five minutes.**

■ Two-way communication is important.

In this scenario the problem was cleared up with two-way communication feedback. With this in mind, it is possible to expand Figure 9.1 to illustrate communication in action, as in Figure 9.2. Not only is there feedback between the two parties, but *both* are encoders, decoders, and interpreters in the process.

Figure 9.2
Communication in Action

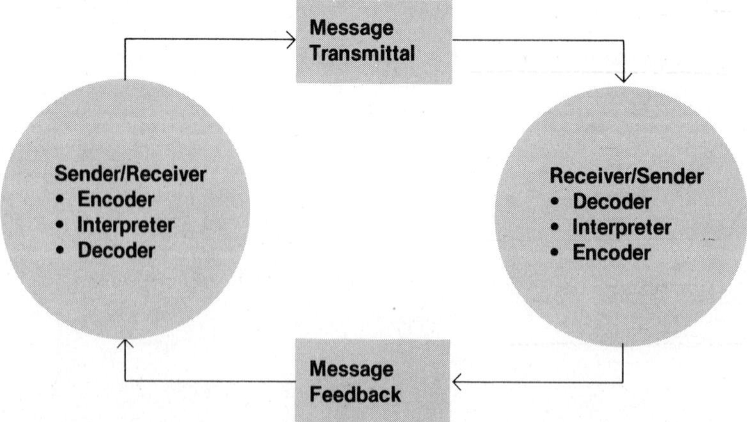

Therefore, if the managers are to be effective when communicating they must realize that the process involves more than just conveying information to subordinates. It involves the transmitting of meanings and the securing of feedback with which to gauge the accuracy of message reception.

Communication Flows

The communication process is used in organizations for carrying messages both to and from individuals and groups. These *communication flows* move in four basic directions: downward, upward, laterally, and horizontally. Figure 9.3 illustrates each of these.

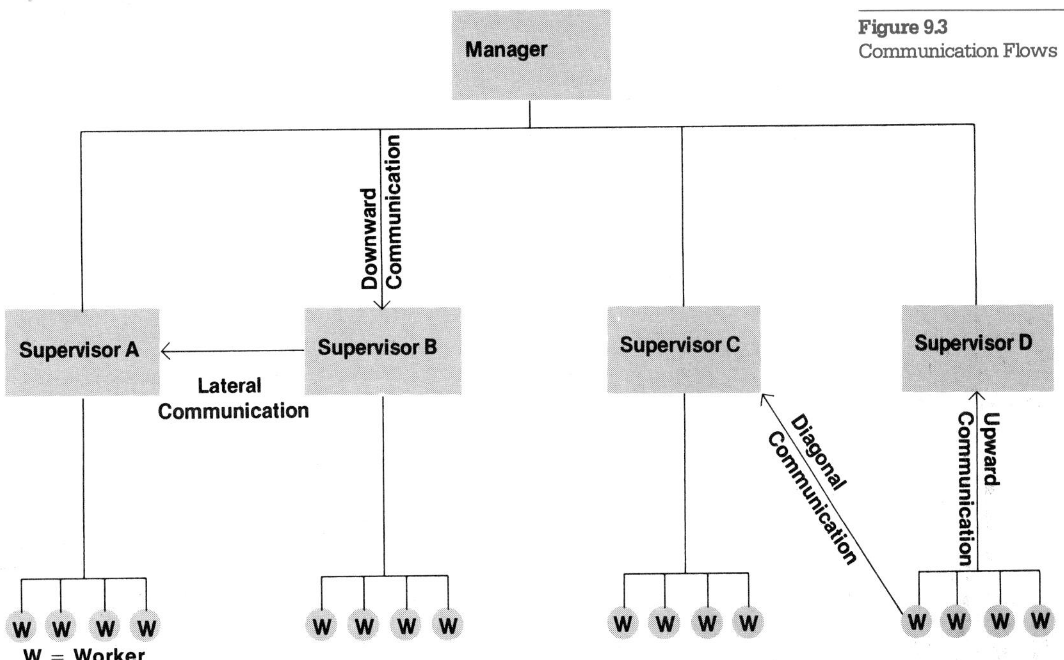

Figure 9.3
Communication Flows

Downward Communication

Downward communication takes place between the superior, who initiates, and the subordinate. The most common reason for this communication flow is to *transmit information* and/or *instruct subordinates in the performance of their jobs.* Typical communication channels used for this purpose include written directives, face-to-face talks, public address systems, bulletin boards, and company newspapers. These flows provide for direction and control of subordinates.

Upward Communication

Upward communication takes place between subordinate (the initiator) and superior. The purpose of this information flow is to provide *feedback* on how

▪ Feedback is provided.

things are going. This information not only keeps the superior aware of what is going on, but provides the individual with input for representing the subordinates to his or her superior. Armed with performance-related statistics, the manager is in a much better position to argue for raises and benefits for these workers.

Lateral Communication

▪ Teamwork is promoted.

Lateral communication takes place between people on the *same* level of the hierarchy. The most common reason for this communication flow is to *promote coordination and teamwork.* As shown in Figure 9.3, Supervisor B will often communicate with Supervisor A for such things as obtaining support or checking on when Supervisor A's people will be finished assembling certain units so that they can be sent over for testing by Supervisor B's workers.

Diagonal Communication

▪ Organizational efficiency is increased.

Diagonal communication occurs between people who are *neither* in the same department *nor* on the same level of the hierarchy. The basic purpose of this communication flow is to *increase organizational efficiency* by cutting across departmental lines and minimizing red tape. For example, one of Supervisor D's people contacts Supervisor C about some materials that were supposed to be sent over yesterday. Supervisor C checks with the appropriate subordinate and tells the worker that they are on their way. Does this communication flow not violate the chain of command? It certainly does, but it is used all the time because it is a fast, efficient way of communicating. However, the subordinate should always follow two rules:

1. Get permission from the direct supervisor (in this case Supervisor D) before undertaking the communication.
2. Keep the direct supervisor informed of any results that have occurred because of the communication.

Why Are There Communication Problems?

Communication problems can be divided into two categories: those created by the physical setting and those brought about by the psychological setting. The former can be dealt with more easily than the latter. However, sometimes the two *overlap* and it becomes necessary to deal with them *simultaneously.* The following sections examine both settings.

The Physical Setting

Sometimes communication problems are brought about by the physical environment in which the contact occurs. Four of the most common are noise, the room itself, seating arrangements, and the specific type of message transmission being used.

Noise. It is difficult to communicate when there is a lot of racket in the room. Communication is most effective when the sender and receiver can easily hear each other in surroundings that are pleasant.

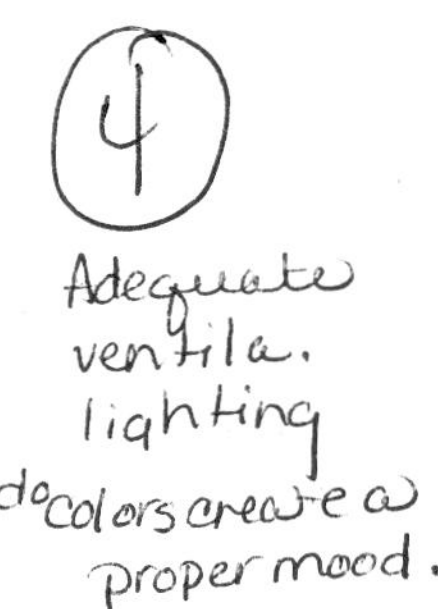

The Room. A related factor, often overlooked by managers wishing to improve their communication skills, is the *room* itself. Is there adequate ventilation and lighting? Are the chairs comfortable? Do the colors of the room help create the right mood? All of these are important, although in some cases one may be more so. For example, a dentist's waiting room must be designed and laid out in such a way as to generate trust and confidence. Many people believe the dentist will hurt them, and the doctor needs to start winning them over with the waiting room. The same is true for organizational managers. Psychologists have found that office colors can help create certain moods in people. Look at the list in Table 9.1 and see if you can match the colors with their respective moods. The answers are given at the bottom of the table.

Table 9.1
A Test of Colors and Moods

Color		Mood
1. Purple	____	a. Exciting, stimulating
2. Orange	____	b. Secure, comfortable
3. Red	____	c. Distressed, disturbed, upset
4. Yellow	____	d. Despondent, dejected, unhappy, melancholy
5. Black, brown	____	e. Dignified, stately
6. Blue	____	f. Cheerful, jovial, joyful

Source: L. B. Wexner, "The Degree to Which Colors (Hues) Are Associated with Mood-Tones," *Journal of Applied Psychology,* December 1954, pp. 433–434. Copyright 1954 by the American Psychological Association. Reprinted by permission.

The answers to the matching assignment are: 1-e; 2-c; 3-a; 4-f; 5-d; 6-b.

Seating Arrangements. A third factor is the *seating arrangements,* which have psychological, as well as physical, meaning. If the manager remains behind the desk, there is a greater degree of formality than if the individual comes out and sits directly opposite the subordinate. An individual who is in trouble will usually find the manager staying behind the desk. There is also the matter of standing up. This is commonly a sign of authority; so the manager may stand, but the subordinate usually remains seated. In this way, the boss can literally talk down to the worker.

Form of Message Transmission. A fourth physical problem is the *message transmission.* Sometimes the wrong form will be used. Instead of sending a memo, which is likely to sit on the receiver's desk, it is better to telephone the individual. Sometimes, it will be appropriate to send a letter. But if there is bad weather in the area and the letter is not delivered for three days, a problem results. In still other cases, an order placed by phone but not confirmed by telegram as required by the firm fails to be processed through human error, either by the order clerk or the telegraph transmitter. In short, the method of transmission is less than ideal.

The Psychological Setting

Other communication problems are brought about by the individuals themselves. Three of the most important aspects of this are the private and public self, timing, and body language.

Private and Public Self. Another important communication variable is the relationship between the manager's *public self* and *private self*. This distinction is well illustrated by the Johari window, designed by Joseph Luft and Harrington Ingham.[1] The window, shown as Figure 9.4, compares aspects of open (public) versus closed (private) communication relationships.

Figure 9.4
The Johari Window

	Known to Self	Not Known to Self
Not Known to Others	**Hidden**	**Unknown**
Known to Others	**Open**	**Blind**

As seen in the figure, there is an *open* part of oneself that all of us know about and are willing to share. There is a *hidden* part of which we are aware but unwilling to share. There is a *blind* part which we do not know about but which others see. Finally shown is an *unknown* part, which neither we nor others know.

To some degree, managers are open in their communications. However, sometimes they hide things because they feel the subordinate does not need to know this information. Other times, they believe they are open while they are not; and the subordinates realize that the manager is not communicating everything to them (the blind part of the window). Still other times, the manager innocently misleads the subordinate and both parties are unaware of it. In short, there are many reasons for communication failure and some of them are best described by the *blind* or *unknown* parts of the Johari window. In order to reduce these parts, managers need to increase their self-awareness. The better managers understand themselves, the more likely it is that they will communicate effectively.

■ The Johari window provides personal insights.

Timing. Another problem is *timing.* When a message is received can be as important as its content. If the receiver is not in the right frame of mind, the message may fall on deaf ears. For example, a manager who has just received word that he did not receive a promotion is unlikely to give favorable attention to a subordinate's request for assistance on a project. The latter should wait a few days and give the manager time to recover from the bad news.

On the other hand, if the manager did receive the promotion, this could be an ideal time to request such support. The boss is likely to be in very good spirits and more than usually willing to be supportive. Remember the cliché "misery loves company"? Well, not only is it accurate, but it can also be extended to "misery loves other miserable company."[2] Unless managers can make themselves aware of these problems and work to sidestep them, message timing will jeopardize message content.

Nonverbal Language. Another reason for communication breakdown is the failure to read *nonverbal language.* The ways people sit, use eye contact, smile, gesture, and even remain silent have meaning.

■ Nonverbal cues communicate ideas.

A large area of nonverbal communication is body language. How people walk tells something about them. A manager who is thinking through a problem may walk slowly, with head down. An executive who is very happy will walk sprightly, head up and arms swinging. Commenting on this area, Larry Baker, a communications expert, notes:

> **We all know how to "read" . . . obvious nonverbal cues, but conscious and sustained effort can help you pick up even more subtle expressions of nonverbal language. For example, you sometimes use your body parts to show that you are or are not associated with the people near you. Thus, crossing your legs in the same way the person next to you crosses hers may indicate identification with that person. Or, if you are standing and arguing with three people, you may soon find yourself assuming the body posture of the person with whom you agree—both of you standing with your hands on your hips, for instance, while your two opponents may also assume like postures.**
>
> **Other gestures show openness and honesty. Holding the hands open while talking indicates sincerity; hands clenched into fists do the opposite. Similarly, if someone unbuttons or even takes off his or her coat in your presence, this conveys openness and friendliness towards you.[3]**

Much of organizational communication, especially face-to-face communication, involves nonverbal transmission of meanings. If either party fails to read these transmissions, communication can break down.

Specific Communication Barriers

Communication problems can create barriers that prevent the receiver from understanding the message. Such barriers can be illustrated as in Figure 9.5.

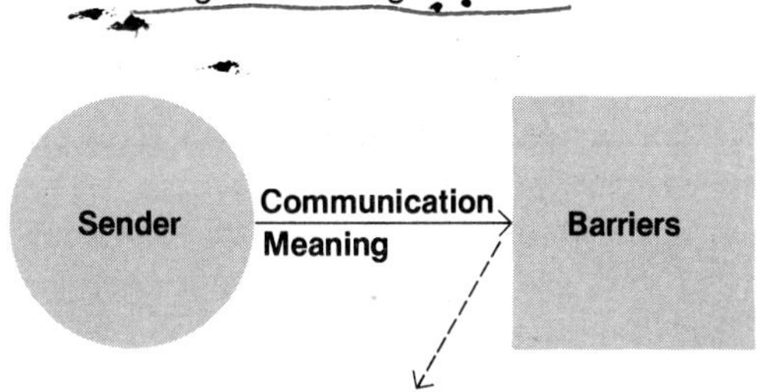

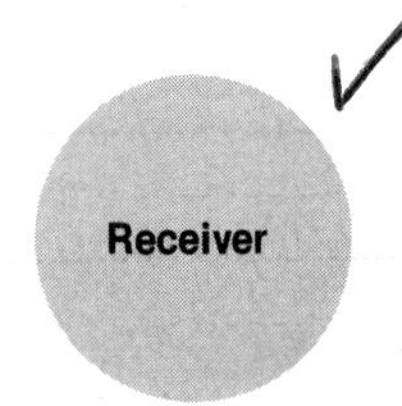

Figure 9.5 Communication Barriers

The barriers create a wall that blocks out communication meaning. As a result, whatever part of the message that does reach the receiver is, for one reason or another, misunderstood.

What kinds of barriers are there? Some of the major ones, which will be examined here, are perception, inference, and language.

Perception

▪ Perception is a person's view of reality.

Perception is a person's view of reality. Of course, no two people have had all the same experiences and training in life, so no two are going to see everything *exactly* the same way. However, for effective communication, it is often sufficient if the sender and receiver are "in the ballpark." A manager who tells a subordinate, "Meet me for lunch," may think the subordinate knows what time to show up. If the individual does not, a call to the manager's secretary may resolve the problem. Other times, however, more accurate and immediate interpretations are necessary. When outlining criteria for raises and promotions, the manager must be very careful to spell out precisely how personnel will be evaluated. This is the only way to prevent morale problems among disgruntled employees who feel they are being denied equitable raises or being systematically passed over for promotion.

In drawing together these two illustrations, it becomes obvious that the *field of understanding* between sender and receiver can sometimes be small, while at other times it must be great. For example, in illustrating the luncheon meeting time problem, Figure 9.6 shows that the field of understanding was, at least initially, not that great. And yet the outcome was appropriate. In the case of raise and promotion criteria, represented in Figure 9.7, the overlap must be very great. In both

Figure 9.6
Overlapping Fields of Understanding—Needed on Minor Issues

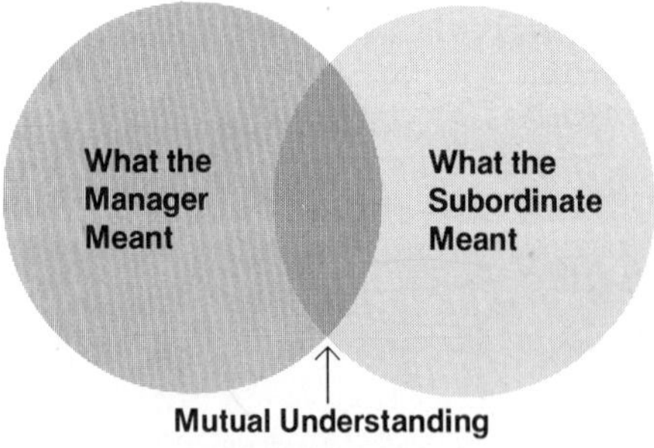

Figure 9.7
Overlapping Fields of Understanding—Needed on Major Issues

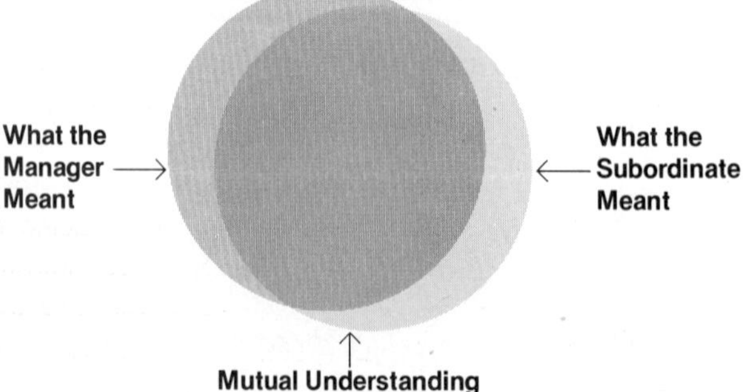

cases the receiver perceived the message the manager was sending. However, different degrees of mutual understanding were required.

On another, more specific level, perception explains why different people will see the same thing and interpret it differently. Surprising as it seems, this is true for both physical as well as more clearly interpretive events. For example, a sentence below appears in all capital letters. Read this sentence for content and then continue on:

FLEXIBLE WORK SCHEDULES FOR EMPLOYEES OF MANUFACTURING FIRMS CAN OFTEN RESULT IN BOTH PRODUCTION INCREASES AND HIGHER DEGREES OF MORALE.

Now that you have read the capitalized sentence, go back and count the number of times a particular letter appears. Here are your ground rules. In counting the number of times the letter appears, you may *not* use a pen, pencil, or finger. You may use only your eyes. You may read the sentence one more time, but take no more than ten seconds to do so.

Finished? Okay, now go back and reread the capitalized sentence, counting the number of times the letter F appears. Go!

Finished? How many Fs did you find? Most people say five. These are found in the words *flexible, for, manufacturing, firms,* and *often.* However, there are actually seven. Most people miss the F in the word *of,* which appears twice. Sometimes people do not perceive what is *actually* there.

The other side of perception, which calls for interpreting meanings, raises common questions, such as "What is being said?" "What is going on?" Figure 9.8 provides an example. What do you see in this figure?

Figure 9.8
Goblet and Twins

Some people see a goblet. Others see the profile of twins facing each other. What did you see? The picture is deliberately vague, hence interpretive. Many communications are the same way. It is difficult to understand the message because it has more than one meaning. When it does, people will perceive different answers.

Inference

An inference is an assumption

An *inference* is an assumption made by the receiver of a message. Inferences are commonly present in communications that are very long and/or involve a large number of facts. Unsure of the entire message content, the receiver reads into the communication and bases an interpretation on some assumptions. For example, a large eastern corporation has a travel-related rule which states that the company will pay all reasonable travel-related expenses. What does *reasonable* mean? One executive went to London, found the weather unseasonably cold for that time of year, and bought a raincoat. Upon returning, he filed the cost of the raincoat with his expenses, but the firm refused to pay it. In anger, he filed another travel expense two months later for a ten-day trip to the West Coast. Attached to the voucher was a note to the person who validates expense-related items. The note read, "Here are my expenses for my ten-day trip. Can you find the raincoat?"

Another common inference problem arises when people use words that have interpretive meanings. For example, a manager told an assistant, "Send this package to Ralph in the home office. It should get to him as soon as possible." Unsure of what "as soon as possible" meant, the assistant sent it air express. The cost was four times what it would have been had it been sent air parcel post. The manager then called in the assistant and chastised him for wasting money. "You should have sent it regular air mail. There wasn't that much of a rush." However, the assistant thought there was. He made an assumption, and he was wrong.

Language

Another common communication barrier is *language.* Words are often misunderstood or not understood at all. For example, what does the word *biweekly* mean? Most people know it means either twice a week or every other week. However, they are unsure. Therefore, if biweekly meetings are scheduled, people are likely to show up twice the first week and, if there are no meetings, then every other week.

In other cases, people use words to impress others, failing to realize that the words have no real meanings in their context. Often referred to as *buzz words,* such words are shown in Table 9.2.

People have different meanings for the same words.

Finally, there are technical words that are understood by members of a profession or organization but are unclear to outsiders. For example, in management training terminology, an OD (organizational development) specialist is a behaviorally trained person who seeks to improve organization climate by working with individuals and groups in achieving greater intraorganizational harmony. However, to another person, the term *OD specialist* may mean an individual who works in a drug program dealing with people who have overdosed. Or consider the term *OB,* which in the management field means organizational behavior but in medicine refers to obstetrics. Of course, the misuse of these terms will not likely get anyone in trouble. However, consider the case of the new secretary who was hired by a drafting department, given some blueprints, and told to burn them. Imagine her boss's surprise when he asked her if she had finished burning

Table 9.2
Buzz-Word Jargon

Many people will stop a conversation the minute the speaker begins to confuse them by throwing out too many ideas or events at the same time. However, few will stop the individual and ask what a particular word means. The listener hopes that the word eventually will make sense when considered in the overall context of the message.

As a result of such reluctance, buzz-word jargon has emerged. These words are used in groups of three and are designed both to confuse and impress the listener. The following are an example.

Column I	Column II	Column III
0. integrated	0. management	0. options
1. heuristic	1. organizational	1. flexibility
2. systematized	2. monitored	2. capability
3. parallel	3. reciprocal	3. mobility
4. functional	4. digital	4. programming
5. responsive	5. logistical	5. scenarios
6. optional	6. transitional	6. time-phase
7. synchronized	7. incremental	7. projective
8. compatible	8. third-generation	8. hardware
9. futuristic	9. policy	9. contingency

Here is how the game is played. Choose one word from the first column, one from the second, and one from the third. For example, combination 6–2–2 produces "optional monitored capability," while option 4–9–6 gives "functional policy time-phase." These phrases can be dropped into virtually any conversation or report, and they carry a ring of decisive, knowledgeable authority. Rather than ask what they mean, most people let them go by. If any anxiety is produced, it is within the receiver who thinks, "Wow, I'd better brush up in this field. I'm getting in over my head. I can't follow some of this." Few people, for fear of looking foolish, are willing to admit that they are lost. Yet, as can be seen, the phrases have no real substance. They are there to simply impress and/or confuse the receiver. And the best part is that 1,000 combinations can be made with the above group of 30 words.

them—that is, making a Xeroxed copy of them—only to learn that she had taken them outside and literally burned them. The two individuals knew different meanings for the same word.

Overcoming Communication Barriers

There are a number of ways of overcoming these communication barriers. Three of the most important are (1) understanding the steps in the communication process, (2) use of empathy, and (3) developing effective listening habits. The following sections examine each.

Understanding the Steps in the Communication Process

One of the first places to start to develop effective communication skills is with the communications process itself. Exactly what happens in this process, and where is communication breakdown most likely to occur?

The first step in the communication process is that of getting the receiver's *attention.* Is the party to whom the message is directed alert and prepared to

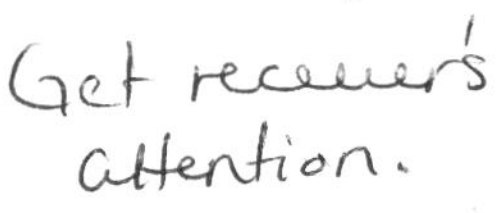

receive it? Or is the receiver daydreaming, looking out the window, or upset over some matter and unwilling to listen? In communication theory terms, attention can only be secured after *message competition* is overcome. Many things vie for the receiver's attention, and the manager must be able to win out over them.

■ Message competition must be overcome.

The second step in the communication process is *understanding.* Does the receiver comprehend the message? Does the person know what is being communicated? Many times, managers are convinced that the receiver does not understand the message. In an effort to prevent communication breakdown, they ask subordinates, "Did you understand what I just told you?" The subordinate often answers yes and then goes out and carries out the order incorrectly. Why? Because the receiver really did not understand, and the manager failed to follow up correctly. Never ask people *whether* they understand a message, for all of the pressure is on them to say yes. Always ask people *what* they understood. Have them repeat messages in their own words. In this way, managers can find out whether subordinates really know what was being communicated.

■ Never ask if, ask what.

The third step in communication is *acceptance.* Is the person willing to carry out the directive or take the required action? The manager should be particularly sensitive to signs that the receiver does not like what is being asked. If there is hesitancy on the part of the other party, the manager should follow through and determine why the receiver is reluctant to carry out the directive. If the individual cannot be persuaded to accept the order, now is the time to get someone else to do the job.

■ Is the receiver reluctant?

The last step is *action.* Was the appropriate action taken? Did the receiver do what was desired? Sometimes the individual will have trouble carrying out the directive. Other times, the person will be confused as to how to continue. In any case, the manager should be prepared to jump in and help out if trouble develops. Remember, the communication process does not end until the action desired by the communicator has been completed.

■ Follow-up action is required.

Empathy. *Empathy* is the process of putting oneself in another's shoes and trying to see things from that person's point of view. (See Table 9.3.) In the communication process, empathy plays a key role in two places: acceptance and action. When the manager gives an order that the subordinate is reluctant to accept, the boss should be tuned in and pick up the hesitancy. Empathy can help do this. In the action stage, empathy plays a key role in helping sensitize the manager to the subordinate's needs. When does the latter require some assistance, and what type of help should this be?

■ Empathy requires putting one's self in another's shoes.

One of the best ways of developing empathy is through the use of transactional analysis. *Transactional analysis,* or TA, as it is often called, is a method of examining interpersonal communication. At the heart of TA are what are called *ego states.* Everyone has three basic ego states: parent, child, and adult.[4]

People are said to be in their *parent ego state* when they act the way they feel their parents did. Generally, this occurs whenever someone acts officious or assumes the dominant role. (You do it the way I say!)

The *child ego state* contains many of the impulses of the infant. People are said

Table 9.3 Communication Games

There are many standard approaches to dealing with communication problems. The most common is that of showing people how to spot and avoid common barriers to understanding. Recently, however, communication experts have been coming up with new, innovative ways of training managers to deal with communication problems. These approaches use games that are both fun and educational.

One of the games involves giving all the participants a slip of paper with a song title on it. Each manager's job is to hum the melody and walk around the room and find the other manager who is humming the same tune. How can this help managers become better communicators? The answer is that it helps them come out from behind their managerial roles and let their hair down. Thus it is a good opener for communication sessions. Then the program gets down to more serious business. And depending on what the organization's problems are, the games will differ. A popular one is to have managers divide into two groups and work on a problem which requires a series of decisions. The team with the highest score wins the game. However, in order to get a high score, it is necessary to cooperate with the other team. Thus, it is a matter of winning through cooperation and effective communication. As the managers play these kinds of games, they begin to realize that communication is not only an effective managerial tool but also that cooperation can often help in getting the job done. The games show the importance of team play.

Do these communication games really help? Business firms report they do, citing declines in complaints from their personnel and increases in overall efficiency. As a result, it is likely that in the future we will see even greater use made of this approach to teaching effective communication to practicing managers.

Source: "Game-Playing to Help Managers Communicate," *Business Week,* April 9, 1979, pp. 76–78.

to be in this state whenever they are curious, impulsive, sensuous, or affectionate. The person is acting just the way he or she did as a child. (Let's leave work early and go bowling!)

The *adult ego state* is characterized by attention to fact gathering and objective analysis. Regardless of prejudice or emotion, a person who is in the adult ego state deals with reality from an objective standpoint. The individual analyzes the situation as dispassionately and realistically as possible. (Let's look at the facts!)

When people communicate with one another, they work out of one of these three ego states. For example, the manager may be speaking from his or her adult ego state, and the subordinate may be doing the same. Of course, this is only one of many TA transactions that can take place. However, when categorized, it turns out that there are three *basic* types of TA transactions: complementary, crossed, and ulterior.

■ Complementary transactions follow expected lines.

A *complementary transaction* is one which is considered appropriate and follows expected lines. Figure 9.9 provides an example. In the first part, the manager talks to the subordinate on an adult-to-adult basis, and the latter responds in the same way. In the second part, the manager and subordinate use a parent-to-child combination. When managers use complementary transactions, they are able to empathize with the receivers of their messages and respond appropriately to situations.

■ Crossed transactions involve unexpected responses.

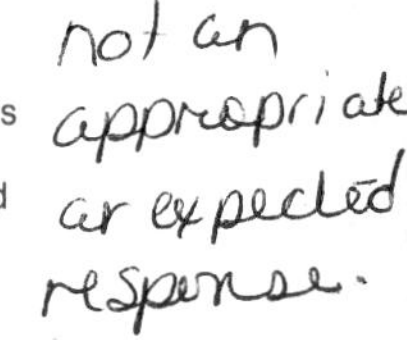

Crossed transactions occur when there is not an appropriate or expected response. Figure 9.10 provides illustrations. Notice that the responses are not what was expected. There is a problem, and by empathizing with the subordinate the manager can get the communication back on track. In particular, by analyzing the transaction and realizing that it has broken down, the manager can straighten out the situation.

Figure 9.9
A Complementary Transaction

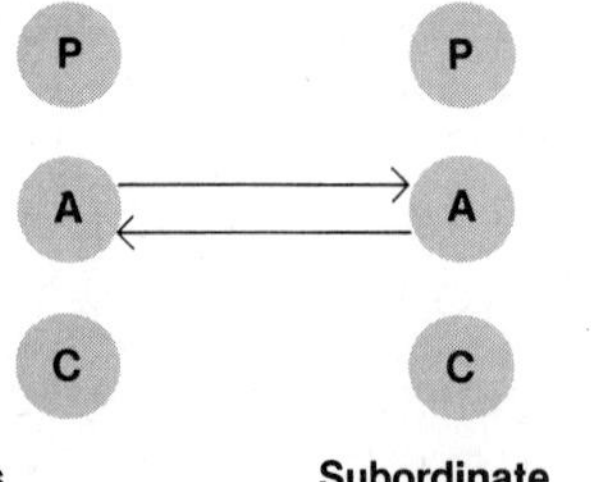

Boss
When will you be finished with that report?

Subordinate
I'll have it for you by 3:00 P.M.

Boss
I want you to handle this matter immediately.

Subordinate
Okay, boss. Whatever you say.

Figure 9.10
A Crossed Transaction

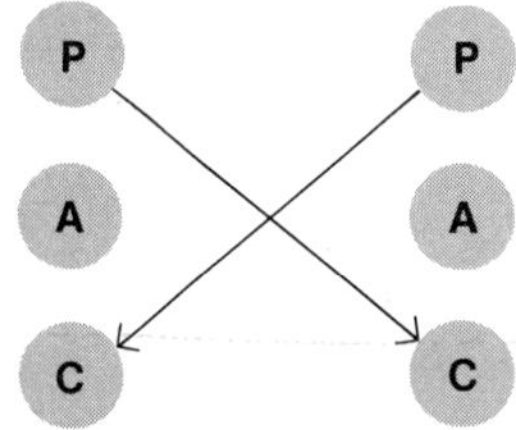

Boss
Your work is going to have to improve.

Subordinate
Where do you get off with that remark? My work is good and you know it.

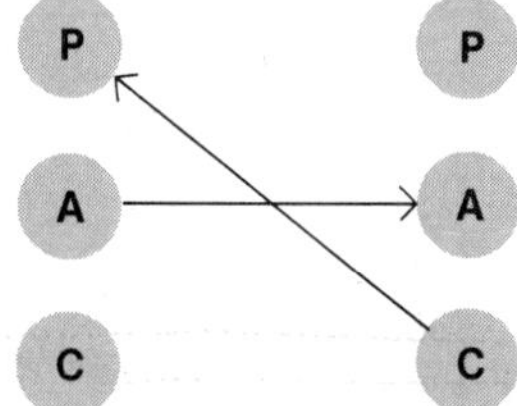

Boss
I'd like you to stay late this evening.

Subordinate
Oh, c'mon boss, I've got a heavy date. Why not ask Barney?

Figure 9.11
An Ulterior Transaction

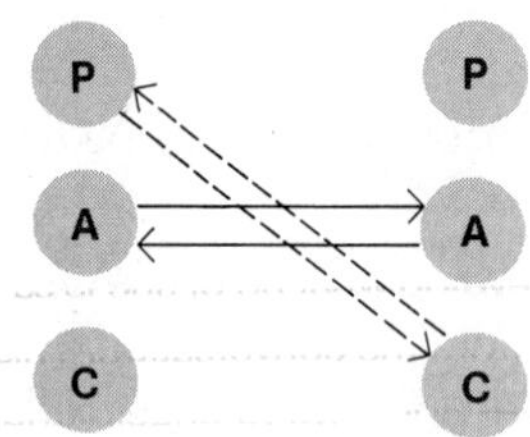

Boss
Do you know what time it is?

Subordinate
Yes, it's four o'clock. I have one hour left to get this job finished.

P = Parent A = Adult C = Child

The last type of transaction is known as *ulterior.* These are often referred to as disguised transactions, since one message is being spoken but another is being sent. Figure 9.11 provides an example. This is the most dangerous type of communication, because there are things going on behind the scenes. The manager in Figure 9.11 seems to be asking the individual about the time but is really saying, "Get moving!" The transaction is a disguised parent-child interaction.

How can a manager deal with crossed and ulterior transactions? First, the individual should refrain from personally using them. They are not helpful in getting things done. Second, when the manager encounters them, he or she should work to get the transaction back to a complementary one. Also, when appropriate, the manager should use the adult-to-adult complementary transaction. Most resistance comes from the parent and child ego states; and this can be overcome by moving into the adult state.

■ Ulterior transactions have disguised messages.

Developing Effective Listening Habits

Listening is difficult business. Research reveals that most people speak approximately 125 words a minute but are capable of listening to over 600 words a minute. This provides what can be thought of as "brain slack," which can be used for such things as daydreaming or thinking up responses to issues being raised by the speaker.[5] The best way to overcome these problems is to develop what are called effective listening habits. Often referred to as the ten commandments of good listening, the following are excellent guidelines for becoming an effective listener.

■ Guidelines for effective listening.

1. Stop talking. As long as you are talking, there is no chance for you to listen.
2. Put the speaker at ease. Let the other person know that he or she is free to talk.
3. Show the speaker that you are interested in what is being said. Do not read your mail or talk on the telephone while listening. Look and act interested. Also, listen for the purpose of understanding, rather than for a way to find things wrong with what is being said.

4. Remove distractions. Close the door or screen out noise. Tell the secretary to hold all calls. This creates the right environment for listening.
5. Empathize with the speaker. Put yourself in this person's shoes and try to see things from his or her point of view.
6. Be patient. Allow the individual plenty of time to develop what he or she is saying. Do not interrupt the person or start walking away from the conversation. This will simply turn the person off and diminish the chances you have to understand.
7. Hold your temper. An angry person often takes the wrong meaning from what is being said. Remain calm.
8. Go easy on criticism and argument, as these things put people on edge and make them defensive. If they have a problem which they relate and then find themselves getting yelled at, it is unlikely that they will come by to discuss such matters in the future. They will bottle it all up inside themselves and let it affect their work. Remember also: If you quarrel and win, you still lose.

9. Ask questions. This encourages the speaker to develop his or her ideas and shows that you are interested in what is being said. It encourages the person to go on with the conversation.
10. Stop talking. This is not only the first rule of effective listening, it is the last. All other commandments of effective listening depend on it.

Summary

Communication is the process by which meanings are conveyed from sender to receiver. This process has five basic elements: a source, encoding, message transmission, decoding, and a receiver. When viewed as a dynamic process, communication also includes feedback, so that the sender also becomes a receiver and vice versa.

The communication process is used in organizations for carrying messages both to and from individuals and groups. These communication flows move in four basic directions: downward, upward, laterally, and horizontally.

Sometimes, communication problems develop. These problems are a result of the physical and/or psychological setting. Examples of the former include noise, the room itself, seating arrangements, and the specific message transmission. Examples of the latter include the private and public self, timing, and body language.

More specifically, these communication problems bring about what are called communication barriers. Three of the most common are perception, inference, and inappropriate language. Perception is a person's view of reality. When the sender and receiver of a message do not have the same perception of what is being transmitted, communication breakdown is likely. An inference is an assumption made by the receiver of a message. When this assumption is incorrect, the receiver is likely to interpret the message *and* handle the situation incorrectly. Language is a problem when people use words inappropriately or interpret them inaccurately. In particular, whenever people have different meanings for the same words, communication breakdown is likely.

How can these problems be overcome? One way is through an understanding of the communication process: attention, understanding, acceptance, and action. If a manager understands these four steps and what should occur in each, the individual is in a good position to meet many of these problems. A second way of overcoming communication problems is by empathizing with the other person. The use of transactional analysis is especially helpful in this regard. Finally, the manager must develop effective listening habits. The ten commandments of effective listening can help here.

Review and Study Questions

1. What is meant by the term *communication*? Put it in your own words.

2. There are five basic elements in the communication process. What are they? Define them.
3. How do each of the following communication flows work: downward, upward, lateral, and horizontal? Explain each.
4. In what way can the following bring about communication problems: noise, the room, seating arrangements, and the form of message transmission?
5. How can an understanding of public self and private self be of value to the manager in communicating? Explain.
6. Timing and nonverbal language are two key areas which should be understood by managers wishing to communicate effectively. What does this statement mean?
7. In what way is perception often a communication problem? Explain.
8. What is an inference? How can it lead to communication breakdown?
9. Sometimes language causes communication breakdown. Describe what takes place when this happens.
10. What are the four steps in the communication process? Describe what takes place in each.
11. In your own words, what is meant by the term *empathy?*
12. In TA there are three ego states. What does this statement mean?
13. How does a complementary transaction differ from a crossed transaction? How does it differ from an ulterior transaction? Explain.
14. How can a manager develop effective listening habits? Cite at least five ways.

Key Terms in the Chapter

communication
encode
decode
downward communication
upward communication
lateral communication
diagonal communication
Johari window
perception
inference
language
attention
message competition
understanding
acceptance
action
empathy
transactional analysis
parent ego state
adult ego state
child ego state
complementary transaction
crossed transaction
ulterior transaction

Notes

1. Joseph Luft, *Of Human Interaction* (Palo Alto, Calif.: National Press Books, 1969).
2. Stanley Schachter, *The Psychology of Affiliation* (Stanford, Calif.: Stanford University Press, 1959), p. 24.
3. Larry L. Barker, *Communication* (Englewood Cliffs, N.J.: Prentice-Hall, 1978), p. 79.
4. For more on how TA works, see Muriel James and Dorothy Jongeward, *Born to Win* (Reading, Mass.: Addison-Wesley, 1971); and *Winning with People* (Reading, Mass.: Addison-Wesley, 1973).
5. Ralph G. Nichols, "Listening, What Price Inefficiency?" *Office Executive,* April 1959, pp. 15–22.

Case: A Communication Breakdown

Don't cross any bridges that someone else can burn in front of you.

Six months ago a midwestern city announced plans to build a bridge connecting the south side of the city with the community located on the other side of the river. This bridge will reduce commuting time for those residents who work in the city.

One of the local construction firms decided to make a bid for the project. As required by the city, the firm submitted a preliminary blueprint and plan of action. After the city council reviewed all of the plans, it reduced the number of companies to a final list of three. Tom Kemp was delighted with the news since his firm was one of the three. He hoped that the firm would get the job.

Soon after the final list was announced, Tom received a call from one of the people on the city council. The woman was a personal friend of Tom's. The two had gone to school together. She told Tom that his company's plan was ranked first by the city council and there was a very good chance that they would be given the job. However, no final decision would be made until more study had been undertaken. This would require about three weeks.

Upon hearing the news, Tom shared it with his boss Tony Farina, and the two of them decided to get a jump on the project. The bridge had to be built within nine months of the contract date. While this was possible, if the design and construction department started finalizing the blueprints and firming up contracts for materials and supplies now, they would be able to finish the bridge early and pick up some bonus money, since the contract would have a bonus clause for early completion and a penalty for late completion. Tony gave the okay and work began in earnest, although it was made clear that no one in the department was to say anything for fear that the city council would learn of it, resulting in a backlash against the company.

Just two days ago the council made its decision. To Tom and Tony's surprise, their firm did not get the contract. Furthermore, because they had invested so much time and money in finalizing the plans and making contracts for the materials, the company was in some financial trouble. The president called Tony into his office this morning and chewed him out. "You should never have proceeded with the bridge project without having the contract in hand. I realize you meant well and were trying to save the company money, but you should have at least cleared it with me or the vice-president of finance. It's going to take us three or four months to crawl out of the financial bind you've got us in. Now don't misunderstand me. You're a good manager and I'm going to keep you. However, I want you to use better judgment in the future. Remember, politics is a funny game. Just because you're number one on the list today doesn't mean you'll be there tomorrow." Tony promised to remember this advice and not make such a mistake again.

Questions

1. How did Tom and Tony get into this problem in the first place? What commun-

ication barriers brought this about? Explain, incorporating the communication process into your answer.

2. How could this problem have been avoided? What should Tom and Tony have done? In your answer, discuss communication flows.
3. What recommendations would you make to Tom and Tony to prevent problems like this from occurring in the future? Explain.

Case: The Busy Boss

Try to miss a good man before he's gone.

Andre Lefevere is considered a very competent manager. He has been given maximum salary raises during each of the last four years and received a major promotion last year. Three months ago Andre's boss left and another man replaced him. Andre had hoped for this promotion but realized that he did not have enough job experience to really do the job.

Last week Andre received a call from a competitor. This company offered him a position equivalent to that of his new boss. This would mean a large increase in both responsibility and salary. Andre is not sure he is ready for such a promotion. On the other hand, he has noticed that the new boss is not treating him as well as the old one did. In fact, he is certain that his chance of promotion is now less than it was under the old boss.

After thinking the matter over, Andre decided to have a talk with his new boss so that he could tell him about the competitive offer and get some input regarding his own future in the company if he stays. The meeting was set up for 9:00 A.M. However, the boss was late getting in and so it did not start until 9:30. Additionally, during their conversation people kept coming in and out of the office, interrupting the boss for his signature on a form or a fast comment on a particular decision. Andre found all of this disturbing. And the phone calls did not help, either. Nevertheless, Andre pushed on and tried to get his message across. The boss listened as best he could and told Andre that he thought Andre should stay with the firm. "You are certainly going to be moving up in this organization. It's simply a matter of time." However, the boss did not elaborate on this statement, and Andre could not get any type of promise out of him regarding when his next promotion might be coming. When he left the office, Andre felt defeated.

After lunch today, he called his wife and spoke with her about the meeting. "I don't know how far I'm going to go in this organization," he told her. "I can't get any promises or counteroffers to what the other firm has offered me. Nor can I get the boss's attention long enough to convince him that I'm going to move if I feel things are not going to go well for me here. I don't know. He just seems so busy with all of his work that he doesn't have time for me. I felt if I left the room it would have taken him five minutes to realize I had gone. This evening, let's talk things over. We may be making a change." His wife said that she thought this would be a good idea.

Questions

1. What physical and psychological setting problems were present during Andre's meeting that have given him cause for alarm?
2. What principles, or commandments, of listening does Andre's boss need to learn about? Could TA also help? How?
3. What would you recommend Andre do now? Explain.

Chapter 10 Motivation

Objectives of the Chapter
The overall objective of this chapter is to study motivation. How do you get people to increase their effort and work harder? In answering this question, attention will first be focused on what motivation is all about and why people often confuse motivation and movement. Then some of the basic theories of motivation, including Maslow's need hierarchy, Herzberg's two-factor theory, and McClelland's learned needs theory, will be reviewed. Next, attention will be directed to expectancy theory, which helps explain individual motivation and offers some guidelines for analyzing and increasing worker motivation. Finally, before concluding the discussion of motivation, everything will be tied together with an overall model of motivation in action.

When you have finished studying the material in this chapter, you should be able to:

1 Explain the two sides of motivation: movement and motive.
2 Identify and describe the five needs in Maslow's hierarchy.
3 Explain the two-factor theory of motivation and relate its value to the practicing manager.
4 Identify some of the learned needs people have and explain how an understanding of them can help managers motivate their workers.
5 Compare and contrast Maslow's, Herzberg's, and McClelland's theories of motivation.
6 Describe how expectancy theory can help the manager understand individual motivation.
7 Discuss the importance of equity in the motivation process.
8 Construct an overall model of motivation in action, drawing together much of what is currently known about the topic.

What Is Motivation?

■ Motivation involves movement and motive.

People who are hard at work are often referred to as *motivated,* while those sitting around doing very little are sometimes called *unmotivated.* The problem with using the term *motivation* this way, however, is that one is really measuring movement. Can a person who is quietly studying a book be motivated? If so, then motivation must consist of more than just movement. And it does; for there are two sides to motivation: *movement* and *motive.* The former can be seen, while the latter can only be inferred. Yet motives are important because they are the whys of behavior. They help explain why people act as they do.

Motives are the needs, drives, wants, and impulses within the individual that arouse and maintain activity. How do motives prompt people to action? In order to answer this question, it is necessary to realize that all motives are directed toward goals. Figure 10.1 provides an illustration. Another example is this: Roger needs money (motive) and so is willing to work overtime (goal). Harriett desires status (motive) and so will strive for promotion (goal).

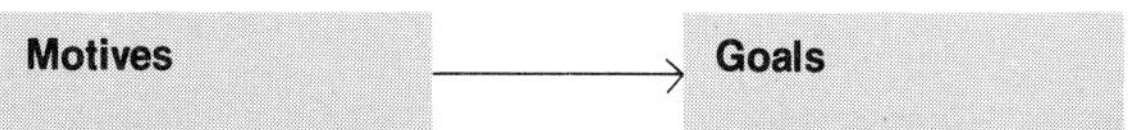

Figure 10.1
Motives and Goals

■ Need strength dictates action.

Of course, an individual often has *many* motives or needs and cannot actively pursue all of them simultaneously. In deciding which will be pursued, the person will opt for the one with the *greatest motive strength.* Using Figure 10.2 as an illustration, the individual will pursue Motive 5, since it has the greatest strength. Having satisfied this need, the individual will then move on to Motives 3, 6, 1, 2, and finally, 4.

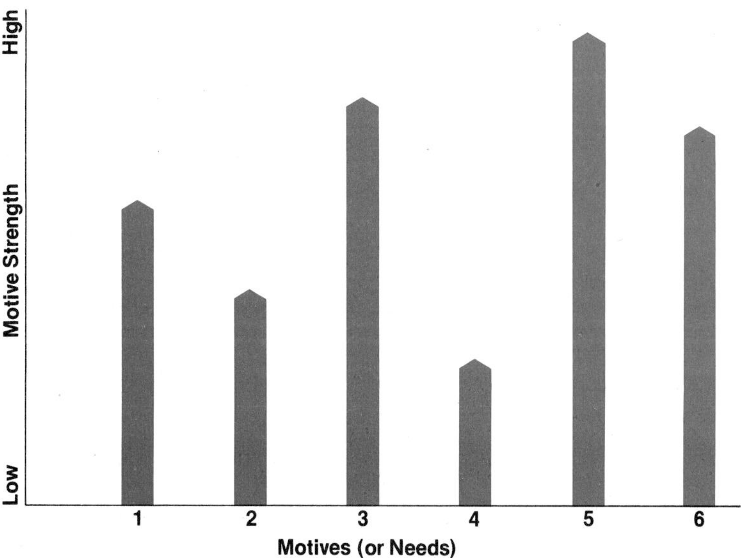

Figure 10.2
Motives and Motive Strengths

Drawing together this preliminary discussion, it is possible to explain motivation in terms of needs. Simply put, people do things that help them fulfill their needs, with the need having the greatest strength receiving priority. Having attained the strongest need, a person will then move on to the need with the next highest strength. This approach to motivation can be illustrated as in Figure 10.3.

Figure 10.3
Need Satisfaction and Behavior

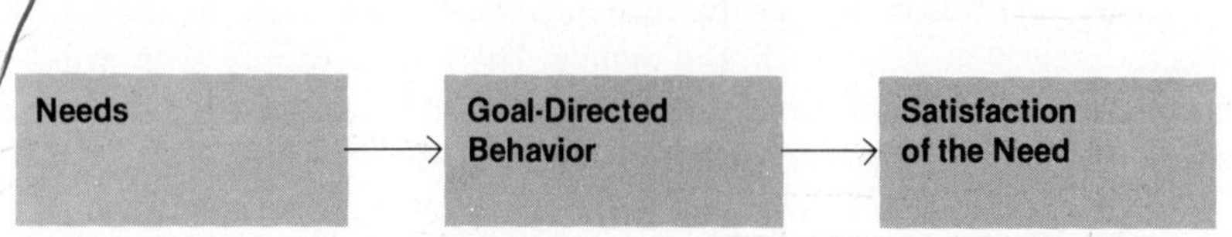

Of course, in order to determine what motivates someone, it is necessary to know the need the individual is pursuing. What types of needs do people pursue? Abraham Maslow has provided some answers to this question.

Maslow's Need Hierarchy

Abraham Maslow, the noted psychologist, set forth five needs which he contended were universal to everyone. These are (1) physiological, (2) safety, (3) social, (4) esteem, and (5) self-actualization.[1]

Physiological Needs

▪ Physiological needs are most fundamental.

According to Maslow, the most fundamental of all needs are *physiological.* Food, clothing, and shelter are illustrations. Deprived of everything, a person would try to satisfy these basic needs first, everything else being of secondary importance, as Figure 10.4 illustrates.

Figure 10.4
The Basic Need Hierarchy

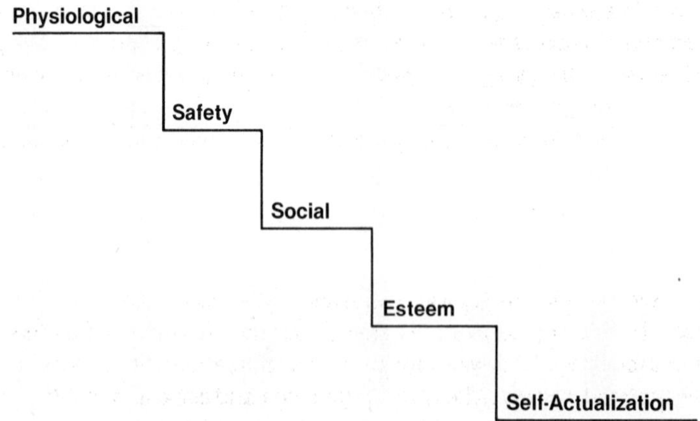

How do organizations help their people satisfy these needs? Many do so by providing adequate working facilities with good ventilation, heating, lighting; vending machines; cafeterias; and competitive salaries with which employees can purchase food and clothing.

Safety Needs

Once physiological needs are basically satisfied, *safety needs* will replace them. One of the greatest safety needs is *survival*. On the job this need is addressed through organizational efforts in providing safety equipment and safety rules. The other safety need is *security*. This is more important for most people, since there is a greater chance of losing one's job than in being injured at work. And if one is injured, a great fear is that of losing pay while recovering from the injury. As a result, many modern organizations provide security in the form of accident, health, and life insurance and retirement programs. Additionally, many of them often ensure job security through programs designed to guarantee employment to their people. In case of a cutback, the last hired is the first let go, thus providing jobs for those with seniority.

■ Then comes survival and security.

Social Needs

When physiological and safety needs are basically satisfied, *social needs* become important. These needs are satisfied through interaction with others. In their daily lives people socialize with their friends and neighbors. At work, they do the same with co-workers. This type of interaction is very important to them, especially if the work is boring or routine. Social affiliation helps make the job livable.

■ Followed by social interaction.

Esteem Needs

When physiological, safety, and social needs are basically satisfied, *esteem needs* move to the fore. These needs are psychological in nature, for esteem relates to self-respect. These needs can be satisfied *only* by the individual. However, organizations can help by creating the right climate for allowing people to satisfy these needs. One way is by giving promotions, so that individuals have something to point to when saying to themselves, "I'm really good. Look, I just got a promotion." Another way is by providing status symbols such as offices, rugs, and keys to the executive washroom.

■ And then comes self-respect.

Self-Actualization Needs

When all other needs are basically satisfied, *self-actualization* needs manifest themselves. Meeting these needs is often described as becoming all that one is capable of becoming. While not very much is known about these needs, research reveals two related motives. They are *competence* and *achievement*. People strive to be competent and master such things as work-related activities. Many also

■ Followed by needs like competence and achievement.

strive to achieve material things. More will be said about achievement in a later section.

The Hierarchy and the Worker

Maslow's need hierarchy provides an interesting point of departure in the study of motivation. It points out that people are motivated by unfulfilled needs. It also postulates that as lower-level needs are filled, upper-level needs replace them and remain important until lower-level ones again demand satisfaction. For example, sooner or later an individual will have to eat or sleep (physiological needs); so, regardless of where the individual is in the hierarchy, he or she then will drop back to the first level.

■ Maslow's approach needs modification.

However, a few parts of Maslow's approach are simplistic and warrant modification. First, while employees may have five basic needs, although this has never been proved to be true for all people, most U.S. workers do not spend very much time worrying about their physiological and safety needs. They tend to operate more at the middle and upper levels of the hierarchy. Therefore, in studying how to motivate people, it is necessary to devote greater attention to the psychological needs—social, esteem, and self-actualization. Finally, there are some need satisfiers that seem to affect *more* than one level of the hierarchy. Money is an example. With a million dollars, some people might be able to satisfy all of their needs from the lower-level physical ones to the upper-level psychological ones. For example, while money can buy food, clothing, and shelter, it can also lead to feelings of self-esteem ("I'm really important") and self-actualization ("with this money I can help make this world a better place in which to live"). As a result, while Maslow's approach is an interesting start, it is important to examine other motivation theories in order to supplement it.

The Two-Factor Theory

Another popular motivation theory is Frederick Herzberg's *two-factor theory.*[2] Based on research initially conducted by him and his colleagues among 200 accountants and engineers, the theory holds that two types of factors affect motivation. One of these is referred to as *hygiene factors* and the other is called *motivators.*

Hygiene Factors

When one hears the word *hygiene,* it is typical to think of such things as brushing one's teeth, taking a prescribed medicine for bronchitis, and putting a bandage on a cut. These hygienic steps all have one thing in common. They will either maintain or return the person to his or her *original* health. Brushing your teeth will not make them any stronger, but it will help prevent tooth decay. Thus, the individual has a choice: brush and maintain healthy teeth or take a chance on losing them. The same is true for a prescribed medicine. If the individual takes the medicine, the bronchitis will probably go away and the person will be as healthy as before. If the individual does not take the medication, pneumonia may set in and the person could die. Thus, hygiene merely returns things to their original state.

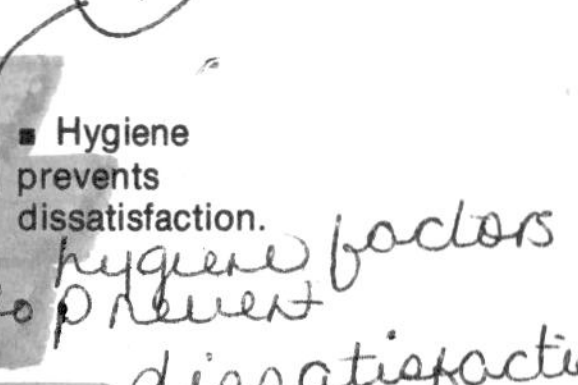

■ Hygiene prevents dissatisfaction.

When Herzberg used the term *hygiene* in his motivation theory, he was referring to things the company can do for the worker that will not motivate the person but which will stop the individual from becoming dissatisfied or unmotivated. Like physical hygiene, these remedies stop things from getting worse. Herzberg would put it this way: "If you give people these things I call *hygiene*, the result will not be motivation. But if you do not give them these hygiene factors, it will result in dissatisfaction and they will do less work." Table 10.1 shows some of the factors that Herzberg claims are hygiene factors.

Table 10.1
The Two-Factor Theory

Hygiene Factors	Motivators
Salary	Recognition
Technical supervision	Advancement
Working conditions	Possibility of growth
Company policies and administration	Achievement
Interpersonal relations	Work itself

Motivators

■ Motivators bring about positive feelings.

Motivators are those factors associated with positive feelings. These are things that stimulate people to do more and better work. Illustrations include recognition for a job well done, advancement, the possibility of growth, achievement, and the work itself. In explaining how motivators work, Herzberg would say, "If you give people motivators, they will do more and better work; but if you do not give them motivators, they will just keep working at their old level." In short, motivators tell the story.

The Two-Factor Theory and the Worker

The two-factor theory is an interesting one and has proved very popular with practicing managers. However, there are a few problems with it. In particular, one must be very careful about assuming that hygiene factors have *no* motivational force, while motivators will indeed bring about increased satisfaction and output. The list set forth by Herzberg represents findings from only 200 engineers and accountants; and while the study has been replicated with other groups, the findings are not universally applicable. Some workers feel that salary is indeed a motivator, although Herzberg lists it as a hygiene factor. Furthermore, other workers do not feel that increased responsibility, the chance for advancement, or recognition for a job well done are motivators. In short, Herzberg's list cannot be applied universally. The manager first needs to know the workers and, based on this knowledge, then can construct a list of what motivates each of them and what does not.

■ The theory has value.

On the positive side, Herzberg's theory does have value for managers. Perhaps its major contribution is the two groups into which job-related factors are divided: those that motivate and those that do not. What it says to the manager is that *not everything* a manager does for the workers will motivate them. Some of these things the workers expect, and so they will have no motivating potential. People expect good working conditions and technical supervision. Others, such as money, are short-run motivators, at best. A person getting a salary raise of $500 will be motivated to work harder, but how long will this motivation last? Research shows that it gradually begins to wear off, and soon there is no motivational potential left. Furthermore, if a person was given a $500 raise last year and this year the individual gets $300, the worker has just taken a psychological cut. People expect at least to keep getting what they have got in the past. Thus, money and other hygiene factors identified by Herzberg may increase over time, but their motivational potential is at best short-lived. And *the zero point escalates,* so that you can never give people less than what they currently have; you must always give them more.

■ But there are shortcomings.

On the other hand, there are many things that truly motivate people. For some it is job security; for others it is challenging work; and for still others it is recognition for a job well done. The manager needs to determine, to recast Herzberg's theory, what is a hygiene factor for each worker and what is a motivator. The list may not agree with Herzberg's findings, but that is not important. What counts is that the manager understands that whatever is a hygiene factor is expected by the worker but has no real motivating potential. As Herzberg says in his famous film, KITA, "Give them hygiene and shut up about it." Then the manager can concentrate on the motivators. Table 10.2 discusses some motivating factors.

Table 10.2
What Workers *Really* Want

A recent survey of American workers asked, "How satisfied are you with each of the following aspects of your job? And how important to you is each of them?" Here is how they responded.

	How Important Is It?	How Satisfied Are You with It?
Chances to do something that makes you feel good about yourself	1	8
Chances to accomplish something worthwhile	2	6
Chances to learn new things	3	10
The opportunity to develop your abilities and skills	4	12
The amount of freedom you have on your job	5	2
Chances that you have to do those things that you do best	6	11

	How Important Is It?	How Satisfied Are You with It?
The resources that are available to you in doing this job	7	9
The respect that you receive from the people with whom you work	8	3
The amount of information you get regarding your job performance	9	17
Your chances for participating in decision making	10	14
The amount of job security that you have	11	5
The amount of pay you receive	12	16
The way you are treated by the people with whom you work	13	4
The friendliness of the people with whom you work	15	1
The amount of praise you get for a job well done	16	15
The amount of benefits you get	16	7
The chances for obtaining a promotion	17	18
The physical surroundings of your job	18	13

The things that respondents liked best about their jobs were related to the friendliness of their fellow workers. When asked to rate the things they felt were most important, however, it was a different story. The respondents listed such things as the possibilities of self-growth, opportunities to develop their abilities and skills, to learn new things, and to accomplish something that makes them feel good about themselves. As seen above, fringe benefits, chances for promotion, and the physical surroundings of the job were very far down the list. Furthermore, report the people who conducted this study, 46 percent of the respondents said they would take a more interesting job even if it paid less than their present one.

Source: Patricia A. Renwick, Edward E. Lawler, and the *Physiology Today* staff, "What You Really Want from Your Job," *Psychology Today* Magazine, May 1978, pp. 56–57. Copyright © 1978 Ziff-Davis Publishing Company.

Learned Needs

Some researchers believe that many of our needs are a result of culture.[3] We learn them as we grow up in society. David McClelland believes that three of these learned needs are (1) the need for achievement, (2) the need for power, and (3) the need for affiliation.

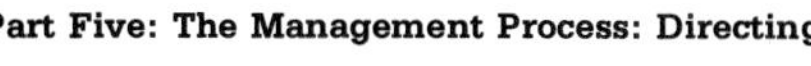

One way of determining whether an individual is higher in one of these needs than the other two is to give the person the Thematic Apperception Test (TAT). Figure 10.5 contains a picture similar to one on the TAT. Look at this picture and then, on a separate piece of paper, write down your answers to the following questions:

1. What is happening?
2. What has led up to this situation?
3. What is the individual in the picture thinking?
4. What will now happen?

Allow yourself no more than five minutes to answer these questions.

Figure 10.5
Photo for Interpretation

Need for Achievement

Are you achievement oriented? Do you have a need to achieve? If so, your answers to the questions should have included such things as: (1) the person wants to do a good job; (2) he is involved in a competition and would like to win; and (3) whether or not he wins, he will go on trying to succeed. The important thing is that the person wants to achieve an objective. He is goal oriented.

Of course, it is impossible to say whether someone is a high achiever by merely having the person interpret one picture. By seeing that individual's interpretations of a half dozen, however, a researcher could obtain quite a bit of information regarding whether the individual is achievement oriented. In addition to goal direction, some other characteristics of high achievers include:

■ Characteristics of high achievers.

1. A desire to take personal responsibility for success or failure, as opposed to depending on luck.
2. Moderate risk taking, as opposed to high or low risk taking.
3. A desire for concrete feedback on how well the person is doing.[4]

While only around 10 to 15 percent of the U.S. population has a strong desire to achieve, this need, or drive, can be both encouraged and developed. To do so, McClelland has recommended the following:

■ How to develop high achievement characteristics.

1. Strive to attain feedback so you know how well you are doing.
2. Pick out successful people and model yourself after them.
3. Imagine yourself as someone who needs challenge and success.
4. Control your daydreams by talking and thinking to yourself in positive terms.

The drive to achieve has at times been criticized as a factor leading to undue stress and even early deaths. Table 10.3 discusses those issues.

Table 10.3
It's Not All Bad

Talk to the average person on the street and the individual probably will tell you that stress is bad for people. In particular, people believe stress leads to such problems as heart attacks, alcoholism, nervous breakdowns, and flameouts (in terms of drive), to say nothing of death. Now, however, such thinking is beginning to come under attack. Some experts in the area are finding that executive stress may not be all bad. In fact, some argue that it is downright necessary, and high-powered achievers thrive on it! Take away the stress and you take away the motivation. Furthermore, evidence that has recently come to light shows that executives have a much lower rate of fatal heart attacks than do middle managers in the same companies. And what about alcoholism? Do not top executives have a much higher rate than that in the general population? Recent statistics show that they do not. Nor is the divorce rate any higher than the average for the population.

What do executives think about these findings? They agree. If a job lacks stress, they claim it lacks motivation. An individual cannot remain mentally sharp on a dull job. Of course, stress can result in physical problems but the key is learning to manage it. Good executives do not try to eliminate stress, they work on learning to live with it.

Source: "Executive Stress May Not Be All Bad," *Business Week,* April 30, 1979, pp. 96–103.

Need for Power

■ These people need to control or influence situations.

While the achieving individual wants to attain specific objectives—such as sell $1 million worth of goods this year or design two new products for the consumer market—the individual with a high need for power is interested in controlling or influencing situations. This person is often a more effective manager than the high achieving individual. The latter tends to be more interested in personal success while the power motivated manager gets things done through other people.

In interpreting the picture in Figure 10.5, people with high power needs see many things. A great number of them see the individual wanting to win a point, show dominance, convince someone about something, or gain a position of control. While not as strong a power motivated statement, interpretations related to wanting to teach or inspire other people also count in this category.

Another common interpretation is that the individual is thinking about how the reports in front of him can help him develop an action plan and, as a result, get him a big promotion. He is also thinking about how he will use this promotion as a stepping stone to the top. Notice in this analysis that the individual is interested in power. This is what is motivating him.

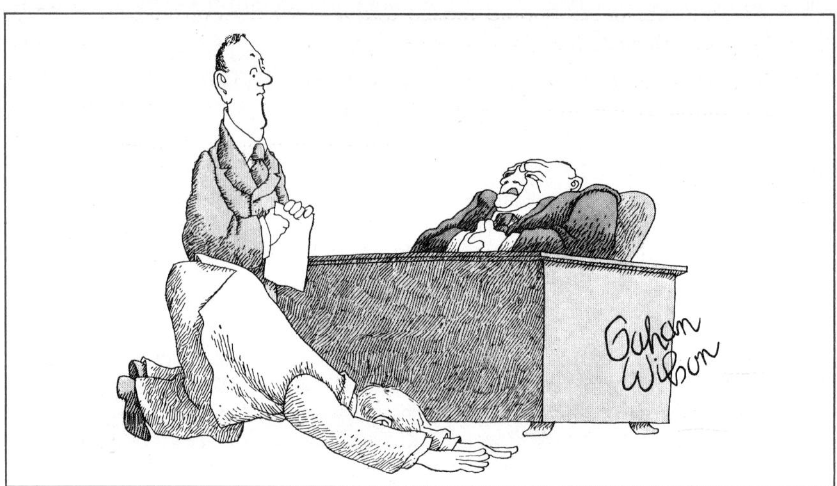

"You could learn a thing or two from Harrington, here, Wiltz."

Source: *Playboy*, February 1977, p. 184. Reproduced by special permission of PLAYBOY Magazine, copyright © 1977 by Playboy.

Need for Affiliation

■ These individuals like warm, friendly relationships.

People who have a high need for affiliation are interested in warm, friendly relationships. They like social interaction. In contrast to high achievement and power motivated people, they tend to spend more time communicating and collaborating with subordinates. They are very much interested in improving the overall climate of the organization and are often very good managers because of their concern for their people.

In interpreting the picture in Figure 10.5, individuals with a high need for affiliation see the man as thinking about his family and how proud they are of him. He misses them very much and will be happy when he can return home this evening and spend time with them. Notice that in these interpretations the responding individual is socially oriented. He or she is interested in being with other people.

Learned Needs and Motivation

The three learned needs just discussed are those that fit into the upper level of Maslow's hierarchy. The first two, achievement and power, come under

Herzberg's definition of motivators. The other, affiliation, is part of Herzberg's hygiene factors. Figure 10.6 provides a comparison of these three theories of motivation.

McClelland's research is useful in understanding motivation because it illustrates that some of the upper-level needs, to a large extent, may be learned. For example, in the United States many people spend a great deal of their time at the upper levels of the hierarchy, while in India this is not common. One reason is undoubtedly the climate, both economic and psychological, in which the individual grows up. If many Americans do have affiliation, power, and/or achievement needs, then the manager should realize that a good deal of time needs to be devoted to determining how these needs can be fulfilled. To a large degree, managers can provide for this type of need fulfillment by making the right climate available. Some of the ways in which this can be done include allowing the workers to interact among themselves (affiliation), giving recognition and advancement for a job well done (power), and providing workers the opportunity for personal growth on the job (achievement).

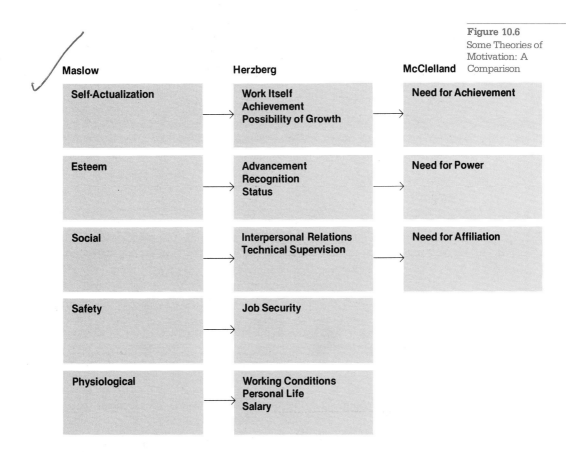

Figure 10.6
Some Theories of Motivation: A Comparison

Maslow		Herzberg		McClelland
Self-Actualization	→	Work Itself Achievement Possibility of Growth	→	Need for Achievement
Esteem	→	Advancement Recognition Status	→	Need for Power
Social	→	Interpersonal Relations Technical Supervision	→	Need for Affiliation
Safety	→	Job Security		
Physiological	→	Working Conditions Personal Life Salary		

Expectancy Theory

■ Content theories tell what motivates people.

The three theories that have just been examined are known as *content theories.* They have one thing in common: They are concerned with *what* it is within the individual or environment that stimulates or sustains behavior. They try to pinpoint the specific things that motivate people.

■ Process theories explain how motivation works.

Today a complementary approach is being used to explain motivation. The theories that fit within this domain are called *process theories.* Such theories are concerned with explaining *how* behavior is initiated, directed, sustained, and halted. The best known process theory is *expectancy theory,* which will be discussed here. A second popular one is *equity* theory, which will also be explained. The important thing to remember about process theory is that it takes into account learned behavior. People are motivated to behave in various ways based on the rewards associated with that behavior. How do they know what the rewards are? Either they have seen others rewarded for such performance, or they have been told what the reward is and they believe they can trust the individual who has told them. Note that these ideas are not addressed by the content theories examined thus far.

There is a great deal to expectancy theory, and much of it is beyond our scope of interest. However, it is currently very popular, especially among researchers in the field. Developed by Victor Vroom and based on earlier work by others, it has been expanded and refined by individuals such as Lyman Porter and Edward Lawler.[5] The essence of expectancy theory is expressed in the following formula:

$$\text{Motivation} = \text{Valence} \times \text{Expectancy}.$$

Motivation is equal to valence times expectancy. An understanding of these two terms, valence and expectancy, are basic to the study of expectancy theory.

Valence

■ Valence is preference for an outcome.

Valence is a person's preference for a particular outcome. This preference can be measured on a scale from +1 to −1. For example, consider the case of Andy, who has learned that he is about to be sent to one of his organization's three branch offices. He would very much like to go to the San Francisco branch, is indifferent about the Chicago branch, and does not want to go to the Dallas branch. Figure 10.7 illustrates Andy's valence for each outcome.

Expectancy

■ Expectancy is the perceived likelihood that a specific outcome follows from a specific act.

Expectancy refers to a person's perception of the probability that a specific outcome will follow from a specific act. This is a fairly complex definition. It says that in motivation people assign probabilities to rewards or outcomes. They learn the likelihood of pay increases or promotions. For example, Mary is pursuing a master's degree in business. She believes that with such a degree she will be given a promotion. What makes her think so? The fact that the last five people in the

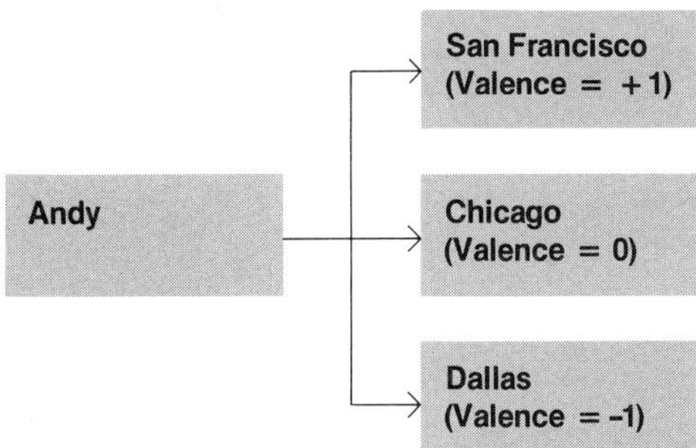

Figure 10.7
Andy's Valence

organization who received this degree were promoted. Thus, Mary has assigned a high probability to the relationship between finishing her master's degree and getting a promotion. Other alternatives were also available to her, including learning a foreign language, since there are occasional openings in the overseas branch offices, and agreeing to take on a new major assignment which would take a great deal of time but increase her chances for promotion. Mary has decided that the best way to get promoted is with the master's degree. Her expectancies can be illustrated as in Figure 10.8

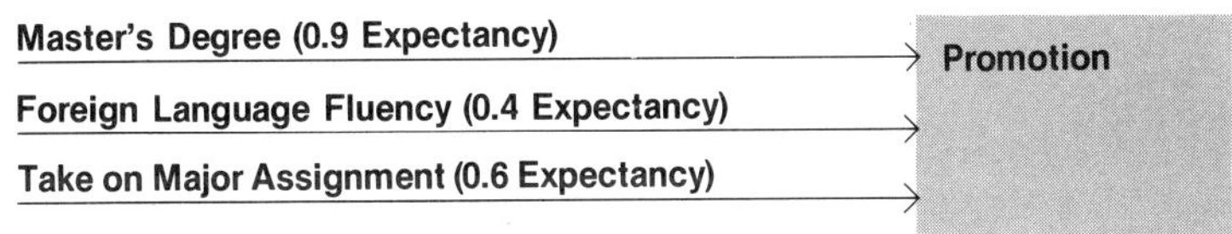

Figure 10.8
Mary's Expectancies

Remember that expectancy is a *perceived* probability and that it is influenced by what has happened in the past. People establish relationships between their acts and the rewards that follow based on what they have seen others receive. If George, the manager, says he rewards high performance with increased salaries, but everyone sees that he gives no greater increases to outstanding performers than he does to average performers, those who want money will not stay with George. They will go elsewhere because their perceived expectancy (probability) between higher performance and increased salaries will be low.

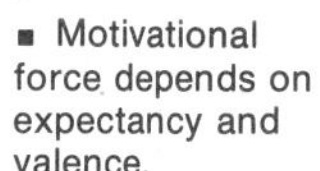

Motivational Force

The expectancy theory formula holds that motivation is a result of both valence and expectancy. This motivational effort, or force, will be high or low based on the values of valence and expectancy. In computing this motivational force, it is necessary to multiply one by the other. The following provides an example.

■ Motivational force depends on expectancy and valence.

Ralph has learned of a new sales force contest. It will start next week and run for two months. Whichever salesperson has the highest sales during this period will receive an all-expenses-paid two-week vacation for two to London, Paris, and

Amsterdam. Ralph has never been to Europe and would like very much to go. His valence is +1.0. However, while the vice-president of sales has announced the contest, Ralph is not sure that the contest has been cleared with the vice-president of finance. This happened once before and the company refused to award the prize, a trip to Hawaii, choosing instead to give the winner $500. For this reason Ralph has assigned the probability of winning the contest *and* getting the reward (expectancy) as 0.6.

Sara, another salesperson, has been to Europe and would like to return. Her valence for the trip is 0.85. However, like Ralph, she remembers the last time something like this happened and is concerned that it could occur again. On the other hand, she thinks it is unlikely that the vice-president would make the same mistake twice. Sara feels the contest has undoubtedly been cleared in advance with the vice-president of finance. Thus Sara's expectancy is 0.8.

Clark, a third salesperson, has just returned from Europe. He vacationed there with his family two months ago. His valence for the trip is 0.5. However, he knows the vice-president of sales very well and is convinced that the contest would not have been announced without having been cleared with the head of finance. As a result, Clark's expectancy is 1.0. He is certain that the winner of the contest will be given the all-expenses-paid trip.

Which of these three people is most motivated to pursue the prize? The answer can be found by multiplying their respective valences and expectancies:

	Valence	×	Expectancy	=	Motivational Force
Ralph	1.0		0.6		0.6
Sara	0.85		0.8		0.68
Clark	0.5		1.0		0.5

Based on the above calculations, Sara has the greatest motivational force. This means that she will be most likely to pursue high sales. Keep in mind, of course, that Ralph and Clark will also be interested in selling. But they will not be as motivated as Sara. Note also that while Clark has the highest expectancy and Ralph has the highest valence, Sara has the highest motivational force. Both expectancy and valence are important to motivation.

Expectancy Theory and Worker Motivation

Expectancy theory encourages the manager to look at two critical areas of motivation: (1) the worker's preference for a particular reward or outcome, and (2) the likelihood in the worker's mind that a particular act, such as high sales, will result in a particular outcome, such as a free vacation. Of course, no manager is going to walk around trying to determine the motivational force of each worker for every objective. However, there are several important reasons that expectancy theory is useful in understanding the motivation process.

First, most workers are at least minimally motivated to perform. They may not do the best possible job, but they are adequate. Thus motivation is a relative concept. It is present in some people more than in others, but it is present to some degree in just about everyone. The manager's job is one of determining how to increase this force.

Second, Maslow, Herzberg, and McClelland take a needs approach to examining motivation. This is an inner way of looking at the subject. How do you know when someone is motivated and what will keep the person turned on? With a needs approach, the manager takes an educated guess at which needs the individual worker is trying to fulfill. Expectancy theory approaches the subject from outside the individual. Rather than talking about unfulfilled needs, it examines motivation as a force that pulls the individual toward an objective. This force will be high if expectancy and valence are high and low if one or both of the factors are low.

Third, a needs approach examines motivation from a very general standpoint. Expectancy theory helps focus in on individual motivation. Some people may be more motivated by certain rewards than others, and this is reflected in their valences for their particular outcomes. Others realize that no matter how well they perform their jobs, everyone will receive the same rewards. When they do, will they work harder? Part of the answer is often found in the work itself. Those individuals who like their jobs and receive intrinsic satisfaction from doing them will work harder. If the worker enjoys a job and finds it satisfying, the individual's valence for carrying it out will increase. This will lead to higher motivation and an increase in output. Using a needs approach to motivation, it is difficult to see how techniques such as job enrichment can lead to increased satisfaction. With an expectancy approach, however, this is possible.

■ Expectancy theory also examines the issue of equity.

Finally, there is the topic of *equity,* which is really not discussed by the needs approach. Many times people are motivated or turned off not by what they are getting but by what others are getting. For example, Sam does an outstanding job and is given a 15 percent raise. Charlie does an adequate job and is given a 14 percent raise. Harry does a poor job and is given a 10 percent raise. Are these raises equitable? If Sam thinks they are, he will continue to work hard. If he feels that he is being shortchanged, this will negatively affect his performance. Do people really compare their rewards against those of others in the organization? They certainly do! In fact there is an entire theory of motivation, called *equity theory,* that describes and explains this process. We can diagram Sam's comparison technique in very simple terms as in Figure 10.9.

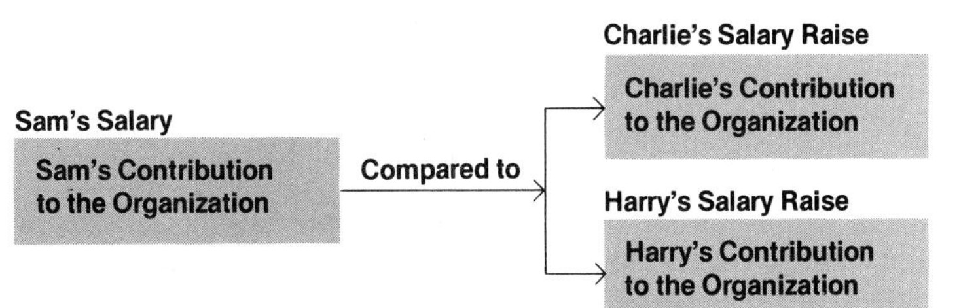

Figure 10.9
Equity Theory in Action

If Sam finds that either Charlie or Harry is getting more than his fair share of salary raises, Sam will modify his work output. Sam will either work less or try to figure out some way of getting more from the organization. If these courses of action are not possible, Sam will either stop comparing himself with these two people or he will leave the organization.

In any event, in order for there to be equity, Sam must feel that his ratio of salary to contribution is equal to those of the other two people. If not, there is inequity.[6] This will result in a decline in expectancy. Remember, Sam will now see less chance of high output bringing about high salary raises. He will come to believe that average output will bring about high salary raises.

Consideration of these kinds of issues has made expectancy theory an integral part of the current study of motivation. The theory has also been favorably received by researchers who want to study motivation at work. By concentrating on expectancy and valence, they hope to learn more about how to initiate, direct, and sustain worker motivation.

Motivation: An Overview

Motivation is a very complex subject. There is a great deal to it, and to put everything into an overall framework can be quite difficult. However, a sufficient amount of research has been done to allow us to construct an overall model of motivation. Figure 10.10 illustrates such a model.

Figure 10.10
Motivation in Action

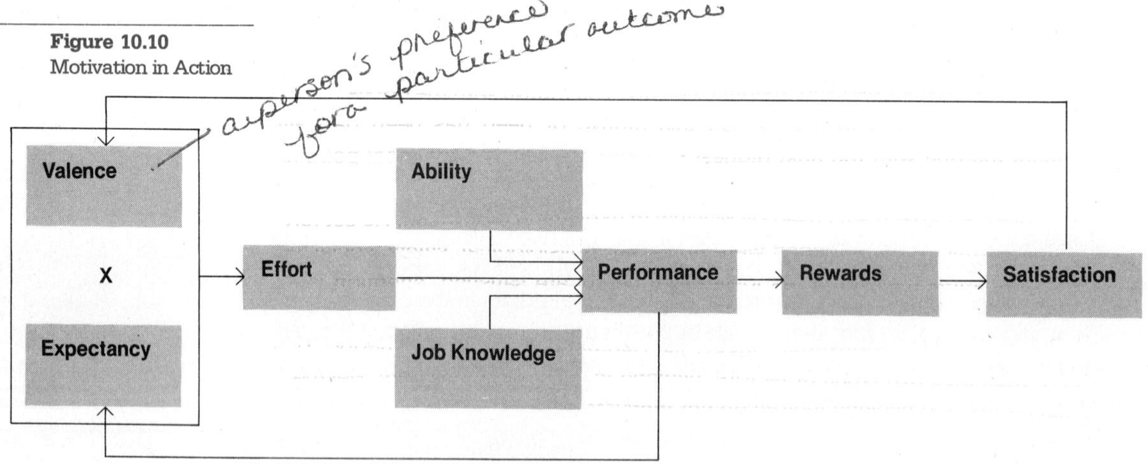

Note in the figure that an expectancy theory approach has been taken. This is because the needs approaches discussed by Maslow, Herzberg, and McClelland can be integrated under the topic of valence. Remember, if people have certain needs that require fulfillment, they will prefer those behaviors that help them satisfy these needs.

Expectancy, as was noted earlier, is the perceived relationship of probability between a specific act and a specific outcome that may follow it. When coupled with valence, the result is effort or drive toward a given objective.

The outcome of effort is performance. Notice, however, that ability and job knowledge have been placed in Figure 10.10. This is because effort alone will not generate performance. The individual also needs to have certain abilities and job knowledge in attaining performance.

Performance, in turn, leads to rewards. These rewards should be administered equitably; and based on the rewards that are given, workers will determine their expectancy. (Notice the arrow in Figure 10.10 running back to expectancy.) People will determine the relationship that exists between performance and rewards.

Finally, rewards lead to satisfaction. The subordinates will either feel they are being treated properly or being handled poorly. In either event, these feelings will affect their valence. This, of course, will affect effort, and the process begins anew.

Figure 10.10 incorporates everything that has been discussed in this chapter. It also provides a framework for analyzing the motivation process in action and for pinpointing where problems can occur and how they can be corrected.

Summary

Motivation has two parts: movement and motive. Movement can be seen, while motive cannot. However, motive contains the why of behavior. It explains why people act as they do. Motives are the needs, drives, wants, and impulses within the individual that arouse and maintain activity. The motive with the greatest need strength will be pursued first. When this motive or need has been basically satisfied, the one with the next highest strength will become the focal point for action.

This need approach was used by Maslow in explaining motivation. He set forth five needs which he contended were universal: physiological, safety, social, esteem, and self-actualization. As lower-level needs are satisfied, attention is focused further up the hierarchy.

Another popular motivation theory is Herzberg's two-factor theory. This theory examines two types of factors: hygiene factors and motivators. Herzberg contends that the hygiene factors do not motivate people but will be a source of dissatisfaction if they are not present. Illustrations of hygiene factors include salary, technical supervision, working conditions, company policies, and interpersonal relations. Motivators, meanwhile, are sources of satisfaction. If they are present there will be motivation, but their absence will not automatically cause dissatisfaction. Illustrations of motivators are recognition, advancement, possibility of growth, and achievement. While Herzberg's initial findings are under attack today, his basic idea of some factors having no motivational potential and others being very important does have merit. The manager's job is to determine which factors are motivational for the individual worker.

Some researchers believe that some needs are a result of culture. McClelland has identified three: the need for achievement, the need for power, and the need for affiliation. If the manager knows how motivational each of these is for the worker, it is possible to use this information in getting things done.

Recently, the content theories have been supplemented with process theories, which seek to explain how behavior is initiated, directed, sustained, and halted. At the heart of expectancy theory is a concern for valence and expectancy. The motivational force of each worker can be determined by multiplying the person's valence and expectancy. The higher the result, the greater the individual motivation.

As noted in the chapter, motivation is a very complex subject. However, by drawing together the concepts of valence and expectancy and relating them to effort, performance, rewards, and satisfaction, it is possible to get a picture of motivation in action, as was done in Figure 10.10.

Review and Study Questions

1. There are two aspects of motivation: movement and motive. What does this statement mean?
2. What are the five needs in Maslow's need hierarchy? Describe each.
3. How can a modern organization help its employees meet their needs at each level of Maslow's hierarchy?
4. In Herzberg's terms, what is a hygiene factor? What is a motivator? Cite some examples of each.
5. How can an understanding of the two-factor theory help managers more effectively motivate their subordinates?
6. What is a high achiever? Describe some of the individual's characteristics. Also, explain how people can develop the high achievement characteristics within themselves.
7. In your own words, how can a manager motivate an individual with a high need for power? What about someone with a high need for affiliation?
8. How does expectancy theory help explain individual motivation? Use valence and expectancy in your answer.
9. In what way does equity theory help explain motivation?
10. In your own words, what is motivation all about? Explain, drawing together all of your ideas into an overall model of motivation.

Key Terms in the Chapter

motive
physiological need
safety need

need for achievement
high achiever
need for power

social need
esteem need
self-actualization need
hygiene factors
motivators
need for affiliation
valence
expectancy
motivational force
equity theory

Notes

1. Abraham H. Maslow, *Motivation and Personality,* 2d ed. (New York: Harper & Bros., 1954).
2. Frederick Herzberg, Bernard Mausner, and Barbara Block Snyderman, *The Motivation to Work,* 2d ed. (New York: Wiley, 1959).
3. David C. McClelland, "Business Drive and National Achievement," *Harvard Business Review,* July–August 1962, pp. 99–112.
4. For more on this subject, see David C. McClelland, J. W. Atkinson, R. A. Clark, and E. L. Lowell, *The Achievement Motive* (New York: Appleton-Century-Crofts, 1953); and David C. McClelland, *The Achieving Society* (Princeton, N.J.: Van Nostrand, 1961).
5. For more on expectancy theory, see Victor H. Vroom, *Work and Motivation* (New York: Wiley, 1964); and Lyman W. Porter and Edward E. Lawler III, *Management Attitudes and Performance* (Homewood, Ill.: Irwin-Dorsey, 1968).
6. For more on this equity theory, see Stacy Adams, "Inequity in Social Exchange," in *Advances in Experimental Social Psychology,* ed. L. Berkowitz (New York: Academic Press, 1965).

Case: Take It from Harvey

How do I motivate the permanents, the power drivers, and the salespeople?

Managing a sales office is probably the most difficult thing Harvey Hendrix has ever done. At least it sounded that way to Tim Flanagan, who is to replace Harvey next week. Tim came on board a few days ago to get a feel for the job, and Harvey has been explaining the ropes to him. From what Tim can make out, Harvey has all kinds of people reporting to him, and each one seems to require a different approach.

For example, in the office there are two types of people. Harvey refers to them as "the permanents" and "those who are on the way up." The former are typists, secretaries, and people who are going to work at the office indefinitely. While money motivates them and they are looking for job security, they also want the chance to socialize with their fellow workers. Those on the way up, on the other hand, seem more interested in power. "You can pick them out right away," says Harvey, "because they do not spend too much time socializing. They are very businesslike and want to influence or control situations, in contrast to the others, who just want to get along with everyone."

Finally, there are the salespeople in the field. These individuals constitute a third type. They tend to be very much interested in success and achievement. They want feedback on how well they are doing, like to strive after difficult but achievable objectives, and do not seem to hold power or affiliation in as high esteem as do the people in the office.

"You'll be working with a lot of different groups of people in this office," Harvey told Tim. "What you need to do is to pinpoint what motivates each and give it to them. If you do, you'll find it easy to manage them. However, if you ruffle their feathers you could be in for a lot of trouble." Tim has promised to take Harvey's advice to heart and keep alert regarding what motivates each of these three groups.

Questions

1. Using McClelland's learned needs as your guide, what motivates the permanents? The people on the way up? The salespeople?
2. Applying Maslow's need hierarchy to the three groups, how should Tim go about trying to motivate each group?
3. Using Herzberg's two-factor theory, how can Tim apply these ideas to the three groups? Would he use the same approach with each, or would there be a need to tailor each approach? Explain.

Case: Ruth's Way

How do you remotivate the highly motivated after someone frustrates them for two years?

Things had not been going well in the department when Ruth Walpole took over. Production output was at an all-time low, and there were tardiness and absenteeism problems with most of the workers.

Ruth decided to start off by talking to some of the workers and trying to find out what the real causes of the problems were. After a week of investigation, she felt she had a pretty good idea of what had gone wrong. It seemed that the last department head's philosophy had been to keep everything running smoothly. In doing so, he spent most of his time praising and giving support to those workers who were either friendly to him or did not cause him any problems. Unfortunately, most of the people in this group were the low producers. The individuals who did most of the work were always on his back to get better equipment, to fight for them for higher budgets, and to recommend them for merit pay increases and/or promotions. The boss did not like this approach, and he went out of his way to treat these people poorly.

During the two years that this individual was in charge of the department, no high producer was recommended for a promotion and few received merit increases. All of these rewards went to the low producers. As a result, the high producers began making even more trouble for the department manager and doing less and less work. Overall output began to drop, problems began to increase, and the company finally stepped in and replaced this individual with Ruth.

Ruth decided to quickly turn the department around. To start, she has called everyone together and told them that from now on merit pay increases and promotions would be based strictly on output. Tardiness and absenteeism would no longer be tolerated, and she would dismiss anyone who continually showed up late.

During the last five weeks Ruth has lived up to these promises. In turn, output is now increasing, and the high producers report that they like her methods very much.

Questions

1. Using valence and expectancy in your answer, explain how Ruth has managed to increase the motivational forces of the high producers.
2. Is Ruth taking equity theory into account? Explain your answers.
3. In overall terms, what is Ruth's philosophy of motivation? Use Figure 10.10 to explain your answer.

Chapter 11 Leadership

Objectives of the Chapter

As we saw in the previous chapter, it is important to have motivated personnel. However, motivation is not enough. There must also be effective leadership. Employees have to be directed. The first objective of this chapter is to study the nature of leadership. In doing so, we will review some of the basic philosophies that managers have about their subordinates and see how these affect their leadership style. Then we will study the types of power that leaders have over their people.

The second objective is to examine the traits and characteristics often found among successful leaders. Particular attention will be directed toward studying both leadership characteristics and personal characteristics.

The third objective of this chapter is to look at leadership behavior. How do leaders act? In answering this question, we will look at authoritarian, paternalistic, and participative leadership. We will also study a two-dimensional approach to leadership, looking at the importance to the leader of concern for work and concern for people.

Finally, an examination of contingency leadership will be undertaken. Two of the most popular contingency theories will be studied, as we attempt to discover in what settings an autocratic leader and a participative leader will be most effective.

When you have finished studying the material in this chapter, you should be able to:

1. Define the term *leadership.*
2. Compare and contrast the tenets of Theory X and Theory Y.
3. Identify the five basic types of power.
4. Describe some of the most common leadership and personal characteristics found among successful leaders.
5. Explain how authoritarian leaders go about directing their people and compare this to the approach used by paternalistic and participative leaders.
6. Describe leadership in two-dimensional terms and relate the value of the managerial grid to the study of leadership.
7. Explain Fred Fiedler's contingency theory of leadership and tell how it can be of value to practicing managers.
8. Briefly describe the path-goal theory of leadership and explain how it can be of value to the modern supervisor.
9. Present an integrative model of leadership, pulling together much of what is currently known about effective leadership styles in the work place.

The Nature of Leadership

Leadership is the process of influencing people to direct their effort toward the achievement of some particular goal(s). How does the leader do this? There are various ways, but all are influenced by two factors: (1) the individual's personality and (2) the power the person wields.

■ Leadership is an influence process.

Some people seem to have an inborn leadership personality. They know when to praise people and encourage them to try harder and when to keep them on a short leash and control their activities very closely. Most successful leaders use the first of these approaches when possible, believing that it is better to treat people well than to use fear or threats of punishment. Nevertheless, there are times when it is necessary to employ control. For example, during crisis situations, effective leaders are very autocratic. A democratic, participative approach will not work well because there is no time to seek group consensus. (See Table 11.1.) The leader must act firmly and decisively. However, since most situations do not involve crises, a participative approach tends to be more effective in most cases.

Table 11.1
Making Winners out of Losers

While autocratic management may not work well in most situations, there are times when it is an ideal style. The classic case is that of turning losing firms into winners. And this is what Miller Myers does for a living. Buying firms that are in financial difficulty, weeding out the losing segments of the operation, building up the winning part, and then selling the firm is what it is all about in his book.

Starting out in the early 1960s Myers secured a large ice cream retailer from a nearly fatal struggle with the original franchisers. From here he went on to gain control of an incinerator manufacturer, a furnace designer, and a manufacturer of oil refinery cracking equipment, to name but three others. In each case he has put the firm back into the profit column, and in some instances then sold it off to provide funds for still other acquisitions.

And while his purchasing strategy may change, his leadership style remains the same. Using a "get tough" approach, he manages to turn losers into winners. Some people do not like this approach, feeling Myers is not humanistic enough. However, judging by the results, it is obvious that he knows how to turn losers around, something that would not be possible if he were to employ a very democratic easygoing style.

Source: "The Miller Myers Formula for a Turn-Around," *Business Week,* September 11, 1978, pp. 108–109.

Theory X and Theory Y

Why are some managers more autocratic or democratic than others? In addition to the environment in which the managers work, one must consider their basic leadership style. Do they tend to favor one style over another? If so, then it is likely that they will use this one more often.

In describing these styles, it is helpful to use Douglas McGregor's Theory X and Theory Y paradigm. These two terms relate to basic philosophies that managers have regarding why employees work and how they can be motivated. *Theory X* holds the following:

■ Theory X tenets.

1. People have an inherent dislike of work and will avoid it where possible.
2. To get these individuals to work, it is necessary to use coercion and threats of punishment.

3. The workers actually like to be directed.
4. The average person has little ambition and above all else, wants security.[1]

As can be seen from the above description, managers who subscribe to Theory X believe that the worker is lazy, uncreative, and in need of constant prodding. This calls for a specific type of leadership style.

On the other hand, there are some managers who subscribe to what is called *Theory Y*. This theory holds the following:

■ Theory Y tenets.

1. Work is as natural as rest or play and people do not inherently dislike it.
2. Coercion and threats of punishment are not the only ways to get people to work.
3. Under the right conditions, individuals not only seek responsibility, but willingly pursue organizational goals.
4. The ability to exercise a relatively high degree of imagination, ingenuity, and creativity in the solution of organizational problems is widely distributed in the population.[2]

These assumptions lead the manager to be much more open and trusting in his or her relationships with the subordinates. The managers see the subordinates as creative, interested in doing a good job, and capable of being motivated.

What do most managers believe in: Theory X or Theory Y? While Theory Y sounds logical to most students of management, in practice most managers are Theory X types. They do not totally believe the theory, but they do feel that there is a great deal of truth in it. Thus, while they may not use an exploitive, autocratic style with their employees—that is to say, they do not take deliberate advantage of workers and treat them terribly on principle—they are "soft Theory X" types. This means that they tend to use close control with their employees, not giving them much of a free rein. They also believe that while the subordinates might work hard on occasion, the individuals will not sustain this effort for very long. As a result, the manager needs to remain alert so that employees will not try to take advantage of any situation. Of course, in some cases this soft Theory X description is an accurate one. However, it does not hold in every situation. In fact, in many cases the Theory Y description is a more accurate one.

Power and Leadership

Regardless of whether they subscribe to Theory X or Theory Y, leaders, by definition, have power. This power can take various forms. There are five basic types in all: reward power, coercive power, legitimate power, referent power, and expert power. They can be described this way:

■ Types of power.

- Reward power. This is power held by leaders who can give rewards such as increases in pay, bonuses, or promotions to those who do a good job. Most managers have this type of power.
- Coercive power. This is power held by those who can fire, demote or dock the pay of subordinates who do not comply with orders. Many managers also have this type of power.

- Legitimate power. This is power that is vested in the manager's position. For example, a vice-president has more legitimate power than a supervisor. This power comes with the position and all managers have it.
- Referent power. This is power based on followers' identification with the leader. If the followers believe the leader is competent, interested in their welfare as well as that of the organization, and has a pleasing personality, referent power is likely to be high. Not all leaders have this power, although it is something the managers should strive to acquire.
- Expert power. This is power held by those individuals who are viewed by their subordinates as competent in their job. Leaders who have demonstrated the ability to implement, analyze, evaluate, and control group tasks are often seen as knowledgeable in their jobs and they acquire expert power. Not all leaders have this power, although they should strive for it.[3]

Research shows that of all five types of power, expert power has been found to be strongly and consistently related to satisfaction and performance. Legitimate power is also very important. Referent power and reward power have been found to be of intermediate importance. Coercive power is the least valuable in bringing about compliance to leader directives. Nevertheless, depending on the situation, any one of the five can be of value to the leader.

Traits and Characteristics

While an understanding of Theory X, Theory Y, and power helps explain the nature of leadership, there has been one overriding question that both students and practitioners have asked about leadership: Are there any traits or characteristics that tend to differentiate the effective from the ineffective leader? From 1920 to 1950 a great deal of research was conducted on this topic, and some still continues today. Popularly known as *trait theory*, it seeks to discover a list of universal traits which distinguish successful and unsuccessful leaders. The findings to date can be divided into two categories: leadership characteristics and personal characteristics.

Leadership Characteristics

Leadership characteristics are those qualities that are required in successful leaders. Are there such characteristics? Ralph Stogdill, one of the leading authorities in the field of leadership study, reviewed the literature and found that there is no universal list of characteristics possessed by successful leaders and not possessed by the others. However, he has concluded that some characteristics seem to differentiate leaders from followers, effective leaders from ineffective leaders, and high-echelon from low-echelon leaders. Some of these are the following:

■ Common leadership characteristics.

1. A strong desire for responsibility and task completion.

2. Vigor and persistence in the pursuit of goals.
3. Venturesomeness.
4. Originality.
5. Drive to exercise initiative in social situations.
6. Self-confidence.
7. A sense of personal identity.
8. Willingness to accept the consequences of one's decisions.
9. Readiness to absorb interpersonal stress.
10. A willingness to tolerate frustration and delay.
11. The ability to influence behavior.
12. The capacity to structure social interaction systems to the purpose at hand.[4]

Personal Characteristics

Personal characteristics are not found only in leaders. They occur throughout the population. However, they are of particular importance to leaders because without them the individual would be less effective. Some of those most commonly cited include the following: (1) superior mental ability, (2) emotional maturity, (3) motivation drive, and (4) problem-solving skills.[5]

■ Leaders have above average mental ability.

Superior Mental Ability. Successful leaders tend to have superior mental ability. This finding is well supported by research. For example, after reviewing hundreds of studies, E. E. Ghiselli has reported that success in a management position can be forecast by, among other things, intellectual ability.[6] Some of the studies also found that high verbal ability is a useful predictor of top management success. Of course, mental ability is not the *only* factor that helps predict managerial performance; but it is certainly an important one.[7]

■ Are self-confident.

Emotional Maturity. Leaders are self-confident and able to direct their people in a calm, conscientious manner. They do not fly off the handle or act irrationally. They maintain control of both themselves and the situation. Additionally, to the surprise of many management students, they are neither ulcer prone nor workaholics.

■ Have high motivation drive.

Motivation Drive. Effective leaders have high motivation drive. They are particularly interested in achieving power and self-actualization over situations they control. In fact, successful leaders tend to be more interested than their less successful counterparts in upper-level need satisfaction (self-actualization and esteem) and have subordinates with the same interests. What about lower-level need satisfaction? This, the successful leader feels, should be taken care of automatically, so as to free up the entire work group to pursue these higher-level needs.

■ And problem-solving skills.

Problem-Solving Skills. Effective leaders also have problem-solving skills. They see a problem as both a challenge and an opportunity to prove their managerial abilities. In approaching problem solving, they research the matter carefully, deciding the best approach to use. Then they move into action. If the problem is too complex or if they feel they are unprepared to deal with it, they either postpone action or bring in additional assistance. However, they do not go in unprepared. They know what they are doing.

Leaders: Born or Made?

Leaders are born and made.

Based on the leadership and personal characteristics just examined, one might ask: Are leaders born or made? The answer is a combination of the two. A person born with low mental ability may have great difficulty filling a leadership position. However, to a large degree, intelligence merely opens the door to leadership. After the initial breakthrough, it is a matter of how the person will respond to the challenges that he or she faces. This is where the leader is made or fashioned by the environment. The process starts when the person is quite young, with the parents serving as role models. The child learns from the parents. The child also is influenced by the environment in which he or she grows up. To a large degree, the desires to assume responsibility, to be venturesome, to develop one's originality, to absorb stress, to solve problems, and to be a high achiever can be taught. In the right environment an individual's chances of developing the right leadership and personal characteristics can be improved.

In most organizations, however, little attention is given to whether the individual is a born leader or has developed many of the necessary traits. The important thing is whether the person is effective in getting things done. Additionally, it is easier, and to some more logical, to study leadership behavior on the job, noting what works and what does not work. As a result, while an analysis of the characteristics presented here provides an introduction to the study of leadership, it is equally important to understand leadership behavior at work.

Leadership Behavior

Trait theory is concerned with what leaders *are*. A leadership behavior approach is concerned with what leaders *do*. While there are a number of ways of studying leadership behavior, the following will examine two of the most popular. The first is a one-dimensional model and the second is a two-dimensional model.

Continuum of Leadership Behavior: A One-Dimensional Model

One of the most basic ways of examining leadership behavior is to look at the various styles that can be used. Figure 11.1 provides an example of a leadership continuum. Notice on the left of this figure that the manager is making all decisions and then announcing them to the subordinates. On the right side of the figure the manager is permitting subordinates to function within defined limits. The manager who operates on the left side of the continuum is often referred to as boss-centered, or authoritarian, while the person on the right side is subordinate-centered, or participative.

Figure 11.1
A Continuum of Leadership Behavior

Use of Authority by the Manager | **Area of Freedom for Subordinates**

Boss-Centered Leadership | **Subordinate-Centered Leadership**

Manager makes decision and announces it.	Manager "sells" decision.	Manager presents ideas and invites questions.	Manager presents tentative decision subject to change.	Manager presents problem, gets suggestions, makes decisions.	Manager defines limits; asks groups to make decision.	Manager permits subordinates to function within limits defined by superior.

Source: Reprinted by permission of the Harvard Business Review. The exhibit is from "How to Choose a Leadership Pattern" by Robert Tannenbaum and Warren H. Schmidt (May–June 1973), p. 164.

■ Authoritarian leaders are work centered.

Authoritarian Leadership. Authoritarian leaders tend to be heavily work centered with major emphasis given to task accomplishment but little concern to the human element. As was noted earlier, these managers can be very effective in crisis situations. They are also ideal in cases calling for maximum attention to efficiency, profits, objectives, and other task-related activities. Unfortunately, there are not a great many cases where the authoritarian leader is superior to the participative leader—although there are a large number of managers in modern organizations who are authoritative in nature.

■ Paternalistic leaders are soft Theory X types.

Paternalistic Leadership. Many managers are best described as paternalistic. While they are heavily work centered, they also have consideration for the personnel. They tend to look after their workers the way a father does his family. Their basic philosophy is best described with a cliché: Work hard and I'll take care of you. These are the individuals we referred to earlier as soft Theory X types. While they like to be in charge, they also want subordinates to follow their leadership direction. In contrast to authoritarian leaders, who may force their style on the followers, paternalistic leaders encourage the subordinates to go along for everyone's sake. They like people to be team players, while they decide what the team will do. This manager functions in the middle of the continuum in Figure 11.1.

Source: *Saturday Evening Post*, May-June 1973, p. 76. Reprinted with permission from the Saturday Evening Post Company, © 1973.

"Believe me Jones, I'd quit this job tomorrow if it wasn't for the money, prestige and power."

Participative Leadership. Participative leaders have a high concern for both people and work. Note in Figure 11.1 that while this manager delegates a lot of authority to subordinates, the individual still defines the limits within which the people can function. This approach is often considered to be more effective than the other two we have just examined, although it should be pointed out that the overall situation will dictate the actual effectiveness of the styles. If subordinates like working under a paternalistic manager, they will not perform as well for a participative leader. Likewise, if the workers do not like feedback or increased responsibility, they will perform poorly for the participative leader. However, many workers do like a participative approach, and it offers some very distinct advantages:

■ Participative leaders are concerned with people and work.

1. Improved decision making. Managers often make better decisions when they include their subordinates in the process. There are now a number of people contributing their efforts to the decision-making process.
2. Willingness to accept change. Getting the employees involved creates a greater likelihood that the subordinates will be willing to accept those changes necessary to implement the agreed upon decisions.
3. Leadership identification. Now that the workers feel they are trusted, defensiveness is reduced and a positive relationship develops between the leaders and the followers.

■ Advantages of participative leadership.

4. Development of high achievement drive. Now that the subordinates know what is expected of them and have the necessary freedom to attain it, they can begin to develop high achievement drive. (The ways in which this can be done were discussed in the last chapter.)

■ It is not always an ideal style.

Before finishing our discussion of participative leadership, it is important to remember that participative leadership is not always ideal. Some special conditions have to be present for it to succeed. One is that the leader must be willing to invest the time necessary to anticipate problems, discuss them with the subordinates, and develop a team approach to problem solving. Second, the subordinates have to believe that the leadership behavior will be beneficial to them and that it is the right style to use. Finally, the leader has to feel a responsibility to both the subordinates and the organization. The individual has to be concerned with both the people and the work.

A Two-Dimensional Approach

■ Leadership has two independent dimensions.

Another way of examining leadership behavior is to take a two-dimensional approach. What do leaders do? As we just stated, the leader has to have two concerns: the people and the work. These are often referred to as *leadership dimensions,* and research reveals that they are not only important for effective leadership but they are *independent* dimensions. This means that the leader can be high on one of these dimensions without having to be low on the other. The result is four basic leadership behaviors, as illustrated in Figure 11.2. Which is the best? This will depend on the situation. Many practicing managers report that they are most effective when using a style that calls for high concern for both the people and the work. However, research does not universally support this. Sometimes leaders are most effective when they have a high concern for work but low concern for people; other times they are most effective when they use a high concern for people and low concern for work; and still other times they are most

Figure 11.2
A Leadership Grid

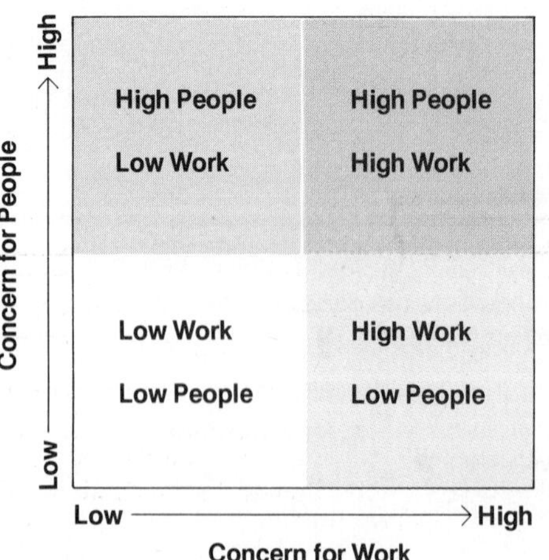

effective when they have a low concern for both the people and the work. While we will not investigate all these combinations and explain the conditions under which each is superior, suffice it to say that effective leadership style is *situationally determined.* Before turning to the subject of situational or contingency leadership, however, let us look at the managerial grid, the most famous two-dimensional description of leadership behavior.

The Managerial Grid. The Managerial Grid ® was developed by Robert R. Blake and Jane S. Mouton.[8] After undertaking research of their own, they developed the grid presented in Figure 11.3. Along the horizontal axis they placed *concern for production* and along the vertical axis they put *concern for people.* As can be seen, they have identified five basic leadership styles. And their Grid has proved so

Figure 11.3
The Managerial Grid

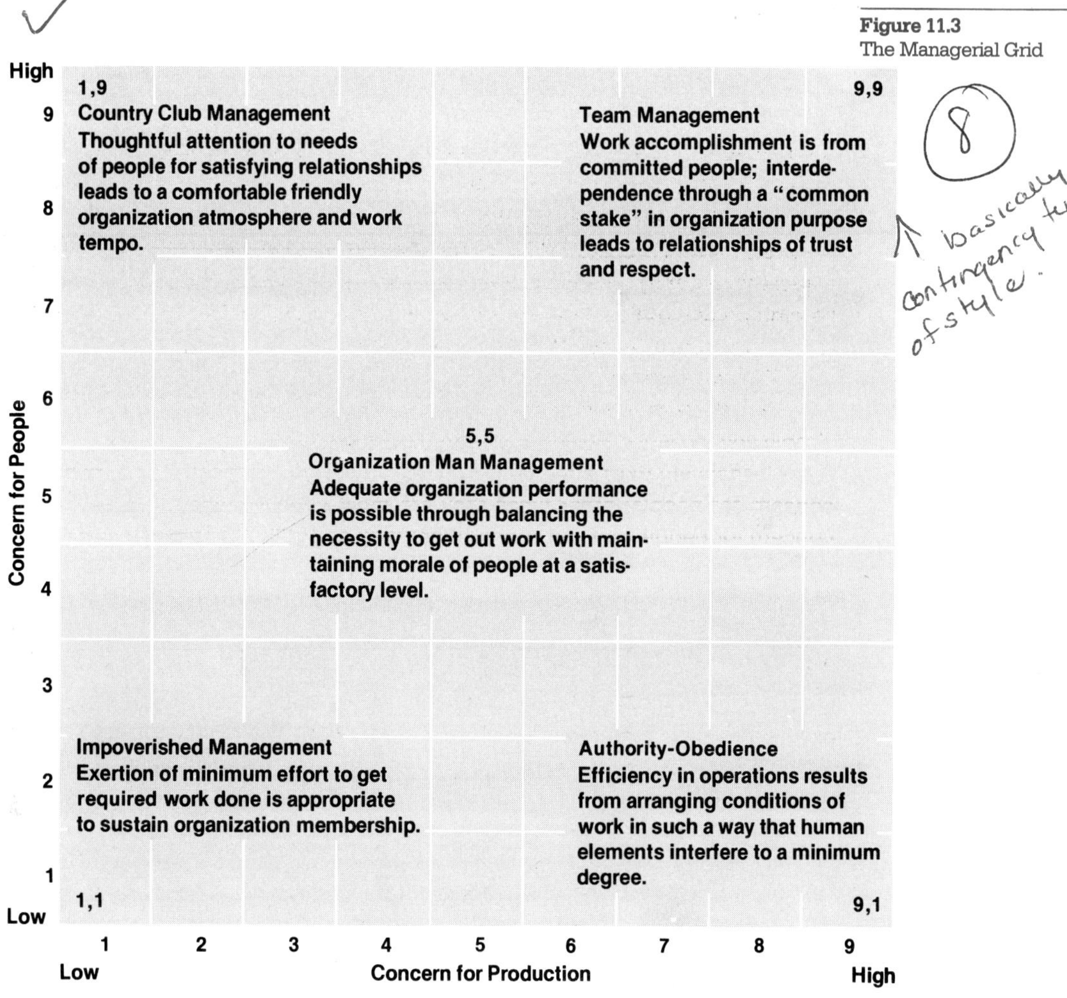

Source: The Managerial Grid figure from *The New Managerial Grid,* by Robert R. Blake and Jane Srygley Mouton. Houston: Gulf Publishing Company, Copyright © 1978, page 11. Reproduced by permission.

popular that it is common to find managers who are familiar with the Grid referring to leadership style by number. For example, a *9,9 manager* refers to a person who has a high concern for both people and work. A *9,1 manager* has high concern for work and low concern for people. A *1,9 manager* is just the reverse, having a high concern for people but low concern for work. A *5.5 manager* is a middle-of-the-road leader with moderate concern for both people and work. Finally, a *1,1, manager* has low concern for both people and work.

Using the Managerial Grid as the basis for their training, Blake and Mouton developed a six-phase program to train leaders to become more effective. Thus their Grid not only describes typical leadership patterns. It also serves as a basis for getting leaders to examine their current styles in order to identify those that would be of the greatest value to them and then start working from the former to the latter. For example, the manager who is heavily 9,1 but believes that a 9,9 style would be most effective needs to start increasing concern for people. The individual already has maximum concern for work; what the person needs to do is determine how to become more people-oriented.

▪ Managers like the 9,9 style best.

In the Grid, there are actually eighty-one total combinations, given the fact there are nine degrees of each dimension. However, it should be noted that Blake and Mouton report that 99.5 percent of the participants say that a 9,9 style is the soundest way to manage. Thus while any one of the styles can be used, they have found that high concern for both people and work is still the most popular among practicing managers.

In perspective, Blake and Mouton have developed an applied approach to leadership by blending theory and practice. This approach helps the manager identify the most effective personal leadership style and then develop a strategy for implementing it. The emphasis is on using what works.

Contingency Leadership

The latest research and writing on leadership is being done from a *contingency standpoint.* In essence, the contingency approach holds that managers must adapt their style to meet the specific needs of situations. The question that has most concerned these contingency-oriented researchers is: What specific style of leadership is most effective in which type of situation? There are thus two parts to their investigation: (1) the *leadership style* and (2) the *situation in which the leader operates.* These are areas which researchers of personality and leadership characteristics and leadership behavior have not really investigated. Additionally, while the trait theory people are interested in what leaders are and the behavioral theory people are concerned with what leaders do, the contingency people are interested in how leaders ought to act in order to lead most effectively. While a number of contingency theories have been developed, we shall confine our attention to two of the most significant: Fred Fiedler's contingency theory and Robert House's path-goal theory.

Fiedler's Contingency Theory

After years of empirical research, Professor Fred Fiedler has developed what is commonly referred to as a *contingency model of leadership effectiveness.*[9] Currently, Fiedler's is the most thoroughly researched contingency model. It concerns itself with the environment in which the leader functions and the way the individual carries out the leadership role.

■ Leader-member relations are the most important variable.

The Environment. From his research, Fiedler has identified three major situational variables that describe the environment in which leaders function: (1) leader-member relations, (2) task structure, and (3) position power. According to him, *leader-member relations* are the most important influence on the manager's power and effectiveness. These relations determine how well the leader will be accepted by the subordinates. If this acceptance is high, the leader may not need to rely on formal rank or authority to get things done. The individual's personality, character, and/or ability may be all that is necessary. On the other hand, if the manager is not liked or trusted, such informal means will be worthless. The leader will have to rely on the power of his or her managerial position, what has earlier been defined as legitimate power.

■ Task structure is the second most important variable.

Task structure is the second most important variable in the environment. If the task is highly structured, there are step-by-step procedures or instructions to be followed in doing the job, and group members will have a very clear idea of what they are supposed to be doing. Mechanical chores, for example, tend to be highly structured, both because it is possible to develop a series of sequential steps for doing the job and because this is often the most efficient way to carry out the task. When jobs are set out this way, the manager has a great deal of authority; for the individual knows how to measure work performance. When things are not going well, the leader can easily identify the problem. Conversely, when the task is unstructured, group member jobs are ambiguous and there are no clear guidelines regarding how to proceed. In these instances the workers can disagree with the leader's instructions and the latter's power is diminished.

■ Position power is the formal position authority.

Position power is the amount of formal authority provided to the leader by virtue of his or her position. The president of the organization, for example, will have a lot of position power. Referring to our earlier discussion of types of power, this person will have legitimate, reward, and coercive power and may have referent and expert power as well. In any event, the individual's position power is high. This is in contrast to a supervisor who works in a unionized shop and has little power over the workers, all of the hirings, firings, promotions, and raises having been determined by the union contract.

These three situational variables can create any of *eight* different conditions. This is done simply by mixing combinations of the following situations: (1) leader-member relations are good, task structure is high, and leader position power is strong, on down to (2) leader-member relations are poor, task structure is low, and leader position power is weak. (See the conditions in Figure 11.4).

The Leader's Style. What kind of style do leaders employ? In answering this question Fiedler and his colleagues designed and used what is called the *least preferred*

Figure 11.4
Effective Leadership Style and the Situation

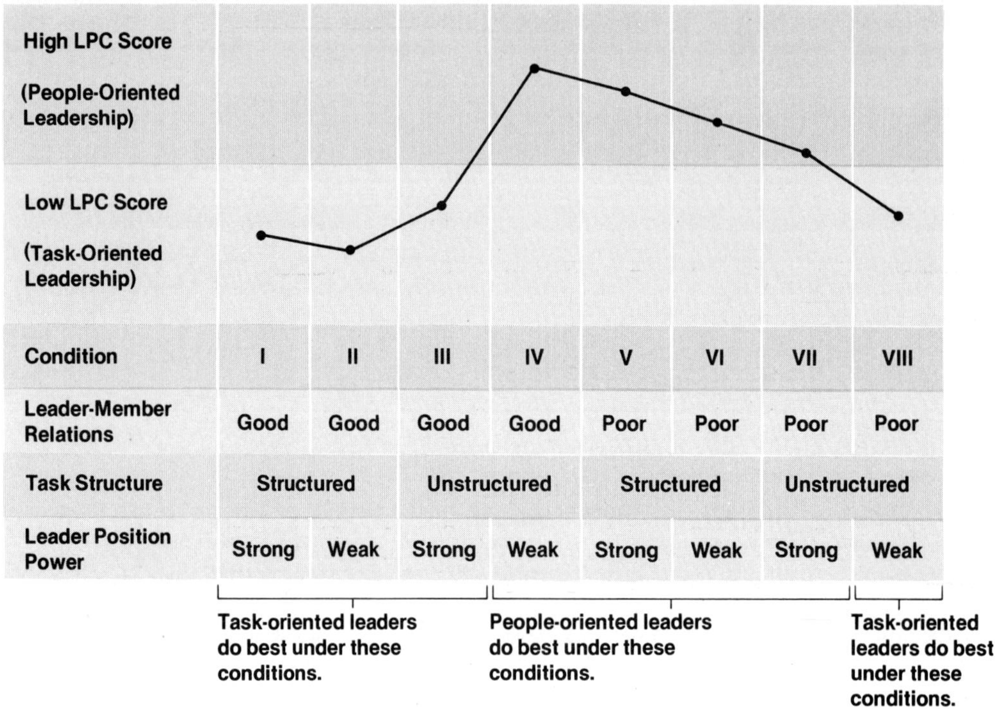

■ An LPC score was determined.

co-worker scale (LPC). This scale, shown in Table 11.2, is a questionnaire which asks the leader to describe the person with whom he or she can work least well. From these responses an LPC score is determined. Looking at Table 11.2, you can see that if the leader is an easygoing person who describes the least preferred co-worker in warm or kind terms, the individual will get a very high LPC score. Conversely, if the leader describes the least preferred co-worker in harsh, negative terms, the overall LPC score will be low. Fiedler put it this way:

> **A person who describes his least preferred co-workers in a relatively favorable manner tends to be permissive, human relations-oriented and considerate of the feelings of his men. But a person who describes his least preferred co-worker in an unfavorable manner—who has a what we have come to call a low LPC rating—tends to be managing, task-controlling, and less concerned with the human relations aspects of the job.[10]**

In Fiedler's view, a high LPC manager wants to establish warm relations with co-workers. The leader sees this as an important part of being an effective manager. The low LPC manager, on the other hand, puts primary emphasis on getting the job done. The work emphasis comes ahead of the concern for people.

Table 11.2
The Least Preferred Co-Worker Scale

Think of the person *with whom you can work least well.* This individual may be someone you work with now or someone you knew in the past. The individual does not have to be the person you like least well, but should be the person with whom you had the most difficulty in getting a job done. Describe this person as he or she appears to you by placing an X on the appropriate place along the respective continuum.

Pleasant	8	7	6	5	4	3	2	1	Unpleasant
Unfriendly	1	2	3	4	5	6	7	8	Friendly
Accepting	8	7	6	5	4	3	2	1	Rejecting
Frustrating	1	2	3	4	5	6	7	8	Helpful
Enthusiastic	8	7	6	5	4	3	2	1	Unenthusiastic
Tense	1	2	3	4	5	6	7	8	Relaxed
Close	8	7	6	5	4	3	2	1	Distant
Cold	1	2	3	4	5	6	7	8	Warm
Cooperative	8	7	6	5	4	3	2	1	Uncooperative
Hostile	1	2	3	4	5	6	7	8	Supportive
Interesting	8	7	6	5	4	3	2	1	Boring
Quarrelsome	1	2	3	4	5	6	7	8	Harmonious
Self-Assured	8	7	6	5	4	3	2	1	Hesitant
Inefficient	1	2	3	4	5	6	7	8	Efficient
Cheerful	8	7	6	5	4	3	2	1	Gloomy
Guarded	1	2	3	4	5	6	7	8	Open

Source: Adapted from Fred E. Fiedler, *A Theory of Leadership Effectiveness* (New York: McGraw-Hill, 1967), Table 3.1, pp. 40–41. Reprinted by permission.

Bringing the Situation and the Leader Together. Drawing together the three major environmental and situational variables and the leader's style, as reflected by the LPC score, Fiedler has constructed his contingency theory of leadership. It has been represented graphically in Figure 11.4, and it shows that the leader with the high LPC score tends to be most effective working in situations that are moderately good or moderately poor. Meanwhile, leaders with low LPC scores tend to be most effective in situations that are either very good or very bad. Fiedler has put it this way:

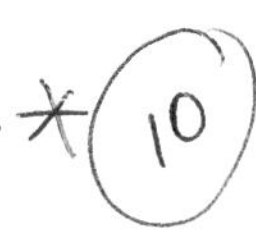

▪ Fiedler's results.

The results show that a task-oriented leader performs best in situations at both extremes—those in which he has a great deal of influence and power, and also in situations where he has no influence and power over the group members.

Relationship-oriented leaders tend to perform best in mixed situations where they have only moderate influence over the group. A number of subsequent studies by us and others have confirmed these findings.

The results show that we cannot talk about simply good leaders or poor leaders. A leader who is effective in one situation may or may not be effective in another. Therefore, we must specify the situations in which a leader performs well or badly.[11]

How can the findings in Figure 11.4 be of value in promoting leadership effectiveness? The answer is found *not* in changing the leader's personality or trying to train him or her to act a different way but rather in *matching the leader and the situation.* If the situation is very good or very bad, use a task-oriented leader. If the situation is between these two extremes, use a people-oriented leader.

How accurate is Fiedler's theory? The testing goes on. Some people have argued that the theory is incomplete. Others argue that it does not adequately explain why a leadership style that is most effective in very favorable situations is also effective in very unfavorable situations. Still others point out that Fiedler has changed his interpretation of what the LPC scale means, so that it is difficult to know exactly what the instrument measures. Fiedler is currently working on answering these criticisms. And to date, his theory offers one of the most comprehensive and best researched contingency approaches to leadership.

Table 11.3 illustrates the importance that the leadership of a single top manager may exert on a large corporation.

Table 11.3
Leadership at Firestone

Small firms often seem to have leadership problems. But this never happens with big corporations, right? Wrong! Not too long ago the Firestone Tire & Rubber Company provided an excellent illustration of a large firm with leadership problems. Its president had taken early retirement and the company had seen over half the senior managers leave within a 36-month period.

What led to all this? Numerous causes can be cited, from an extended labor strike to the revelation that Firestone had been making illegal domestic political contributions and foreign payoffs (one of the officers drew a four-year jail term for this) to an investigation by federal authorities into design problems that allegedly caused an abnormally high rate of blowouts and resulted in the industry's largest tire recall. The result: a $148 million loss in 1978. And after this things did not really seem to improve much. Executives leaving the firm reported interdepartmental fights, lack of communication, and general chaos.

As the next year rolled on, everyone waited for the new president and chief executive officer to be chosen. Would he be able to straighten out the situation? Firestone executives were hoping for the best. There were a lot of problems to be confronted—and it was going to take a dynamic leader to meet the challenge. And the lesson to be learned was clear: leadership is a major factor in the success of every firm—small or big.

Source: "Firestone's Search for Stability," *Business Week,* July 9, 1979, pp. 44–49.

Path-Goal Theory of Leadership

Another recent contingency theory of leadership is the *path-goal theory.* Originally proposed by Robert House, it has been refined and extended in collaboration with others.[12] This theory is based on the expectancy-valence model of motivation that was described in Chapter 10.

In essence, this theory holds that the leader's job is one of clarifying what the subordinate is supposed to be doing, clearing away any roadblocks that prevent goal attainment, and increasing the subordinate's opportunity to obtain personal satisfaction. Thus, the best style of leader behavior is seen as a function of the subordinate and the task.

The Subordinate. According to the path-goal theory, the subordinate will see the leader's behavior as acceptable to the extent that such behavior is either an immediate or future source of satisfaction. If the leader helps the subordinate fill out a cost control report that is due in two hours, the subordinate will like this because it provides an immediate source of satisfaction. Likewise, if the leader provides the subordinate with assistance in finding information needed for next month's job evaluation report, this will provide a future source of satisfaction. Furthermore, those individuals who have a high need for affiliation or esteem will be motivated by leaders who provide close interpersonal interaction, while those who prefer autonomy or self-actualization will like it best if the leader provides work-related assistance and then leaves them alone. Thus, some subordinates like leaders who are friendly and approachable, while others prefer leaders who tell them what is expected and then leave them alone to accomplish these objectives.

■ Subordinates want leadership behavior that results in satisfaction.

The Task. Additionally, to the extent that the subordinates see the leader's behavior as helping clarify path-goal relationships, they will like it. Particularly when the goal is unclear or the task is ambiguous, they will welcome assistance from the leader. However, if the task is already clear and the workers know what is expected of them, they will prefer loose control. If the leader is too work-centered, they will see this as excessive control and it will turn them off. What, then, is the best amount of directiveness to use? Figure 11.5 provides the answer initially provided by the path-goal theory people. Note that when the task is unstructured, high leader directiveness will result in high worker satisfaction, and low leader directiveness will bring about low worker satisfaction. Conversely, if the task is basically structured, low leader directiveness brings about high work satisfaction and high leader directiveness will cause low worker satisfaction.

■ They also want leaders to clarify path-goal relationships.

Applying the Path-Goal Theory. As can be seen, the path-goal theory is less a leadership theory than it is a *supervisory* theory of leadership. It postulates a right way to lead lower-level subordinates. How accurate is the theory? While current research is showing a few problems with it, such as subordinates who seem to need less leader directiveness on unstructured tasks than was initially thought, the theory does provide some interesting insights to leader-subordinate relations. On the positive side, the theory helps integrate the expectancy theory of motivation with contingency leadership style. It also reemphasizes the importance of leader concern for both the work and the people. Finally, it encourages the leader to analyze the situation in determining the right degree of each—concern for structure and people—that will be required.

■ Basically, it is a supervisory theory of leadership.

Figure 11.5
Path-Goal Theory in Action

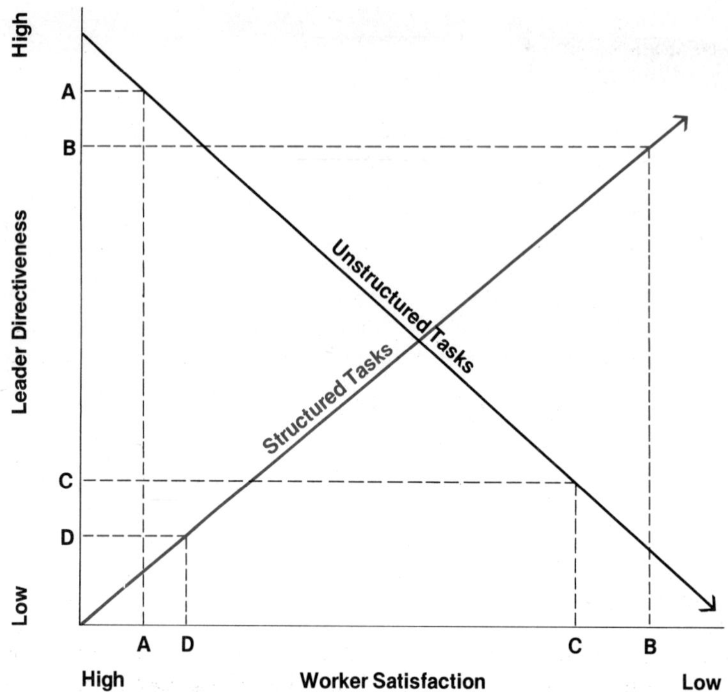

Leadership: An Integrative Approach

As we have just seen, the study of leadership has actually gone through three phases. First there were the trait theorists, who sought to uncover universal traits or characteristics common to all successful leaders. Then there were the behavioral theory people, who sought to explain how leaders behave. Now, there are the contingency leadership people who seek to answer the question: Under what conditions are various types of leaders effective?

Drawing together all of what is known about leadership, it is possible to construct an integrative model. Remember, the effective leadership style is a function of three variables: the leader, the subordinates, and the work environment. This is illustrated in Figure 11.6.

The *leader* has to be competent. The individual must know what he or she is supposed to be doing. Additionally, the individual must be able to reward the followers. After all, why should people respond to the leader's command if the latter does not reward them for doing so? Finally, the leader must have influence with upper management. The individual must be able to support the workers and fight for them with higher management. The leader must represent the workers to the boss.

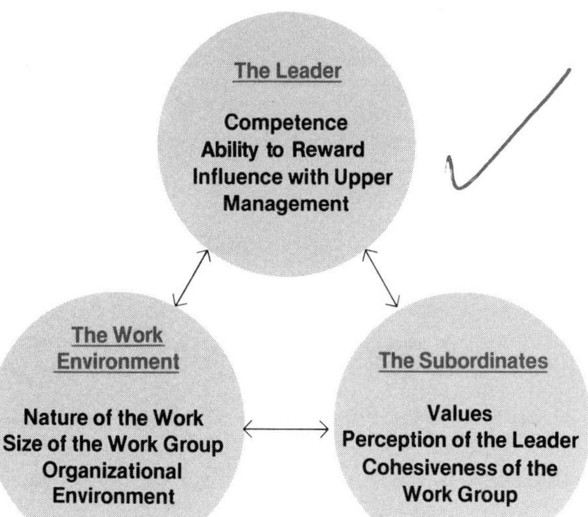

Figure 11.6
An Integrative Leadership Model

Then there are the *subordinates.* The most important subordinate-related factor is the values of the subordinates. What do the subordinates want? What things do they place in high regard? What turns them on? Additionally, their perception of the leader is important. Do they see the leader as someone who fights for their best interests, or do they believe that the leader sells them out to upper management in the hope that this approach will lead to further personal promotions? Finally, there is the cohesiveness of the work group. If it is cohesive, the leader has the best chance of motivating its members to attain organizational goals. If they are fighting among themselves, the leader is likely to find that most of his or her time is spent trying to settle disputes, with little progress being made toward objectives.

Finally, there is the *work environment.* What are the conditions under which the leader and the subordinates come together? The nature of the work is an important factor. Are the jobs routine and well structured, or do they require that the leader be available for continual assistance and consultation? Given the type of work, what style of leadership is most likely to be effective? Then there is the size of the work group. If the group is very large, the leader cannot use the same close, interpersonal style that can be employed with a small group. Finally, there is the organizational environment. If upper management insists on a lot of rules and regulations, it may be necessary to use an autocratic style. However, if decentralization is encouraged, a democratic style is best.

The material we have examined in this chapter can be integrated into this model and used to explain effective leadership. The important thing to remember is that the effective leader is a contingency-oriented person. A good leader is able to adjust personal leadership style to meet the needs of the subordinates and the work environment.

Summary

Leadership is the process of influencing people to direct their efforts toward the achievement of some particular goal(s). In doing so, most managers have a basic style that is a result of assumptions they hold regarding their subordinates. Some believe their employees are basically lazy, have to be coerced and threatened with punishment, and want security above all else. These leaders subscribe to Theory X. Others feel that people do not inherently dislike work and under the right conditions will seek responsibility and pursue organizational goals. These individuals subscribe to Theory Y.

In addition to the assumptions they have about their subordinates, all leaders can exercise power. This power can take any of five types: reward, coercive, legitimate, referent, and expert. All were described in this chapter. So were some of the common leadership and personal characteristics that typify leaders.

The next part of the chapter examined leadership behavior. First, authoritarian leaders were described, followed by paternalistic leaders and participative leaders. A two-dimensional model was also presented, in which it was shown that leadership consists of two independent dimensions: concern for people and concern for work.

The last part of the chapter was devoted to contingency leadership. Two popular theories were examined. First, attention was focused on Fiedler's theory, which attempts to match the leader to the situation. It was shown that his research suggests that participative leaders be used in situations which are of moderate favorableness or unfavorableness, while work-centered leaders be used in situations which are highly favorable or unfavorable. The path-goal theory, meanwhile, suggests that on unstructured tasks the leader should be highly directive, while on structured tasks the individual should offer low direction.

The last part of the chapter was given over to an integrative model of leadership. Pulling together the three most important leadership variables—the leader, the subordinates, and the work environment—we considered how each has an effect on the other. In the final analysis, there needs to be a right fit among the three in order for the leader to be most effective.

Review and Study Questions

1. In your own words, exlain what is meant by the term *leadership.*
2. What is meant by the statement that a person is a Theory X manager? How would this person differ from a Theory Y manager? Explain.
3. What are the five basic types of power? Define each. Then explain which are most effective in getting motivated people to do things.
4. Of all the leadership traits, which do you think are of most value to modern leaders? Defend your answer.
5. Of all the personal characteristics discussed in this chapter, which are of most value to the modern leader? Explain your answer.

6. How does an authoritarian leader differ from a paternalistic leader? How does a paternalistic leader differ from a participative leader?
7. Leadership has two independent dimensions: concern for work and concern for people. What does this statement mean?
8. Perhaps the most popular approach to studying leadership styles is the managerial grid developed by Robert R. Blake and Jane S. Mouton. What is meant by the term *managerial grid?* What are the five basic leadership styles on the grid? Which is the most effective style? Defend your answer.
9. In Fiedler's contingency theory, what are the three major situational variables? Explain each.
10. In Fiedler's contingency theory, what style of leadership is most effective when the situation is very good or very bad? What about when the situation is only moderately good or moderately bad? Explain.
11. In what way can the path-goal theory of leadership help a supervisor lead subordinates? What type of leadership style would be most effective if the task is highly structured? What if the task is highly unstructured? Explain your answer.

Key Terms in the Chapter

leadership
Theory X
Theory Y
reward power
coercive power
legitimate power
referent power
expert power
leadership characteristics
personal characteristics
authoritarian leadership
paternalistic leadership
participative leadership
managerial grid
9,9 manager
9,1 manager
1,9 manager
5,5 manager
1,1 manager
Fiedler's contingency theory
LPC scale
path-goal theory of leadership

Notes

1. Douglas McGregor, *The Human Side of Enterprise* (New York: McGraw-Hill, 1960), pp. 33–34.
2. Ibid., pp. 47–48.
3. John R. P. French, Jr., and Bertram Ruane, "The Bases of Social Power," in *Studies in Social Power,* ed. D. Cartwright (Ann Arbor: University of Michigan, Institute for Social Research, 1959), pp. 150–167.
4. Ralph Stogdill, *Handbook of Leadership* (New York: Free Press, 1974), p. 81.
5. Richard M. Hodgetts, *Modern Human Relations* (Hinsdale, Ill.: Dryden Press, 1980), Chapter 12.
6. E. E. Ghiselli, "The Validity of Aptitude Tests in Personnel Selection," *Personnel Psychology,* Winter 1973, pp. 461–467.

7. For more on this subject, see Wayne F. Cascio, *Applied Psychology in Personnel Management* (Reston, Va.: Reston Publishing, 1978), pp. 237–239.

8. Robert R. Blake and Jane Srygley Mouton. *The New Managerial Grid* (Houston, Tex.: Gulf Publishing Company, 1978), p. 11.

9. Fred E. Fiedler, *A Theory of Leadership Effectiveness* (New York: McGraw-Hill, 1967).

10. Fred E. Fiedler, "Engineer the Job to Fit the Manager," *Harvard Business Review,* September–October 1965, p. 116.

11. Fred E. Fiedler, "Style or Circumstance: The Leadership Enigma," *Psychology Today,* March 1969, p. 42.

12. Robert J. House, "A Path-Goal Theory of Leader Effectiveness," *Administrative Science Quarterly,* September 1971, pp. 321–338; Robert J. House and Gary Dessler, "The Path-Goal Theory of Leadership: Some Post-Hoc and A Priori Tests," in *Contingency Approaches to Leadership,* ed. James G. Hunt and Lars L. Larson (Carbondale, Ill.: Southern Illinois University Press, 1974), pp. 29–55.

Case: Curly's Matrix

Curly's moving up . . . and so is someone else.

Curly O'Brien is being promoted to company headquarters. He has done a fine job as head of the firm's largest retail store, and it was only a matter of time before he got this promotion. Even Curly knew the home office would be impressed with his store's sales record.

Now, however, Curly has to choose a replacement. He has narrowed the list to three heads of the major departments and his assistant, Sam Headley. Who should be the new store manager? Curly knows that a leader should have certain characteristics or traits. He also knows that there are some personal characteristics or traits the individual should possess.

In an effort to systematically choose his successor, Curly has listed six traits or characteristics. They are the following:

1. Mental ability. In order to be a successful store manager, an IQ of at least 110 is required. These scores can be obtained from the personnel department, since everyone who holds a managerial position has taken such a test.
2. Problem solving. The store manager must be capable of facing and solving complex problems.
3. Personality and maturity. The manager must be able to effectively relate to people and be mature enough to deal with subordinates at the appropriate level.
4. Creativity. Creativity is required in both problem solving and judging product lines. This skill can often mean the difference between an average and a superior manager.
5. Ability to withstand stress. The manager must be able to face the rigors of the job. Store managers are exposed to quite a few.
6. Motivation drive. The manager must be highly motivated in order to meet the personal demands of the job. Also, this motivation will spur on the subordinates. Therefore, it is one of the most important characteristics.

After reviewing the above, Curly has put together the following matrix:

	Mental Ability	Problem Solving	Personality and Maturity	Creativity	Ability to Withstand Stress	Motivation Drive
Sally	125	O	G	G	G	O
George	111	G	O	A	G	O
Andy	139	O	P	O	G	G
Sam	128	G	A	G	O	G

Outstanding: O Good: G Average: A Poor: P

Questions

1. In addition to the characteristics listed by Curly, are there any others you think would be important? What are they?
2. Based on Curly's matrix, which manager should be recommended for the job? Explain your reasoning.
3. In addition to the matrix, what other things would you recommend Curly do in deciding whom to choose? Explain.

Case: Short-Run Success

Does Intertown need Cutter Bill or Secretariat?

Things were really going downhill at Intertown Inc. when Lyle Norman took over as president. The first thing Lyle did was get rid of the deadwood. All the people who were unable to pull their own weight were let go. The secretarial staff was cut in half, and the budget was trimmed by 40 percent.

Working with the reduced work force, Lyle slowly began to turn the company around. The first thing he did was buy better machinery and equipment, while increasing the working hours from 8:00 AM to 6:00 PM. Overtime was paid, but everyone was required to stay and put in these hours. Next, Lyle started hiring more salespeople and picking out the accounts that were most likely to generate the greatest amount of sales. Finally, he worked closely with the bank, insuring that an adequate line of credit was available to keep the firm afloat long enough for all of these strategic changes to take effect.

During all of this time, Lyle proved himself a hard taskmaster. He yelled, screamed, fired some people on the spot, and demanded that things be done his way. However, his behavior did not greatly upset the workers. They understood that things were in poor shape and someone had to take the bull by the horns.

By early last year, things were much better. The firm showed a very nice profit. The board of directors was so pleased that they gave Lyle and the management staff a bonus, and everyone in the company received an overall 12 percent increase in salary. The business had certainly come a long way since Lyle took over.

However, a new problem has begun to develop. While everyone was willing to put up with Lyle's autocratic style when things were going poorly, people thought it would change when the operation was straightened out. Then, they had thought, Lyle would use a more participative approach with them. But it hasn't happened. Lyle is as autocratic as ever, and this is now starting to have an effect on the work force. Some of them are threatening to quit, and overall efficiency is beginning to slip. One of the top managers, who is sympathetic with the worker gripes, has put it this way: "Lyle's a great guy when you have a big problem. But for ordinary day-to-day business, he has problems in leading. He's a troubleshooter, not a professional manager. In race-horse terminology, he's a quarter horse, not a thoroughbred. He's only good for the short run."

Questions

1. Why was Lyle successful in turning the firm around? Explain.
2. Why are the workers now upset? Integrate the manager's comment about Lyle being a quarter horse into your answer.
3. Can the situation be straightened out? What would you recommend? Explain.

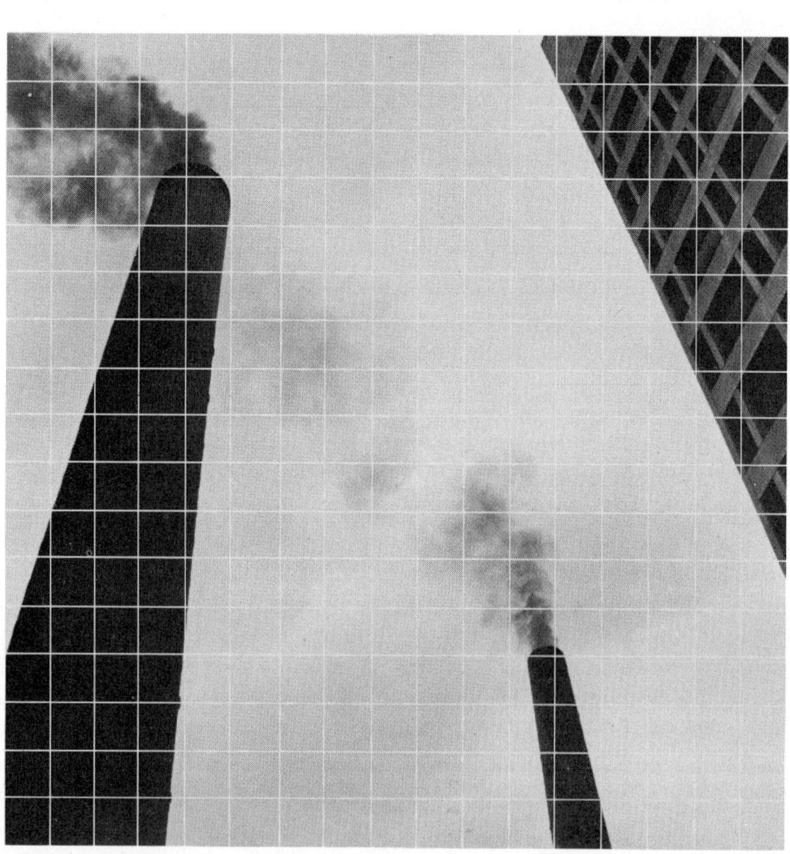

327.

Part Six

The Management Process: Controlling

The overall objective of this part of the book is to study the controlling process. During this process the organization compares what it did with what it planned to do. This function serves to close the loop between planning and performance. For example, Company A set an objective of $50,000 profit for the last fiscal year. When this period was over, the company determined how well it had done by examining the income statement and looking at the net profits.

There are two important areas that organizations need to control: operations and people. Although these two overlap, for purposes of analysis we can break them into separate groups. In this way control techniques and behavioral performance can both be studied.

Chapter 12 The Basics of Control

Objectives of the Chapter

There are two important areas that need to be controlled in every organization: operations and people. These two generally overlap. However, for purposes of analysis we are going to examine the basics of control and the various techniques that can be used in controlling operations in this chapter and study the behavioral side of control in the next chapter. The first objective of this chapter is to review the basics of the controlling process. Then traditional control techniques will be examined, including budgeting, breakeven point analysis, and financial statement analysis. The final objective of the chapter is to examine overall control techniques, including return on investment, key area control, and auditing.

When you have finished studying the material in this chapter, you should be able to:

1 Describe how the controlling process works.
2 Explain how organizations use the budget process, with attention given to both flexible budgets and zero-based budgeting.
3 Illustrate how to compute a breakeven point.
4 Describe financial statement analysis, using some typical ratio analysis to illustrate the point.
5 Discuss the value of return on investment as an overall control technique.
6 Tell how key area control works.
7 Explain how internal and management audits can be of value to the organization in controlling its operations.

The Controlling Process

The *controlling process* involves the measurement of performance against objectives. During this process the organization compares what actually happened with what was expected. The three basic steps in this process are: (1) the establishment of standards, (2) the comparison of results against standards, and (3) the correction of deviations. Figure 12.1 illustrates the process, beginning with the formulation of the plan.

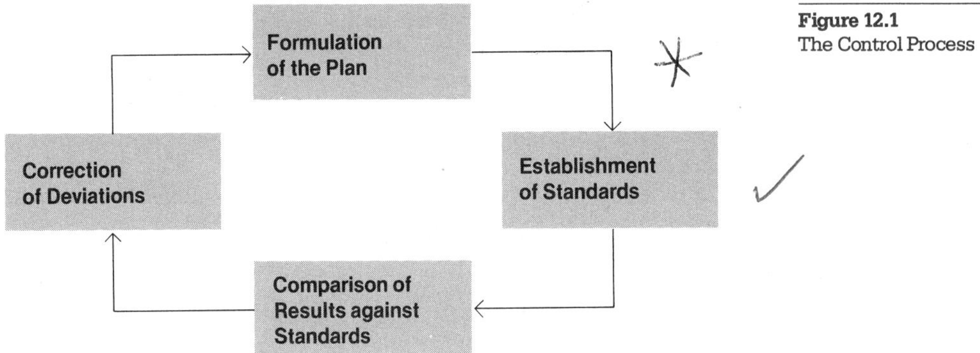

Figure 12.1
The Control Process

Establishment of Standards

Standards are actually set in the planning process. In some cases these standards are very specific and are presented in terms of costs, revenues, products, or hours worked. The following are typical kinds of standards written in such a way as to facilitate control:

▪ Typical standards.

- Reduce overtime among the supervisory staff by 30 percent during the next fiscal year.
- Increase the number of production hours from 32,000 to 40,000 by April 15 of this year.
- Increase sales by 20 percent during the current fiscal year.
- Increase overall profit by $35,000 by the end of the fiscal year.
- Cut scrap cost from 6 percent of overall production cost down to 2 percent by the end of December.

Notice that in each case the objective has been written in such a way as to make control easier. The statement tells us what is to be done and by when.

However, not all objectives or standards are as measurable as those above. Many of them relate to areas such as developing higher morale among the employees or designing a public relations program for gaining community goodwill.

In these cases it is difficult to quantify the standard. Nevertheless, objectives such as these cannot be overlooked, so the organization will have to control them as best it can.

Comparison of Results against Standards

The purpose of comparing performance against standards is to answer the question: How well have we done? Sometimes this comparison is not difficult to make, because the objective has been stated quantitatively and feedback is available for comparison purposes. For example, it is often easy to evaluate sales performance since the quota is set in terms of sales dollars or units and all the manager has to do is compare them. However, there are times when it is difficult to measure actual performance, as in the case of comparing one vice-president's performance with another's for the purpose of determining which is superior. Of course, we could look at the performance of their subordinates and judge from that. But what if one of the executives is in sales and there is currently a recession, while the other is in research and development and the firm has just won an R&D grant from the government? In this case, it may be difficult to say which executive is superior.

Furthermore, effective comparison of performance with standards is sometimes a result of the evaluation form being used. What type of information is being collected for comparison purposes? How detailed are the data? Do they tell us what we need to know to make an intelligent comparison? If these roadblocks can be surmounted, the results will be useful. If not, a new evaluation form or method of gathering the data should be determined. Only in this way can the organization be sure that the data are valuable for comparison purposes.

■ Standards and performance evaluation should be tied together.

One way of dealing with this particular issue is to face it at the same time that the standard is established. How will we evaluate our performance in this area? What kinds of feedback or information will we need? Then an instrument or approach can be formulated. By doing it this way, the organization avoids having to face the problem later on, only to realize that it is unsure of how the standard can really be evaluated.

Correction of Deviations

■ Then corrective action should be determined.

If there is a deviation between the standard and the performance, the organization has to decide whether corrective action should be taken. Remember, as we noted in Chapter 1, only significant deviations should be controlled. If things are outside acceptable boundaries, they need to be investigated. For example, the organization may be willing to accept a return on investment of between 13 and 15 percent. If the results are any lower than 13 or higher than 15, the manager will want to look into the situation.

Also remember that sometimes a problem is no one's fault. For example, a new product may be marketed vigorously, only to flop. Who should be responsible for the loss? Some people may point the finger at the vice-president of marketing. Others will say that it is the people in advertising or marketing research. However, the truth of the matter may be that public tastes suddenly changed in a way that was not identifiable beforehand, and no one is really to blame. All the organization does by pointing an accusing finger is to find a scapegoat, but the problem itself may have been one that even the best managers could not have avoided. In other cases, of course, there may be someone who was to blame for the mistake; and this should be noted.

However, control should not be used for the purpose of being punitive. Once a mistake has occurred, the damage is already done. The organization should now concentrate on preventing similar problems in the future. Perhaps the subordinate needs more training. Maybe the manager misunderstood a directive. If the organization spends all of its time reprimanding or penalizing those who have done things wrong, it will soon find that control is looked on as a means of punishment instead of as a basis for improving things for everyone.

Traditional Control Techniques

How does the organization implement the control process? What kinds of tools and techniques are employed? Some of the most popular control methods include the budget, breakeven point, and financial statement analysis. These are commonly referred to as traditional control techniques.

The Budget

■ It is the most widely used control technique.

The budget is a formal, financial expression of a plan, used for both setting objectives and evaluating results. Some of the most common budgetary targets include revenues, expenditures, and profits, all of which usually are expressed in dollar terms. Because of the simplicity with which it can be constructed, the budget is the most widely used control technique. While there are various types of budgets, as we shall see shortly, all of them work the same. First, a financial allocation is made; then the actual expenditures are computed; and finally, variances are determined and explanations are provided. Table 12.1 illustrates an

Table 12.1
Budget for New Product Line

	Budget	Actual	Variance	Explanation
Research and development	$50,000	$55,000	$5,000	Unforeseen technical problems were encountered.
Development of prototypes	10,000	10,000	—	
Marketing research	25,000	27,500	2,500	For statistical reasons the size of the research sample had to be increased.
Production of 20,000 units	75,000	60,000	(15,000)	Increased production efficiency resulted in lower than expected cost per unit.
	$160,000	$157,500	$(2,500)	

overall example of a budget for the development and production of a new product line.

Note that the new product was developed and produced for less than the overall budget. Within the budget, there were some cost overruns, but these were offset by the efficiency savings in the production process.

■ It all begins with a forecast.

How Budgeting Is Done. The overall budgeting process starts with a forecast of sales or other sources of revenue. The organization first needs to determine how much money it can afford to spend.

From this sales forecast a production and materials budget is drawn up. How much will it cost to generate the forecasted sales? If this budget is being drawn up by a public or service organization, there is a slight difference. Now the organization must compare services such as fire and police protection against tax revenues to see what can be afforded.

■ Followed by projected revenues and expenses.

From here the overall budget, with both the projected revenues and expenses, is broken down by division, department, and unit. There is also a monthly or quarterly breakdown so that the organization can control operations on a short-run basis. For example, instead of waiting until the end of the year to see if a sales division is successful in meeting its targets, a review is conducted on a quarterly basis. Figure 12.2 provides an illustration.

Figure 12.2
Division A Sales Budget (Thousands of Dollars)

	Quarter 1			Quarter 2			Quarter 3			Quarter 4		
	Budget	Actual	Variance	Budget	Actual	Variance	Budget	Actual	Variance	Budget	Actual	Variance
Sales revenue	900	1,000	+100	1,200	1,300	+100	2,800	3,000	+200	900	750	-150
Salespeople's expenses	600	650	+50	900	975	+75	2,000	2,100	+100	600	550	-50
Advertising expenses	50	50	—	75	75	—	150	150	—	50	50	—
General and administrative expenses	200	200	—	200	200	—	200	210	+10	200	200	—
Total	1,750	1,900	+150	2,375	2,550	+175	5,150	5,460	+310	1,750	1,550	-200
Net effect		+100			+25			+90			-100	

As seen in Figure 12.2, the sales revenues and expenses of Division A are computed and analyzed quarterly. During the first three quarters the division generated a profit, but during the last quarter it cost more to operate the division than was obtained through sales revenue. All of this was expected; however, the division did even better than budgeted in terms of sales revenue. The overall effect was a net gain of $115,000. By anticipating the quarterly peaks and troughs of its sales, the division is able to budget expenses appropriately. The organization, meanwhile, knows how much revenue can be expected from the division and will take this into account in its overall budget.

Flexible Budgets. There are many types of budgets: marketing, administrative, manufacturing, cash, and so on. All of these budgets are designed to help the organization control a specific aspect of its operations; and all are established using the approach described above. However, in recent years many firms have adjusted their budgetary process through the use of *flexible budgets*. With this approach, a basic budget is determined and then adjusted, based on the various levels of activity. If sales are much higher than anticipated, the budget is raised accordingly. In this way, the budget responds to operations rather than vice versa. Table 12.2 gives an illustration of how a budget can be tied to the production level.

▪ The budget responds to operations.

Table 12.2
Flexible Budget Based on Production Level

Levels of Production				
Units manufactured	10,000	20,000	30,000	40,000
Labor cost	$20,000	$ 38,000	$ 54,000	$ 70,000
Materials and supplies	50,000	95,000	135,000	160,000
Repairs	1,500	4,000	8,000	15,000
Administrative overhead	4,000	4,500	5,000	5,500
Total budget	$75,500	$141,500	$202,000	$250,500

As units manufactured rise, so does the budget under which the department operates. Notice that as the level of production increases, the cost per unit declines. That is, 10,000 units cost $75,500, or $7.55 each, while 40,000 units cost $250,500, or $6.26 each. All departments or units which face varying levels of activity would have similar kinds of budgets.

Zero-Based Budgeting. In recent years there has been a growing popularity for zero-based budgeting (ZBB). One of the primary differences between ZBB and traditional forms of budgeting is that the latter work from the assumption that whatever amount of money the department or unit received last year will serve as a base for the amount it will be getting this year. The only exceptions to this rule of thumb occur when a product line or unit is eliminated because of organizational cutbacks or when there is a reorganization, in which case units or departments end up reporting to different executives. However, once the reorganization is over, the budgeting process proceeds from there and budgets grow annually.

■ Each year is a new beginning.

ZBB works from a different philosophy. Each year is viewed as a new beginning. Rather than starting with the old budget and adding on new expenditures, each manager has to justify his or her entire budget request each year. Then working on the basis of cost-benefit analysis, each department's requests are reviewed and evaluated. From here budgets are funded, either totally or partially. Three basic steps are followed in this process.

■ Decision packages are formed.

First, each organization's activities are broken down into what are called *decision packages.* A decision package includes all the information about the activity that the management needs in order to evaluate and compare the cost and benefits of that activity with those of other activities. Additionally, consideration is given to the consequences that can be expected if the activity is not approved and alternative activities are used in its place.

■ Then evaluated and ranked.

Second, all the activities are evaluated and ranked in order of importance, starting with the first and working on down to the last. Usually each supervisor ranks those activities for which he or she is responsible. These are then passed on to the manager who, working with the subordinate, establishes rankings for all of the activities in the department. This process continues up the line, with each manager meeting with his or her superior. When the process is over, all the organizational activities have been reviewed and ranked.

■ Then resources are allocated.

Third, resources are allocated. The organization has only a limited amount of money to spend. By budgeting these funds in accord with the established priorities, the organization ensures that highly important activities are fully funded, while low priority activities are funded only if there are sufficient monies left.[1]

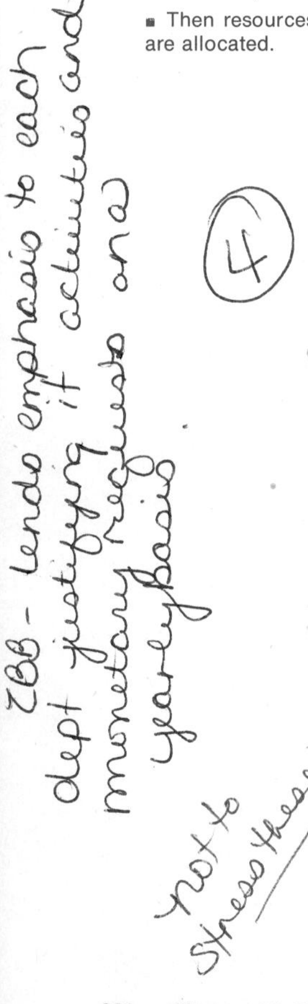

ZBB - lends emphasis to each dept justifying it activities and monetary requests on a yearly basis
4
not to stress these

Why do practicing managers like ZBB? One of the major reasons is the emphasis it gives to justifying one's activities. Just because some department got a large budget last year does not mean that it will be funded again this year. Second, all activities are subjected to close scrutiny and units have to explain why they should be funded again. Third, low-priority programs can be cut or eliminated with more confidence. On the other side, it should be noted that managers do dislike the amount of paperwork associated with the entire process. Until the program is up and going for a couple of years, supervisory employees must give a tremendous investment of time and effort. Everything must be evaluated, justified, and prioritized. However, once the process has been done a few times, it becomes much simpler and the overall benefits can be more objectively measured.

Breakeven Point

Another important control technique is the breakeven point (BEP). This point occurs when the firm's sales revenue is equal to its total costs. By definition, then, the company will lose money if its sales are less than this amount and make money if its sales are greater than this amount. This becomes clear if we examine the two types of costs which are fundamental to an understanding of the breakeven point—fixed expenses and variable expenses—and then follow with a computation of the BEP.

Fixed and Variable Expenses. A fixed expense is one which will remain constant, at least in the short run. Property taxes, property insurance, and administrative salaries are all examples. For example, property taxes will not change regardless of the firm's level of production. If it has a good year or a bad year, the company pays this amount of tax and no more.

▪ Fixed expenses remain constant in the short run.

A variable expense is one which changes in relation to output. When production is low, these costs are low; when production goes up, so do these costs. Labor salaries and materials are examples. As a firm hires more workers and goes to a second shift, labor salaries will increase; as the company reduces production and lays off workers, these costs will decline.

▪ Variable expenses change in relation to output.

Breakeven Point Computation. In computing a breakeven point, three cost-revenue components are of major importance: (1) total fixed cost, (2) selling price per unit, and (3) variable cost per unit. Once these three are determined, the variable cost per unit can be subtracted from the selling price to determine a margin above cost. This margin can then be applied to the fixed cost. Breakeven occurs at that point at which total fixed cost is equal to the total of these margins above cost.

Before examining the formula for computing breakeven, let us first look at these three major cost revenue components. Total fixed costs are those the firm has to cover, regardless of how many units it produces. Selling price is the revenue the firm obtains from the buyer. Variable costs are those that fluctuate in relation to production. Let us take an example. A firm has total fixed costs of $180,000, a selling price of $15 and a variable cost of $6. How many units will it have to sell in order to break even? The formula for computing the breakeven point in units is:

$$\text{Breakeven point (in units)} = \frac{\text{Total fixed cost}}{\text{Selling price minus variable cost}}.$$

In this example the computation is:

$$\text{Breakeven point} = \frac{\$180{,}000}{\$15 - \$6}$$

$$= \frac{180{,}000}{9}$$

$$= 20{,}000.$$

If the firm can sell 20,000 units it will break even. Anything less than this, as seen in Figure 12.3, will result in a loss, while anything greater than this will produce a profit.

Value of the Breakeven. The breakeven point is a valuable control technique because it helps the firm identify the *minimum* number of units which must be sold. If sales ever dip below 20,000, the company should stop production and limit its losses.

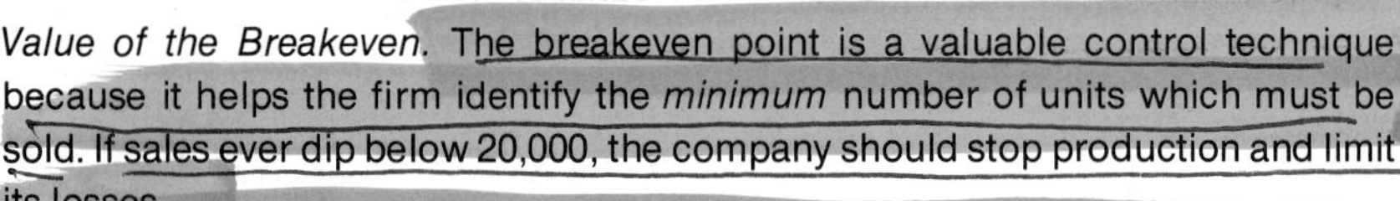

Of course, no company will produce merely to break even. Rather, it will establish a *feasibility range* above breakeven, such as 25,000 to 30,000 units of sales. If

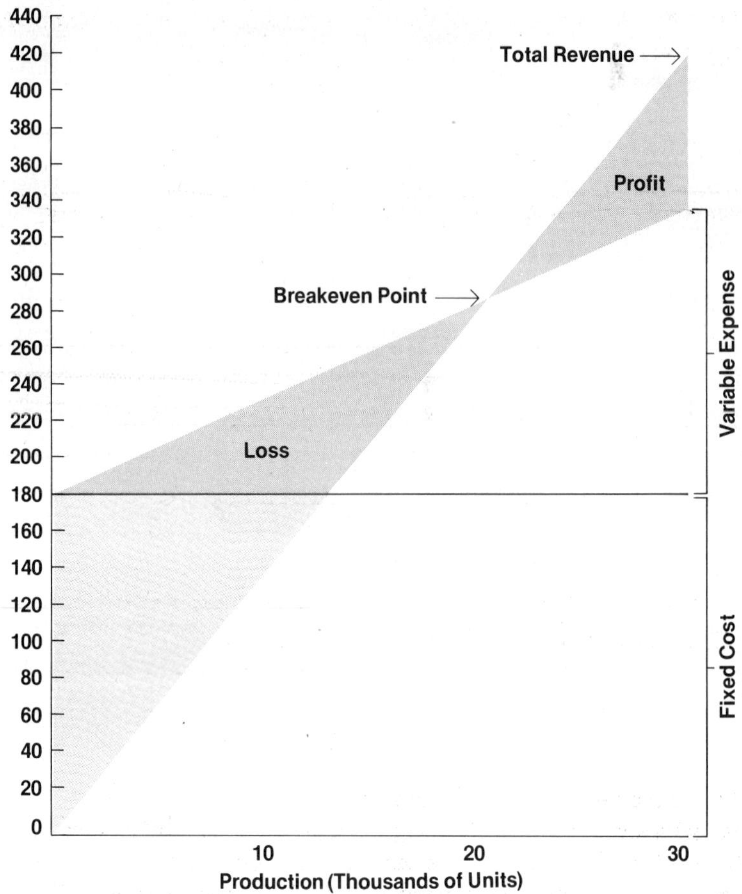

Figure 12.3
Breakeven Point Computation

▪ A feasibility range is determined.

sales drop below this range, the profit margin will be too low to justify the time, effort, and risk involved with producing the product. For example, if the firm sells 25,000 units, it will make a profit of $9 per unit (selling price minus variable cost) on the last 5,000 units, or $45,000. If it sells 30,000 units, profit will be $90,000. What is the minimum profit acceptable to the firm? If the management sets it at $18,000 to $27,000, at which time an evaluation of the situation will be made, then it will continue with this product line until overall sales fall below 23,000 units. (Remember for each 1,000 units over 20,000 units, the firm will make $9,000; so in this case 22,000 to 23,000 is the feasibility range.) Once sales forecasts indicate that sales will be less than this, the company will start winding down its production of the line. In this case, the feasibility range helps the firm control operations through the development of production and sales targets. If these targets are reached, profits are acceptable; if they are not attained, the product line is dismantled and the firm turns its attention to other lines worthy of consideration. In short, the breakeven point can help the firm push its winners and prune its losers. Table 12.3 provides a current example of this.

Table 12.3
Where Volume Makes the Difference

When the Guardian Industries Corporation, a Detroit-based glassmaker and photo processor, bought the GAF Corporation's photo-finishing operations, many people thought they had made a mistake. These GAF plants had been suffering heavy losses and the $6 million that Guardian paid looked like money being thrown away. Now, however, it seems as if Guardian made a very wise decision.

By closing some of these newly purchased facilities and getting rid of wasteful operations in the others, Guardian has managed to get them into the profit column. As a result, the company is now vying for the number two spot in the industry. Only Eastman Kodak is ahead of it. How has Guardian managed to do this? The answer is by determining its breakeven point and then getting volume above this level. This has been done by sticking to big volume product lines and staying away from "one of a kind" things. For example, the firm sells only the most common sizes and thicknesses of glass so that its products appeal to the largest segment of the market. And in the photo division, the company sticks strictly to wholesale processing for large retail chains such as K mart and Revco.

This strategy does not seem very sophisticated—and it is not. However, the results are certainly outstanding. Earnings are almost 20 percent of sales and the corporation should be grossing over a half billion dollars by the early 1980s. Using traditional control techniques, Guardian is managing to build an empire by turning losers into winners!

Source: "Guardian Industries: Focusing on Volume Turns Losers Around," *Business Week,* March 12, 1979, pp. 120–122, 123–125.

Financial Statement Analysis

One of the most fundamental methods of controlling is through the use of the financial statements. Is the firm making money? Can it meet its current financial obligations? What product lines are the winners, worthy of further investment? Which are marginal lines or losers, those that should be eliminated? How much return are the owners getting? These types of questions can be answered through what is called *financial statement analysis.*

Table 12.4 provides an example of a balance sheet and Table 12.5 illustrates an income statement. These financial statements provide the organization with feedback on how well it has performed and help the management develop future courses of action.

The *balance sheet* provides the organization a picture of its assets, liabilities, and owners' equity at a particular time, such as December 31. The *assets* are the "things" the company owns. They extend from current assets, which consist of cash or items that can be turned into cash within the next year, to fixed assets, which are used for producing the firm's goods and services. *Liabilities* are the debts of the organization, ranging from current liabilities to long-term liabilities. Finally, there is *owners' equity,* which is the difference between total assets and total liabilities and represents the owners' investment in the business.

The *income statement* shows the company's revenues and expenses over a particular period of time. From the revenues are subtracted the various expenses associated with obtaining these revenues. The result is income after taxes.

Table 12.4
A Balance Sheet

Hobner Manufacturing

Balance Sheet
as of December 31, 1980

Assets		Liabilities and Net Worth	
Current Assets		Current Liabilities	
Cash	$ 500,000	Accounts Payable	$ 700,000
Accounts Receivable	1,250,000	Accrued Expenses	
Inventories	300,000	Payable	300,000
Total Current Assets	$2,050,000	Total Current	
		Liabilities	$1,000,000
Fixed Assets			
Land	$550,000	Long-Term Liabilities	
Plant and Equipment	6,500,000	Total Long-Term	
Less Accumulated		Liabilities	$5,000,000
Depreciation	300,000		
Total Fixed Assets	$6,750,000	Stockholders' Equity	
		Common Stock at Par	$1,000,000
Other Assets		Accumulated Retained	
Patents and Goodwill	$ 200,000	Earnings	2,000,000
		Total Stockholders'	
		Equity	$3,000,000
		Total Liabilities and	
Total Assets	$9,000,000	Net Worth	$9,000,000

Table 12.5
An Income Statement

Hobner Manufacturing

Statement of Income
for the Year Ended December 31, 1980

Net Revenue		$5,000,000
Less Cost of Sales and Operating Expenses		
Cost of Goods Sold	$2,500,000	
Selling, Administrative, and Other Expenses	500,000	3,000,000
Operating Profit		2,000,000
Other Income	100,000	
Gross Income		2,100,000
Less Interest Expense	600,000	
Income before Taxes		1,500,000
Less Income Taxes	713,000	
Income after Taxes		$ 787,000

While there are many ways to use financial statements for control purposes, one of the most common is *ratio analysis*. Such analysis involves the comparison of data on either or both of these financial statements for the purpose of determining how well the organization is performing. Keeping in mind that there are far too many ratios to warrant our attention here, let us look at four of the most popular.

Current Ratio. The current ratio is computed by dividing current assets by current liabilities. This ratio measures the firm's ability to pay its current debts. Remember, since current assets consist of cash or things that can be quickly turned into cash, the ratio reveals the organization's ability to cover these debts. Drawing on the data in Table 12.4, the current ratio is computed as follows:

$$\frac{\text{Current assets}}{\text{Current liabilities}} = \frac{\$2{,}050{,}000}{\$1{,}000{,}000} = 2.05.$$

The firm has twice as much in current assets as in current liabilities. This 2.05 ratio is standard for the industry and indicates the firm should have no trouble meeting its short-term obligations.

Inventory Turnover. Another important control ratio is inventory turnover, which reveals the number of times the company is selling the inventory. In some industries such as the furniture and jewelry business, turnover averages around once a year. In other industries it is much higher. For Hobner Manufacturing the turnover should be in the vicinity of six to nine. The computation for the firm follows:

$$\text{Inventory turnover} = \frac{\text{Cost of goods sold}}{\text{Ending inventory}}$$

$$= \frac{\$2{,}500{,}000}{300{,}000}$$

$$= 8.3 \text{ times.}$$

The turnover is very good. The firm does not have the problem that faces many companies, namely slow-moving merchandise that ties up money and keeps profits down.

Debt/Equity Ratio. A third common control ratio is the debt/equity ratio. This measures the percentage of the business that is a result of debt and the amount that is contributed by equity. Remember, there are only two ways to increase the firm's overall assets: increase debt by borrowing or increase equity through either selling stock or retaining profits in the company. The lower the debt /equity ratio, the more the firm is financed by equity and, if problems develop, the more likely it is that the business can borrow money. Conversely, the higher this ratio, the less likely that banks or other lenders will be willing to advance more money. Before examining Hobner Manufacturing's ratio, however, one thing should be kept in mind. Debt can be an ideal way to raise money for expansion, and if the interest rate on the loans is 10 percent and the business is making a 20 percent return from its operations, borrowing is a wise

strategy. The problem occurs when the firm borrows too much and its profitability declines. What then is a good debt/equity ratio? In many industries a 1:1 ratio is considered the limit and 0.5:1 is considered a safe, conservative ratio. For Hobner Manufacturing it is:

$$\frac{\text{Debt}}{\text{Equity}} = \frac{\$6{,}000{,}000}{\$3{,}000{,}000} = 2{:}1.$$

Hobner is very heavily debt-financed. The company should consider paying off some of these financial obligations, especially the long-term ones, and getting this ratio down to 1:1.

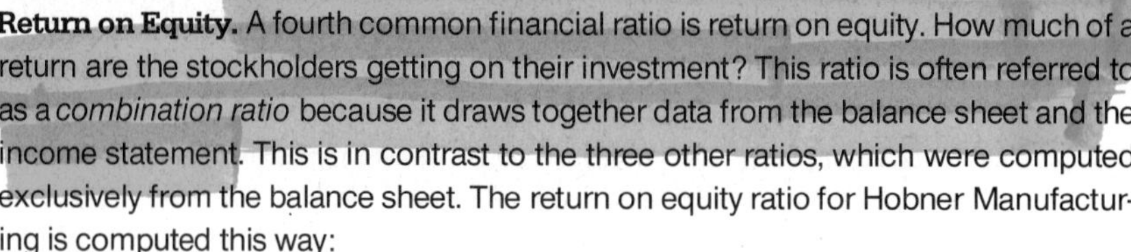

Return on Equity. A fourth common financial ratio is return on equity. How much of a return are the stockholders getting on their investment? This ratio is often referred to as a *combination ratio* because it draws together data from the balance sheet and the income statement. This is in contrast to the three other ratios, which were computed exclusively from the balance sheet. The return on equity ratio for Hobner Manufacturing is computed this way:

$$\frac{\text{Net profit}}{\text{Stockholders' equity}} = \frac{\$787{,}000}{\$3{,}000{,}000} = 26.2 \text{ percent.}$$

This is a very good return. Note that the stockholders have made a net profit of $787,000 on an investment of $3 million. This 26.2 percent return is far higher than what is being paid on Hobner's loans, which is undoubtedly the reason the company owners are willing to use debt financing. Also remember that the above ratio used net profit. If it used gross income, which some firms prefer to use, the return would rise to 70 percent. In any event, the firm's return is excellent.

Value of Ratio Analysis. Ratio analysis helps pinpoint strengths and weaknesses in the firm's financial position. In particular, it assists the company in measuring current performance against desired objectives. Is the current ratio adequate? Is inventory turnover high enough? Are we reducing our debt/equity ratio? Is our return on equity sufficiently high? These ratios provide guidelines for control. Obviously, we have not covered all of them here. We have been most interested in those that reflect current operating performance. One other popular one which measures overall performance is the return on investment, which we will examine shortly.

Ratio analysis is so important to both managers and investors that many businesses have begun trying to improve the "understandability" of their financial statement so that this analysis can be conducted. For an example, see Table 12.6.

Controlling Overall Operations

The control techniques we have just examined are designed to help the organization control specific areas of its operations. However, many businesses are also interested in controlling *overall* operations. They feel that concentrating on

Table 12.6
Telling It Like It Is

Financial statement analysis is of importance not only to managers but to investors as well. In recent years many firms have begun changing the makeup of their annual reports so that they are now understandable and both managers and investors who want to learn how the firm is doing can pick up the report and read it without having to wade their way through a lot of legal or accounting jargon. In fact, firms are going out of their way to explain their strategy and operational successes. Reports are now 10 to 40 percent larger than those of just a few years ago. Commenting on this, *Business Week* reports that:

Corporations seem to be a bit more imaginative and expansive in providing sales and earnings breakdowns by product segment and geographical location. . . . W. R. Grace & Company and Gulf Oil Corp. go even further and combine two concepts, giving investors a picture of foreign operations by individual major product or service.

Furthermore, almost half the companies surveyed by *Business Week* had tax disclosure, generally in the form of a three-part table. These notes first divided the tax figure from the income statement into taxes currently payable and deferred taxes, then went ahead and analyzed the individual elements that gave rise to tax deferral, and finally reconciled these figures with the U.S. amount in both dollar and percentage terms. Additionally, 8 percent of the firms carried special sections describing the work of individual board committees, letting the reader know what the board of directors was doing. Finally, noted *Business Week,* some of the firms gave a great deal of attention to explaining just what goes into a balance sheet, income statement, and other basic financial documents. Koppers Co. carried line-by-line explanations in the margins of each of its key financial statements, and General Electric, National Can, and the Celanese Corporation took extra pains to assist shareholders in using the financial footnotes. And AT&T again produced special versions of its annual report on both records and in Braille.

Developments such as these are allowing people to perform financial statement analysis on the corporations of their choice. The result is a more informed investor, who can invest more money in the winners and prune investments in the marginal and losing firms.

Source: "The Annual Report 1978: Thick and Innovative," *Business Week,* April 16, 1979, pp. 114+.

piecemeal control can be dangerous to the overall success of their operation. Three of the most popular overall control techniques are return on investment, key area control, and auditing.

Return on Investment

▪ ROI is a comprehensive control measure.

One common overall approach to controlling operations is *return on investment.* As seen in Figure 12.4, return on investment (ROI) is equal to the profit margin on sales multiplied by capital turnover. Notice, however, that a great many inputs affect ROI, making it a very comprehensive type of control.

In particular, many firms like return on investment because it helps them answer the question: How well are we doing with what we have invested? A careful analysis of the figure shows that ROI can be expressed this way:

$$\frac{\text{Profit}}{\text{Sales}} \times \frac{\text{Sales}}{\text{Investment}}.$$

The return on investment will be a percentage, such as 12 percent, 15.2 percent, or 18.7 percent.

▪ It has many benefits.

ROI is useful in helping the organization assess the overall effectiveness of its various product lines or divisions. For example, a small firm might have three

Figure 12.4
Return on Investment

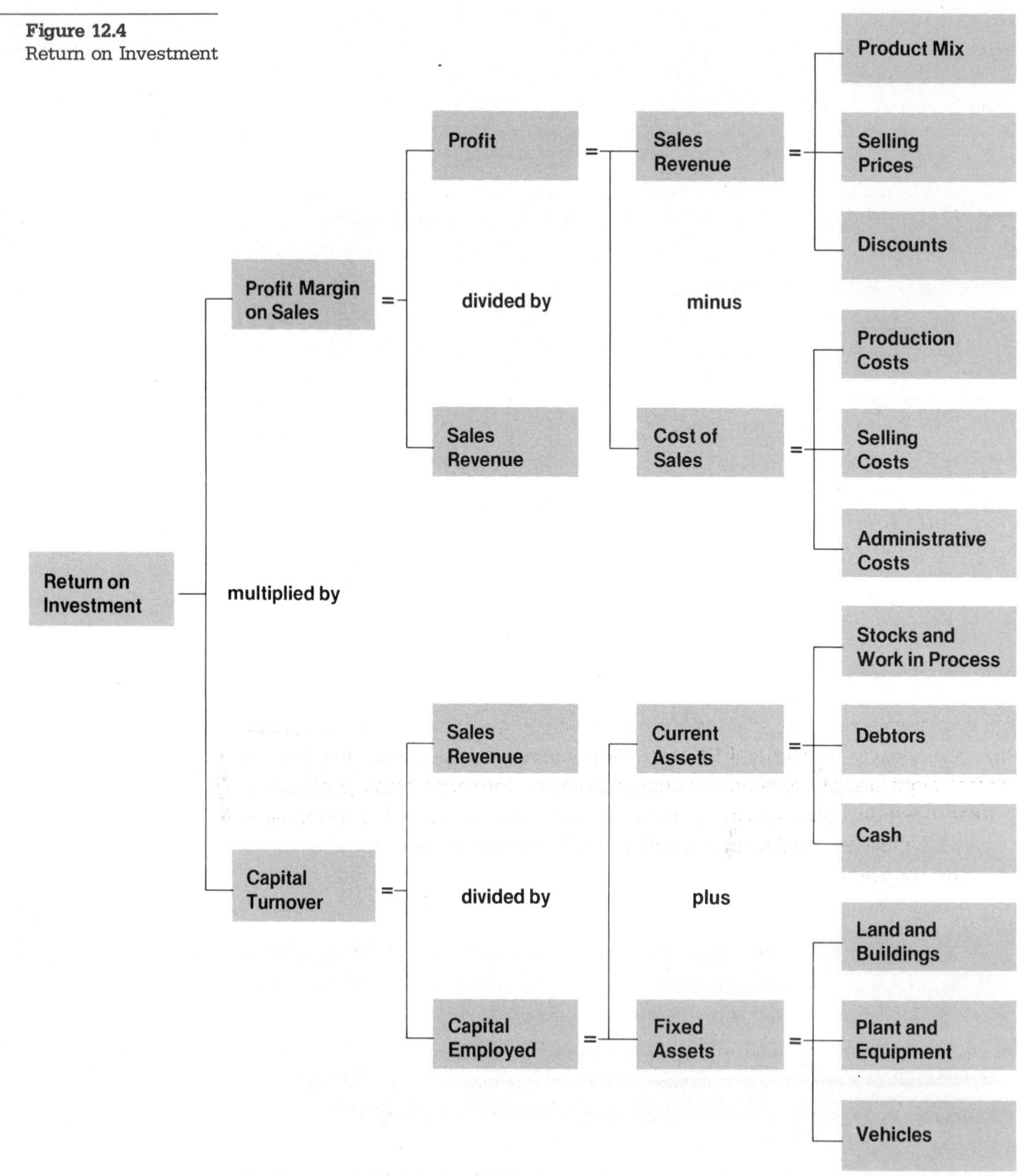

product lines, while a large competitor has eleven. The small one will not be able to capture as large a share of the market as the competition. Nor can it make as much money. However, the small firm could compare its performance to the large one by looking at its ROI. After all, the small company should have less money invested in its product lines, and so profit as a percentage of investment may well be about the same as that of the large firm.

Another benefit of ROI is that when there is poor performance from one of the product lines or divisions, the organization can backtrack and find out what is causing the problem. For example, looking at Figure 12.4, the sales revenue might be down, the cost of sales might be up, or the amount of investment might be too high for the amount of sales revenue generated by the product line. In any event, by examining the various aspects of the return on investment formula, it is possible to pinpoint areas that require attention.

Many firms use ROI as a control measure in determining whether to invest more money in a product line, leave the line alone, or sell it away. By comparing expected and actual ROI, and then looking at what the rest of the firms in the industry did, the top management can make the final decision about the various lines. In short, controlling of ROI can be very helpful. However, it is not the only type of overall control technique available, and it is often supplemented by others such as key area control.

Key Area Control

Key area control consists of identifying key areas of operations and then monitoring them closely. At General Electric, most famous for its use of this kind of control, eight areas have been designated as key performance areas: profitability, market position, productivity, product leadership, personnel development, employee attitudes, public responsibility, and the balance between short-range and long-range goals.

- Profitability. GE uses total dollar profit rather than return on investment. This profit, minus a charge for capital investment, takes into account the cost of the investment. It also helps management focus directly on increasing dollar profits rather than on improving the appearance of return on investment.
- Market position. This measures how well the firm is doing in relation to other companies in the industry. Share of the market is one of the key criteria here. In addition, the company attempts to measure customer satisfaction and to discover what the consumer wants but is not getting.
- Productivity. In this area, the company attempts to measure how efficiently its resources are being used. Two of the major areas the firm concentrates on are payroll costs and the efficient use of plant and machinery.
- Product leadership. This is the ability to lead an industry in engineering, manufacturing, and marketing of new products, and the improvement of old products. In measuring such performance, members of these three departments

evaluate the cost, quality, and market position of a product and decide what improvements, if any, are needed.

■ GE's key performance areas.

- Personnel development. GE measures its performance in this area by determining whether its recruitment and on-the-job training programs are well designed and whether there is an adequate number of people to fill vacancies.
- Employee attitudes. Some of the areas the company keeps its eye on here include absenteeism, labor turnover, and safety records. Using attitude surveys, which are taken on a regular basis, the firm tries to gauge how content the workers are with the organization.
- Public responsibility. GE defines this area in terms of relationship to its employees, suppliers, local communities, and business community. In each case, indexes have been developed to evaluate how well the company is doing.
- Balance between short-range and long-range goals. In this area, the firm attempts to blend its current and future objectives by encouraging the formulation of long-range planning. For example, if the organization wants to increase its market share in a particular area during the next two years, current objectives must be formulated so as to lead toward this long-range objective. Likewise, if the company wants to achieve this objective, it may be necessary to invest a great deal of money now with no return for the next twenty-four months. By balancing the short- and long-range goals, the firm is able to see the impact each has on the other.

This approach is only one of the many that can be used for key area control. Other firms will identify other areas on which they want to concentrate their attention. However, all have one thing in common: Realizing that it cannot control every element of its operations, the firm highlights those that are most important and proceeds under the philosophy that if things are all right in the key control areas, they are all right throughout the organization.

Auditing

Still another overall control measure is that of auditing. The term *auditing* usually brings to mind a financial audit, such as that carried out by the Internal Revenue Service or the company's own certified public accounting firm. These are external financial audits and are designed to examine and evaluate the firm's financial transactions and accounts. However, of greater value to the organization are internal audits and management audits.

■ The organization's staff specialists can do it.

Internal Audit. An *internal audit* is conducted by the organization's own staff specialists. The auditing team examines and evaluates the firm's operations, determining where things have gone well and where corrective action is needed. In most cases, these audits are of a financial nature, but they need not be restricted solely to such matters. Nonquantitative areas can also be evaluated. When they are, the firm uses what is commonly called the management audit.

Management Audit. A *management audit* provides a broader, more detailed evaluation of the organization than either the external financial audit or internal audit. While the specific form may vary, it is commonly carried out by outside experts and is seldom done more than once every three to five years. Perhaps the best known are those conducted by the American Institute of Management (AIM). The AIM audit is based on the evaluation of the following operational categories:

■ Or an outside organization can.

1. Economic function. The audit evaluates the usefulness of the organization's goods and services to the public, as well as the contribution it makes to the national economy.

■ AIM's operational categories.

2. Corporate structure. The audit assesses the overal efficiency and effectiveness of the organization design.
3. Health of earnings. The quantity, quality, consistency, and stability of the company's earnings are evaluated. Measures such as return on investment are compared with those of similar organizations in the same industry.
4. Service to stockholders. The audit assesses the degree to which management provides the stockholders with investment security, capital growth, and reasonable dividends.
5. Research and development. The audit evaluates the company's R&D efforts and preparedness for the future.
6. Directorate analysis. The individual contribution, team effort, integrity, and acceptance of responsibility of each director are evaluated.
7. Fiscal policies. The financial structure of the firm and its application of fiscal policies and control to the attainment of both short- and long-term objectives are reviewed by the AIM team.
8. Production efficiency. The operating efficiency of the enterprise is evaluated for the purpose of determining how well the organization is maintaining its competitive position.
9. Sales vigor. The expertise, enthusiasm, and efficiency of the sales effort is assessed in an effort to evaluate the firm's ability to realize its full sales potential.
10. Executive evaluation. In this area the ability, industry, and integrity of the firm's executives are evaluated.[2]

Each of these categories has a point score, and the total figure can be compared to past performance or industry standards. However, this is not the only approach that can be used. For example, Robert Buchele has set forth a series of auditing categories, although he concentrates more on the organization's ability to meet future challenges than on previous performance (in contrast to the AIM audit).[3]

■ Common characteristics of audits.

Regardless of the type of audit, all have three common characteristics:

1. They encourage a systematic analysis of where the organization is and should be heading over the next three to five years.
2. They evaluate a series of organizational performance factors.
3. They assess top management's performance.

The result is an overall evaluation of the organization's operations.

"Try as we might, sir, our team of management consultants has been unable to find a single fault in the manner in which you conduct your business. Everything you do is a hundred per cent right. Keep it up! That will be eleven thousand dollars."

Summary

The control process consists of three basic steps: (1) the establishment of standards, (2) the comparison of results against standards, and (3) the correction of deviations. One of the most common control techniques is the budget, a formal, financial expression of a plan that is used for both setting objectives and evaluating results. The budgeting process starts with a forecast of sales or other sources of revenue. Then a determination of the costs associated with generating or earning this revenue is computed. From here the overall budget, with both the projected revenue and expenses, is broken down by division, department, or unit. In many organizations, flexible budgets are used so as to adjust for various levels of activity. Additionally, some organizations are now using zero-based budgeting (ZBB) because of the benefit it provides in helping identify and prune low-priority or wasteful programs.

Another important control technique is the breakeven point (BEP). The computation of this BEP is determined by dividing total fixed costs by the difference between selling price and variable cost. The BEP helps the firm identify the minimum number of units that must be sold if it is to break even. From here the organization can decide the minimum sales that will return it an acceptable profit and drop the line should sales fall below this amount.

Another traditional control technique is financial statement analysis. Using the balance sheet and income statement, the firm can conduct ratio analysis. Some of the examples provided in this chapter included the current ratio, inventory turnover, the debt/equity ratio, and the return on owner's equity.

The latter part of the chapter examined some of the techniques used for controlling overall operations. One of these is return on investment (ROI), which is the profit the firm obtains on its overall investment. Many firms use ROI as a control measure in determining whether to invest more money in a product line, leave the line alone, or sell it away.

The last technique examined in this chapter was auditing. While an internal audit can be useful, an external management audit can provide the firm a broader, more detailed evaluation. As used by organizations like the American Institute of Management, these units generally focus on a series of areas and evaluate how well management is doing in each. This systematic analysis of where the organization is and where it should be heading can be very beneficial to organizations interested in improving their overall performance.

Review and Study Questions

1. How does the controlling process work? Explain it in your own words.
2. How does an organization put together a budget? Describe the steps involved.
3. What is a flexible budget? How do organizations use them?
4. Why is zero-based budgeting popular? What do managers like about it?
5. Describe in your own words how the breakeven point can be calculated. Of what value is the breakeven point to the organization for control purposes?
6. In financial statement analysis, what would the following ratios tell the manager: the current ratio, the inventory turnover, debt/equity ratio, return on equity?
7. How is return on investment computed? What does it tell the manager?
8. What are some of the key control areas of interest to General Electric? Why does the organization use this form of control?
9. How does an internal audit differ from a management audit? Compare and contrast the two.

Key Terms in the Chapter

controlling process
budget
flexible budget
zero-based budgeting
breakeven point
balance sheet
income statement
asset
liability
owners' equity
current ratio
inventory turnover
debt /equity ratio
return on equity
return on investment
key area control
internal audit
management audit

Notes

1. For more on zero-based budgeting, see Peter A. Pyhrr, "Zero-Base Budgeting," *Harvard Business Review,* November-December 1970, pp. 111–121.
2. Jackson Martindell, "The Management Audit," *Proceedings of the Annual Meeting, Academy of Management* (1962, pp. 164–171; Jackson Martindell, *The Appraisal of Management* (New York: Harper & Row, 1962).
3. Robert R. Buchele, "How to Evaluate a Firm," *California Management Review,* Fall 1962, pp. 5–17.

Case: The Inflexible Budget

"We can't just draw up a budget and chisel it in stone."

The Perondi Company had a sales increase last year, but it could have been a lot greater had it not been for the firm's budgeting process. At Perondi, managers submit proposed budgets for their departments. These budgets are usually a reflection of the previous year, with an increase built in for inflation and growth.

The production department's budget this year was increased by 12 percent. This budget was premised on increases in sales of the product lines as follows:

Line	Sales (Percent) Increase
A	+20
B	+18
C	+12
D	+ 8
E	+ 1

However, this is not what happened. To management's surprise, Products A and B had very big sales years—at least on paper. The marketing department had orders that would have resulted in increases of 33 percent in Product A's sales and 27 percent in Product B's. Unfortunately, the production department did not have the budget to manufacture the units necessary to meet this demand.

Once the sales orders started coming in, the production department realized that it could not keep up with the orders. The head of the department called the vice-president of marketing and asked for an increase in the production budget, but the request was rejected. "We budget based on a 15 percent ROI," the vice-president told the production head, "and if we can get this, we're happy." In an effort to make the most of its success, the marketing department received an okay to raise prices. However, demand still remained strong and in some cases customers left their orders with the company on a "fill it as soon as you can" basis. Nevertheless, the inflexible budgeting strategy of the firm cost it money.

At the end-of-the-year management meeting, Frank Perondi admitted that the budgeting approach was a poor one. "We need a more flexible method of dealing with sales increases or decreases. We can't just draw up a budget and chisel it in stone," he said. "Let's have some ideas for preventing this in the future. And let's talk about replacing Product E. Its sales growth and profitability are too low." The meeting then turned to consideration of these issues.

Questions

1. How can Frank's company avoid the budgeting problem it had this year? Bring flexible budgeting into your answer.
2. How could ZBB help the firm in deciding which lines to keep and which to drop? Explain.
3. Is ROI a useful control technique for the Perondi Company? Why or why not?

Case: The Proposed Audit

Is it worth spending a lot of money to see whether more can be made?

Anne Fairchild is a hospital administrator; her 750-bed facility is located in a major metropolitan area. Anne has three associate administrators who report directly to her. These administrators supervise between four and seven departments each.

At weekly administrative meetings, Anne has computer printouts on all costs and revenues, and she discusses these with the other administrators. However, most of her time is spent talking about key area control factors: major cost items, spiraling inflation, the number of available patient beds, community relations, public image, and employee relations. The specific cost factors related to the individual departments are left to the associate administrators and the specific department heads. Anne does not get into the finer points of control; she concerns herself with these key areas only.

Last week Anne had a visit from an outside consulting firm. This company conducts management audits. It has proposed an overall audit of the hospital. The price quoted for the audit is well within the hospital's budget, and Anne is sure she can get approval from the board of directors for such an expenditure. However, she is somewhat unclear regarding the value of such an audit. She wonders whether the hospital could really benefit from such an audit. After all, the institution currently uses key area control and, when measured in terms of profitability, is in the top 20 percent of the nation's hospitals. Furthermore, the organization has never had a loss, has increased its bed facilities by 25 percent in the last five years, and is considered to be the best hospital in the city based on a recent newspaper poll taken among doctors and members of the community. On the other hand, Anne is wondering if a management audit might not help her improve operations even more. Before making a decision, she has decided to discuss the matter with her associate administrators.

Questions

1. How does key area control work? Explain.
2. What is a management audit? What would the outside consultants be doing for the hospital?
3. Do you think Anne would be wise to go ahead with the management audit? Why or why not? Would her associate administrators agree with your answer? Explain.

Chapter 13

Performance Appraisal and Organizational Development

Objectives of the Chapter

The traditional control techniques examined in the previous chapter will help the organization monitor its production and financial performance. However, there is also the human side of controlling, in which the manager examines how well the subordinate has performed and decides what kinds of rewards the individual should receive. This is called performance appraisal and will be the initial focus of our attention in this chapter. In carrying out this appraisal, managers use numerous instruments including graphic rating scales, the paired comparison method, behaviorally anchored rating scales, and management by objectives. The first objective of this chapter is to examine these appraisal instruments.

The second is to identify and discuss some of the common performance appraisal problems. Primary in this regard are the clarity of the appraisal form, the halo effect, central tendency, leniency, validity, and reliability. All will be examined in this chapter.

The third objective is to examine what is meant by organizational climate and look at the ways in which this climate can be measured.

The final objective is to study organizational development and review some of the common organizational development interventions that can be used in improving the organization's human resources.

When you have finished studying the material in this chapter, you should be able to:

1 Describe how the performance appraisal process works.
2 Describe the graphic rating scale, the paired comparison method, behaviorally anchored rating scales, and management by objectives.
3 Explain some of the common performance appraisal problems, including clarity of the appraisal form, the halo effect, central tendency, leniency, validity, and reliability.
4 Discuss whether pay should be directly linked to performance.
5 Define the term *organizational climate* and explain how it can be measured.
6 Define the term *organizational development* and describe some of the commonly used organizational development interventions.

Performance Appraisal

The basic control process studied in the previous chapter is used by the manager to compare expected and actual performance, and the results serve as the basis for setting further organizational objectives. At the same time, the results can be used for appraising the work force. In this way, the employees learn how well they are doing and are given feedback regarding how they can improve future performance. This process, known as *performance appraisal,* usually takes place once a year. It involves comparing the subordinate's expected and actual performance. In carrying out this appraisal, many managers commonly use a formal appraisal instrument to rank or rate the individual employee. One of the most popular appraisal instruments is the graphic rating scale.

Graphic Rating Scale

■ The graphic rating scale is easy to use.

The *graphic rating scale* is not only easy to understand but easy to use. Figure 13.1 provides an illustration. As seen in the figure, a series of job-related factors are identified and described. The manager is asked to rate each of the employees on these factors. The latter are usually placed on a continuum that ranges from outstanding to unsatisfactory or very good to extremely poor. In any event, an overall rating can be attained by simply noting the subordinate's performance on each of the factors. In developing this rating some organizations weight the factors for examining by giving 5 points for an outstanding rating on a factor, 4 for a good rating, and so on down to a 1 for an unsatisfactory rating. Then an overall weighted score is determined by adding up the totals and dividing by the number of factors. For example, in Figure 13.1, if the individual was outstanding on two factors, good on one factor, and satisfactory on the last, the point total and

Figure 13.1
Graphic Rating Scale (Partial Form)

Name____________ Department____________ Date________

	Outstanding	Good	Satisfactory	Fair	Unsatisfactory
Quantity of Work Volume of work under usual conditions	___	___	___	___	___
Quality of Work Accuracy, neatness, and thoroughness of work	___	___	___	___	___
Job Knowledge Understanding of facts and factors relevant to the job	___	___	___	___	___
Dependability Conscientiousness, thoroughness, accurateness, and reliability	___	___	___	___	___

weighted average score would be: 5 + 5 + 4 + 3 ÷ 4 = 4.25. The weighted scores of all the employees could then be determined and everyone eventually ranked from highest to lowest based on this score.

Paired Comparison Method

Another common method of performance appraisal is the *paired comparison.* In the graphic rating scale, everyone could be rated excellent or unsatisfactory on all factors with the result being identically weighted scores. The paired comparison prevents this from happening. Each individual is compared against all the others in the respective unit or department. An example is provided in Figure 13.2. Notice that in this particular figure Gentry has the highest rating for work quality. The individual is ranked superior to all of the others. Of course, this paired comparison is only for work quality. The manager can use a series of these comparisons for such things as work quantity and job knowledge and then average the rankings.

▪ Paired comparison ranks the workers from first to last.

Figure 13.2
Paired Comparison Method Used for Work Quality

	Personnel Being Rated				
As Compared To:	Franklin	Gentry	Harding	Ivory	Jackson
Franklin		+	−	+	+
Gentry	−		−	−	−
Harding	+	+		+	+
Ivory	−	+	−		+
Jackson	−	+	−	−	

Gentry has the highest ranking for work quality.

Behaviorally Anchored Rating Scales

In recent years a new appraisal method, known as *behaviorally anchored rating scales,* or BARS for short, has become popular. Advocates of this appraisal method claim that it provides more detailed and equitable evaluations than anything else in the field. On the one hand, the approach can be time-consuming to develop and implement. On the other hand, however, it is systematic and ties performance *directly* to job related behaviors. The manager does not search his or her mind asking, "Exactly how effective is Harry as a worker?" With the use of BARS, the manager knows what to look for and how to make the evaluation. Figure 13.3 provides an example of a behaviorally anchored rating scale used for measuring interpersonal relations among interviewers and claims deputies in a public sector agency.

▪ BARS ties performance to job-related behaviors.

Note that the rating scale spells out nine different types of interpersonal behavior. This helps the manager evaluate the subordinate, for the individual now knows the various types of behavior that should be rated and the value that is associated with each.

Figure 13.3
Behaviorally
Anchored Rating Scale
(Partial Form)

Interpersonal Relationships—Behaves in a manner appropriate to the situation and individuals involved.

Employment interviewers and claims deputies must possess interpersonal skills in performing their work. Some people can initiate and maintain effective relations with job applicants, employers and co-workers. Others have difficulty establishing effective relations with outside groups and their associates. When making this rating, evaluate each person only on skill in human relationships.

Interpersonal relations with others (applicants, employers, co-workers) not only alleviates but often prevents difficult emotional and social situations; this implies a sensitivity to and understanding of the behavior of others.

9 With a demanding or complaining client, could be expected to gain control of the interview and direct it toward employment assistance.

8 This interviewer, in charge of a program, could be expected to offer full assistance to co-workers in understanding program content.

7 If an employer complained about a filed claim, interviewer could be expected to initially listen and then calmly discuss unemployment insurance, rules and regulations with the employer.

Interpersonal relations with others (applicants, employers, co-workers) is such that it does not complicate difficult emotional and social situations; this implies usually working effectively and cooperatively with others.

6 In the presence of an individual crying over the loss of a much needed job, could be expected to respond sympathetically.

5 In interviewing an applicant who talks rapidly and continuously about his employment problems, could be expected to listen attentively.

4 If an applicant complains about Employment Office service, interviewer/claims deputy could be expected to become rather impatient and antagonistic toward client.

3 Would expect this interviewer to fail to properly explain Employment Office functions to a new applicant.

Interpersonal relations with others (applicants, employers, co-workers) is such that it frequently complicates or creates difficult emotional or social situations.

2 If claimant had problems with claim, interviewer could be expected to reply: "Read the instructions and then come back."

1 If a repeater applicant came in after failing to report for a job, interviewer could be expected to tell him not to come in again.

Source: Cheedle W. Millard, "The Development and Evaluation of Behavioral Criteria for Measuring the Performance of Non-Operational Employees," University of Nebraska, Ph.D. dissertation, 1974, p. 183.

By constructing a series of these rating scales, the organization can have the manager evaluate the subordinates along such key performance-related areas as quality of work, quantity of work, knowledge, judgment, and the like.

Who constructs these rating scales? The managers or others who have knowledge of the job do. They begin by identifying specific behaviors that are both effective and ineffective. They then cluster these behaviors into performance-related groups (work quality, work quantity) and then construct a continuum of seven to nine statements ranging from highly ineffective behavior (one point) to highly effective behavior (nine points).

BARS can be an expensive approach to performance evaluation because of all the time and effort involved in constructing the various rating scales. However, practicing managers report that they like the approach because:

■ Benefits of BARS.

1. Standards for performance appraisal are spelled out.
2. The instrument is put together by individuals who are familiar with the job, so the form tends to be both valid and reliable.
3. The approach takes much of the subjectivity out of the appraisal.

The manager can be objective and comprehensive in evaluating the subordinate.

Management by Objectives

Management by objectives (MBO) is an overall appraisal system used at all levels of the hierarchy.[1] The process is really quite simple, consisting of but three major steps:

■ Steps in MBO.

1. The superior and the subordinate jointly identify the objectives that the latter is to pursue.
2. The subordinate's areas of responsibility are spelled out in terms of specific expected results.
3. These measures are used as guides in operating the unit and evaluating the subordinate's contribution.

Figure 13.4 illustrates the sequential order in which the process is carried out.

The objectives are, whenever possible, spelled out in quantitative terms by describing what is to be done and by when it will be accomplished. If the production output in Unit 6 is to be increased by 30 percent by the end of the year, this is the way the objective is written. Furthermore, it is common to find the manager breaking this objective down into three-month segments so that it can be analyzed on a quarterly basis. In this way if there are some progress problems, corrective action can be taken immediately.

It is also common to find the manager and the subordinate working to spell out exactly how progress will be evaluated. In our above example, output could be measured from production records. This is easy to do. However, what if the subordinate is in the public relations department and has an objective of improving the company's image in the local area? How can this objective be measured? This is more difficult to do. The manager might be content to say, "Okay, if you give ten speeches in front of civic groups and finish that new public relations ad campaign you are working on, we will agree that you have met the objective of improving the company image." Obviously, this objective does not directly lend itself to a quantitative approach and so progress is measured indirectly.

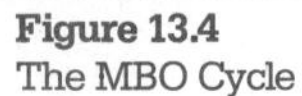
Figure 13.4
The MBO Cycle

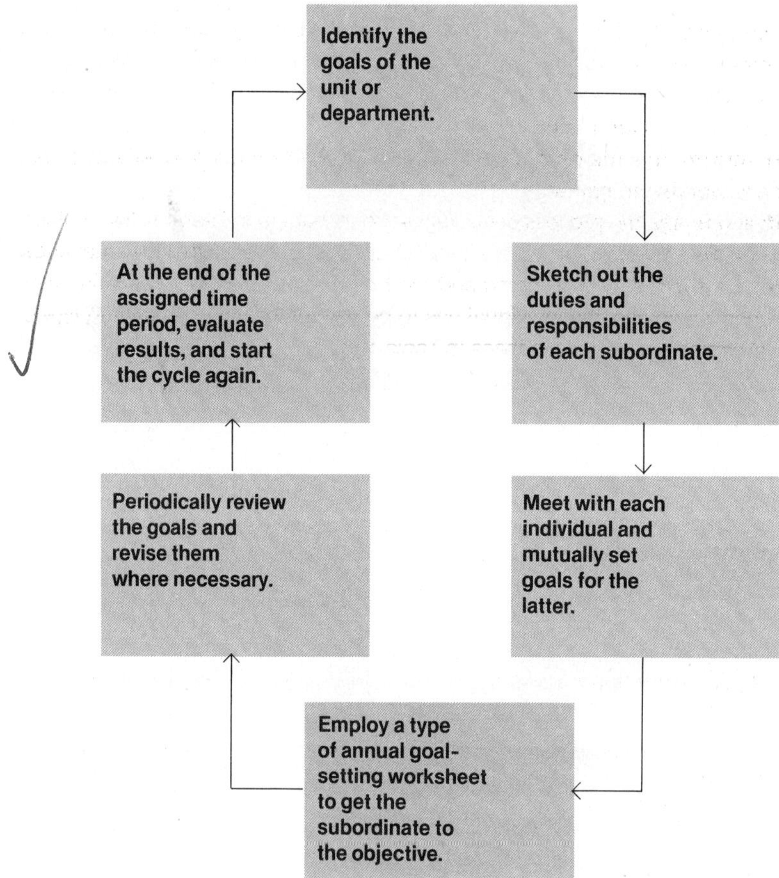
Identify the goals of the unit or department.
Sketch out the duties and responsibilities of each subordinate.
Meet with each individual and mutually set goals for the latter.
Employ a type of annual goal-setting worksheet to get the subordinate to the objective.
Periodically review the goals and revise them where necessary.
At the end of the assigned time period, evaluate results, and start the cycle again.

Finally, once the manager and the subordinate agree on what the latter is to do, it is typical to find these objectives typed up and a copy given to each party. In fact, some organizations have the subordinate read the objectives and then sign his or her name. In this way the manager has a copy that shows that the subordinate understood and agreed to pursue these particular objectives.

■ It is easy to understand.

What Makes MBO Popular? Why is MBO so popular in organizations today? Four reasons can be cited. First, it is both comprehensive and easy to understand. The process can be used with every boss and subordinate throughout the structure so that all employees know what they are supposed to be doing; it is easy to follow the logic of the process; and all know how they are going to be evaluated.

■ Emphasizes quantifiable objectives.

Second, MBO puts strong emphasis on quantifiable objectives which are tied to a time dimension. It relates both what is to be accomplished and by when.

Third, every superior asks the same questions: What are the overall objectives of this department? In light of this answer, what objectives should each of my subordinates be pursuing to ensure that I meet these overall objectives? Employing these answers as a guideline, the superior identifies those things the subordinates need to do. Continuing this process up the line, MBO keeps everyone focused toward the major objectives of the organization and ensures that everyone is working in harmony.

■ Provides overall direction.

Fourth and finally, the process encourages the managers to keep the list of objectives assigned to the subordinates to a handful, say, four to five, so that the latter know what they are supposed to be doing and the boss has little trouble evaluating their performance. Of course, the individual has to be careful to avoid committing typical MBO goal-setting errors such as those in Table 13.1.

■ Makes evaluation easier.

Table 13.1
MBO Goal Setting—Doing It Right

George S. Odiorne is perhaps the best known individual in the area of management by objectives (MBO). Writing recently about the problems that can be encountered in setting up an MBO system, he has noted that organizations make many errors in establishing goals in the MBO process. The following constitute some of the most common and offer suggestions for overcoming them.

1. Don't stress the obvious—set progressive, innovative goals. Do not just repeat what was done last year or modify it slightly.
2. Every goal accepted means the rejecting of others—know why you accepted the goals you did and rejected the others. In doing so, look at all of the objectives.
3. A mistake in goals will produce a mistake in activity—if people are heading toward the wrong goal, a lot of time and effort are being wasted. Choose the right goals.
4. Goals are most useful when they are stated as indicators. Say what you are going to do. Spell it out, and where possible quantify it.
5. Some objectives are an ego trip—stay away from these.
6. Other things equal, participative goal setting should be tried first—get the subordinate involved in the goal-setting process. If the individual drags his or her feet, then impose the goals on the individual.
7. If a goal will make somebody important uneasy, tone it down—don't develop criticism or hostility among upper-level managers. You need them to support your efforts.
8. Experience is a pretty good teacher, and experienced goal setters set better goals—thus the more you get people involved in goal setting, the more meaningful the process will become.
9. Goals are a means of attaining power—people set goals to help themselves in their drive for power, and managers have this kind of drive. Thus you help develop management talent through goal setting.
10. Good goals always create the resources to produce them—a good idea is almost always funded, especially if it is a necessary and potentially productive one.
11. Goals which are routine won't excite anybody—effective goal setting allows people to "stretch" their abilities and forces them to develop their talents.
12. Let people overstate themselves a little bit in their goals—if someone's objectives are too optimistic, let the person try to attain them anyway. You might be pleasantly surprised, and if not, the person will learn a lesson for the next time.

Source: Adapted from George S. Odiorne, "How to Succeed in MBO Goal-Setting," *Personnel Journal*, August 1978, pp. 427–429. Reprinted with permission, *Personnel Journal*, Costa Mesa, CA, copyright August 1978.

Performance Appraisal Problems

■ The form can be unclear.

Before concluding our discussion of the performance appraisal process, it is important to briefly discuss some of the common performance appraisal problems with which the manager should be familiar. One of these is the *clarity of the appraisal form.* If the form does not spell out the factors to be used in rating the subordinate and what each of these factors contains, the manager may end up giving subjective evaluations based on how well he or she remembers the worker's performance.

■ Subjective appraisal is not totally accurate.

A second problem is the *halo effect,* which exists when the manager appraises an individual the same on all traits regardless of the person's actual performance on these traits. For example, Ralph is always on time with his reports and the manager lets this affect Ralph's overall performance rating, resulting in a very high evaluation. And this can occur despite the fact that Ralph is not a very productive worker. This is in contrast to Marie, who is always late with her reports but, otherwise, is an excellent performer. She continually receives poor performance ratings because the manager lets her tardiness in turning in her reports negatively influence the overall evaluation.

Source: Motley's Crew, December 16, 1977. Reprinted by permission of Chicago Tribune–N.Y. News Syndicate.

■ Everyone is rated average.

A third common problem is called the *central tendency;* it describes those managers who rate everyone as average, regardless of actual performance. Such an approach, of course, punishes the superior workers and rewards the poor ones.

■ Or very high.

A fourth performance appraisal problem is that of *leniency.* In this case, the manager gives all subordinates the highest possible rating. Here again, the high performers are being shortchanged and the lower performers are being rewarded.

■ Validity and reliability are important.

How can the organization prevent these problems? In addition to providing training for the managers on how to evaluate people, there is the need to build validity and reliability into the performance appraisal instruments. By *validity* we mean that the instrument measures what we want it to measure. If work quality is important, this factor is evaluated by the rating form. By *reliability* we mean that the instrument measures the same thing over and over. If Jane's output is high every month, she should get high ratings for work quality regardless of the manager who is performing the rating.

In recent years a great deal of attention has been directed toward dealing with these kinds of performance appraisal problems. Today it is common to find behavioral scientists playing an active role in designing these instruments and also advising organizations on how to carry out their evaluation process. Gone is the day when a manager could say "Barry is a real nice guy, while Henry has no real social skills; so I gave all the merit money to Barry and none to Henry." Rather, it is typical to find many organizations carefully evaluating organizational performance and giving the greatest rewards to the most effective personnel. Table 13.2 shows how this works out in the evaluative procedures of some of the nation's biggest businesses.

Organizational Climate

Evaluation is one of several significant factors in creating worker feelings about a firm. Managers must ask: Are the workers satisfied with their conditions? Do they believe the organization has their best interests at heart? Do they feel that the management will give them a fair deal? Do they trust the management? Answers to these types of questions tell us about the *organizational climate.* This climate contains both observable and nonobservable aspects. In this regard, as seen in Figure 13.5, we can represent this climate in the form of an iceberg.

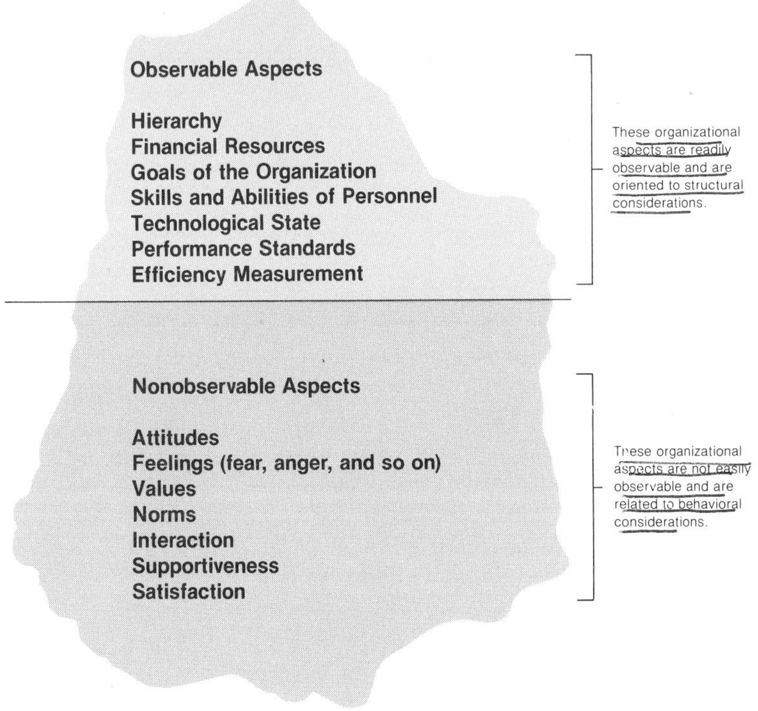

Figure 13.5
The Organizational Iceberg

Table 13.2
How to Get Ahead

A poll was taken recently among top corporate executives selected from a *Fortune 500* listing These managers were all asked to take a list of questionnaire items consisting of promotion-related statements selected from a wide variety of sources related to career advancement. The items were intended to provide a wide spectrum of factors that were representative of diverse schools of thought. What were the important promotion factors? The executives listed the following thirteen at the top of the list, while indicating what the situation in the firm is currently and what it should be.

	Is Currently	Should Be	Difference (Percent)
1. Comes up with new ways to handle problems.	100	99	−1
2. Is cooperative; has the spirit of teamwork.	100	99	−1
3. Has a good record of accomplishments.	100	99	−1
4. Is able to operate with a minimum of direction.	100	99	−1
5. Is able to argue logically.	100	99	−1
6. Is able to meet deadlines.	99	98	−2
7. Is able to communicate clearly and concisely.	99	90	−9
8. Is tactful in making suggestions to superiors.	98	82	−16
9. Is able to take suggestions from subordinates.	98	99	+1
10. Has the respect of colleagues.	98	99	+1
11. Has the respect of subordinates.	98	99	+1
12. Is able to sell his or her ideas.	98	99	+1
13. Understands the emotional makeup of people.	98	98	0
At the other extreme were the lowest-ranked items. They were the following:			
41. Is married.	24	14	−10
42. Has received job offers from other companies.	23	21	−2
43. Has a similar social background to those already at the top.	22	6	−16
44. Is white.	22	8	−14
45. Was born in the U.S.A.	16	12	−4
46. Has never been divorced.	14	15	+1
47. Regularly attends a house of worship.	14	18	+4
48. Lives in a residential area similar in quality to those already at the top.	5	3	−2
49. Belongs to the same club or lodge as those already at the top.	8	2	−6
50. Is a Republican.	3	3	0

The study found that competency-based promotion systems factors were more important than social, political, or religious factors. What you are or can do is more important than where you live, which country club (if any) you belong to, or what your religion or political affiliation is.

Source: Adapted from W. J. Heisler, "Promotion: What Does It Take To Get Ahead?" *Business Horizons*, April 1978, pp. 57–63. Reprinted by permission.

Some of the observable aspects include the hierarchy, financial resources, and goals of the organization. Some of the unobservable aspects include attitudes, feelings, and values. The former are easy to identify and when there are problems with them, direct control steps can be taken. The nonobservable cannot be seen; they must be measured with attitude questionnaires or some other instrument that helps identify and describe them. The approach is much more indirect. Before looking at how this can be done, however, let us examine how these nonobservable aspects change.

Causal, Intervening, and End-Result Variables

▪ Intervening variables are psychological.

In Figure 13.5 there is a series of identified nonobservable aspects. These are called *intervening variables.* They are internal psychological factors that describe how the employees feel about the organization.

▪ Causal variables affect intervening variables.

How do these intervening variables change? The answer is found in such *causal variables* as leadership styles, business strategies, and management decisions. When these variables change, they affect the intervening variables. For example, bringing in an autocratic leader to replace a democratic leader can lead to decline in attitude, feelings, and worker satisfaction. Thus, the causal variable of leadership style would affect the intervening variables.

▪ End-result variables are measurable.

The full impact is found in the *end-result variables* such as costs, output, tardiness, and absenteeism. If the leadership style changes from democratic to autocratic and costs and intervening variables decline, then costs will go up, output will decline, tardiness and absenteeism will rise, and so on. The three variables can be diagrammed as in Figure 13.6.

Causal Variables → **Intervening Variables** → **End-Result Variables**

Figure 13.6
Organizational Climate Linkage

The biggest problem in dealing with organizational climate is that changes in the causal variable may take months before showing their effect on the end-result variables. For example, from the time the organization announces that it is cutting back its contribution to the employee retirement program until the time the employees begin venting their anger by reducing their production output may take a total of eight weeks. How, then, can the organization know the current state of the organizational climate? How can they anticipate changes in this climate? The answers are found in measurement instruments like the Likert profile.

The Likert Profile

▪ Management systems.

The Likert profile is an instrument used to gather information about key organizational variables. In particular, the profile attempts to identify the type of leadership style and conditions under which the organization is currently operating. Table 13.3 shows the four basic systems. *System I* is called the *exploitive autocratic* approach. The management has virtually no trust or confidence in the subordinates. People are treated very badly. *System II* is the *benevolent autocratic* approach. Under this approach some confidence and trust in the employees are shown. *System III* is the *consultative democratic* approach. An increasing amount of confidence and trust is shown in the subordinates. Finally, in *System IV*, the *participative democratic* approach is used. Here one finds complete confidence and trust in the subordinates.

Likert has found that by asking people to fill out a profile of organizational characteristics, a partial form of which is shown in Table 13.3, it is possible to monitor and predict changes in organizational performance. For example, if the

Table 13.3
A Profile of Organizational Characteristics

Organizational Variables	System I Exploitive Autocratic	System II Benevolent Autocratic	System III Consultative Democratic	System IV Participative Democratic
Leadership How much confidence and trust are shown in the subordinates?	Almost none.	Some.	A substantial amount.	A great deal.
Motivation Is predominant use made of: (1) fear, (2) threats, (3) punishment, (4) rewards, (5) involvement?	1, 2, 3, and occasionally 4.	4 and sometimes 3.	4 and sometimes 3 and 5.	5 and 4 predominantly.
Communication What is the usual flow of information in the organization?	Down.	Mostly down.	Down and up.	Down, up, and sideways.
Decision Making At what levels are decisions made?	Mostly at the top.	Policy is set at the top; some delegation occurs.	Broad policy is set at the top; more delegation occurs.	Decisions are made throughout the entire organization.
Goal Setting How are goals determined?	Orders are issued from the top.	Orders are issued; some comments are invited.	After discussion, orders are issued.	Except in crisis situations, there is group action.
Control How concentrated are the review and control functions?	Very highly at the top.	Quite highly at the top.	Moderately; delegation to the lower level.	Widely shared.

last profile showed that the organization was operating under a System II management and is currently operating under a System III management, Likert would predict that things are getting better and output will soon be increasing. If the reverse is taking place, he would predict that the output will soon start to fall off.

While the Likert instrument is only one of the many that can be used in measuring the organizational climate, the enterprise can remain alert to impending problems by monitoring climate factors. What can it do if it finds that things are going badly? For example, suppose a change in operating procedures was announced four months ago and there is still a great deal of worker resistance. One thing the organization can do is measure the department's attitudes and see whether they are declining. If so, it can work through the manager to try to straighten out the problem. However, sometimes outside assistance can be most helpful in controlling these situations. This is particularly true when the department or division has been having behavioral problems for some time. The management may not be able to straighten the situation out; it may require an outside change agent. This is where organizational development comes in.

Organizational Development

Organizational development, or OD, as it is commonly called, is a long-range effort to improve the organization's performance. The approach is very behavioral in orientation and seeks to overcome many of the problems that are so common to modern organizations: intragroup and intergroup conflict, lack of cooperative relationships throughout the organization, and uncertainty regarding what the unit or department should be doing. The basic premise of organizational development is that from time to time the climate in the organization is going to break down, and the organization must work to correct these problems before they become very serious. In doing so, it is common to find a *change agent* or *organizational development intervention specialist* being called in.

How OD Works

■ First is diagnosis.

This change agent, who may work within the firm on a full-time basis but more likely is brought in from the outside to deal with the problems, uses a three-part process: (1) diagnosis, (2) action, and (3) maintenance of the new situation. Here is how it works. First, the management, realizing that there are organizational behavior problems, brings in the change agent and the individual diagnoses the situation, finding out exactly what types of problems exist in the organization. Why is there a decline in output? Why is there increased tardiness or turnover? During this *diagnostic phase* the individual focuses on the groups or departments in which there seem to be problems. The change agent looks at the decision-making processes, communication patterns, and leadership styles that exist there, and studies the relationships that exist within the unit and between other units with which it interacts. At this stage the individual is very much like a doctor who is diagnosing a patient's condition.

Then comes the OD intervention.

The next stage is the *action phase.* This phase is characterized by what are called *OD interventions.* This is a catchall term used to describe the types of activities that the change agent will have the targeted individuals, groups, or departments engage in. Depending on the type of intervention used, and we shall be examining some of them very shortly, the change agent works to overcome the unit's current problems and get everyone working in a unified manner.

Followed by situation maintenance.

The final phase is one of *maintaining the new situation.* This is done by monitoring progress and seeing that everything is going according to plan. Now that the change agent has the various groups working in harmony, can the situation be maintained? Is there continued involvement, commitment, and investment in the program by the members? During this phase, the change agent works to keep employees from slipping back into their old ways.

OD Interventions

The specific type of OD intervention that is used will depend on the particular problem(s) the organization is facing. However, some of the typical goals of OD include the following:

Typical OD goals.

- To create an open, problem-solving climate.
- To supplement the authority associated with role or status with the authority of knowledge and competence.
- To locate decision-making and problem-solving responsibilities as close to the information source as possible.
- To build trust among persons and groups throughout an organization.
- To make competition more relevant to work goals and to maximize collaborative efforts.
- To develop a reward system which recognizes both the achievement of the organization's goals (profits or service) and the development of the people.
- To increase the sense of "ownership" of organizational objectives throughout the work force.
- To help managers to manage according to relevant objectives rather than according to "past practices" or according to objectives which do not make sense for one's areas of responsibilities.
- To increase self-direction for people within the organization.[2]

Specific OD interventions commonly fall into one of three types: personal interventions, intra- or intergroup interventions, or total interventions.

Personal Interventions. The personal intervention is used to improve individual performance. There are people in the organization, for example, who are concerned about what the future holds for them. They do not know whether they should stay with the firm or move to another organization. What will be best for their career? Their concerns are having an effect on their work output and the organization would like to help them make a decision. In this case, it is typical to see the change agent use what is called a *life and career planning intervention*. This intervention tries to draw together the past, present, and future by getting the individuals to concentrate on: (1) what they have done thus far in their careers, (2) where they currently are in their careers, and (3) where they hope to go in the future.

■ Career direction is determined.

While there are many types of life and career planning exercises, they almost all follow the same basic pattern. The participating individuals begin by putting together a life inventory, in which they note peak career experiences, the things they do well and poorly, and what they would still like to do. This provides a basis for discussing future career direction. Then the change agent and the participants talk about the likelihood of reaching these future goals. Can the person do it? Is the individual truly top management timber? If so, then the question is: Can the person attain this position if he or she remains with this organization? If the answer is yes, attempts are made to sketch out the path that will have to be taken. If the answer is no, the question is whether there are any other organizations the individual could move to where this route to the top would be available.

Typically, these life and career planning exercises take only a day, although they can last as long as a week, with a great deal of time spent generating data about oneself, analyzing the results individually and in groups, and then formulating goals and action plans. In any event, the value of the intervention is that it helps individuals who are contemplating career changes or who feel they are in a rut think through their life-style and career patterns. The intervention helps management control operations by straightening out employee career-related problems.

Intragroup Interventions. Intragroup interventions take place *within* a particular group. A typical illustration is *role analysis technique* (RAT), which is designed to clarify both role expectations and role obligations of team members. This kind of intervention is useful when the members of the work group are unclear as to their roles and do not know how they are supposed to be working with each other.

The first step in the intervention is to choose one of the workers and discuss the duties and behaviors in which this individual should engage in order to fulfill his or her role. The individual explains what he or she thinks the job consists of and how it should be carried out. Then all the other members of the group get the opportunity to either add or delete some of these duties so that the final role description is one that is understood by all members of the group. This procedure is then continued, in a round-robin fashion, until everyone in the group has had his or her job analyzed.

■ Work roles are clarified.

When the intervention is over, the group members understand their own jobs and those of everyone else in the group. Additionally, each worker knows what he or she is supposed to be doing and what can be expected of the others in the group. As a result, RAT serves not only to clarify work roles but to ensure commitment to them as well.

Intergroup Interventions. Sometimes there are organizational problems that arise *between* work groups. In these cases an intergroup intervention can be helpful. While numerous interventions can be used, one of the most popular is called *intergroup team building*.

Typically, the intervention begins with the change agent meeting with the groups and trying to determine whether relations between them can be improved. If this appears to be possible, the formal intervention starts. It usually begins with each of the groups being put in separate rooms and asked to construct two lists. The first contains their perceptions, attitudes, and feelings about the other group(s). This list relates such things as what they like about the other group and what about the other group upsets them. The second list contains the group's predictions of what the other group(s) may be saying about them on their particular list. In constructing this second list, the group asks questions, such as: What does the other group like about us? What do they dislike? Exactly how do they see us?

■ Groups work out their differences.

The groups are then brought together to share the information on their respective lists. When this is over, the groups then return to their individual meeting places to discuss what they have learned about themselves and the other groups. Often the areas of disagreement or friction between them are seen to rest on erroneous perceptions and communication breakdowns. Once this is realized, each group becomes aware that there is far less friction than they initially perceived. The groups then construct a list of priority issues which still need to be resolved, and they meet again. At this point they share their lists and decide what they need to do to improve their relations. The ideas are written down and put in order of priority. Then an action plan for dealing with them is drawn up.

For all practical purposes, this ends the team building intervention. However, in many cases the OD change agent comes back again to check on the progress of the teams. Is everything going according to plan? Do they need any further help in meeting their agreed upon objectives?

Total Organizational Interventions. Some OD interventions are designed to cover the entire organization and, as such, are referred to as total OD interventions. One of the most common is the *grid OD.* This approach was discussed earlier when we studied the managerial grid in our discussion of leadership. As we noted then, the objective of the grid is to (1) examine which leadership style is being currently used by the manager, (2) determine which would be most effective, and (3) then develop a plan to move from the former to the latter. The grid approach to OD consists of six basic phases.[3]

■ There are six grid phases.

The first phase of this intervention is basically a seminar diagnosing the current leadership styles of the organization's managers and developing team-action skills. Then, during phase two, the focus is turned to perfecting teamwork. The third phase is given over to developing intergroup teamwork, with each group individually analyzing what an ideal relationship would be and sharing these ideas with the other groups. Representatives from units in direct contact are asked to develop these ideal relationships by discussing the problems associated with attaining them and then formulating a plan of action for moving toward them. Phase four, which can take up to one year, focuses on developing an ideal overall organization strategic plan. Phase five requires the greatest amount of time, often two to three years, and is concerned with closing the gap between where the organization is and where it wants to go. Finally, in phase six, after the organization is well into its implementation of the ideal strategic mode, a systematic critique of the five phases is begun. Progress is evaluated, barriers are identified, and further action steps are determined. Primary attention is given to reinforcing the new methods that have been developed during the initial five phases so that they become standard practices. During this phase the organization tries very hard to prevent any pressure toward slipping back to its old ways of doing things.

OD Evaluation

■ Varying levels of success have been reported.

How well do OD interventions work? Organizations report varying levels of success, depending on how well particular interventions are designed and implemented. The important thing is that the specific intervention address the organization's problems. For example, it does no good to use an intragroup intervention to deal with an intergroup problem. Additionally, there must be the requisite attention to the diagnosis part of the process. Unless the OD change agent carefully studies the organization's problems, it is virtually impossible to know what type of intervention will work best. Finally, some of the OD interventions, as in the case of grid OD, take quite a bit of time to implement. Unless the intervention has the support of top management and unless the organization is willing to stay with the intervention until it has been finished, it is likely that the entire process will prove to be a waste of both time and money.

For control purposes, OD is an important area of consideration. Many problems are people problems that cannot be solved by more careful budgeting, a lowering of the breakeven point, or a more detailed approach to zero-based budgeting. When there are people problems, the organization needs to recognize them and determine how to deal with them. No organization will be performing at maximum efficiency unless adequate consideration is given to both the work environment and the people who operate there. And when there are people problems, they often require more than a promise from management that things will get better or a training program to improve the manager's leadership style. Many times an OD approach is needed to straighten out the situation. Thus, OD can be an important part of an organization's control process.

Summary

When the control process is applied to the individual employee, it takes the form of a performance appraisal and involves comparing the subordinate's expected and actual performance. In doing this, the manager can use a number of different methods or instruments. One of the most popular is the graphic rating scale, which is easy not only to understand but to use. Another is the paired comparison method, in which everyone is ranked against everyone else in a particular work group. A third is behaviorally anchored rating scales, which identify performance-related behavior and ask the manager to evaluate each individual in relation to these behaviors. A fourth is management by objectives, which is an overall appraisal system that can be used at all levels of the hierarchy. All four of these were discussed in the chapter.

In carrying out performance appraisals, the manager must contend with a number of problems. These include the clarity of the appraisal form, the halo effect, central tendency, leniency, validity, and reliability.

The latter part of the chapter examined organizational climate and the need for the enterprise to be aware of climate factors. Using instruments like the Likert profile to examine and monitor intervening variables, one can measure this climate. When it gets out of line, organizational development interventions can be used in restoring organizational equilibrium. Some of the commonly used OD interventions include life and career planning, role analysis technique, intergroup team building, and grid OD. These kinds of interventions help the organization deal with people problems that cannot be handled with traditional control techniques such as budgeting, lowering of the breakeven point, or a more detailed approach to zero-based budgeting.

Review and Study Questions

1. How does performance appraisal work? What are the steps that are carried out in this process?
2. Describe the graphic rating scale.
3. Why is the graphic rating scale so widely used in performance appraisal?
4. How is a behaviorally anchored rating scale put together? Discuss the process. Also explain why practicing managers like this approach to performance evaluation.
5. How does the management by objectives process work? Discuss its major steps. Why is MBO so popular among modern managers?
6. What is meant by each of the following: halo effect, central tendency, leniency, validity, and reliability?
7. In your own words, what is meant by the term *organizational climate?*
8. In what way are causal, intervening, and end-result variables related? Explain.
9. Of what value is the Likert profile to the modern manager? Explain, incorporating into your answer the four management systems used in the profile.
10. How does organizational development intervention work? Be sure to define the term *OD* in your answer.
11. How do each of the following OD interventions work: life and career planning intervention, role analysis technique, intergroup team building, and grid OD.
12. Of what value is OD in the control process? Explain.

Key Terms in the Chapter

performance appraisal
graphic rating scale
paired comparison method
behaviorally anchored rating scales
management by objectives
halo effect
central tendency
leniency
validity
reliability
organizational climate
causal variable
intervening variable
end-result variable
System I
System II
System III
System IV
organizational development
change agent
life and career planning intervention
role analysis technique
intergroup team building
grid OD

Notes

1. George S. Odiorne, *Management by Objectives* (New York: Pitman Publishing, 1969).
2. Warren Bennis, *Organization Development* (Reading, Mass.: Addison-Wesley, 1969), pp. 36–37.
3. Robert R. Blake and Jane S. Mouton, *Building a Dynamic Corporation through Grid Organization Development* (Reading, Mass.: Addison-Wesley, 1969), pp. 76–109.

Performance Appraisal Techniques

Graphic Rating Scale
Paired Comparison method
Behaviorally Anchored Rating Scales (BARS)
management By objectives (MBO)

Performance appraisal Problems –
① clarity of appraisal form
② halo effect
③ central tendency
④ leniency

validity and reliability need to be built into the performance appraisal tool.

Case: Evaluating Evaluation Methods

Finding the right way to evaluate people depends on the evaluation of the evaluators.

All of the employees in the Compton Insurance Company are guaranteed cost-of-living adjustments. Once a year the firm raises all salaries by whatever percentage living costs have risen. Thus there is never any fear on the part of the workers that their salaries will be eroded by inflation.

In addition to these adjustments, Compton offers merit pay. Usually it averages between 5 and 7 percent, although some people get nothing and others receive as much as 20 percent. The very large increases are usually given only at the lower levels where salaries are most likely to need adjustments, so there is a gap between new employees and those who have been with the firm for some time.

In the past, merit increases have been given on the basis of informal evaluations. Each manager would look over people in his or her unit and decide who should get merit increases and how much it should be. Many people would get 2 to 3 percent and a small number would get more. The higher the percentage, of course, the smaller the number of people who would get it. Furthermore, merit increases over 6 percent had to be cleared with the manager's boss.

Four months ago, the company started looking into a formal performance evaluation system. The president believes that the evaluation process must be more objective and thorough than is currently the case. At the present time, there is more support for using a graphic rating scale than any other evaluation system, although some line managers believe a paired comparison approach is superior. None are particularly interested in either BARS or MBO. The head of the personnel department is concerned about this because he feels that these first two methods lack the rigor of the latter two. There is a greater likelihood, in his opinion, of validity and reliability problems with the graphic rating and paired comparison methods than with BARS and MBO. He would like to see attention given to a more detailed, rigorous evaluation of all employees and then have merit increases tied directly to these evaluations. However, he is in the minority among all the managers.

Questions

1. How does the graphic rating scale work? Paired comparison? BARS? MBO?
2. When is validity a performance appraisal problem? When is reliability a problem in performance appraisal? Would BARS or MBO or better appraisal instruments than the graphic rating scale or paired comparison in overcoming validity and performance appraisal problems?
3. Should merit pay be tied directly to performance? Explain.

Case: Up and Down Again

"We're right back where we started when we bought Clyde's firm." Why?

The employees at Clyde Whelan's Company were a very close group, even though there were over 400 workers and 50 managers in the firm. About two years ago Clyde sold the company to a large organization which put in its own top management team to run the operation. Before the sale, Clyde's management team was best described as System III, while the new top management team uses basically a System I approach. They believe that a "get tough" philosophy is needed to achieve maximum output, which they have estimated to be 1,750,000 units every three months. When they took over the company, quarterly output was 1,100,000 units. Since then the output has changed as follows:

	Units Manufactured
Year 1	
Quarter 1	1,000,000
Quarter 2[a]	1,100,000
Quarter 3	1,400,000
Quarter 4	1,650,000
Year 2	
Quarter 1	1,750,000
Quarter 2	1,650,000
Quarter 3	1,500,000
Quarter 4	1,400,000

[a]Point at which the new management took over.

During all this time the number of workers declined by 35 percent. Only half of these people were replaced. At the management levels, 20 percent of the old managerial staff has resigned and none of their positions has been filled. The firm has simply reorganized so as to do more work with less people.

As seen by the data above, output went up for three quarters and has now turned around. In an effort to turn things around, the firm brought in a new top manager last week. The man's philosophy is quite interesting. He intends to go back to the old way of doing things. "We're right back where we started when we bought Clyde's firm. All we've done during this period is increase production in the short run and alienate the workers. We have to start rebuilding this company and stop trying to exploit the work force. We can't even produce 1,400,000 units unless we get more help and stop cracking the whip so hard. If we don't loosen up and start treating the people here like important assets, output will drop below 1,000,000 units quarterly." The new president then ordered his staff to start filling current vacancies, while he scheduled a meeting with the work force to discuss future plans.

Questions

1. At the present time, how would you describe the organizational climate in this firm? Be specific.
2. Why did output go up under the new management? Why is it now dropping off? Include a discussion of causal, intervening, and end-result variables in your answer.
3. How could an OD change agent help this company? Explain.

- diagnose
- take action
- evaluate and maintain new situation

organizational climate - evaluation of the environment is a significant factor in creating worker feelings in a firm

absenvable and non absenvable aspects

hierarchy
goals of organiza

attitudes
feelings
values

Causal Variables → Intervening Variables - End Result Variables

① Leadership styles
② mgmt decisions

internal psycholog factors that describe how the employees feel about the organization

tardiness
absenteism
↓ in production

causal variables affect intervening variables

Likert Profile - by asking people to fill out a profile of organizational characteristics it is possible to monitor and predict changes in organizational performance.

System I - exploitive autocratic
System II benevolant "
System III consultive democratic
System IV participative democratic

Organizational development - a long range effort to improve organizational performance.

- change agent - (1) diagnosis (2) action (3) maintenance of new situation

Personal Interventians
Intra group "
Inter group "
Total organizational Interventions

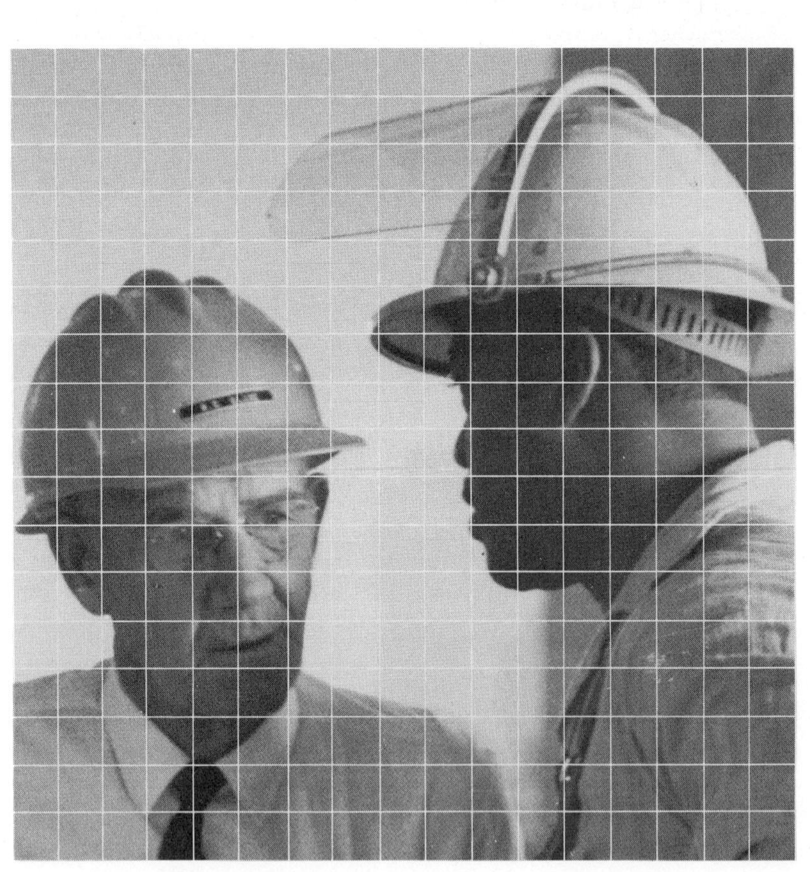

Part Seven

Management and You

During the last eleven chapters you have studied the functions in the management process. You know quite a bit about what managers do. However, there are still a few areas that warrant attention. One is that of management's changing world. Management does not operate in a vacuum. There are a great many changes going on and the modern executive must be able to adjust to them. These range from those brought about by external factors such as the general economy to those caused by internal factors such as changing workers' values. These environmental changes affect the manager's job and before concluding our study of basic management, we need to address them. Then we want to step back and look at the overall field of management and pose a question to you: Would you like a career in management? Before answering this question you may feel there is more you need to find out about the field.

Chapter 14

Management's Changing World

Objectives of the Chapter

Management does not operate in a vacuum. A great many external forces of change, from the economy to government legislation and from changing work values to challenges to the private enterprise system, promise to make the manager's world an interesting one. The first objective of this chapter is to study some of these overall challenges that will confront the manager of the 1980s. The second objective is to study the area of worker values and investigate whether these values are changing. The third objective is to examine the area of managerial ethics and see whether the ethics of today's manager are higher than those of previous decades. The fourth objective is to look at social responsibility and its component parts, noting the social challenges management faces and what is being done about them. The last objective is to answer the question: Is business more socially responsible than it was a decade ago?

When you have finished studying the material in this chapter, you should be able to:

1. Discuss five of the significant challenges management will face during the 1980s in the political, economic, and social arenas.
2. Define the term *values* and relate the values of young workers to those of older workers.
3. Explain what is meant by the term *ethics* and what the 1977 Harvard study reveals about management ethics.
4. Identify the three main areas of social responsibility, discuss the challenges each presents, and tell what business is doing in each area.
5. Answer the question: Is business more socially responsible than it was a decade ago?

Some Overall Challenges of the 1980s

The current decade will see significant changes in the political, economic, and social arenas. The following briefly examines some of the major challenges that will face the manager in each of these areas.

High Political Turbulence and Uncertainty

■ There will be inflation and unemployment.

One of the major challenges that will confront business during the current decade is that of operating at a profit in a very dynamic political environment. Like other industrial democracies, the U.S. will face inflation, unemployment, energy shortages, and social challenges. At the same time, businesses will find themselves trying to reconcile competing claims from stockholders, public employees, farmers, minorities, labor, and other interest groups. Meanwhile, college graduates will be streaming out into the work place to compete for available jobs and finding that the number of openings is insufficient to meet the demand. When one also considers such changes as increased unionization of professional and public employees resulting in labor and public confrontations, and the likelihood that major cities will be undergoing financial crises, it should be evident that business will indeed be operating in a highly turbulent environment.

Slow Economic Growth

■ Productivity gains will be small.

The 1960s and 1970s were growth years for many businesses, but the 1980s will not be. Productivity gains will be relatively small, and there will be less money available for new research and development. The result will be a decline in the number of launchings of new technologies, industries, and products. And with this slower growth, managers will find that they have to be more concerned with managing stability or decline than with managing growth.

Expensive Capital and Credit

■ Capital will become more expensive.

Capital and credit will become more expensive as the demand for funds increases but the amount saved declines. The result will be higher interest rates and the large sums of money needed for such undertakings as energy development, mass transportation systems, urban renewal, and plant modernization will not always be available.

Weakening Industrial Discipline and Support for the Work Ethic

■ Workers will question the system.

As will be seen shortly, there will continue to be a weakening of industrial discipline. Modern employees, especially the young, are less willing to blindly accept organizational demands. They continually question the system, desire more authority over their jobs, and want to work in an environment in which the task is both challenging and meaningful. They want to feel that what they do is important. No longer will they put up with unacceptable working conditions and poor treatment by management just because the latter is paying their salaries. Today's workers feel they are important and they want to be treated as such.

Challenge to the Private Enterprise System

■ Company profits will also be questioned.

Still another challenge will be to the private enterprise system itself. Recent public opinion polls reveal that Americans in general, and young people in particular, have a limited understanding of the private enterprise system. As a result, they are suspicious and hostile toward business managers. For example, many question why the oil companies should be making large profits from the sale of a natural resource that is needed for survival. Few believe that the oil firms are really reinvesting their funds back into exploration and trying to provide the lowest possible prices to the public; rather, they believe that the oil firms are gouging them. In an effort to combat this negative business attitude and acquaint the public with the free enterprise system, the Advertising Council and the federal government have come out with a booklet entitled "The American Economic System . . . and Your Part in It." The purpose of the booklet is to explain the free enterprise system and how it works. As explained in the foreword to the booklet, it has been prepared "to provide a quick and simple description of the American economic system. It can serve as one step in a journey to better economic understanding—a journey which should be a continuing one for all of us."[1] The point, of course, is to present the positive side of free enterprise, showing the reader that it is the best economic system for meeting the needs of all people. Twenty years ago a pamphlet such as this would have been totally unnecessary. Today even the federal government feels that free enterprise is under such strong attack that it requires defense.

These five challenges provide a general overview of what is facing management. However, on a more specific level, consideration of such topics as values and ethics provides more insight to these challenges.

Changing Values

■ Values are changing.

Values are those things that are important to people. Some illustrations include money, power, status, friendship, and religion. Recent research shows that the values of young workers are changing. Years ago people used to be strong advocates of the Protestant work ethic. Today individuals entering the work force have a striking difference in attitudes. Findings from a recent study conducted among workers from the manufacturing, mining, insurance, banking, construction, and airline industries, among others, produced the results in Table 14.1. While data from male workers only are reported in the table, in almost all cases similar responses were given by female workers. Thus the key criterion proved to be not sex but age. Young workers had similar responses; older workers had similar responses; and there are noticeable differences between the two. The following discussion examines each of the six areas covered in this study.[2]

Table 14.1
Values among Male Workers

	Males, by Age		
	17–26	27–39	40–65
Money			
Getting more money or a larger pay increase[a]	86.20	82.60	76.10
My pay: satisfying/dissatisfying[b]	4.05	4.22	4.56
When you are making enough money to get along, making more money is not very important.[c]	2.99	3.22	3.39
Work Ethic			
If you do an especially good job, what are the chances that you will feel greater pride in craftsmanship?[d]	5.69	6.01	6.09
Working harder makes an individual a better person.[c]	5.08	5.36	5.65
A good indication of a person's worth is how well he does his job.[c]	5.39	5.65	6.04
Even if you do not like your work, you should do your best.[c]	5.72	5.82	6.12
Work should be one of the most important parts of a person's life.[c]	4.75	4.83	5.40
If a person can get away with it, there is nothing wrong with doing a poor job at work.[c]	1.88	1.53	1.38
It is more important to get along with your friends than to work hard at your job.[c]	3.59	3.00	2.78
Job Attitudes			
My job is: attractive/repulsive.[b]	4.74	5.30	5.59
My job is: interesting/boring.[b]	4.33	5.22	5.55
How much job responsibility do you have?[e]	4.58	5.10	5.19
How much job responsibility would you like?[e]	5.59	5.81	5.55
Attitudes toward the Company[c]			
Considering everything about this firm, I'm very well satisfied with it.	4.30	4.76	5.27
My company is just a place to work and is separate from my personal interests.	4.24	3.42	3.20
This community is a better place to live because of this firm.	3.69	4.47	5.33
Acceptability of Welfare[f]			
Accepting government welfare.	2.51	2.09	2.14
Accepting help from family or friends.	2.99	2.71	2.41
Working more hours or getting a second job.	5.15	5.26	5.32
Background Characteristics			
I feel very much that I belong in this community.[c]	4.02	4.64	5.20
My family expects me to perform well on the job.[c]	5.36	5.69	6.03
How important is religion in your life?[c]	4.47	4.83	5.30

[a]This scale ranged from 0 (extremely undesirable) to 100 (extremely desirable).

[b]This was a 7-point semantic differential scale where 7 was the most favorable end of the scale.

[c]This scale ranged from 1 = Strongly Disagree to 7 = Strongly Agree.

[d]Probability was indicated on a 7-point scale where 1 = Never and 7 = 100 percent certain.

[e]This was a 7-point scale where 7 represented Very Much (that is, high job enrichment) and 1 = Very Little.

[f]This was a 7-point scale where 1 = Very Undesirable and 7 = Very Desirable.

Source: David Cherrington, "The Values of Younger Workers," *Business Horizons,* December 1977, pp. 24–25. An adaption of a table. Reprinted by permission.

Pay

The David Cherrington study found that money is desired by young workers. In fact, young people are more interested in money than any other age group. Additionally, the accumulation of wealth was slightly more important to young workers than to old ones.

Work Ethic Attitudes

■ Young workers are less work oriented.

Younger workers were found to be less work oriented than middle-aged workers, and the latter were less work oriented than older ones. Furthermore, pride in craftsmanship was less important to younger workers than to older ones. Young workers also gave a lower score to "being of service," while rating leisure time as highly desirable. And in contrast to the other age groups, they felt it was more acceptable to do a poor job.

Job Attitudes

■ Less job satisfied.

Older workers are more satisfied with their jobs than younger workers. They report that their work is interesting, exciting, and attractive. They also had more favorable attitudes toward their jobs than did the middle age group which, in turn, reported more favorable attitudes than the younger workers.

Attitudes toward Business

■ Less conforming.

Older workers were much more satisfied with the company than were younger workers and felt that top management had respect for their personal rights and kept them informed about what was going on. They also expressed a greater commitment to the company than did the younger workers and thought it was a better place to get ahead than most other firms.

Acceptability of Welfare

■ More willing to accept welfare.

The survey also found that all the workers agreed on one thing: If a person needed more money, the best way to get it was to work more hours, get a second job, or get more training or education. However, when it came to accepting welfare, there was a difference of opinion. The younger workers were more agreeable to accepting help from the government, the church, family, and friends than were older workers.

Attitudes on Work and Social Pressure

■ Less willing to work hard.

Older workers indicated that it was more important to work hard at a job than it was to get along with one's friends. Younger workers were not this strong in their beliefs. Additionally, the latter were less willing to incur the dislike of fellow workers than were older employees.

Background Characteristics

■ And have different background characteristics.

Older workers reported that they came from a family unit that was close-knit and happy. They also tended to come from towns with small populations, and religion was a more important part of their lives than it was among younger workers. These background characteristics suggest that the developmental experiences of early life and the influence of the family are related to the attitudes and values of workers. The data also suggest that family expectations, early work experiences, and discipline are important factors which result in people believing in the importance of hard work and the dignity of labor.

What Does It All Mean?

■ Young workers expect more.

Drawing together the data in this study provides us with a general picture of the young worker in America today. This picture is not unlike that reported by other writers, and it indicates work values in America are changing.[3] What is causing these changes? One primary answer is found in the life-style in which people are raised. *Affluence affects values.* If individuals are raised in an environment where they do not have to worry about basic needs, then food, clothing, and shelter are no concern for them; and when they get on the job, they are not greatly interested in earning money to buy these things. They *expect* them to be provided, if only through a sufficiently high wage. What they are looking for is an enjoyable life, similar to the one they had while growing up. The result is an individual more interested in quality of life than in survival strategy.

■ Have had different education.

Nor can we overlook the type of education and training that today's young workers have had. Hard work, perseverance, and industry are not taught as frequently or as enthusiastically as they were prior to 1950. Young adults have been reared on a different philosophy.

■ And are just starting out.

Finally, we have to keep in mind that, as people get older, their interests tend to change. Many older workers can afford to be less concerned with money. Over the span of a lifetime, the normal, healthy, fully employed worker makes quite a bit of money. Those who can usually save some of it. Younger workers are just starting out. Older workers have less time before retirement, so they are more likely to feel they need to be content with their jobs. After all, why would they want to leave? They are staying to ensure their retirement benefits, and a time comes when they realistically assume other firms will not hire them, perhaps despite age discrimination policies to the contrary. Conversely, younger workers have decades before retirement, so they are more likely to be choosy about working conditions, salary, and promotion opportunities.

What does all of this mean for the modern manager? It means that the individual faces a tremendous number of worker-related challenges, because there are young, middle-aged, and older workers in the organization. Each has different values, different objectives, and different work philosophies. The manager's job is to bring all these people together into a well-knit group. Finally, to compound the problem even further, the manager is more likely to be middle-aged or older, while new workers are more likely to be young. Most managers are hiring individuals with values that are more than likely different from their own.

Ethics

■ Ethics is defined as right and wrong conduct.

Another major management challenge is that of maintaining ethical standards of behavior. *Ethics* can be defined as a set of principles used to identify right and wrong conduct. The major dilemma that faces the modern manager is determining exactly what is right and wrong. For example, if a business finds that it must give bribes to foreign government officials in order to do business in that country, is it ethical to give the bribe or should the firm simply refuse to do business there? What if everyone else is giving bribes? Is it then ethical to follow suit? What about giving kickbacks to purchasing managers in order to get business from their firms? Is that all right? What about padding one's expense account? Can one ethically do any padding of it?

As you can see, ethics covers a wide range of management behaviors. And given some of the latest news about rising oil prices and foreign bribery payments, one wonders exactly how ethical managers are. Everyone reads such news as that in Table 14.2. A recent study at Harvard shed some light on the area of business ethics.

Table 14.2
Let This Be a Lesson

While many businesspeople argue that they have very high standards of ethical conduct, not everyone would agree. In fact, some would point to the recent decision by a federal jury in the case of five Texas oilmen who were charged with a conspiracy to illegally raise the price of oil sold to the Florida Power Corporation during the 1973–74 fuel crisis. The jury found four of the defendants guilty.

The government charged them with conspiring to pass oil shipment through a "daisy chain" of companies, raising prices to enrich themselves before selling to the utility. As a result of the jury's decision, each faces up to 35 years in prison and a $70,000 fine. Two other people indicted in the case, including the former president and chairman of the Florida Power Corporation, pleaded guilty to conspiracy and agreed to testify for the government. A government spokesman said he hoped that the decision would serve as a deterrent to such unethical conduct in the future.

Source: "4 Oilmen Convicted in Fuel Oil Scandal," *The Miami Herald,* March 4, 1979, Section AA, p. 1.

The Harvard Study

■ Unethical practices still exist.

In an effort to study whether the ethics of business is changing, the *Harvard Business Review* recently undertook a survey of 1,200 readers and compared their responses to those of executives seventeen years before.[4] The following overall conclusions were reached.

First, business people still feel that there are unethical practices in industry, although the percentage of executives who feel this way has declined. For example, in 1961, 68 percent of the respondents said that there were at least some unethical practices, while the latest poll shows that only 55 percent now feel this way.

Second, the types of unethical practices have changed. For example, while gifts, gratuities, and bribes still head the list, unfair pricing and dishonest advertising have declined in importance. On the other hand, unfair competitive practices, the cheating of customers, the use of unfair credit practices, and prejudice in hiring have increased.

■ But the types of practice are changing.

Third, it is difficult to say whether ethical standards are higher today than they were twenty years ago. Approximately one-third of the respondents thought that ethical standards were lower today, 41 percent thought they were about the same, and 25 percent thought they were higher. Those factors influencing higher or lower standards are found in Table 14.3.

■ It is tough to say whether ethical standards have improved.

Fourth, many managers feel that they are more ethical than the average manager. For example, as seen in Table 14.4, when comparing responses by executives in 1961 and 1976, more executives now believe that (1) they would be more ethical than their earlier counterparts and (2) other managers would be less ethical than they.

■ Managers personally believe they are ethical.

Fifth, the responsibility that managers today feel toward various groups has changed. In the past, managers always reported that their primary responsibility was to the stockholders. Today, the customer occupies the top slot. On a scale of 1 (most responsibility) to 7 (least responsibility), the respondents gave the following answers:

■ And their responsibilities have changed.

Customers	1.83
Stockholders	2.52
Employees	2.86
Local community where the company operates	4.44
Society in general	4.97
Suppliers	5.10
Government	5.72

Overall, the Harvard study found that ethical issues will continue to be problems for the manager of the eighties to deal with. There is less agreement regarding what is right and wrong conduct, less chance to permanently label things as ethical or unethical. Furthermore, the study found that managers now place less reliance on industry codes of conduct, feeling that the mere existence of a list of ethical acts that people should follow is no assurance that everyone will abide by them. Codes of ethics sometimes create a false sense of security and lead to the encouragement of violations. What, then, can the manager of the eighties do in dealing with the issue of managerial ethics? The *Review* recommended the following:

■ Ethics will be a problem for the 1980s.

1. Deal fairly with customers and employees; this is the most direct way to restore confidence in business morality.
2. Corporate steps have to be taken to improve ethical behavior, and these must come from the top and be part of the reward and punishment system.
3. If an ethical code is developed and implemented, the firm should have an accompanying information system to detect violations and treat these violators equitably.

4. Test decisions against what is right rather than against what is expedient or what helps solve a problem right now but is really unethical behavior.
5. Do not force others into unethical conduct.[5]

Table 14.3
Factors That Influence Ethical Standards

Factors Causing Higher Standards	Percentage of Respondents Listing Factor
Public disclosure; publicity; media coverage; better communication	31%
Increased public concern; public awareness, consciousness, and scrutiny; better informed public; societal pressures	20
Government regulation, legislation, and intervention; federal courts	10
Education of business managers; increase in manager professionalism and education	9
New social expectations for the role business is to play in society; young adults' attitudes; consumerism	5
Business's greater sense of social responsibility and greater awareness of the implications of its acts; business responsiveness; corporate policy changes; top management emphasis on ethical action	5
Other	20
Factors Causing Lower Standards	
Society's standards are lower; social decay; more permissive society; materialism and hedonism have grown; loss of church and home influence; less quality, more quantity desires	34%
Competition; pace of life; stress to succeed; current economic conditions; costs of doing business; more businesses compete for less	13
Political corruption; loss of confidence in government; Watergate; politics; political ethics and climate	9
People more aware of unethical acts; constant media coverage; TV; communications create atmosphere for crime	9
Greed; desire for gain; worship the dollar as measure of success; selfishness of the individual; lack of personal integrity and moral fiber	8
Pressure for profit from within the organization from superiors or from stockholders; corporate influences on managers; corporate policies	7
Other	21

Note: Some respondents listed more than one factor, so there were 353 factors in all listed as causing higher standards and 411 in all listed as causing lower ones.

Source: Reprinted by permission of the *Harvard Business Review.* The exhibit is from "Is the Ethics of Business Changing?" by Steven N. Brenner and Earl A. Molander (January–February 1977), p. 63.

Table 14.4
How Managers View Their Ethical Practices versus Those of Other Managers

Situation: An executive earning $30,000 a year has been padding his expense account by about $1,500 a year.

What I Think			What the Average Executive Thinks	
1961	6%	Acceptable if other executives in the company do the same thing.	27%	1961
1976	4		28	1976
1961	11	Unacceptable, regardless of the situation.	28	1961
1976	9		33	1976
1961	86	Acceptable if the executive's boss knows about it and says nothing.	60	1961
1976	89		53	1976

Social Responsibility

Another major challenge for business is that of *social responsibility.* In meeting its obligations to society, business has found three main areas of concern today: (1) equal opportunity, (2) ecology, and (3) consumerism. The following examines each of these.

Equal Opportunity

The term *equal opportunity* refers to two main benefits in work. First, people are entitled to *job opportunities* without regard to non-performance-related factors such as race, religion, color, political beliefs, or sex. Second, they are entitled to *salaries* equal to those of others doing the same work under the same conditions. One of the ways in which these rights are being ensured is through legislation.

■ Discrimination is forbidden.

Legislation. A number of major laws ensure equal job-related opportunity for everyone. The most important is the *Civil Rights Act of 1964.* This act has eleven major sections. Title VII is the most important for business, because it forbids discrimination on the basis of race, color, religion, sex, or national origin. In addition, the act established an Equal Employment Opportunity Commission to investigate complaints, seek to end violations through conciliation, and ask the U.S. Attorney General to bring suit if such conciliation efforts are unsuccessful.

■ Equal pay is required.

The other important act is the *Equal Pay Act.* The purpose of this act is to correct wage differentials that are based on sex. Specifically, the act forbids discrimination on the basis of sex for doing equal work on jobs that require equal skills, effort, and responsibility and that are performed under similar working conditions. Particularly in the case of women, this act has been used to adjust salaries on jobs where a woman was paid much less than a man when both were doing basically the same thing. The latest court rulings require equal pay for approximately the same work.

Courts have acted in other ways to ensure the job opportunities of persons who have been traditionally discriminated against. Table 14.5 gives one illustration.

Table 14.5
Reverse Discrimination?

Brian F. Weber was a lab analyst with ten years of experience at the Kaiser Aluminum and Chemical Corporation in Gramercy, Louisiana. He wanted a skilled-craft job in which he could double his pay, escape the grind of night work, and obtain greater job security. However, when he applied for a craft-retraining program he was rejected. The program called for at least 50 percent black and female trainees and Weber was white. Angered over the situation, he filed a lawsuit claiming reverse discrimination and his charge was upheld in federal district court in New Orleans and in the Fifth Circuit Court of Appeals. From here the case went to the Supreme Court.

Attorneys for the company warned that if the high court ruled against the firm, it would destroy affirmative action as practiced by the company. Attorneys for the defendant claimed that he was being discriminated against.

In a 5–2 decision the Supreme Court ruled that private employers can legally give special preferences to black workers to eliminate what it called "manifest racial imbalance" in traditionally white-only jobs. Overturning the two lower courts, and writing for the majority, Justice William J. Brennan, Jr., wrote, "It would indeed be ironic if a law triggered by a nation's concern over centuries of racial injustice and intended to improve the lot of those who have 'been excluded from the American dream for so long' constituted the first legislation prohibition of a voluntary, private, traditional pattern of racial segregation. . . ." In short, voluntary affirmative action plans do not violate the Civil Rights Act.

Source: Linda Greenhouse, "High Court Backs a Preference Plan for Blacks in Jobs," *New York Times*, June 28, 1979, p. 1.

▪ Minorities have higher unemployment.

Minorities in the Work Force. While many people in the work force are better off than they were ten years ago, many ethnic minorities and women are still denied equal opportunity and suffer greater economic hardship than most other working people. For example, over the last twenty years nonwhite unemployment has *always* been higher than white unemployment. Nonwhites constitute approximately 12 percent of the civilian labor force but account for around 22 percent of total unemployment.[6]

Salaries are also lower for minorities. For example, during the last twenty years black income has, on the average, never been higher than 62 percent of white income. Furthermore, recent statistics show that the gap between black and white family income is again beginning to widen.[7]

▪ Women have fewer opportunities.

And then there are women, who constitute over 40 percent of the total work force and are paid, on the average, less than men and have poorer chances for promotion. One of the reasons for this can be traced to sex-role stereotyping, in which women are seen by their male counterparts as emotional, overly sensitive, and lacking in aggressiveness, ambition, and drive. In many organizations, either managerial positions are not filled by females, or a few women are given limited opportunities for advancement up the ranks.

▪ Career-goal workshops are being provided.

Current Responses. At the present time, businesses are taking steps to ensure that minorities and women are indeed given equal opportunity. For example, the National Alliance of Business, which consists of firms throughout American industry, is work-

"Just between us, Don, *are* we ripping off the public?"

ing to find jobs for the hard-core unemployed. Many companies are also trying to establish affirmative action programs aimed at their minority employees. General Foods is an illustration. The company uses self-assessment and career goal-setting workshops, job fairs, and job clinics to indicate the job openings that are available in the firm and the types of skills required for these jobs. Job posting is used to publicize open positions throughout the company, and movement between departments is both encouraged and made as smooth as possible. In addition, special courses are offered on college campuses to introduce employees to particular topics and to the collegiate life experience. Special attention is also given to a positive, pragmatic approach to learning and career choices. The results of this approach are a high degree of acceptance and greater job mobility for minority and female employees throughout the firm.

■ Minority supply companies are being used.

Other companies are directing their efforts toward helping minority entrepreneurs. For example, General Motors maintains a list of items that it buys preferentially from black suppliers. General Electric helps sponsor fairs at which minority businesses present their wares and get advice from GE's purchasing agents.

■ Women are being promoted.

In dealing with the challenge of women in business, many firms are making it clear that they want people promoted on the basis of ability. If a woman is the best person for the job, she is to get it. By letting the word filter down from the top, the firm ensures that this will indeed be company policy. Despite such progress, however, equal opportunity will still be a major issue for business throughout the 1980s.

Ecology

Ecology is a term that refers to interrelationships of organisms and their environments. As used in social responsibility terms, it refers to the relationship between the business firm and the environment in which the firm operates. For business, ecology became an issue about twenty years ago, when the matter of pesticides and their impact on the environment was raised by Rachel Carson in her book *Silent Spring.*[8] Since that time, DDT and other pesticides have been greatly restricted as to use. However, ecological issues have spread much further than simply the pesticide question.

▪ Oil usage is tremendous.

Raw Material Depletion. Today business firms are being asked to restrict their use of energy so as to reduce the amount of oil that must be imported from overseas. In 1970 the United States imported 26 percent of its oil. By 1976 this was up to 42 percent and, if it continued at this rate, by 1985 the import volume would have been over 50 percent. And while U.S. consumption is beginning to slow, America today uses up to 500 times more fuel per capita than some of the world's less developed countries.[9]

▪ So is that of other resources.

And oil is not the only resource problem. In virtually any resource you can name, from aluminum to copper to nickel to tin, the United States uses more of the resource than any other country of the world. Obviously, this nation cannot go on doing so indefinitely. New ways of producing current products must be devised.

▪ Including land.

Another important raw material is land. Every year, developers move in and turn virgin farmland into housing developments. However, only so much land can be converted to this use before food production is seriously affected.

▪ The auto is a big polluter.

Pollution. Another common ecological problem is *air pollution,* with the automobile being one of the primary culprits. At the present time auto manufacturers are trying to reduce the amount of pollution caused by their cars. Industrial smokestacks are another primary polluter. Large copper refineries and smelters throw tons of pollution into the air every year, as do many utilities and other manufacturing firms.

▪ Then there is industrial waste dumping.

And then there are *water pollution* and *thermal pollution.* A recent Harris Poll indicated that water pollution was a serious concern to over 69 percent of those surveyed, an increase of 15 percent over those surveyed in 1971.[10] Water pollution takes numerous forms. One of the most common is the result of industrial waste dumping. Businesses used to dump their industrial garbage into rivers and lakes, with no thought given to the side effects. Today they either treat this waste before dumping it or simply find another way to get rid of the material. Nevertheless, there is still the problem caused by years of such dumping. For example, wonder many ecologists, can the Great Lakes ever be restored to their original state, or are they polluted beyond restoration?

▪ Thermal pollution.

Thermal (warm water) pollution is less well known. One common cause of thermal pollution is utilities that take water out of a lake, use it to run their turbine engines to generate electricity, and then return it to the lake at a higher temperature. In the process, the overall temperature of the lake is raised.

▪ And solid waste pollution.

Finally, there are pollution problems which often go unnoticed by many of us. One is solid waste disposal. What should be done with all the garbage created by the population? And what about noise pollution? People are being subjected to more and more noise, both at home and in the work place. The effects of this pollution are many and varied, but they include impaired hearing, difficulty in remaining alert, sleeplessness, and irritability.

Current Responses. Business is taking many steps in dealing with ecological issues. For example, in trying to reduce raw material depletion, many firms are now seeking ways to recycle unused raw materials and are reclaiming the materials in used products. In the area of energy conservation, they are looking for new supplies of existing energy fuels, seeking out new sources of energy, and trying to conserve existing supplies through the curtailment of current usage. In regard to the latter, for example, many business firms have raised their thermostats to 80 degrees during the summer, dispensing with formal dress codes, while in the winter the thermostats are lowered to 68 degrees. In dealing with air pollution, the auto firms are redesigning engines so that they are more efficient and less polluting. Meanwhile, manufacturing firms are installing equipment to reduce the amount of air and water pollution caused by their production facilities. And when it comes to noise pollution, many companies are taking measures to reduce the noise to a level that is commensurate with work productivity and work safety.

■ Special equipment is being installed.

Consumerism

Consumerism is the most prominent of the three major social issues. This is because it directly affects every individual in the country. The sub-issues consumerism addresses today include advertising claims, pricing policies, product safety, product and service warranties, and service activities.

The Issues. Advertising is a consumerism area because many people feel that businesses are deliberately misleading them with their ad claims. One of the commonest unethical practices is called bait and switch. Under this practice, the consumer is lured into the store by an ad that promises special merchandise at a very low price. Once there, however, the consumer is told that the merchandise has been sold or is of such low quality that the buyer would be better off purchasing an alternative product at a higher price. Other common ad-related complaints include incomplete advertising, ambiguous wording of the ad, and claims that cannot be backed up.

■ Bait and switch is used.

Pricing policies have been a constant source of concern for consumers. For example, some people claim that discounts are given to some customers but not others. Or business firms agree among themselves that they will charge no less than a designated price for their product so that their consumers are faced with an artificially high price regardless of where they shop.

■ Special discounts are given.

Product safety is another key issue in the consumer movement. If a product does not work properly and someone is hurt as a result, who is responsible? Recently, the courts have held that the manufacturer is because it has unlimited liability for the product's safety. The result has been a host of lawsuits against manufacturers accused of producing inherently dangerous or defective products. The same develop-

■ Some products work improperly.

ment has occurred in the area of auto safety. Individuals buying cars that do not operate as they should are bringing suit against the manufacturers.

■ Warranties are not honored.

Another consumer issue is that of product and service warranties. A warranty is an obligation that the seller assumes to the buyer. Sometimes this warranty is written, while at other times it is implied. A written warranty is a statement from a company promising to fix or replace a product if it breaks within a certain time after purchase. When a company sells the consumer a product that does not work as it should, the company has violated its implicit warranty. The firm did not say it would replace defective products, but this is really implied in the sales agreement. Many consumers contend that companies do not stand behind their warranties.

■ Informational ads are used.

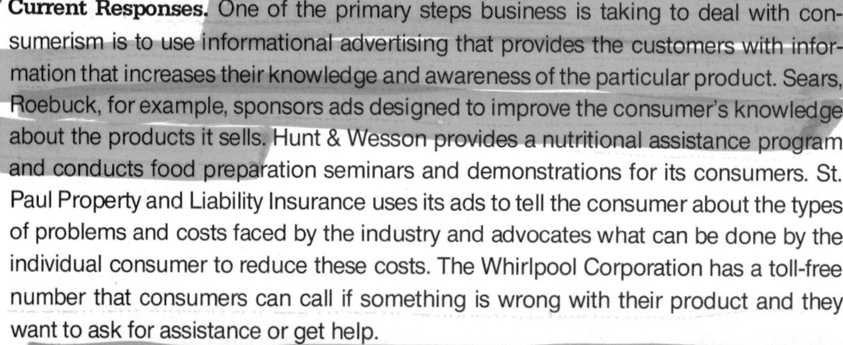

Current Responses. One of the primary steps business is taking to deal with consumerism is to use informational advertising that provides the customers with information that increases their knowledge and awareness of the particular product. Sears, Roebuck, for example, sponsors ads designed to improve the consumer's knowledge about the products it sells. Hunt & Wesson provides a nutritional assistance program and conducts food preparation seminars and demonstrations for its consumers. St. Paul Property and Liability Insurance uses its ads to tell the consumer about the types of problems and costs faced by the industry and advocates what can be done by the individual consumer to reduce these costs. The Whirlpool Corporation has a toll-free number that consumers can call if something is wrong with their product and they want to ask for assistance or get help.

■ Complaints handled.

Another area in which business has concentrated its attention is that of handling complaints. If something goes wrong or the customer has a gripe, the individual wants someone to listen and take corrective action. In addition to 24-hour toll-free telephone lines, many firms have a central customer relations department that listens to complaints from all over the country and then works with customers to ensure that their problems are resolved.

■ Safety features built into products.

A third common method is to study both the product and the production process in order to identify ways of reducing safety problems. For example, when it comes to auto safety, the major auto firms have come up with all sorts of changes on recent model cars, ranging from new bumpers to energy steering columns to passive passenger restraint systems. In the area of product safety, businesses are now studying the various ways in which their products are used and trying to anticipate dangers before they happen. For example, one lawn mower manufacturer now calls to the attention of the user that the machine should not be picked off the ground and used for trimming hedges. Another points out that its vacuum cleaner, unlike industrial vacuums, should not be used for picking up puddles of water. Others concentrate more on designing safety into the product, looking over the prototype, and trying to figure out everything that can go wrong with the product. Finally, some firms have gone to the trouble of developing product recall strategies. In this way, if something does go wrong, the company has a plan for identifying who owns the product, where they live, and how they can be quickly contacted.

Summary

Management operates in a changing world. Some of the major challenges it will have to cope with during the 1980s include high political turbulence and uncertainty, slow economic growth, expensive capital and credit, weakening industrial discipline and support for the work ethic, and challenges to the private enterprise system.

One of the specific challenges is changing values. Research shows that young employees, regardless of sex, have different values from middle-aged employees who, in turn, have different values from older employees. These changes can be found in attitudes toward such areas as pay, the work ethic, the job, and the acceptability of welfare.

A second challenge is ethics. How should managers conduct themselves and their businesses? Recent research shows that unethical practices are changing. Also, while it is difficult to say whether ethical standards are higher today than twenty years ago, many managers feel that they, personally, are more ethical than the average manager. Additionally, they feel a greater obligation to customers than to any other group. Overall, however, the study found that current, workable definitions of ethical policy will be a problem for the manager of the eighties.

The last challenge examined in this chapter was that of social responsibility. This responsibility can be divided into three main areas of concern: (1) equal opportunity, (2) ecology, and (3) consumerism. Each was examined with attention to both the issue and business's response. In each case, it is obvious that there are problems facing business and that business is attempting to deal with them. However, there is still a great deal more to be done. We can conclude that while business is meeting many of its external challenges, the battle will continue throughout the decade.

Review and Study Questions

1. What are some of the political and economic challenges that will confront business during the current decade? Identify and describe four of them.
2. Are work values in America changing? Explain your answer.
3. How do young workers and old workers feel about the following: pay, the work ethic, the job, the acceptability of welfare. Compare and contrast the answers from the two groups.
4. Is business ethics today higher than it was twenty years ago? Explain.
5. What can a manager do in dealing with the issue of ethical practices? Offer at least four guidelines.
6. In what way is equal opportunity a challenge for business? Incorporate into your answer a discussion of traditional work conditions among women and minorities and be clear as to the relationship between this history and current legislation on equal job opportunity.
7. What is business doing to ensure equal opportunity in the work place? Explain.

8. In what way is ecology a challenge for the modern manager? Be complete in your answer.
9. What is business doing to meet this ecological challenge? Explain.
10. In what way is consumerism a challenge for business?
11. What is business doing to meet the consumer challenge? Explain.
12. Overall, is business more socially responsible today than it was ten years ago? Defend your answer.

Key Terms in the Chapter

values
ethics
social responsibility
equal opportunity
Civil Rights Act of 1964
Equal Pay Act
ecology
consumerism

Notes

1. *The American Economic System . . . and Your Part in It,* pamphlet prepared by the Advertising Council and the U.S. Department of Commerce in cooperation with the U.S. Department of Labor, n.d.
2. David Cherrington, "The Values of Younger Workers," *Business Horizons,* December 1977, pp. 18–30.
3. Richard M. Hodgetts and Steven Altman, *Organizational Behavior* (Philadelphia: Saunders, 1979), Chapter 6.
4. Steven N. Brenner and Earl A. Molander, "Is the Ethics of Business Changing?" *Harvard Business Review,* January–February 1977, pp. 57–71.
5. Ibid., p. 71.
6. Research and Policy Committee of the Committee for Economic Development, *Jobs for the Hard to Employ: New Directions for a Public-Private Partnership* (New York: Committee for Economic Development, January 1978), p. 23.
7. Alfred L. Malabre, "After Shrinking, the Gap Widens Again between Black and White Family Income," *Wall Street Journal,* March 6, 1979, p. 48.
8. Rachel Carson, *Silent Spring* (Boston: Houghton Mifflin, 1962).
9. Arthur Elkins and Dennis W. Callaghan, eds., *A Managerial Odyssey: Problems in Business and Its Environment* (Reading, Mass.: Addison-Wesley, 1978), p. 245.
10. Louis Harris, "Pure Water of Concern," *Chicago Tribune,* July 20, 1978, Section 4, p. 3.

Case: Price Rebates

"Do you mean, am I going to kick you back 5 percent under the table?"

Jill Compton is a salesperson for a large auto supply dealer. This dealer is the largest in a 6-state area, although in recent years it has been losing ground to one of the competitors.

Last week Jill called on one of her regular customers, a purchasing agent, and felt sure that she would get the sale. However, as the meeting came to a close, the customer asked, "Are you offering a 5 percent rebate off the books?" Jill was shocked. "Do you mean, am I going to kick you back 5 percent under the table?" The customer said yes and went on to explain that the other major competitor had already made such an offer to him. "Of course, I've been doing business with your firm for so long," he said, "that I told the salesman that I'd have to get back with him." Jill said she did not know whether her company would match this offer but she would check it out and be back with an answer within a few days.

Jill explained the situation to her boss, who became very angry. "So that's how those guys have been managing to take away our customers for the last three years. This type of activity is illegal. There are fixed prices in the industry. I'll bet if that guy's boss found out that he was taking money under the table, he'd be fired. On the other hand, if we don't want to get anyone fired, we can't blow the whistle; so we'll have to just meet the competition by offering similar kickbacks. I don't know what to do. This is a decision that will have to be made by the owner himself."

Questions

1. How common do you think these types of pricing practices are in business today? Why?
2. If you were the owner of the auto supply firm, what would you do about the situation? Explain.
3. How can these pricing practices be eliminated? Be complete in your answer.

Case: Future Challenges

"Things have certainly changed for us over the past ten years."

The president of a large manufacturing firm was recently talking to a group of college students during an annual Careers Day program. Part of his talk went as follows:

Things certainly have changed for us during the past ten years. For example, we now no longer just try to hire minorities; we have a formal program for ensuring that there is representation of minorities from the local area. For example, if 10 percent of the local population is black, we want to have 10 percent black employees. And, of course, we are trying very hard to hire more women, especially in the management ranks.

Meanwhile, air and water pollution laws have had an effect on the way we manufacture our products. We have spent quite a bit of money on special filtering systems and other programs designed to reduce or eliminate pollution.

And then there is consumerism. We can be sued if our products don't work right, and we could lose quite a bit of money. For this reason, we have established a very sophisticated control procedure for ensuring that our products are safe and work properly. Over the past five years we have not had one lawsuit because of product performance.

The future looks like it's going to be more of the same. In particular, ecology and consumerism head the list of our concerns and we intend to keep our eye on them.

Questions

1. What is equal opportunity all about? Will it continue to be an issue for firms such as the one in this case during the 1980s?
2. What kinds of ecology problems do manufacturing firms have? Explain.
3. If a product does not work properly, what legal problems can this create for firms like the one in this case? Explain your answer.

Chapter 15 Management as a Career

Objectives of the Chapter

After studying throughout this book what management is all about, you can ask the question: Would I like a career in management? The overall objective of this chapter is to help you answer this question. Of course, it is really too early for you to make any final decision on the matter but you can learn a great deal about a career in management, from how to get ready to some of the initial shocks you are likely to encounter during your first couple of months on the job to early career problems to various ways of managing your career and improving your chances for advancement up the ranks.

When you have finished studying the material in this chapter, you should know a great deal about management as a career and should be able to:

1 Discuss the current trend toward practicality in schools of business.
2 Describe some of the major factors that can cause reality shock among new managerial recruits.
3 Discuss some of the early career problems that are likely to be confronted by young managers today.
4 Explain what a typical career pattern looks like, noting some of the major events that occur at each of the various stages of the pattern.
5 Present a series of steps that will be useful for individuals who want to manage their own careers, rather than waiting and hoping that things will turn out for the best.

Get Ready!

Thus far we have studied five basic functions of the management process: planning, organizing, staffing, directing, and controlling. These functions are carried out through other people in the sense that the manager does not perform all of them personally but has assistance. Do you think you might like a career in management? Does it offer some initial appeal for you? If so, there are a number of other things that you should know in order to get ready for such a career.

■ Formally prepare yourself.

First, you should concentrate on formally preparing yourself to become a manager. The initial step in doing so is to keep on studying management. Remember, there are two ways of learning how to be a manager: (1) learn all you can about management and then go out and apply it in a work setting and (2) learn all about management on the job. The first is preferable because you will have the fundamentals under your belt and you can concentrate on modifying what you have learned to fit the situation. On-the-job experience is not going to teach you as much as fast, and a lot of what you learn may not be as useful as what can be picked up in the classroom.

What types of management courses should you now take? Regardless of whether you are pursuing a two-year or four-year degree, this will depend on your particular interests. However, you should study human relations or organizational behavior; for no matter where you work in the hierarchy, you will be interacting with people. Also, you should take at least one course in quantitative science or production-operations management. Additionally, if you pursue a four-year degree, you should take a course in business policy, an integrative course that helps you apply everything you have learned by analyzing business cases and offering recommendations for action. These three courses cover, at least partly, the three basic areas a manager needs to know about: the management of people, the management of things, and general concepts of the overall organization.

With a solid management education behind you, many organizations may be interested in hiring you. However, it will not always be a rosy picture. There are some things about first jobs and career development you should be aware of before you begin your career in management, and for the rest of the chapter we will examine these, starting, in Table 15.1, with some things you may be now participating in as you go through school.

Reality Can Be a Shocker

■ Low initial challenge.

One of the first things you should realize about getting into any organization is that it will probably be quite different from what you initially expect. This phenomenon is commonly referred to as *reality shock,* and it has been attributed to any of six factors.[1]

■ Low level of satisfaction.

One of these factors is the *low initial challenge* presented by the work. Many organizations oversell the challenge of their jobs. Then new recruits find that things are not only fairly easy but are downright boring.

A second factor is *low level of satisfaction.* Many new employees go into the job

Table 15.1
Practicality in the Business Schools

One of the big complaints made by opponents of B-schools (schools of business) is that the course material is too theoretical and does not really teach the student a whole lot about what to expect on the job. However, they are wrong! The current trend in B-schools is toward practicality. For example, some of the topics that have been added to the average curriculum in the last ten years include computers as management tools, government regulation, consumerism, and the impact of growing internationalization on American business. The result is a greater balance between theory and practice.

Furthermore, this trend is leading practicing executives to evaluate their own need for B-school training. Many of them are finding that after five to ten years on the job, they are out of touch with a lot of things happening in areas other than those they work in on a day-to-day basis. How can they retool and learn about new management developments? Why, by taking a course or executive seminar offered at a local B-school. After all, with the current blend of theory and practice, these schools are proving to be an ideal jumping off point for both the young manager just starting out as well as the practicing executive who wants to learn more about the field of management. And this trend is welcome news to university administrators who know that during the 1980s the undergraduate enrollments are going to drop and then taper off. With this new executive development market, however, they believe they can continue to fill the classrooms with individuals interested in learning about the field of management.

Source: "The Swing to Practicality in the B-Schools," *Business Week,* July 23, 1979, pp. 191–192.

expecting to find growth and self-fulfillment, only to discover that the organization not only fails to offer these but rewards conformity and the willingness to be a team player. If recruits want more independence or freedom, they are not very likely to remain with the organization.

▪ Lack of performance appraisal.

A third factor is *lack of performance appraisal,* a topic we examined earlier in the book. Most organizations promise their new people that they will be told how well they are doing and that they can use this information as a guide for improving their future performance. However, this is not what happens. Most managers do not do performance appraisal very well, and some neglect it entirely. The result is that young managers are not sure how well they are doing or what they need to do to improve future performance.

▪ Unrealistically high aspirations.

A fourth factor is *unrealistically high aspirations.* Many new college graduates start out feeling that they have the necessary skills and techniques to do a first-rate job. However, many of them are generally unskilled in the practical application of these ideas. They have the necessary theory, but they do not know how to shape it to the practical world. The rude awakening for them comes when they realize that they are not yet as good as they initially thought, and their peers and superiors do not rate them as high as they still feel they should be rated.

▪ Inability to create challenge.

A fifth factor is *inability to create challenge.* During their school years, most students are given challenges by their teachers. However, in the work place, they have rather boring, basic tasks and are unable to figure out how to make them more challenging.

▪ Threats to the superior.

Finally, some new recruits find that they are *threats to their superiors.* They know quite a bit more, at least from a theoretical or technical standpoint, than their bosses. Additionally, many of them enter the organization at a salary that is much higher than their boss's initial salary. For all these reasons, their relationship with the bosses can become strained.

How can problems like these be overcome or reduced? Some firms try to accomplish this by using what is called a *realistic job interview.* During this session with prospective employees, the interviewer tells them about both the positive and negative aspects of the job they have applied for. Additionally, they are told the types of conditions under which they will be working. For example, if the job requires close supervision, the recruiter will make this clear. If there are any boring aspects of the job, this too is explained. In this way, the individual goes in with both eyes open. There is not the big letdown after the first couple of weeks, followed by the all-too-typical response, "This isn't the type of job I interviewed for. The company really misled me."

First Impressions Really Count

Early job experiences are very important in influencing the new employee's adjustment to the organization and the person's subsequent career success. An individual's first impressions form a lasting imprint. If things go well, the person is more likely to have a different type of career than if things go poorly.

The First Job

▪ Initial success is important.

As we noted earlier, one of the biggest disappointments for most new employees is the lack of job challenge. One research study reported that of over 1,000 college graduates hired by a large manufacturing company, almost half left within a three-year period because the lack of job challenge resulted in disenchantment with the firm.[2] (See Figure 15.1.) These findings support those of David Berlew and Douglas Hall, who followed the careers of 62 junior executives over a five-year period and found that the degree of challenge given to these executives in their first jobs correlated closely with both how successfully they performed subsequent assignments and how their careers advanced.[3] This led the researchers to conclude that the successful accomplishment of initially challenging tasks results in individuals realizing high performance standards and setting higher goals for themselves in the future. In addition, as the organization realizes that these people are indeed very capable, it gives them more in the way of challenging assignments. There is thus a blend of high achievers and difficult jobs, resulting in an ideal mix for both the individuals and the organization. Meanwhile, what happens to those young managers who have been given unchallenging jobs? These people do not realize high standards; nor do they receive much recognition for their work. As a result, they are not designated as management timber, and they fail to keep up with the other group. Given the fact that most organizations do not provide their new people with very challenging initial tasks, it should be evident that the small number of top management jobs is not the only reason that many people do not end up in top management positions.

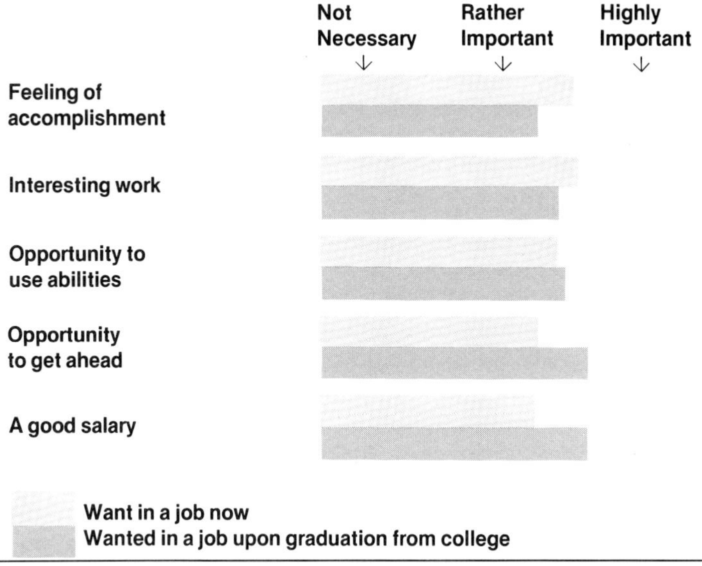

	Not Necessary ↓	Rather Important ↓	Highly Important ↓
Feeling of accomplishment			
Interesting work			
Opportunity to use abilities			
Opportunity to get ahead			
A good salary			

Want in a job now
Wanted in a job upon graduation from college

Figure 15.1
Job Features Most Important to 495 Employees Now and When They Graduated from College

Source: Reprinted by permission of the publisher, from "Why Do They Leave?" *Personnel*, May-June 1973, p. 28, © 1973 by AMACOM, a division of American Management Associations. All rights reserved.

The First Boss

One's first boss can also have a significant effect on an individual's performance. The superior embodies all that is good and bad with the organization. If the boss is lazy, spiteful, or a stern taskmaster, this image will influence the subordinate's view of the entire organization. Conversely, if the superior is helpful, trusting, attentive, and concerned with the new employee, this too will affect the person's view of the overall organization. It all depends on the boss.

The big problem in many organizations is that a new recruit is likely to make a higher-than-average number of mistakes and the boss must be patient with the individual. Unfortunately, some supervisors overreact and weaken the new employee's self-image and enthusiasm for the job. For example, many supervisors like to use close control in an effort to keep the employee from making errors. However, all they end up doing is preventing the new employee from learning. There is no positive feedback or feeling of "I've really learned a lot since I've been here." Instead, the individual feels that the boss does not trust him or her. Sometimes there is really no recognition given by the superior. How can there be? The person never really completes a job personally. The boss is always there to help out.

■ The boss will influence the subordinate.

Finally, the expectations of the boss will greatly affect the new employee's attitudes and performance. Employees tend to fulfill the expectations of their superior. If the person treats the subordinate as a slow learner, this will reduce the latter's motivation. Conversely, if the employee is treated like a potentially high performer, the latter is more likely to act this way. The boss plays a great role in molding the new employee. Research by Jay Hall suggests that bosses who are interested only in low-level satisfaction needs, such as physiological and safety needs, will have employees who feel the same way. The latter will either have these feelings before coming to work for this boss or will develop them on the job. In either event, the subordinates will all feel the same way about need satisfaction. Those who do not will quit or get jobs elsewhere in the organization. The managers who fit into this category tend to be the lowest producers of all.[4]

Managers who rate average in Hall's research tend to be most interested in satisfying those needs that fit into the middle of Maslow's hierarchy, especially social needs. They want everyone to get along with each other. "Let us all be one big happy family," seems to be their motto. They, like their counterpart managers, tend to be surrounded by individuals who think and act the way they do.

Finally, there are the most successful managers that Hall found. These individuals are high achievers and are most motivated by upper-level need satisfaction. They demand performance and work to ensure that ego needs and self-actualization desires are fulfilled. Drawing together all three categories, Hall has written:

> **High Achievers place major emphasis on the actualization, belonging and ego-status needs composing the motivator package, paying only average attention to the hygiene factors. Low Achievers, on the other hand, virtually ignore motivators while stressing the importance of creature comfort and, particularly, safety and security issues having hygiene significance. Average Achievers stress ego-status, giving adequate attention to the actualization needs of their subordinates, essentially promoting motivator seeking among those they manage. As . . . expected, managerial achievement is linked to the motivational climate one creates for . . . subordinates as well as to personal striving.[5]**

In short, there tends to be a self-fulfilling prophecy. Managers who have a strong desire for lower-level need satisfaction surround themselves with subordinates who have or develop the same needs, and together they tend to be low performers. The same holds for average and superior performers. Thus, a manager's subordinates really say as much about the manager as about the workers. Thus, we can return to our earlier proposition: The influence of one's first boss can have a significant effect on the new employee's performance.

Early Career Problems

After surviving these first impressions, many young managers face early career dilemmas. These include (1) insensitivity and passivity, (2) loyalty dilemmas, and (3) personal anxiety.[6]

Insensitivity and Passivity

▪ Some people are manipulative.

One of the biggest complaints made by practicing managers about new recruits to the organization is that they overemphasize analytical tools and rational decision making while underemphasizing human understanding. They tend to be too manipulative in their dealings with others.

Young managers who are insensitive to the political environment are also frequently characterized by personal passivity and inadequate probing of the world around them. They seem to fear what they may discover about themselves and often assume that good intentions are enough to make everyone think that they are doing a fine job. Instead of trying to shape events, they are led by them. Many times they feel that they are helpless to cope in an organization that is confining because of its many rules and traditions. Also, they are afraid that, if they are different, they will be labeled nonconformists. As a result, while many organizations reward independence and encourage initiative, many young managers refuse to take the chance. And it is always easier to drift with the times and hope that everything will work out for the best. Unfortunately, this is not the strategy for a successful career.

▪ Insensitive to the political environment.

Another problem faced by new employees is ignorance of how they will be evaluated. Many managers place high value on such performance related areas as profits, sales, and productivity. However, what happens when subordinates occupy positions where results cannot be easily measured? They too face the problem of how the boss will evaluate them. In many cases, we find that the superiors tend to be biased, evaluating others as they see themselves. For example, most managers see themselves as successful, and there is a tendency to rate others who act as they do as also successful. Thus such things as speech habits, clothing, academic background, and point of view often influence the superior's evaluation of the new employee.

▪ Unsure of how they will be evaluated.

Loyalty Dilemmas

Another major problem is that of loyalty dilemmas. Loyalty can be interpreted in many different ways, but the way the superior chooses to define it is going to be the most important for the new employee.

▪ Loyalty has many meanings.

Some superiors equate loyalty with obedience. Sometimes, of course, the subordinate winds up falling into the "yes man" trap. The problem here is that the boss fails to distinguish between obedience and honest disagreement and ends up not tolerating the latter.

Another way in which loyalty is often measured is in the form of effort. Does the individual work hard in the interest of the organization? Some managers operate under the philosophy that everyone should get to the office early and not leave until well past quitting time. Anyone who holds regular nine to five hours is seen as lazy or disloyal to the company. Other managers are more concerned with work than hours, though no new employee should disregard hours.

A third way loyalty is viewed is as synonymous with reliability and successful performance. Work is to be done on time; jobs are to be completed within budgets; productivity is to be high. If the subordinate fails to achieve any of these objectives, he or she is seen as disloyal to the organization.

A fourth way loyalty is often viewed is by how well the subordinate protects the superior from ridicule or adverse evaluation by others. These managers expect the subordinate never to disagree with a superior in public and always to make excuses for superiors who are late for a meeting or who have failed to complete some assignment. Under this definition of loyalty, everyone is divided into two groups: us and them. With "us," all efforts are to be made to conceal, contain, or cover up mistakes, and leaks about problem areas to outside parties are forbidden; for they threaten the security of the relationship and the working arrangement.

Finally, loyalty is sometimes viewed as honesty. In these cases, bosses expect subordinates to warn them of impending failure before things get out of hand and the whole organization knows about it. This, of course, can be particularly hard on young managers, because it sometimes forces them to admit personal mistakes which can sidetrack their careers before they really get off the ground. It is also threatening in that the bearer of bad news is sometimes confused with the news itself.

For new managers, the dilemma is that of determining which version of loyalty is expected by the organization or the boss. Sometimes subordinates find that the superior uses a combination of views about loyalty. For example, the boss wants you to say so if you have made a serious mistake but will hold this against you when it comes to performance evaluations. Or the boss wants you to cover for him by going to a meeting, but if you do that you will not get your monthly cost control report done and this will come to the attention of higher management. Do you please the boss by going to the meeting or completing the report? Either way, there is going to be a loyalty dilemma.

Personal Anxiety

Another major problem that confronts young managers is that of personal anxiety. This anxiety takes two forms.

▪ Are they selling out?

One is that related to integrity and commitment. Young managers often ask themselves whether they are selling out to the organization in return for promotions and salary increases. Is this job really worth it? Is the product I am selling (or helping produce) really that useful to people? Is what I'm doing a contribution to this society? On the one hand, people do not want to throw away a career. On the other hand, they are concerned with their integrity.

▪ Overdependent?

The other anxiety-causing factor is related to dependence. Young managers like to believe that they are independent and off on their own. They are no longer reliant on their parents for assistance. However, they are dependent on the organization in the sense that they cannot solve all their organizational problems without assistance. They need subordinates to help get the work done and in many cases do not know as much as the subordinates about the technical side of the job. Thus, they cannot personally replace these individuals. They have to work through them. Additionally, subordinates rely on them for assistance, such as going to bat for pay increases, building their career paths, and helping them get promotions.

The feelings associated with others being dependent on them often create great personal anxiety within young managers.

Another kind of anxiety can stem from being in the wrong kind of management. Some people do not work well in organizations. Table 15.2 explores an alternative management form.

Table 15.2
Are You an Entrepreneurial Manager?

Many students of management want to seek a career with an established organization such as General Motors, IBM, or General Electric. They overlook the possibility of going into business for themselves. Do you have that entrepreneurial spirit? Two psychologists, Richard Boyatzis and David Winter, have studied the entrepreneurial character and designed the following questions to reveal whether you have entrepreneurial attitudes. Look over the following fourteen questions and choose the answers that best describe your feelings. The interpretation to the test is given at the end of the chapter.

1. If you had a free evening, would you most likely a) watch TV b) visit a friend c) work on a hobby?
2. In your daydreams, would you most likely appear as a) a millionaire floating on a yacht b) a detective who has solved a difficult case c) a politician giving an election night victory speech?
3. To exercise, would you rather a) join an athletic club b) join a neighborhood team c) do some jogging at your own pace?
4. When asked to work with others on a team, which would you anticipate with most pleasure: a) other people coming up with good ideas b) cooperating with others c) getting other people to do what you want?
5. Which game would you rather play a) Monopoly b) roulette c) bingo?
6. Your employer asks you to take over a company project that is failing. Would you tell him that you will a) take it b) won't take it because you're up to your gills in work c) give him an answer in a couple of days when you have more information?
7. In school, were you more likely to choose courses emphasizing a) fieldwork b) papers c) exams?
8. In buying a refrigerator would you a) stay with an established, well-known brand b) ask your friends what they bought c) compare thoroughly the advantages of different brands?
9. While on a business trip in Europe you are late for an appointment with a client in a neighboring town. Your train has been delayed indefinitely. Would you a) rent a car to get there b) wait for the next scheduled train c) reschedule the appointment?
10. Do you believe that people you know who have succeeded in business a) have connections b) are cleverer than you c) are about the same as you but maybe work a little harder?
11. An employee who is your friend is not doing his job. Would you a) take him out for a drink, hint broadly that things aren't going right and hope he gets the message b) leave him alone and hope he straightens out c) give him a strong warning and fire him if he doesn't shape up?
12. You come home to spend a relaxing evening and find that your toilet has just overflowed. Would you a) study your home-repair book to see if you can fix it yourself b) persuade a handy friend to fix it for you c) call a plumber?
13. Do you enjoy playing cards most when you a) play with good friends b) play with people who challenge you c) play for high stakes?
14. You operate a small office-cleaning business. A close friend and competitor suddenly dies of a heart attack. Would you a) reassure his wife that you will never try to take away any customers b) propose a merger c) go to your former competitor's customers and offer them a better deal?

Source: "Testing the Entrepreneurial You," reprinted from the March 1978 issue of *Money* Magazine by special permission;

Career Patterns—What to Expect

Most people's careers follow a pattern. Before looking at the various ways in which you can manage your own career and turn things to your advantage, let us look at a typical career pattern, describing what you can expect.[7]

Breaking Away

■ Initial self-sufficiency.

The first period of an individual's career actually begins in late adolescence and covers the years between sixteen and twenty-two. During this time people break away from family ties and become more independent than ever before. While many still depend at least partially on their parents during this period, the degree of self-sufficiency increases and these ties start to be broken.

Initial Adulthood

■ Search for career goals.

During this next stage, which often lasts from around the ages of twenty-two to twenty-nine, the individual completes his or her education and begins making commitments for the future. A life-style and career are being chosen, and the person starts getting into the adult world. Those individuals who are uncertain about the course they are to follow often find themselves going through a dogged search for career goals, and for them initial adulthood may last well into their thirties.

The Transition Period

■ Review of progress.

Next comes a transition period during which the individual reviews career progress and evaluates how satisfactorily things have been moving along. This often takes place during the years between twenty-nine and thirty-two. If progress is satisfactory, the person will continue on. If not, the individual will often make a radical change, and turmoil may result. During this state it is not uncommon to find people making changes in career objectives, employment, geographic location, and, in some cases, marital status. Many people feel during this period that it is their last chance to break out of their established pattern and do what they really want to do with their lives.

Becoming One's Own Person

■ The career becomes paramount.

The next phase is characterized by a settling-down period, during which everything else is subordinated to job and career advancement. The person becomes his or her own person and social contacts and friendships are cut or minimized to enable the individual to concentrate on gaining mastery over the job and getting ahead in his or her career. During this period, which covers the years from thirty-two to thirty-nine, it is common to find the person looking for a sponsor who will help in this career climb.

Mid-Life Crisis

■ A crisis may develop.

While it might seem that the individual is now ready to move with no further problems, nothing could be further from the truth. Actually, during the ages of thirty-nine to forty-three many people experience what is called *mid-life crisis.* They again review their careers and, if they feel things are not going well, they go through a crisis of sorts. Feelings of resentment, frustration, or sadness can cause them to lose their emotional equilibrium. Some turn to excessive drinking, others quit their jobs, and still others simply do things like entering a middle-aged hippie life-style or making some spectacular break with the past that messes up their careers. The outcome of all this is traumatic for many of these people.[8]

Reestablishment of Equilibrium

■ A feeling of contentment.

In this last stage of the career pattern, which often occurs between the ages of forty-three and fifty, people experience a sense of contentment over their past achievements. Of course, these are those individuals who have survived their mid-life crisis and are still in the management ranks. These people still have high career interest, and they are often quite open to the many types of satisfactions that life can offer. During this period many managers find that they have arrived. They now take heart in their accomplishments, slow up their competitive drives, and seek to renew old social ties and/or develop new ones. Many of the things that have been neglected over the years, including family relationships, are now renewed. It is a flowering period for the person.

Keep in mind that you may not go through this career cycle. However, it is a typical pattern.

"Well, they haven't repealed mandatory retirement yet, Fernman, so tell me, are you coming out to get your gold watch or not?"

Manage Your Career

The last thing that needs to be said about your career in management is that you must assume personal responsibility for your advancement. Too many people rely on taking advantage of opportunities. This is too passive an approach. Rather than take advantage of opportunities, you must *make opportunities.* In recent years, some writers have set forth guidelines for career advancement. The following are some *career strategies.*

Be a High-Level Performer

▪ Do well!

The first rule of success is: Outperform everyone else. While there are many ways to get promoted up the ranks, nothing succeeds like success. Job-related performance is still the quickest route to the top.

Job competence and talent are still the number one success ingredients in all but the most pathologically political organizations. All other talk about success strategies is fanciful without first assuming that the person on the make is competent in his or her specialty. Before anybody is promoted in any big organization, the prospective new boss asks, "How well did he (or she) perform for you?" Even if you become the most adept office politician (including consorting with people with power), you still have to exhibit job competence to be assigned more responsibility.[9]

Help Your Boss Succeed

▪ Support your boss.

Your boss can make or break your career. By making yourself invaluable to this individual, you can improve your chances for promotion. In particular, when something you do will help the boss and you do it well, the latter is likely to remember. Conversely, if it is a critical matter and you do it poorly, you may jeopardize the boss's career and your own in the process. Individuals in these situations are referred to as *crucial subordinates,* and they are of two types: complementary and supplementary. *Complementary crucial subordinates* help the boss overcome weaknesses; for example, they fill out reports or write memos if the superior is not very good at those jobs. *Supplementary subordinates* help the boss in areas where the individual is capable but wants to expand his or her expertise. Being a complementary or supplementary subordinate is most likely to help you in your career. So too is any emotional support you can give your superior. Of course, this can lead to the charge of apple polishing. However, this is not all bad, depending on the environment in the department. For example, research shows that superiors are prone to favor apple polishers when there is a hostile or disagreeable worker on the scene, although the apple-polishing approach is much less useful when the other workers in the group are simply inept.[10]

Find a Sponsor

▪ Get a mentor.

Sponsors are influential individuals of higher rank than you who will endorse your credentials for promotion. By having a sponsor you greatly increase your chances for promotion; for there is now someone to argue your case. The result is that you are pulled up the organization by your patron, rather than having to push or force your way up all by yourself.

How do you get a sponsor? One way is to make yourself visible. Let people know how well you are doing. No sponsor wants to move along a mediocre performer, for this reflects on both parties. Sponsors would like very much to pick out winners and then give them that extra push they need to make it. Remember, it is not only rewarding but a lot easier to sponsor a high-level performer than an average performer. By letting people know you are a high performer, you improve your chances of getting a sponsor.

Document Your Accomplishments

▪ Keep a hero file.

Do not be bashful. If you are good, be prepared to prove it. Save memos from superiors that tell what a good job you did on a particular project. If you are singled out by the company newspaper as an up-and-coming manager, save the clipping. Often referred to as *hero files,* these documents impress people. Also, if you find your sponsor is leaving the organization and not taking you, at least you have a file to use in convincing the new manager to sponsor you.

Another way of documenting your accomplishments is through empire building. If you have a small group reporting to you and there is a chance of increasing the number, take it. As the number of subordinates increases or the department size grows, you look more powerful. Remember, when top management is casting around for a manager to head a new project or take over a particular division, they are most likely to look at those who currently manage large departments or units. Additionally, there is a tendency to equate department size with contribution. Thus, if you head a large department, the management will believe you are making a much more significant contribution to the organization than someone who is managing a much smaller department.

Give and Get Loyalty

▪ Be loyal to the boss.

Loyalty is an important factor in promotions. People who are looked on as team members are more likely to get top management jobs than are those who are seen as independent thinkers, gadflies, or loners. Superiors feel more psychologically comfortable when they can rely upon a subordinate to support the department in times of organizational warfare. Keep in mind, however, that we are not talking about yes men. Competent superiors can identify these people and will be turned off by them. However, they will reward true loyalty. And if you are loyal, you will end up forming alliances or coalitions with groups and individuals in the organization who have the power to influence your career. The important thing is to form the right coalition. The palace revolt at Ford Motor Company in the early 1970s provides an excellent example of the importance of forming the right coalition. Simon E. Knudsen was brought into the firm as president, after having served in a top-management position with General Motors. However, in less than two years he was fired. Why? Abraham Zaleznik provides the following explanation:

While it is true that Henry Ford II named Knudsen president of the company, Knudsen's ultimate power structure depended on forming an alliance. The particular individual

with whom an alliance seemed crucial was Lee Iacocca. For some reason, Knudsen and Iacocca competed for power and influence instead of using cooperatively a power base to which both contributed, as is the case with most workable coalitions. In the absence of a coalition, the alternate postures of rivalry and battle for control erupted. Ford ultimately responded by weighing his power with one side over the other.[11]

Consider Swimming against the Tide

▪ Look before you leap.

Choosing a nonconventional path can also result in career success. For example, if everyone seems to be flocking to the manufacturing end of the business, go into sales. Remember, sooner or later someone is going to have to sell everything that is being produced, and sales is going to be the critical area. By doing well here, you will come to the attention of your superiors. Or consider the young graduate who agreed to take a position in the firm's South American office. No one else wanted to go; it was considered an outpost. However, within three years the young man was head of the subsidiary, and when he transferred back to the States, he was much further up the hierarchy than those who had opted for stateside jobs.

However, you should be careful about one thing. Sometimes swimming against the tide is a poor career decision because those in the mainstream are more adaptable to what is going on. For example, deciding to go into public relations rather than advertising might be an initially sound move, but if there is a recession, it is the public relations department that often gets cut first. Thus you may end up choosing an area that is popular now but will dry up or be cut back in the near future. This is why it is important to investigate the career path and decide whether it will be as promising in five and ten years as it is today.

Be Mobile

▪ Successful managers are mobile.

Many managers make it to the top by being mobile. Rather than standing in line for thirty years to get into the president's chair, they switch from one firm to another, moving ever higher in the process. Eugene Jennings noted this phenomenon over a decade ago when he studied corporate presidents and found the following:

1. Fewer and fewer of the men emerging at the top have gray hair and stooped shoulders. From 1948 to 1953 the average age of board chairmen was sixty-three; of corporation presidents, fifty-nine; and of new officers, fifty. Fifteen years later, from 1965 to 1968, the average ages of the men in these positions had dropped to fifty-nine, fifty, and forty-one.
2. More and more men who become presidents do so after joining the corporation at a high level rather than after working their way up through the ranks at one company.
3. Fewer and fewer of the men who follow an inside route to the presidency do so by plodding along the straight, upward path of traditional insiders. Instead of boring their way through the center, they whirl around the edges of the middle management spiral.[12]

Despite a move away from this pattern during the recession of the mid-1970s, the description is again accurate. Why is this so? Perhaps it is best described by the adage "the grass is always greener on the other side of the fence." Many organizations hesitate about promoting their own people into top-management, sensitive positions but will bring someone in from the outside for the job. One manager has explained this phenomenon by saying, "The inside person is well known to everyone. We all know the person's strong points and, perhaps more unfortunately, weak points. The person coming in from the outside is something of a mystery to us, and much more emphasis is placed on the individual's strengths. Thus when we're comparing the inside and outside candidates, the latter look better. Of course, this is a silly way to approach top management recruiting, but this is the way it is done in many firms and we're no exception."

▪ Managerial milestones.

When should you become mobile and move to another firm? Numerous suggestions have been set forth. Richard Gleason has developed a set of milestones that a manager can use in deciding if his or her career progress is satisfactory.[13] According to Gleason, the first milestone occurs around the age of twenty-five—the maximum age at which one should remain an individual performer. By thirty the individual wishing to be an executive should have completed his or her tour of duty as a first-level manager. By thirty-five the person should have passed through the second level of management by having held a position such as a district sales managership. By forty management of a broad corporate function, such as general sales manager or director of research and development, should have already taken place. The successful executive should be a vice-president of a functional area by forty-five and president by fifty if he or she wants to stay on plan. These milestones are in line with other research in industry. For example, Eugene Jennings found that among those presidents who were super-mobile, the average age when the person made president was forty-seven.

Of course, position is not everything. People also have to be interested in salary. Sometimes people occupy the upper rungs of the ladder and do not want to leave the firm because they like it there. How then can we measure their career success? This is where salary or financial progress enters the picture. Gleason has suggested that the career people who plan their way to the top should double their salary every seven years. In this plan, if you join an organization in 1981 at $15,000, then by 1988 you should be making $35,000 and by the year 2002 you should be up to $140,000.

▪ Move up or move out.

Many managers, however, feel that they should be able to make these salaries *regardless* of whether they stay in the organization or move to another. Therefore, in determining when to move, let us consider another useful guideline: Move when you feel you have mastered the job and cannot learn any more. Remember that there is an 80–20 theory in management which holds that 20 percent of any job counts for 80 percent of the learning. Thus when you have learned 20 percent of the work, you have basically mastered all there is to know. The rest is minor material. Now the question is, will you be promoted or should you move? A good rule of the road is that if you are not promoted within four years, you need to consider moving to another organization. This is especially true if you have followed the earlier advice about seeking the right type of job. In every organization there are routes to the top. How do you know which ones they are? By simply looking at who are getting the promotions and determining what areas they work in. Some organizations prefer to promote finance types, while others favor marketing managers. If you are in one of these fast-track areas, you should be promoted rather rapidly. If not, move. This is the wrong organization for you, and you will want to find the right one.

Summary

The first step in pursuing a management career is to get ready. This book has started you out in the right direction. However, there are still other courses you should take including human relations or organizational behavior, quantitative methods, and business policy. These three courses cover the behavioral, quantitative, and general management areas and will provide you with a broadly based understanding of what management is all about.

Having completed this academic preparation, you will then be ready to start your formal career. One of the first things you should realize, however, is that the initial job can be a reality shock. Some of the reasons for this initial shock include low challenge of the job, low level of satisfaction, lack of performance appraisal, unrealistically high aspirations, inability to create challenge, and the threat a new employee can present to the superior. Additionally, you should realize that first impressions sometimes count too much, and you should try not to be turned off if your boss gives you the impression that you are not doing a good job. Many superiors simply do not know how to handle new subordinates very well.

Next you should realize that you will undoubtedly have early career problems. Typical illustrations include insensitivity and passivity, loyalty dilemmas caused by a failure to understand exactly what type of loyalty the boss expects, and personal anxiety brought on by the pressures of having other people dependent on you. Nevertheless, if you hang in there and do a good job, you will find that your career will make headway. Of course, this still does not mean that you will not have any problems. As noted in this chapter, there are six basic stages in the typical career pattern and a few of them, such as mid-life crisis, can be especially frustrating.

How can you hope to deal with all of these problems? One way is by taking an active role in managing your own career. Rather than waiting for opportunity to knock, go out and try to make opportunity for yourself. Some of the ways of doing so include being a high-level performer, helping your boss succeed, finding a sponsor, documenting your accomplishments, giving and getting loyalty, considering swimming against the tide, and remaining mobile.

These are only a handful of helpful suggestions. There are many more you will come across as you continue your study of management. For the moment, remember that management is an interesting and dynamic field of endeavor and there is always room for another bright, highly motivated person in its ranks. As you continue your study of management, keep your mind open to management as a career. Many people have found it to be a rewarding, meaningful life—and so can you!

Review and Study Questions

1. Are business schools really incorporating more practicality into their courses? Explain.
2. In what way do new young managers face reality shock when they take first jobs? Incorporate four of the factors that help account for reality shock into your answer.
3. How much of an impact does the first boss have on a young manager's view of the organization? Explain.
4. A manager's subordinates really say more about the manager than about the workers. What does this statement mean?
5. What kinds of loyalty dilemmas are young managers apt to confront on the job today? Identify and describe at least three.
6. In your own words, what does a typical career pattern look like? Start with the breaking away phase and trace the pattern through mid-life crisis and into the reestablishment of equilibrium stage.
7. In giving people advice about ways to manage their careers, what would you tell them? Be specific in your answer.
8. What would you tell someone who said that career success is more a matter of luck than of anything else? Defend your answer.

Key Terms in the Chapter

reality shock
loyalty dilemma
career patterns
mid-life crisis
career strategies
crucial subordinates
complementary crucial subordinates
supplementary subordinates

Notes

1. Douglas T. Hall, *Careers in Organizations* (Pacific Palisades, Calif.: Goodyear, 1976).
2. Marvin D. Dunnette, Richard D. Arvey, and Paul A. Banas, "Why Do They Leave?" *Personnel,* May–June 1973, pp. 25–39.
3. David E. Berlew and Douglas T. Hall, *Some Determinants of Early Managerial Success,* Working Paper No. 81–64 (Cambridge, Mass.: Sloan School of Management, Massachusetts Institute of Technology, 1964).

4. Jay Hall, "To Achieve or Not: The Manager's Choice," *California Management Review,* Summer 1976, pp. 5–18.
5. Ibid., p. 10.
6. Ross A. Webber, *Management: Basic Elements of Managing Organizations,* rev. ed. (Homewood, Ill.: Irwin, 1979), pp. 585–607.
7. Daniel J. Levinson et al., "The Psychological Development of Men in Early Adulthood and the Mid-Life Transition," in *Life History Research in Psychopathology,* vol. 3, eds. D. F. Hicks, A. Thomas, and M. Roff (Minneapolis: University of Minnesota Press, 1974).
8. For more on the topic of the mid-life crisis, see Gail Sheehy, *Passages: Predictable Crises of Adult Life* (New York: Dutton, 1976).
9. Andrew J. DuBrin, *Survival in the Sexist Jungle* (Chatsworth, Calif.: Books for Better Living, 1974), pp. 29–30.
10. "Apple-Polishing Sometimes Pays Off," *OBI Interaction: The Management Psychology Newsletter,* July 16, 1971, pp. 5–6.
11. Abraham Zaleznik, "Power and Politics in Organizational Life," *Harvard Business Review,* May–June 1970, p. 52.
12. Eugene Jennings, "Mobicentric Man," *Psychology Today,* July 1969, p. 70.
13. Richard E. Gleason, "Planning the Way to the Top," *Business Horizons,* June 1971, pp. 60–63.

Answers to Entrepreneurial Quiz

1. c; 2. b; 3. c; 4. c; 5. a; 6. c; 7. a; 8. c; 9. a; 10. c; 11. c; 12. a; 13. b; 14. c.

Score one point for each correct answer. Questions 1, 2, 3, 7, 9, and 12 suggest whether you are a realistic problem solver who can run a business without constant help from others. Questions 5, 6, and 8 probe whether you take calculated risks and seek information before you act. Questions 4, 10, 13, and 14 show whether you, like the classic entrepreneur, find other people most satisfying when they help fulfill your need to win. Question 11 reveals whether you take responsibility for your destiny—and your business. If you score between 11 and 14 points, you could have a good chance to succeed. If you score from 7 to 10 points, you'd better have a superb business idea or a lot of money to help you out. If you score seven or less, stay in someone else's company.

Case: At a Crossroad

Is it all a roll of the dice, or can a 39-year-old man take charge?

It seemed to Jack Baugh that things had never really started off that well for him in his career. Straight out of college, he took a job with a large western-based manufacturing firm. Jack felt that he did very good work, but his boss always watched Jack's performance very closely. When his six months of probation were over, Jack was delighted. He hoped to be able to do more things on his own and, most importantly, he thought perhaps the work would become more interesting and challenging.

However, it did not happen. Jack's boss turned out to be a very stern taskmaster; and when Jack received his semiannual performance evaluation, it indicated that he was a marginal employee. Meanwhile, Jack's friends, who had entered the firm at the same time as he, all had very good performance ratings. Their bosses were apparently much more easy to please than his. "Look on it this way," said one of his friends. "It's all a roll of the dice. You just happened to draw the toughest boss for your training period." Everyone laughed at this remark, but it did not turn out to be a joke for Jack. Based on the evaluations, all new management trainees were given positions throughout the firm. Jack was assigned to a department where morale was poor and output was low.

Aware of the situation, Jack worked hard and managed to turn things around. His boss realized what a good job he had done and Jack's evaluation reflected it. Nevertheless, he never seemed to make up that lost ground. He was always a promotion behind the group he started with.

Last month Jack was thirty-nine years old, and he has been evaluating his career progress. Jack believes that he is not moving along as fast as he should. On the other hand, he wonders if he has not waited too long to make a move to another company. Is life passing him by?

This past weekend Jack saw an ad for a senior vice-president's job with one of his competitors. He is wondering if he might fill the bill but, at the same time, is nervous about leaving a firm where he has been employed for seventeen years. In short, Jack is confused about what career move to make. He is at a crossroad. If he stays with his current firm, the future will be more of the same. But he will have both seniority and security. If he leaves, he will have new opportunities; but there will also be major challenges and he does not know if he is up to facing them. Nevertheless, Jack intends to make a decision within the week.

Questions

1. What particular problems common among new recruits did Jack encounter early in his career?
2. In terms of career cycle, what phase is Jack currently in? Explain your answer.
3. What would you recommend Jack do? Be complete in your answer.

Case: Career Opportunities

She has to choose from too many good things . . . and after three crummy years.

When Christine Stander graduated from college with her bachelor's degree in business administration, she took a job with a large retailing chain in the Chicago area. Chris's initial performance evaluations were very good, and her boss told her that she would have no trouble moving up the organization. And this is what happened—at least for the first two years. During this time Chris was promoted to department head, while her boss moved into upper middle management. However, things then took a turn for the worse. Her boss left for a job with a competitor, and Chris found herself without a mentor.

For a while, Chris thought her track record would speak for itself. Sales in her department were very high, and she had the lowest personnel turnover rate in the store. Nevertheless, none of this seemed to impress her superiors very much, and she has not had a promotion in three years. Several other people, none of whom have as high a performance record as she, have been given promotions; and Chris is concerned that her career has run into a very serious snag.

Last week she called her former mentor and discussed the situation with him. He asked her a number of questions, including whether she could document her accomplishments at the store. Chris said that she could and went on to tell him that those individuals who had moved past her into upper middle management positions all had mentors. "Ever since you left," she told him, "my career has been drifting."

Her old boss asked her if she would consider moving to another retail organization. "We have openings over here for people with your qualifications. However, I never really thought you would be interested in moving or I would have contacted you. There are also a few other organizations I know of that are looking for people like you. I'll contact them and get back to you."

Three days ago Chris's first boss called back and said that he had two possibilities to discuss with her. First there was a job opening with a major retailer across town. If she were interested, an interview could be arranged for early next week. Second, there was an opening as his assistant. His subordinate had just decided to leave, and Chris could have the job. "It'll be like old times," he told her. Chris was elated and told him she'd be back with him next week.

Today, to her surprise, Chris's current boss called her in for a talk. "We've had our eye on you for quite a while," he said. "I'm moving up in the organization and would like you to take my position. You do an excellent job, and I'd like us to work as a team. I'll help you up the organization ladder if you just keep working as effectively as you have in the past. Together we can both succeed. What do you say?"

Questions

1. Does Chris have a promising career? Explain.
2. Why has it taken so long for her organization to give her another promotion?
3. What would you recommend Chris do now? Explain.

Supplementary Cases

The following cases supplement those at the end of the chapters on planning, organizing, staffing, directing, and controlling. However, in contrast to the earlier cases, which reinforced the material in specific chapters, these are designed to handle more broadly based functional areas. The material in this book is adequate to serve as a basis for the solution of these cases, which have been specially written to reinforce the major concepts and problem areas in the five functional areas examined in this text—planning, organizing, staffing, directing, and controlling. Questions designed to direct the analysis appear at the end of each case.

Planning

1 Philosophy of Planning

"Karl, this is only my second month with the company," said Sheila Whittier, a new manager in the corporate R&D office, "so I may be premature in speaking. However, I really think people around here are confused about the concept of planning."

"What makes you think that?" asked Karl Kramer, general manager of Factory 3. "I think we're pretty clear-cut about where we're going and how we're going to get there."

"I disagree. We're tremendous efficiency and control people, but we're terrible when it comes to planning. Here's the problem, at least the way I see it. We put all our emphasis on what we said we were going to do and what we already did. We control our performance. We measure it. But what attention do we give to the long run? Where is this company going to be in ten years? Why, I haven't heard any plan or objective being discussed that would take us more than twelve months into the future."

"Well, then you have to admit we have planning, don't we?"

"Short-run, yes. Long-run, no."

"How do you arrive at those conclusions?"

"I think I need to emphasize the long run, since we seem to agree that there is short-run planning. Therefore, let me illustrate my ideas in this chart." (See Figure 1.)

Figure 1
Planning Flowchart

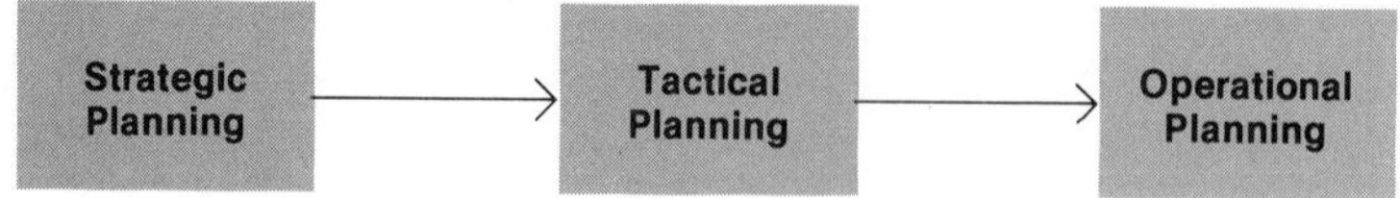

"First of all, we should have strategic planning. This is what I call long-range planning. The company defines its market niche and where it wants to be, say, ten years down the road. Then, in tactical planning we devote attention to allocating the resources necessary to attain these long-range objectives. Finally, in operational planning, we give prime emphasis to efficiency. We look at evaluation and control. And we concentrate our time on this third phase."

"Look, Sheila, we couldn't get to the third phase without the other two. Let me ask you this: How would we know what to evaluate and control if we didn't have strategic and tactical plans? You've defined away the very problem you've identified."

"No, Karl, it just doesn't work that way. If a company once had a strategic plan, that could be the basis for getting this whole process started. You're right about that. However, once strategic planning is deemphasized, the firm starts to operate on a day-to-day or month-to-month basis. For all practical purposes, long-range planning ceases and only operational planning is stressed."

Questions

1. Do you agree or disagree with Kramer's comment that if long-range planning ceases, a company will be operating solely on an efficiency basis?
2. How much strategic planning must be done by a firm such as General Motors? American Motors? Datsun? Explain, bringing into your discussion major points that each would want to consider and, if possible, decide upon in the strategic planning phase.
3. Suppose you were called in as a consultant in the firm in this case. How would you go about determining whether the company was conducting adequate strategic planning? Tactical planning? Operational planning? Be specific.

2 Indirect Strategy

Anthony Ashton had taken over Conglomerates, Inc., two years earlier. During that time he had moved the firm from marginal profitability to the strongest financial position it had ever enjoyed. As a result, he was being hailed as one of the nation's outstanding managers. This was why Rachel Webster, a feature writer for *See* magazine, had been sent to interview him. The business editor of the magazine told Webster, "Call up Anthony Ashton and see if you can get an exclusive interview with him. I think our readers would be interested in learning how he was able to save Conglomerates, Inc., from bankruptcy." Webster had no trouble getting Ashton to agree to an interview. Because the executive was continually on the road, the meeting was held in the executive jet between New York and Los Angeles, where Ashton was to address a business convention. Webster decided to make the best use she could of the time.

"Mr. Ashton, your success with Conglomerates, Inc., is well known. How did you manage it?"

"Rachel, it's no great secret how I turned the company around. I could sum it up in two words: indirect strategy."

"What do you mean by that?"

"Simply this: When I took over the firm, I found every division and subsidiary trying to compete with the competition on a direct basis. If the competition lowered its price, we lowered ours. Whatever they did, we did. Furthermore, when we attempted to break into a market already dominated by another firm, we would find out what that company's strong suit was and then try to match it. For example, if they had low price, we came in with a low price. If they had high quality, we came in with high quality. We were always reacting."

"Why didn't it work?"

"Because it's an absurd strategy. We were playing the game according to someone else's rules. And that's what I changed. Now, when we go into a market, we go on our terms. We find out the competition's weakest point. If they have a very low price, we look at the quality of their product or the service they provide. In other words, we attempt to determine the chink in their armor. And we don't wait for them to move first."

"How do you know the strategy you choose will work?"

"You don't. But you can be very sure that few firms—your own or your competitors'—succeed with strategies that can be easily undermined with direct confrontations. I believe that you have to judge the strongest point your competition has and then stay away from attacking it unless you are willing to pay a ghastly price. Why? Because the castle was built for the purpose of defense against frontal attack. You win by starving out the occupants. They have no way of stopping you if you have the strength to surround them and the patience to wait them out."

"Is this indirect approach workable only for business strategies?"

"That's a good, quick question, and I think you know the answer. No, as I just pointed out, the indirect strategy works in military campaigns as well. The whole point is not to attack your enemies at their strongest point because you are going to deplete your resources faster than theirs. Seek an indirect method."

Questions

1. Do you agree or disagree with Anthony Ashton? Explain your reasons.
2. How might a firm such as Ford Motor use this advice against General Motors? How might Volkswagen use the advice against General Motors?
3. How could this advice be of value to the president of a bank? A retail clothing company? An insurance firm? Give an illustration in each case.

3 The Entrepreneurial Engineer

Dale Mattson had always dreamed of going into business for herself. However, it was a long time before she was to find an opportunity. Mattson graduated from an engineering college and then went to work for a consulting firm.

One day, while visiting her sister, Mattson discovered that her three-year-old niece, Frances, had broken her doll. "It used to walk and talk, Aunt Dale, but now it's sick," the little girl said. Mattson took Frances out and bought her a new doll. When she returned home later that evening, she realized that the broken doll was still in the back of her car. However, just as she was about to throw it away, a thought came to her. Taking a knife, Mattson cut the doll open to look at the insides. The construction proved to be rather simple. In fact, Mattson realized in only a few minutes that some minor design changes could simplify the manufacturing process and greatly reduce the amount of material required.

She was unsure of what to do with this information. She did consider starting her own business; that, after all, was her goal. But she quickly assessed her finances and realized that for now, she seemed to have only two alternatives. First, she could take the doll to a number of manufacturing companies and see if their managements might be willing to enter the doll manufacturing business. Second, she could give her idea to the doll manufacturer in return for some kind of financial remuneration.

The first of the two options was the most appealing to Mattson, and so she spelled out her ideas to one of the firms for which she consulted. However, she had little success. Nor was the second firm any more enthusiastic. The third seemed attracted to the new design. But Mattson was told it would take two to three weeks before a final decision could be made. After the firm had studied her concept, the vice-president of manufacturing sent for Mattson.

"Dale, we've been looking over your design idea, and you have found a way to manufacture children's dolls at a very considerable saving over present methods. I can tell you that I like it. However, I've been overruled by the other members of top management; and actually, they do have a valid argument. Here it is. We could buy your design and manufacture the doll on a competitive basis. But we don't know anything about the toy business. We wouldn't know how to market the doll. In short, we are long on technical experience but short on the managerial and marketing expertise we would need to crack this market. We think your best bet would be to sell your idea to the company that manufactured the doll."

Mattson was disappointed. She had hoped that her idea would be the basis for something big. Now, the prospects looked very dim. However, after giving the matter serious thought, Mattson decided that she was probably better off selling her idea. Therefore, she contacted the doll manufacturing firm. Two months later the company sent Dale Mattson an offer of $15,000, which she accepted.

Questions

1. Was Mattson right in selling her idea? Explain.
2. What do you think of the vice-president's statement regarding the reasons the firm decided not to manufacture the doll? Are they logical, or is the company overlooking an excellent opportunity?
3. What is the main point about planning that this case makes? Be specific.

4 Trade-Offs

The Miller Chemical Corporation was in sound financial condition. It had not missed a dividend payment in fifty years. Furthermore, its profits between 1974 and 1979 had increased, while the competition was feeling the pinch of an economic downturn. When Bradley Washington was appointed the new president in January of 1980, he looked foward to continuing this financial progress. However, it was not long before he began to sense that something was wrong. The rest of the firms in the industry were complaining about the difficulty of making a profit, but Miller continued to report favorable earnings each quarter. To Washington this appeared incongruous. He began wishing that he had spent more time checking out the company before he agreed to leave his old position to come over to Miller. But it was obviously too late for regrets. The best thing to do now would be to obtain a copy of the last five annual reports and try to see what was going on. From them Washington obtained the data in Table 1.

President Washington then sent for his vice-president of finance.

"Viola, I've just been looking over our financial reports. How long has this been going on?"

"If you mean the freeze on research and development and the drive to increase profits, about ten years."

"How much longer do you think it can continue?"

"Maybe fifteen more years. We are really in excellent shape in some of our product areas and could operate at a profit there for quite a while."

"Well, I'm confused as to how we ever adopted such a strategy. All we're doing at present is sacrificing our market position to increase our profits. There is no planning being done! We are in the ridiculous process of liquidating our own company. Look at how much our share of the market has declined. I really can't comprehend this logic. How did Miller Chemical ever get started on this approach?"

"It all began under the old president, Jeff McMullen. His philosophy of management was that the company's first responsibility is to the stockholders. As a result,

Table 1
Annual Report Data, Miller Chemical

	Sales (000's)	Share of Market[a]	Research and Development Expenditure (000's)	Profit (000's)
1974	20,000	11.0	1,000	2,000
1975	20,500	10.8	1,000	2,300
1976	21,000	9.6	1,000	2,500
1977	22,000	8.5	1,000	2,800
1978	23,500	7.4	1,000	3,000
1979	24,000	6.3	1,000	3,200

[a] Since Miller Chemical was a small company in contrast to the giants in the industry, it computed its market share as a percentage of the total demand which existed in the market areas in which it competed. All other market areas were ignored in this calculation.

he put strong emphasis on dividends and the maintenance of a high price/earnings ratio. The result was a dynamic increase in the price of our stock. At one point we were selling for 35 times earnings. You can imagine how the stockholders received this. Some of them had tripled their investment within a year. They were ecstatic. Jeff McMullen was their hero."

"Terrific . . . He was selling their company right out under their noses, and they were cheering."

"I'm not so sure you can blame them. After all, they are interested in seeing their stock go up, and we have a responsibility to these people."

"Sure, but how far do we have to go along these lines? I think it's time we started putting more money in R&D and begin building back our share of the market."

"OK, but I'm not so sure that the stockholders or the directors are going to agree."

Questions

1. How much longer do you think this company can continue to allow its market share to decline? Explain.
2. What do you think of Washington's proposed plan? Do you agree or disagree?
3. What problems will Washington now face? Be explicit. How should he handle the situation?

5 The Backlog Problem

The Cadding Company had been faced with a backlog of orders for over a year. Initially, it was only $30,000 in unfilled requests, but over a twelve-month period, it grew to $150,000. At this point, the company decided that something would have to be done. Ackerman Consulting was brought in to make recommendations. The consulting firm examined the production records for the past year and interviewed Ben Phillips, vice-president of manufacturing, and some of the middle managers and first-line supervisors. The consultants then met with Phillips to talk over their recommendations.

"Mr. Phillips, we've looked your department over very carefully and I think we have pinpointed your problem."

"Fine. But don't tell me it's machine breakdowns, please. We had some consultants in here a few years ago and they told us that. However, we checked into that, and we discovered that the number of times our machines broke down was just about average for a department our size."

The consultants agreed: "Your machines aren't breaking down any more than might be expected. But there is a problem, nonetheless. Instead of undertaking preventive maintenance, you're allowing your machines to operate until they finally go down. Every time this happens, it takes longer to get them up than would have been the case had you opted for preventive maintenance. If you'll start to do this in the future, you can cut your backlog by at least 20 percent in the next six months alone."

"You may be right," said Phillips. "But how do we know when to undertake preventive maintenance? I don't want my people to start making repairs on machines that don't need them."

The consultants were encouraging. "Actually, it's not that difficult. By using a mathematical approach, you can determine an optimum solution. We've done a lot of research on this problem and have come up with the information your people are going to need. You must have noticed that machines are like people. They follow a pattern and break down with systematic regularity. With this in mind, you can see that, for example, machine A might break down every 160 hours on the average. This means that you can run the machine for almost four full weeks before having to do preventive maintenance. Then, if you do the maintenance before the machine goes down, you attain two objectives. First, it takes less time to get the machine back up. Second, you can set up a schedule for your maintenance people so that they know when to make maintenance repairs on each machine. You keep them busy while reducing down time."

"Sounds good to me," said Phillips. "I never thought about doing that. However, how do we know that these machines will go down according to some pattern? Why isn't machine breakdown random? Can't your mathematics be wrong?"

"Sure. We deal in probabilities, not certainties. But if you use this preventive maintenance approach, you are going to do a lot better than if you just sit and wait for the machines to break down before you provide maintenance. Those machines are going to be maintained, whatever you do. If you go toward prevention, you're going to be way ahead in the long run."

"I see. Well, let's go on to the rest of your recommendations, and we'll come back to this problem later."

Questions

1. Why might the vice-president of manufacturing be apprehensive about mathematical decision making?
2. Will Phillips accept this first recommendation or is he going to turn it down? Explain.
3. Should all managers be advocates of mathematical decision making? Explain.

6 Changes in Standards

"We're in trouble," remarked Anita Harding, a personnel specialist. "I've just come from a meeting with the union and they're plenty mad. Something's going to have to be done and done fast!"

Harding was referring to the new production standards that had been issued a few days earlier. These standards called for an across-the-board increase of 25 percent for all lathe operators. The union claimed this was both unfair and unreasonable. Their spokesman, Ned Nelson, put it this way:

"Look, why should the lathe operators be required to do 25 percent more work? We had industrial engineers in here five months ago. They studied the layout and conducted time and motion studies on all the machines. On the basis of their findings, standards were set for all jobs. Now we hear that management isn't happy; they want standards increased by 25 percent on some machines. Why do they tell us now, after five months?"

Harding stated management's differing point of view, trying as she did so to test bargaining possibilities by getting a gauge of union sentiment: "Well, here's how the managers are thinking. When the team of industrial engineers came in, we told them to find out what an average worker could do in an average day. We figured they would certainly take into account the performance on our own lines as they did that. OK? So following that, management set the standard and told all line employees that if they did more than standard, there would be an incentive payment. We figured that if they worked harder, they were entitled to a little something extra. However, the next thing we knew, everyone on the shop floor was averaging $9.75 an hour. Since average hourly base pay was only $7.00, we made an investigation. It turned out that those industrial engineers were wrong. Standard was far too low for the lathe operators. Those guys are presently averaging $10.25 an hour. All we're doing now is raising standard on those machines to its proper levels."

The union representative, hearing this, was angry.

"Listen, we didn't set standard, your consultants did. If they had set it too high for the lathe operators, management wouldn't be griping. No, ma'am, they'd be sitting up there in their offices claiming the industrial engineers had done a good job. Well, sauce for the goose is sauce for the gander. Management set standard and management will just have to live with it."

It turned out that management had no intention of living with it. A memo from the president to the line supervisors on the shop floor indicated that the new lathe standards were going into effect beginning the first of the month. However, after the union expressed its vehement reaction, the company president, Burt Heald, decided to call in the union leaders and see if things couldn't be ironed out.

"Ned," Heald said, "there seems to be some disagreement between the management and workers, and I thought perhaps we could straighten it out before things went any farther."

Nelson said he would like that. "What do you have in mind?"

"Well, I think it's important to realize that standard on the lathe machines was set too low. Will you agree with that?"

"No, I won't, but go ahead with your comments."

"I think standard should be raised by 25 percent. It's only fair. On the other hand, we're willing to increase the productivity bonus by 35 percent for all units over and above standard. What do you think?"

"I think it stinks," Nelson snapped. "You set standard and you ought to be willing to live with it, at least until the present contract expires."

"It's interesting that you raised that contract issue, Ned. As you know, your union negotiated no provision for changing standards. Management has complete flexibility in the area."

"You won't have it in the next contract."

"You may be right. But we do for now, and unless you can give me a good reason for not raising standard, then standard is going up."

"I'm not going to mince words with you, Mr. Heald. You can do anything you want, but if you raise standard for those operators, we're walking out and we're staying out. And while we're gone, you guys in management can see if it's so easy to meet standard."

Questions

1. Which position do you support, that of management or that of the union? Explain.
2. How common do you think this kind of problem is? What can be done to avoid it?
3. What action do you recommend to Heald? Be explicit.

7 Contract Negotiations

The Kelvining Company and its unionized employees were nearing the end of their contract period. With only sixty days left, both sides began to put out feelers regarding the next three-year contract. The management indicated that it was willing to sign a new agreement immediately, calling for an 8 percent increase in wages and an increase in fringe benefits which would apply straight across the board to everyone at the worker level. The union, on the other hand, was asking a 12 percent increase in wages and fringe benefits that would increase costs by another 5 percent.

The margin of difference between the two groups changed little over the next eight weeks. The management agreed to increase its salary offer to 8.5 percent, and the union lowered its fringe benefit request somewhat, but that was all. With four days left before the contract ran out, the union was beginning to reevaluate its strategy. Shirley Petersen, the union representative at Kelvining, and Jim McCracken, a shop steward, were particularly dismayed with the situation.

"Jim, I thought we'd have this new agreement worked out a long time ago, but here it is, four days before the old contract expires, and we and management are still miles apart."

"Well, if they don't come across with a good offer and fast, I think we ought to go out on strike."

"Hold on, Jim. It isn't that easy. I've talked to the officers at our union headquarters, and you know, we're not a very rich union. It isn't as though we were affiliated with the Teamsters. We aren't going to be able to go out for more than three weeks. And even if we do that, we'll only be able to draw $100 per worker per week. In other words, a strike will cost us a whole lot of money."

"I still think it's better to strike than be pushed around by those management fat cats. I'd rather take a hundred a week and wait them out."

"I just can't feel so sure about that. We've got to weigh the extra money we'll get if we win the strike against what we'll give up by striking. How much do you make a week?"

"I average around $235."

"Well, if you go out for three weeks, you'll be giving up $135 a week. Do you think you'll make this up over the next three years if we get the raise we're asking for? If we eventually settle at 10 percent, it will take you about three months to get back what you'll lose in a three-week strike. If we go out for more than three weeks, it will take a lot longer. And we have to remember this: We may not get that 10 percent even if we do strike."

"Well, I don't care. It's a matter of principle with me. I'm not going to be shoved around."

Management and the union continued to talk about contract terms over the next three days, with neither side willing to initiate a new offer or acceptance. Finally, on the day before the contract was to end, management presented a new offer. It promised a 9 percent wage increase and fringe benefits that would add another 3 percent. The company spokesman led the union representatives to believe that this was management's last offer. If the terms were unacceptable, the union would either have to continue working without a contract or strike. Management was leaving the alternative up to the work force.

Questions

1. What do you think of the management's strategy? Why?
2. Should the union accept or reject the contract? Explain.
3. Which side do you think will have gained the most when the issue is finally resolved? Why?

Organizing

8 An Ancient Solution

"Regardless of what kind of problem you face in your management careers," remarked Paul Shearson, president of Namble, Inc., "you can always find a guiding principle in the annals of management history." As Shearson spoke, all eyes were on him and everyone in the room was attentive.

"Let me explain. When I first took over at Namble, Inc., there was little more than autonomous units. In fact, to get something done I had to literally beg the division chiefs to cooperate. Then I started reading about management. And do you know where I obtained the solution I needed? From Diocletian, the Roman emperor.

"Let me tell you about him, because he was quite an organizer. When he became emperor, in 284 A.D., he realized that he faced a formidable task. If Rome attempted to exercise too much control over the empire, there would be trouble; for how could the emperor in Rome know what was best for the people in Britain? On the other hand, if too much authority was delegated, local leaders might well break away from Rome. What was needed was decentralized authority with effective control from a central point. Diocletian attained this by allowing the local areas to be governed with local autonomy. However, to ensure their loyalty to Rome, the emperor placed several hierarchical levels between himself and these local leaders.

"First, Diocletian divided the empire into 100 provinces. Each of these 100 was part of 13 dioceses, and the latter belonged to one of four divisions. By increasing the number of levels between himself and the local areas, he ensured effective control. Now, the number of people who were responsible for managing the empire increased. With more managers involved, each was responsible for a smaller area and could do a much better job than could the emperor alone. In addition, the amount of authority that any one manager had was reduced, thereby increasing the emperor's control over the organization.

"This is exactly the situation I faced at Namble, Inc., and I handled it the same way Diocletian did. I installed two levels of managers between me and my division chiefs. In a matter of months, my control problems were solved. Today we are stronger financially than at any other time in our history. In closing, I leave you with this advice: Stick with basic ideas. Old solutions are often the best solutions."

Questions

1. What problems do you think Shearson faced when he reorganized his firm?
2. What did Shearson mean by "old solutions are often the best solutions"?

9 Organizational Mechanics

The Rodall Corporation board of directors was not happy with its management's performance. Sales were increasing, but expenses were rising at a faster rate, as seen in Table 1.

Table 1
Sales/Profit Data, Rodall Corporation

	Sales	Expenses	Profit	Profit/Sales
1976	$10,500,000	$9,870,000	$630,000	6%
1977	9,200,000	8,464,000	736,000	8%
1978	8,000,000	7,280,000	736,000	9%
1979	7,000,000	6,300,000	700,000	10%
1980	5,400,000	4,860,000	540,000	10%

In discussing this declining performance, two members of the board presented divergent points of view. The first, Eleanor Towne, felt that the company needed more structuring.

"I think our problem is that we have to start organizing ourselves more formally. We need job descriptions and policy manuals so that everyone knows what is expected. Right now there are too many people doing anything they want to."

Ron Trumpe had a different view. "I disagree. The problem with this company is that we are over-organizing. We have more job descriptions and policy manuals than we know what to do with. We ought to reduce this rigidity and give people more freedom. If we would let people do their own thing instead of dictating everything we want done, we would get more personal initiative. This, in turn, will result in decreased expenses."

Questions

1. What are the advantages of using job descriptions and/or policy manuals?
2. What are the disadvantages of using job descriptions and policy manuals?
3. With which of the two board members do you agree? Explain.

10 Authority Delegation

Frank Fischer's Uncle George had been after his nephew for many years to join his company. "Frank," he said, "come over and work in my manufacturing firm. I have no children of my own, and I want someone I know at the helm when I retire." Fischer had always declined. However, as Uncle George neared the age of sixty five, Frank began thinking the situation over once again and decided to take the job. "Great!" replied his uncle. "You'll be my personal assistant. I promise you, within a year you'll be ready to step into my shoes."

Frank expected to turn in his resignation at his old job and be prepared to assume his new position as assistant to the president within ninety days. But before this could take place, his uncle suffered a massive heart attack. He lingered in a coma for a few days and then died. Control of the company went to Uncle George's wife Laura, who decided to abide with the wishes of her late husband. "George wanted Frank to head up the company and that's the way it's going to be."

Fischer was pleased by this show of faith, but the challenge unnerved him. He was not sure he would be up to the task. Nevertheless, he promised to do his best.

His first step was to call in the top executives of the firm and ask for their assistance. All promised to cooperate. His next move was to hire a management consulting firm. Fischer knew that it would take him a year before he really got his feet on the ground. The last thing he wanted during this period was to have to face some major catastrophe. Thus, his instructions to the consulting firm were brief: "I want you to analyze this company and tell me what you think our strong and weak points are. Then I want you to tell me how it can be managed more effectively."

The consultants talked to all of the top executives, interviewed a number of the other managers, analyzed the firm's financial statements, and talked to key members of the sales force. They then submitted their report to Frank. The main points follow:

> The major strong points of your firm are its high quality product and its effective market penetration. In addition, the top staff has an average of eight years with the company, so you have an effective management team.
>
> On the negative side, your uncle built the firm up from the ground. He accomplished much of this through one-man rule. He surrounded himself with competent executives but made all final decisions personally. We think your major problem in running the company is going to be that of decision making. You cannot run the whole show yourself. You are going to have to encourage decentralization, a new concept for your organization.

Frank read the report and agreed with the findings. Decentralization, he felt, was indeed the key to the problem. However, having identified the critical area, he now pondered exactly what to do. How should he implement this recommendation in his organization? As he thought over this question, he studied the company's organization chart (see Figure 1).

Figure 1
Organization Chart, Fischer Manufacturing Firm

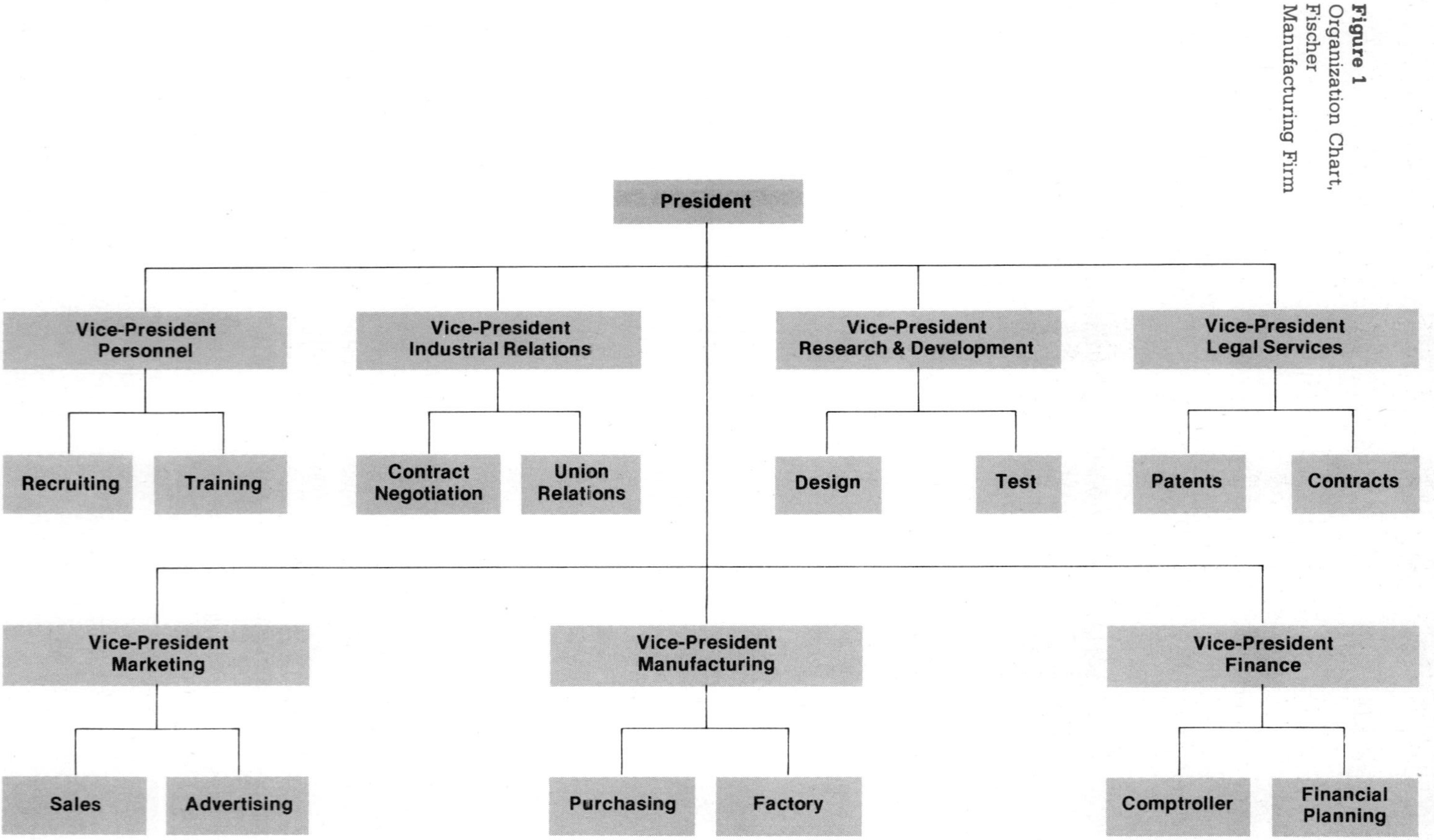

Questions

1. In which of the firm's departments do you think authority would be more centralized? Decentralized? Explain.
2. How would you recommend that Fischer implement the consultants' suggestion regarding decentralization? Defend your answer.

11 Territorial Reorganization

Since its founding in 1950, the Brilly Company had been operating along functional lines. (See Figure 1.) This form of organization had proved very beneficial to the firm. By 1979, it was producing six successful products and selling them in all of the states except Alaska and Hawaii.

Figure 1
Organization Chart, Brilly Company

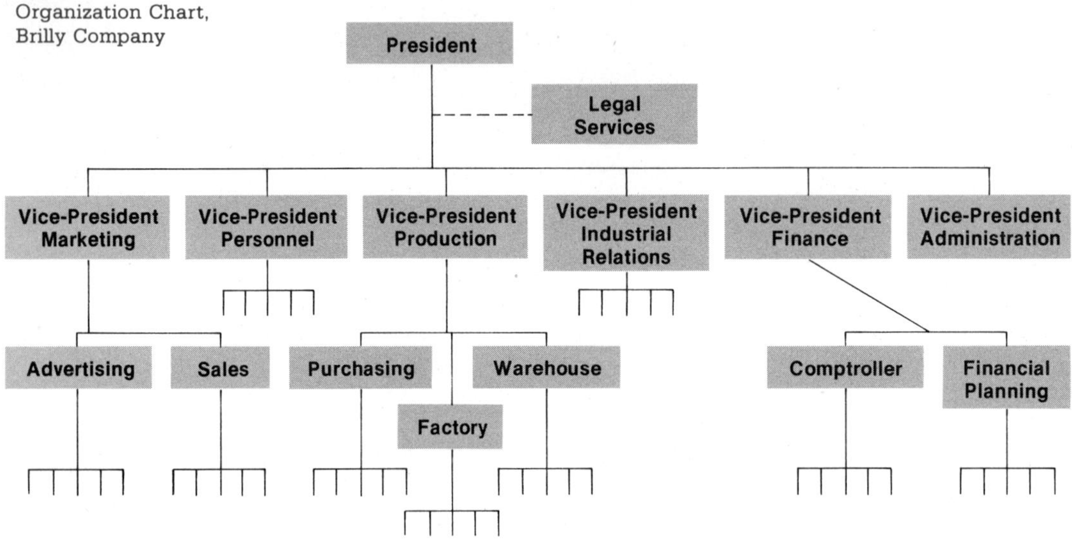

President
Legal Services
Vice-President Marketing
Vice-President Personnel
Vice-President Production
Vice-President Industrial Relations
Vice-President Finance
Vice-President Administration
Advertising
Sales
Purchasing
Warehouse
Factory
Comptroller
Financial Planning

It was at this point that a group of consultants, who had been brought in to study the company's operations and make recommendations for increased efficiency, suggested that the firm reorganize its structure and move from a functional to a geographic or territorial form of departmentalization. The consultants wanted to see the company set up three departments under the president. These were to be: Vice-President of Eastern Operations (New York City), Vice-President of Midwestern Operations (Chicago), and Vice-President of Western Operations (Los Angeles).

Questions

1. Draw the organization chart for the Brilly Company as it would look if the firm decided to adopt a territorial form of organization.
2. Why might a firm change from a functional to a territorial form of departmentalization? Explain.
3. What would be the advantages of remaining with a functional organization? Be explicit.

12 An Advisor's Opinion

The Greshing Corporation is a large pharmaceutical firm headquartered in New York City. However, its operating facilities are located in New Jersey, and some of the company's products are developed and manufactured at the New Jersey site.

A major problem that has troubled the firm is that of patent protection and infringement. It is no easy task deciding at what point a competitor has infringed on one of the firm's patents. Nor is it any easier to determine how far the company can legally progress before it will face an infringement suit from one of the competing firms. It is for these reasons that Greshing maintains a large legal staff. On average, the firm finds itself bringing approximately fifty infringement suits a year against its competitors, and it has to defend itself in about twenty-five court actions a year.

Top management has no qualms about bringing action against other firms, but it dislikes having to defend itself against infringement suits. For this reason, management encourages the marketing and production department vice-presidents to check out all new products with the legal people before proceeding to the manufacturing and selling stages. On some proposed products the legal department has the final word. On others, where patent infringement is highly debatable, the legal people merely give their opinion and leave the decision in the hands of marketing and production. In most cases, this legal advice is accepted.

Product 1A4, however, was considered a borderline case. "Jack," remarked Greta Behls, one of the legal department's top counsel, "we think that you ought to pass up 1A4. The competition has a patent on a process very similar to the one you are proposing. I have no doubt that if you bring out this product we are going to have a lawsuit on our hands." Jack Miller, vice-president of manufacturing, and Bob Tasken, vice-president of marketing, both listened quietly. When Behls was finished, Jack Miller thanked her for her opinion. "Greta, we appreciate your dropping by to give us the legal side of the picture. If we have any further questions, we'll get back with you." Behls then shook hands with both men and left.

"Well," replied Tasken. "I guess that about wraps up 1A4."

But Miller said, "Not so fast. How do you feel about all this?"

"I think 1A4 is a winner. Furthermore, the last time Greta came by and gave us her opinion on that 120Q cough medicine, she told us to lay off. Do you remember?"

"I do."

"Well, do you also know that one of our other competitors came out with a similar product—their own 120Q cough medicine? Did they get hit with a patent infringement lawsuit? No. They had a field day instead. Greta's advice was worthless, and we threw away a chance at a real big winner. With all the push I get from those top execs across the river, you'd think they would get us more competent legal advice."

Miller reflected. "Bob, I feel the same. But remember—we don't have to take Greta's advice. We just have to listen and evaluate. Do you think 1A4 will be a successful product?"

"My research staff tells me it will be."

"Then let's go with it. I have idle capacity I'd like to use; and if you think this product will sell, we can kill two birds with one stone."

Questions

1. Of what value are staff advisors if the line management does not listen? Explain.
2. "Staff people give advice but cannot be held responsible for poor results, so why listen to them? I mean, they're not risking anything; I am." Do you agree or disagree with this line manager's philosophy? Explain by giving both sides of the argument, line management's and staff management's.

13 The Junior Board

Jed Smithson, president and board chairman of Windrom, Inc., was intrigued when he first learned about the concept of junior boards of directors. He asked his secretary to obtain all available information on the subject as soon as possible. Within a week Smithson knew just about everything there was to know about junior boards' function. However, he was still not certain whether the concept would be good for Windrom, Inc. Therefore, he called in his executive vice-president, Fred Frank.

"Fred, I've been reading through a host of materials about junior boards of directors. I think they have real value. I'd like your opinion before I do anything. Read this stuff and give me your candid comments."

Frank returned a few days later, and together the two men began to discuss the issue.

"Jed, I've read all the material you gave me, and I believe that we could use a junior board in our corporation. It would be an excellent method for motivating our young managers, by giving them a chance to participate in the decision-making process. If we structured it properly, we could avoid dual-command problems. That is, we could let it be known from the start that the junior board was advisory only and that any recommendations it made would be forwarded to the corporate board for action. Once these problems were handled, there should be smooth sailing."

"Those are my sentiments exactly, Fred. However, there are a few other items we need to talk about. First, eligibility: Who can serve on the junior board? Also, size is important. How large ought it to be? My feelings are that all managers beneath the rank of vice-president or factory chief should be eligible unless they are already on the corporate board."

"I think that's a good idea. And in regard to your second question about size, I think we should use an odd number, say fifteen."

"OK. So next we need to determine how committee membership should be decided."

"Why not let the managers nominate and elect their own committee?"

"I like your idea. And that takes us to the last point of consideration. What should the duties of the board be?"

"Why enumerate specific duties? Why not leave it all flexible? That is, let the junior board investigate or analyze any aspect of corporate activity it wants to. This could range from a cost per unit analysis of products to investigating ways in which we can improve company morale. The only restriction I would place on this board's activity is that it be cleared with the regular board."

"It sounds good to me. Let's put all of this into a memorandum and circulate it to our managerial staff to see what they think of it."

The response was overwhelmingly favorable and Smithson decided to go ahead and formally establish a junior board of directors. After the ensuing election, he was delighted to see that the majority of the committee was to consist of young, dynamic individuals. He reasoned that the junior board would give these young managers the kind of seasoning they would need in order to move up in the corporation.

The committee seemed to function well for the first year. However, after that Smithson began to hear some grumbling. Unsure of what it all meant, he decided to have the matter investigated by his executive vice-president. It took Frank a week to gather all the pertinent information.

"Jed, I've investigated the junior board situation, and there appear to be two major problems. The first is that some of the corporate board members feel the junior board is too idealistic; they haven't found the junior board's recommendations to be of real use. For example, three months ago the junior board received permission to study ways to improve efficiency at the production level. They recommended a variation of the Scanlon plan whereby all productivity increases would be shared by management and the workers."

"I remember that."

"Well, the board turned it down, as you know. When I talked with the corporate members, three of them told me that they thought the junior board was getting too big for its britches. On the other hand, the junior board members feel that their recommendations are not being given sufficient attention or consideration. Five of the members told me that they believed the junior board was nothing but window dressing. It seems to me that the second problem we must face is bad feeling between the two boards."

Questions

1. Was the formation of a junior board a good idea?
2. What really went wrong? Could it have been avoided? Explain.
3. What recommendations would you make to Smithson to straighten out the situation? Be explicit.

14 Committee Decision Making

Product 42Y appeared to have tremendous prospects. Initial marketing research indicated that annual sales might run as high as $10 million. The marketing approach, however, had not yet been determined because there was uncertainty about the relative importance of price and advertising in the marketing of the product. Vern Clark, vice-president of marketing, had decided how to handle the situation. He explained it to Margaret McKesson, assistant to the president, this way: "I'm going to put together a committee consisting of nine members of my department. Their purpose will be to answer just one question. Should we use price or advertising in moving 42Y? Whatever they say, we'll do."

"How will they make the decision, Vern?"

"On the basis of the market research we've done. They'll have to sift through the data and determine which of the two factors is more important."

"Which do you think it will be?"

"I'm convinced that a strong advertising program is the best road."

"Then why not implement that approach and forget the committee?"

"Oh, I don't want to do that. You see, I've got a group of young people in my department I'm trying to motivate. I want them to feel they are a part of the department team."

Three weeks later Clark received the committee report. Despite his earlier expectation, his group recommended that the company employ a low price strategy. Clark felt this was the wrong approach, but he did not feel strongly enough about it to reverse the committee. When he implemented the decision, the results were disastrous. Product 42Y never got off the ground. In contrast, the product's three major competitors, all using big advertising campaigns, had huge successes. The company president, Fred Ambly, was upset with the results.

"Vern, what happened with 42Y? I thought it was supposed to be a big seller."

"So did I, but we took the wrong approach. We emphasized low price when we should have opted for a strong advertising program."

"Who made that decision?"

"I had a committee examine the matter and make the decision."

"Well, find out who was responsible and do something about it."

Questions

1. Was Clark right in assigning this task to the committee? Explain.
2. What do you think of Ambly's suggestion? Who should be reprimanded for this failure?
3. What lessons should Clark learn from this experience?

Staffing

15 The New Foreman

Chuck Crasser, the head of production at the Caxter Company, asked Personnel to find him a new foreman. "Perhaps a young college graduate would be interested in the job. Jobs are not as plentiful as they once were, and a line manager with a college education might be good for us."

In a few days, Regina Harper, the company college recruiter, hit pay dirt. Gene Machen, a graduating senior with a degree in production management, seemed highly interested in the job.

"Gene, we're looking for someone to come to work as one of our foremen. While I'll concede that the title doesn't sound very appealing, I can assure you that the pay is equivalent to that being offered any graduating senior today. In addition, a foreman's job at Caxter is upwardly mobile. Our president and three of the six vice-presidents all started as foremen."

"Actually, Ms. Harper, the job sounds great. I'm especially impressed with the opportunities for advancement. However, I am concerned about how I'd fit in. Do I have the right kind of training?"

"No problem there at all, Gene. In fact, you'll add quite a bit to our team of foremen. As the only college graduate in the group, you can be sure that they'll look to you for guidance. After all, they have all come up through the ranks and lack your educational stature."

The position seemed ideal to Machen, who accepted the job. However, he was not at Caxter more than a couple of months before he realized that all was not going well. In the beginning, Machen felt he was fairly well accepted, but a kind of coolness had set in. The initial cooperation he received from the other foremen disappeared. In addition, they tended to cluster together during coffee break or lunch hours and Machen was never invited to join. He tried to become a part of the group, but he remained an outsider.

In the beginning, Machen had shrugged it off. But after a while it began to bother him. He no longer looked forward to his work. He began putting in eight hours and going home. The zest was gone. Regina Harper, the interviewer, heard that the young man was looking for a new job, although Machen had given no indication that he was planning a move. In fact, when Chuck Crasser, the vice-president, asked him how he liked his job, Machen had said, "Fine, fine." However, a week later the young foreman submitted his resignation.

Crasser asked him about it. "Gene, I thought you liked your job. What happened?"

"Well, Mr. Crasser, I did like the job, at least in the beginning. But somehow it didn't turn out to be quite what I thought it was going to be."

Questions

1. Why do you think Machen did not fit in well on the job? Explain.
2. Who should be held accountable for the problem? Why?
3. What would you recommend Crasser do in filling Gene's job? Be explicit.

16 A Case of Employment

Tom Jenkins had been sitting at his desk for over an hour. His feet were resting on the desk top, his head drooped on his chest. On the desk were two résumés. The first belonged to Henry Archer, the second to James Rezner. Both were about to receive their undergraduate degrees from accredited schools of business, and both were applying for the one opening in Tom's department. Initially, Jenkins felt that it would be quite simple to choose between the two. Now he was not so sure. He decided to call in Kathleen Adams, his assistant, and solicit an opinion.

"Kathleen, I've got a problem. We have two applicants for that sales trainee opening. I've been reviewing the records of both, and I'm unable to decide which one would be best for us. Why don't you look at their résumés and give me your opinion."

Adams looked over the credentials and then began to read recommendations for each applicant. Two of the letters are shown in Table 1.

Table 1
Letters of Recommendation

Dear Mr. Jenkins:

I am writing to you on behalf of Hency C. Archer, who informs me that he is seeking a position as sales trainee with your firm.

I have known Mr. Archer for three years. He first came to my attention when he was elected president of his dormitory. Henry was a leader from the very beginning. As dorm president he was successful in getting the university administration to alter its rules regarding co-ed visitation privileges. In addition, he was president of the Student Senate during his senior year.

While these tasks have taken much of Henry's time, he has also participated in other university functions. For example, he was assistant editor of the student newspaper during his junior year and wrote a daily column for the paper during his senior year. In addition, he chaired the student multiple sclerosis drive during both of these years, drives which netted over $7,500.

In his last two years he was elected a BMOC (Big Man on Campus) and has been nominated as one of the five all-university finalists in his year's "Outstanding Senior" contest.

His leadership ability and his willingness to give of himself to help others indicate to me that Henry has great future potential. I am delighted to recommend him to you and hope that you will feel free to call on me should you desire any further information.

Sincerely yours,

Frank Fischer
Dean of Students

Dear Mr. Jenkins:

James L. Rezner has asked me to write a recommendation on his behalf, and I am delighted to do so.

Mr. Rezner was a student in two of my courses. The first was a course in basic grammar and essay writing; the second was a course in literary criticism. In both instances Mr. Rezner received an "A." Although he is a business administration student and was not required to take the literary criticism course, he explained to me that he felt businessmen must be well versed in the arts as well as the sciences. I found this to be a refreshing point of view.

Mr. Rezner's work was always of the highest quality. In terms of intelligence and drive, I would rank Mr. Rezner in the top one percent of the graduating class. I had the opportunity to review his scholastic record last year and he had only one "B," that being in physical education. He was elected to Beta Gamma Sigma at the end of his junior year. This, as you may know, is the business school's equivalent to Phi Beta Kappa, and entry at the junior level is reserved for the top 10 percent of that class. Although I have not seen his final semester grade report, I would imagine that his overall GPA must be approximately 3.95 on a 4.0 scale.

When I first talked to Jim, he told me that he had one major objective, that of a bachelor's degree. He has certainly attained that goal and done so with a splendid record. This was quite a feat in light of the fact that his mother died during his senior year in high school, and he has had to spend most of his free time at home helping his father in his grocery store. The family, three boys and three girls, are very close; and Jim, as the oldest, has many responsibilities. Thus, between helping out at home and carrying a full course load, he has performed splendidly.

Jim is the kind of individual who understands responsibility and can be counted on to get the job done. I recommend him to you without reservation.

Yours truly,

George Williams
Associate Professor of English

"Well, I agree that both are fine candidates. However, I have to give the nod to Henry Archer. That guy has leadership ability, and that's important in any marketing job. He also apparently likes to mix with people, and gregariousness certainly can't hurt."

"Fine, but are you overlooking Archer's scholastic record? He has an overall grade point of 2.00. He has 'C' average. He has as many 'D's' as he does 'B's.' The last thing I need in this department is someone who is long on talk and short on brains."

"You have a point."

"Once again, it's not that simple. Sure, Rezner's smart, but does he have the personality that allows him to mix well with people? During his school days he had a reason for not having to join groups or get involved in the university setting. His personal problems provided him with an out if he wanted it."

"You can't throw out the proven strongpoints or the possible weakpoints of either. The two key questions are: (a) Exactly how intelligent is Archer? and (b) Is Rezner a loner, or can he be relied upon to be a member of a company team?"

"Nobody ever told us it gets any easier up on the top of the organization chart. This really is a problem."

Questions

1. Whom would you recommend Jenkins hire?
2. On what basis would you make this recommendation?

17 Grade Point Average

Ralph Richards was a graduating senior with a major in marketing. Realizing that time was growing short, he signed up at his university's placement office for interviews. Richards was not too concerned about the kind of job he might get. He was sure some firm would give him an offer. However, he did have his heart set on going with a big firm.

Richards felt somewhat disappointed when he learned that companies generally sent only a couple of recruiters to the campus and there was, therefore, a limit on the number of interviews they could conduct. The placement office's policy was to have the students sign up for the firms with which they wished to interview. Once the quota was filled, no further applicants were permitted. By the time Richards got over to the placement office, there was only one large firm left that was looking for marketing majors. He quickly signed up.

On the day of the interview, Richards put on his best suit and arrived at Placement thirty minutes early. He was determined to make a good impression on Les Wheaton, the company representative. After preliminaries, the interview went as follows:

"Ralph, I've been looking over your résumé. I see that you're a full-time student. Do you have an outside job?"

"No, sir. I live at home with my folks, and my dad provides me with spending money."

"Do you do much in the way of outside activity?"

"Well, I'm a member of a fraternity."

"With all the time for studying, don't you think your 2.1 grade point average is pretty low?"

"I agree that it's not as high as I'd like it to be, but I don't put too much emphasis on grades."

"What do you mean?"

"Well, grades are okay for some people, Mr. Wheaton, but they aren't a measure of my potential."

"Why not?"

"Because I know I'm better than the grades show."

"Where do you think you'll be in twenty years?"

"I think I'll be vice-president of marketing in a small to medium-sized company or occupying a high level marketing post in a large firm."

"You don't think grades are important?"

"Not at all. Grade point average is okay, but your own basic belief in your ability determines how far you'll go in life."

"Do you believe there is any relationship between grades and success in a company?"

"No direct correlation, certainly. There might be an indication there. For example, someone with a 3.9 certainly isn't stupid. But there might be somebody with a 1.9 who's a genius—just bored stiff."

Questions

1. Is there any correlation between grade point average and business success? Explain.
2. What do you think of Richards's statement that a high grade point average is okay, but less of a prime determiner of how far one will go in life than a basic belief in one's own talent?
3. Would you recommend that Wheaton hire Richards? Why or why not?

18 Free Vacations

Ivanna Wheeler had worked fifteen years for a competitor before Edson & Company hired her. The company president, Roger Fullmore, felt that Wheeler would make an excellent addition to the marketing staff.

On her very first day at Edson, the president made it clear to Wheeler that the company put great stock in subordinate training.

"Ivanna," he said, "I know it's going to take you a while to get the feel of things around here, so take your time. There's only one thing I'm going to demand: Keep your number-one subordinate informed about what's going on at all times. Years ago, one of our vice-presidents had a heart attack and was out of work for nine months. It took us half of that time to figure out what was going on in his department. His subordinates knew nothing. He was a one-man ship. Since then, I tell everybody, 'Make sure your people can carry on if something happens to you.' Wheeler promised the president that she would play by that rule.

That afternoon at lunch, Wheeler got to meet some of the executives from the other departments. As the meal drew to a close, she noticed some friendly bantering between Harold Renter and Jack Goggans, both from Production.

"Hey, Harold, I hear this month you're going to get a free two-week trip."

"Not me, Jack. The name that's due starts with a *G* and ends with an *s*."

"Harold, if I win, I'm sending you."

"Thanks, but I wouldn't hear of it. Not after I've gone to the expense of buying a bottle of champagne to celebrate."

"If I win, I'll hold you to it."

With this exchange, lunch broke up, and everyone started to leave. Renter and Goggans were still laughing and quietly ribbing each other. Wheeler was unsure of what it all meant, but she smiled good-naturedly. On Friday, when her intercom buzzed, she began to find out.

"Ms. Wheeler, Mr. Goggans is on the line."

After thanking her secretary, Wheeler said, "Hello, Jack—what's up?"

"I'm just getting ready to go up to the boardroom for the monthly drawing. Are you coming?"

"I hadn't planned on it. What's going to happen?"

"You mean you really don't know?"

"Nope."

"Didn't the old man give you that talk about training your subordinates?"

"He sure did—emphatically."

"Well, didn't he tell you about our monthly drawing?"

"No, he just told me that story about the vice-president who had the heart attack."

"He left out the best part! Listen, meet me up in the boardroom in ten minutes."

Wheeler told her secretary that she was going up to the boardroom and would be back as soon as she could. By the secretary's smile, she guessed that everyone but her was in on some joke.

On entering the boardroom, she noticed that all the company's senior executives were there. Jack Goggans seemed to be the convenor for the group.

"Ivanna," said Goggans, "I believe you know everyone here."

"I think so. Nice to see all of you again. I take it that I'm now going to be let in on some secret."

"Right. Since the old man didn't tell you, I will. All executives who have been here over six months must have their subordinates sufficiently trained so that they can take over at any time. Since it is highly unlikely that any of us will be severely incapacitated often enough for the old man to know whether we're maintaining the policy, we have these drawings on the last Friday of every month; and we keep him up-to-date. Everyone's name is put into this fishbowl. The only exceptions are those who have been here less than six months or those who have won within the past six months."

"I see. The winner gets something besides a heart attack, I hope?"

"Oh yes—well, see what you think. The drawing is for a two-week, all-expenses-paid trip to Rio de Janeiro for winner and spouse. Also, the company pays if child-care is needed."

"That sounds great. When does the winner leave?"

"Immediately. That part *is* like a heart attack; it doesn't wait. The president's secretary has the tickets; reservations are all made. The winner is driven straight to the airport, and somebody has to see to it that spouse and luggage are there too. Then the two of them catch a 4:00 PM flight. All the recipient has to worry about is whether the chief subordinate can run the department for the two weeks."

Goggans then took the fishbowl and circulated throughout the room until every name was in the bowl. Then the fishbowl was put on a table, and a blindfolded typist was brought in, ready to draw a name. Just as the drawing began, Harold Renter interrupted. "Not so fast, friend. I believe you forgot to put your own card into the bowl."

Amid laughter from the rest of the executives, Goggans tossed in his name. Then came the drawing; and the typist, now not blindfolded, read the name. "The winner is Harold Renter." Goggans was overcome with laughter. He slapped Renter on the back and congratulated him. The others followed, with a wide range of comments. Goggans's response came last: "Hey, Harold, if your subordinate screws up, maybe you can get a full-time job in Rio." All the assembled executives then returned, laughing, to their offices.

Questions

1. Do you think this approach is effective in encouraging executives to train their subordinates? Explain.
2. What other approaches could a firm use in attaining this goal? Be specific.

19 The Salesman-Manager Dilemma

Eduardo Olveira was the Cander Corporation's leading salesman. While his quota for the last fiscal year was 250 machines, he managed to sell 367. No one was able to understand it. Olveira certainly did not have a sales personality. If anything, he was a loner. But no one could argue with his performance, especially not his superior, William Mallon.

Olveira's performance contrasted greatly with Hal Harver's. Harver never seemed to be able to make his quota. On the other hand, everyone liked him. He had a constant smile and a kind word for all. Mallon, realizing that he himself was going to be promoted to the home office in the very near future, wanted to see Harver get his job. For this reason, Mallon went out on the road with Harver on several occasions, helping him close his sales. On these trips, Harver did well; but as soon as he went out on his own again, his record was as dismal as ever. Nevertheless, when Mallon's superior, Albert Syms of the home office, asked about his replacement, Mallon recommended Harver.

"Gee, Bill, I thought you'd want to recommend Ed Olveira for that job."

"Mr. Syms, he's a great salesman, but he has no real managerial ability. He's a loner. What we need is someone who can pull this department together. I think Hal Harver is the right man for the job."

"But his sales record is poor. How can he generate high sales from his staff if he himself can't sell?"

"I'm not sure that it's necessary for a manager to be a super-salesperson."

"Oh, really? You had a terrific sales record and did pretty well as department head. Surely you aren't saying that selling isn't important."

"Not at all. But I don't think we should give it that much attention."

"Look, I'll tell you what. You list the positive and negative points of each of these two men, and let's review the matter next week."

Questions

1. What are Mallon's reasons for supporting Hal Harver?
2. Who do you think would be the better manager, Eduardo Olveira or Hal Harver? Why?
3. Which of the two men do you think will get the promotion—Olveira or Harver? Do you think either of them is certain to get it? Explain.

20 Testing: One, Two, Three

Arthur Higgins had been hired to head up the advertising department of Dale & Dale. "Get in there, Arthur, and get us moving again," the president told him, and Higgins had done just that. Within ninety days of his appointment, the department came out with an entirely new advertising campaign. Sales began to pick up almost immediately. The president was so pleased that he increased the advertising budget by 5 percent. Higgins decided to use this money to hire another copywriter. He knew just the man, William Essex.

The first thing Higgins did was to bring Essex in and introduce him to the staff. The two men then began to talk about Essex's job responsibilities and his salary. After this discussion, Essex indicated to Higgins that he was interested in the job and would take it if offered. Higgins was delighted.

However, before making a formal offer, Higgins told the president of his decisions. The latter agreed. "Anything you want to do is all right with me," he said to his advertising manager. Higgins thereupon contacted the personnel department, told them he was planning to hire Bill Essex, and asked them to put through the necessary paperwork. A couple of days later, the head of personnel called.

"Arthur, this is George Lembke. We're in the process of constructing a personnel file on Bill Essex, and I was wondering what kind of exams you would like us to administer."

"I'm afraid I don't follow you."

"Well, do you want us to give him an intelligence test, aptitude test, or personality test? Or do you want the whole battery administered?"

"Frankly, I hadn't given it any thought. I've known Bill Essex for a number of years, and I don't think the tests can tell me anything I don't already know. Besides, I've seen the kind of copywriting he does, so I'm not sure those tests would be of any value to me."

"Okay, but if you change your mind, call me."

Questions

1. Are tests, such as those being proposed by Personnel, of any value? Explain.
2. What are the drawbacks to using tests as part of a screening process?
3. Did Higgins make a right or wrong decision? Defend your answer.

21 No Right Solutions

Thea Holloway, a trainee at the Sminder Corporation, had just gone through her second week of training. The last hour of these sessions was always devoted to answering questions or providing additional information on the topics that had been discussed during the week. Holloway decided to take the opportunity to ask the training director, James Franklin, a question.

"Mr. Franklin, this week we were introduced to the case approach, and I'm confused in regard to its value."

"Well, Thea, the case approach has many positive points. It's been used at Harvard for over thirty years in educating businesspeople, and many other universities use it as well. All we've done is to apply it to our own company."

"I understand that, but the cases we've been using are incomplete. That is, we aren't given sufficient information for reaching a solution."

"I'm not so sure I agree with you," Franklin responded. "After all, in the business world you never have complete information. You have to use good judgment to fill in those gaps."

"I see your point. But if we lack complete information, how do we know that our solution will be right?" Holloway continued. "For example, this morning we were given two cases. One dealt with linear programming and had a mathematical solution. That one was easy because we knew how to work the problem. The second, however, was concerned with how to handle a problem employee. That one was much more difficult."

"Didn't you discuss possible solutions?"

"Sure, but there were some of us who felt the employee should be fired. The rest, though, believed the individual should be given another chance. The problem, of course, is to decide which of the possible solutions is correct. Now, talking about the problem is helpful, but we never did reach a conclusion on what ought to be done."

"That's because there are no absolute solutions to these cases."

"Well then, why waste our time with them? I mean, what are we supposed to be learning if there are no real solutions to the problems? Is the case method just a basis for asking rhetorical questions which are never answered?

Questions

1. How would you respond to Holloway's questions?
2. What are the advantages of using the case method in training managers? What are the disadvantages?
3. Would you recommend the case approach for training programs? Why or why not?

Directing

22 Managing the Line

Diana Tucker was the new production manager at Jackson & Co., and she wanted to do the best possible job. It had taken her ten years to work herself up to this position. For her, however, this was only the beginning. She had plans to move into a vice-presidency before she retired. This, she knew, meant performance. It was an established fact in the company that only the most successful managers were moved up. Tucker felt that productivity was a major factor in this process and that good supervision on the production line was important. What does a successful line manager do that an unsuccessful one does not? Tucker sought to identify the performance factors that were involved.

She decided it would be wise to spend most of her time in the first month observing the line workers and the supervisors. She asked the line managers many questions about their supervisory techniques, though she was somewhat apprehensive at first, feeling that the supervisors would think she was wasting their time with her questions. Fortunately, it did not turn out this way. In fact, the line managers seemed to like the questions, which gave them an opportunity to verbalize some of their pet management theories.

Tucker recorded the ideas gained from her talks with the supervisory staff. Within a month's time, she had been able to talk to all of them. She then began to look at past productivity records to determine which of the line managers was most successful in terms of output.

She also wrote down the names of the supervisors with the lowest output. Two stood out in terms of productivity. The first was Hal Tendling, whose productivity was the lowest in the company. Tendling's comments on supervision follow:

In this business, it's dog-eat-dog. The workers are really a bunch of goof-offs. Now, don't misunderstand me. There *are* good workers. And then there are goldbricks. They're the ones you have to watch. Take my group. About 80 percent of them are going to quit working the minute I go out for a cup of coffee. Do you know that between 10:00 AM and 10:15, which is the line managers' coffee-break time, I get less output than any other time all morning? The same is true for the afternoon coffee break. This goldbricking is nothing more than the workers' way of testing you. That's why I adhere to two rules. One, always emphasize productivity. Employees like this. It lets them know that you're not going to sit still for horsing around. Two, when someone does something wrong, chew him out good and proper; make an example of it. If you don't, the crew will think you've gone soft. Believe me, workers appreciate a boss they can't shove around. It creates a kind of respect. They do a better job for you. Take my case. My productivity record isn't very good—but can you imagine how much worse it would look if I tried treating these people softly? Nope, no one else in this company could get as much productivity out of my workers as I do.

Steve Jessup, the line manager who had held the highest productivity record in the company during the last six months, summarized his supervisory approach this way:

My approach to managing people is to take it easy with them. The workers want to do a good job. Now, that isn't to say that you won't get a goof-off from time to time. You'll face that situation regardless of what position you're in. The question is how to live with it. I find that employees are basically conscientious. Therefore, my first rule is never to jump on them about output. I spend most of my time trying to be helpful. If they need assistance in repairing a machine, I call maintenance. If they have a family problem, I tell them to check out early. The people on the line don't need to be told that output is important. They know; it's what their jobs are based on. They have a stake in output. Second, if someone messes up, never yell about it. Not only does that embarrass the worker and anybody else around, but it serves no real purpose. If you can't be helpful, say nothing. Believe me, workers like this easy style.

Questions

1. Summarize briefly the leadership style of Steve Jessup; then contrast it to that of Hal Tendling. What do you see as the basic difference?
2. Consider information in addition to that given in the case—be sure to include your own general knowledge and experience. Can you find reasons beyond what the case states for Jessup's effectiveness as a line manager?
3. Are there any times when Tendling would be a more effective manager than Jessup? If yes, when? If no, why not?

23 Money and Motivation

For the better part of an hour Jack Turner and Phil Amber, two line managers in a large manufacturing plant, had been arguing their individual points of view about motivation.

"Look, Phil, you've worked around here long enough to know what really motivates people. It's money, pure and simple."

"I disagree. I know that money is one way of getting people to do things, but it isn't the only way. A pat on the back will also motivate individuals. I've seen it work."

"But how do you account for the fact that every Saturday, when we offer overtime, ninety-five percent of the factory work force shows up?"

"Look, I'm not saying money doesn't make people work. But I *am* saying that it is only one of many factors. Take increased responsibility or job enlargement. One of the major gripes of workers, both here and throughout the country, is that the work is too simple; there is no challenge. If we were to try increasing salaries, do you think this boredom would go away? I doubt it. The only way to handle the situation is to give workers a more challenging job by increasing their responsibilities."

"If you gave them increased responsibilities, you'd have to increase their pay as well. No one is going to do more work for the same pay. And where does that leave you? You're right back where you started, motivating people with money."

"I disagree. Lots of people work because they enjoy it. Increased responsibility is really important. There are many workers who stay after hours cleaning their equipment. How do you figure that out?"

"All they're trying to do is improve their chances of getting a raise or making more money. The worker who cleans company equipment is only making sure that the machine won't break down during working hours. The result is increased chances of producing more than standard and picking up that extra productivity bonus the company gives. The manager who takes work home from the office is doing the same thing—trying to turn out more work, show great efficiency, and get in line for a promotion and raise. Managers are clever people. They know the big money is in the top positions, and that's where they are heading."

"Jack, you're oversimplifying the whole thing. I've admitted that money can be a form of motivation, but I just don't think it's *that* important."

"All right, then tell me what is."

"I'll do more than that. Let's call Nora Mudge in personnel training and ask her if she can bring someone to our next supervisors' training session to talk to us for a few hours on what really motivates people."

"Sounds okay to me. I'd be interested in seeing what these 'other' factors are."

Amber picked up the phone and called Nora Mudge. The two chatted for a few minutes, and by the look on Amber's face Turner could see that Mudge had bad news. Amber quietly hung up.

"Well, is she going to bring someone in?"

"No, she's not. She says that the training department likes to draw on faculty from the university across town. However, Nora's tried before, and it seems that no profs in the business school are willing to talk about nonmonetary motivators for less than $100 an hour."

"See, I told you. Even the guys claiming money is a poor motivator are asking for a bundle to talk about it. Face it, Phil, money is all that motivates people."

Questions

1. Do you agree that money is all that motivates people? If so, defend your position. If not, list five nonmonetary motivational factors.
2. How do you account for the apparent incongruity of the business professor who wants $100 an hour to speak on nonmonetary motivational factors?
3. Is Jack Turner's position unique, or do you think most line managers believe money is the prime motivator of workers? Explain.

24 Work, Work, Work

When Nicole Peters accepted her position as assistant personnel director, she looked forward to an exciting and rewarding career with the firm. She was disappointed. Most of the work was routine, to say the least.

In the beginning, Peters waited patiently, hoping the job would increase in complexity. However, there was simply not enough work for both her and the personnel director, Les Hamlin. In early September Nicole turned in her resignation, effective December 31. "I think it's time that I moved on to another firm," she said. "I'm too young to get tied down to one company." Hamlin decided not to push the matter. His major concern now was that of finding a replacement. However, before he could make any progress toward this objective, the personnel director was called into the president's office.

"Les, I've asked you to come by because I've been going over some of the financial reports. As you know, we've been using an outside training agency to handle all our management development. During the past year we have spent over $25,000 on this training. I think this is much too costly. We ought to be able to do the job for a lot less money. I've been considering alternative approaches, and I think I have one. You and Nicole Peters have college degrees and are both qualified to teach some of the material that these agency people are currently presenting. Furthermore, if you were to send Nicole to a couple of outside training programs sponsored by professional groups, she could pick up important ideas and develop them into a presentation for our managers. I'd say that within a year's time, managerial training could be turned over entirely to the two of you."

"It sounds fine to me, but Nicole has told me she's quitting on December 31."

"I see. Well, let's get going on the development of an in-house training program and see how much progress you can make before she leaves."

Hamlin agreed to do so. However, he felt edgy about the entire matter. Peters had decided to quit, and here came the president, asking Personnel to take on all in-house training. Peters was liable to think that the president had decided to break her back with a lot of work before she left. Nevertheless, Hamlin had to call Peters in and tell her what the president had said.

"I know you're getting ready to leave within a few months," Hamlin said, "but the president wants to see how much headway we can make on this training program before you go. My plan is to have you talk to all division managers and find out the kind of management training they think they will need over the next twelve months. This should give us a basis for putting together a training program for the year. Once we get that done, we'll start to find speakers for the sessions. Some of our top managers can do part of it, some can be handled by professors over at the business school, and this department will take over the rest."

It took Peters two weeks to determine the needs of the various divisions. After another week, she had all the speakers and topics lined up. Peters and Hamlin then got together to discuss the next step.

"Nicole, there are still two months before you leave, and the people over in Industrial Relations are after me to give a one-day workshop to their middle management people. I don't know exactly what to tell them. However, I got this pamphlet in the mail today. One of the big national training associations is sponsoring a weekend conference in New York City on 'New Techniques in Labor Arbitration.' I'd like you to go to the meeting, pick up as much information as you can, and then present it to the department. I think it would be both useful and interesting to them."

Peters agreed to go. However, while she was gone, Hamlin kept feeling that he had been taking advantage of the young woman. "Here she is, getting ready to leave," mused the personnel director. "And I'm working her like a dog. When she gets back, I'm going to tell her that she can have the last week in December off with full pay. She deserves it." However, when Peters returned—and before Hamlin could convey that message—Peters said that she had decided to stay with the firm. The personnel manager was completely puzzled.

Questions

1. Is job enlargement really a motivational tool, or does this case represent an exceptional situation?
2. Why is Hamlin puzzled at the end of the case?
3. What implications for managers does this case have? Explain.

25 Just Obeying Orders

"Al, this is Mr. Odum. What seems to be the trouble on the assembly line?"

"Oh, Mr. Odum. How are you, sir? I'm not sure what the trouble is yet, but we think it's coming from the automatic control unit. We'll know in about an hour. We have a guy down here from maintenance. The minute things started to screw up, I called and asked him to come over."

"Good move, Al. You did the right thing. Now keep on top of this. I want it given first priority. The minute you find out what's causing the problem, let me know."

It took Al and the maintenance engineer an hour to diagnose the situation. Al then called Mr. Odum.

"Mr. Odum? This is Al. We finished looking over the entire operation down here, and it is definitely the automatic control unit. What do you want us to do?"

"You be the judge of that. However, remember, we have a productivity squeeze on. Look the unit over carefully, find out what's causing the problem, and then get rid of it."

"Right."

It was noon the next day before Odum thought about the control unit problem again. He decided to call and find out how everything was going.

"Hello, this is Mr. Odum. Is Al there?"

"No, sir, he's out. But he'll be back in about three hours."

"What's the status of that automatic control unit?"

"Oh, it's coming along fine, Mr. Odum. Al says they'll have a new one in by tomorrow morning."

"What do you mean, a new one?"

"Well, we just got done pulling the old control unit, and Al went over to pick up a new one. He should be back with it later this afternoon."

"What? You mean you guys pulled the unit and are going to put a new one in?"

"Yes, sir."

"Listen, where the hell is Al right now?"

"He's over at the Jayson Company picking up that new unit. Boy, were we lucky that they had one available. But he'll be back with it real soon, Mr. Odum. Do you want to leave a message?"

"Never mind; I'll call him over there."

Odum placed a call to the Jayson Company and asked for Al.

"Al, Mr. Odum here. What the hell have you been doing about that control unit problem?"

"Oh, no problem at all, Mr. Odum. We've got it all straightened out. We'll have a new one installed and operating by morning."

"Are you crazy? Why did you pull the unit in the first place?"

"Why, you said to."

"I did not."

"Sure you did, Mr. Odum. You told me to find out what was causing the problem and get rid of it."

"But I didn't say to get rid of the control unit."

"Well, that's what was causing the problem."

"Couldn't you have fixed it?"

"I suppose so, but you didn't say to do that. You told me to get rid of it."

Realizing that they were not going to make any progress, Odum asked Al to drop by his office after the unit was installed. In the meantime, he decided to try to relax. However, he just couldn't get the problem out of his mind. That evening as he sat sipping a martini, he told his wife what had happened. "You know, Beth," he said, "a guy's got to be really stupid to do what Al did. I'm not so sure he's managerial timber after all."

Questions

1. What is the problem in this case? Explain.
2. Who is responsible for the problem? Defend your answer.
3. What should Odum do now?

26 A Perception Problem

Brownson & Associates had been called to the Webster Company when it became evident that there were some serious production problems. "I've been president of this company only three months," said Keith Peterson, "but it doesn't take very long to realize that we have a problem. I don't know what's bugging the work force; but whatever it is, find it and help us do something about it." With this introduction, Gail Brownson and a team of consultants began their work at Webster. It was six weeks before the team felt ready to make its first report to management. Brownson first spoke for the consultants.

"Ladies and gentlemen, my associates and I have been spending quite a bit of time in your firm, trying to determine how efficiency can be improved. Naturally, there are two sides to the problem—the mechanical and the human. We believe your problem is definitely the latter. Although we have not yet had time to uncover all the problem areas, we would like to show you the results of our early investigation. George, would you take over?"

George Ritter walked up to the podium carrying several overhead transparencies in his hand.

"Thank you, Ms. Brownson. Ladies and gentlemen, I have worked out some tables that I would like to show you. I believe the data should prove quite interesting in pinpointing one of your problem areas."

Ritter then put two transparencies on the overhead projector. The two are reproduced in Tables 1 and 2.

Table 1
Do You Tell Your Subordinates about Changes Which Will Affect Them in Advance of Their Happening?

	Categories						
Responses	Always (100%)	Almost Always (90–99)	Very Often (70–89)	Often (60–69)	Usually (50–59)	Sometimes (21–49)	Seldom (1–20)
Top managers said of themselves	60	40					
Middle managers' rating of top management	30	30	40				
Middle managers said of themselves	71	29					
Lower level managers' rating of middle management	17	27	29	12	10	5	
Lower level managers said of themselves	85	15					
Subordinates' rating of lower level managers	12	18	22	24	18	5	1

Table 2
Do You Encourage Your Subordinates to Speak Freely with You Regarding Any Problems They Might Have?

Responses	Always (100%)	Almost Always (90–99)	Very Often (70–89)	Often (60–69)	Usually (50–59)	Sometimes (21–49)	Seldom (1–20)
Top managers said of themselves	70	30					
Middle managers' rating of top management	55	25	14	6			
Middle managers said of themselves	85	14	1				
Lower level managers' rating of middle management	45	32	12	6	5		
Lower level managers said of themselves	93	7					
Subordinates' rating of lower level managers	31	22	18	10	8	7	4

Questions

1. What are the implications of Table 1? Explain.
2. What are the implications of Table 2? Explain.
3. In light of the two tables, what recommendations would you expect Brownson & Associates to make? Be complete in your answer.

27 What's in a Word?

Every Wednesday afternoon at Indler & Indler the personnel training division conducted a session for line managers. The topic for this day was communication, with major emphasis on word selection. "What you say," stated Carmeda de Vega, the session leader, "will have different meanings for different people. No two individuals are always going to agree, especially when one is a management representative and the other, a union representative. Furthermore, our choice of words is either going to turn people on or shut them off, depending on how they interpret our message. Let me illustrate. Each of you is going to be given a piece of paper with managerial traits on it. I want you to look over these sixteen items and then indicate whether you believe these traits, if found in a line supervisor, would be good, bad, or irrelevant."

Table 1 shows the list de Vega distributed.

	Good	Bad	Irrelevant
1. Self-confident	______	______	______
2. Bureaucratic	______	______	______
3. Truthful	______	______	______
4. Respects authority	______	______	______
5. Weak	______	______	______
6. Petty	______	______	______
7. Firm	______	______	______
8. Willing to bend	______	______	______
9. Good on details	______	______	______
10. Persevering	______	______	______
11. Cocky	______	______	______
12. Blunt		______	______
13. Nonconformist	______	______	______
14. Unyielding	______	______	______
15. Independent thinker	______	______	______
16. Stubborn	______	______	______

After all the papers were completed, the responses were discussed. "How many of you," said de Vega, "said that 'self-confident' was a good trait for a line manager?" Fifteen of the group of twenty raised their hands. "How many of you said it was a bad trait?" The other five raised their hands. A discussion then began on the difference of opinion. It turned out that most of the supervisors felt that managers have to trust themselves, while the others felt that self-confidence implied cockiness, an undesirable trait. One of the line managers said, "Where do you draw the line between self-confidence and cockiness? It's not easy, because the first can lead into the second; and the boundary between the two is easy to cross." Most of the other supervisors disagreed. "Self-confidence," clarified one man, "means knowing what you are capable of doing and what you are not capable of doing. It does not mean that you have a big head."

De Vega then cut off discussion on those two particular traits: "Let's go on to another of these. How many of you feel that 'Bureaucratic' is a good trait?" No one raised a hand. "How many of you feel that 'respects authority' is a desirable trait?" All hands were raised. "How do you separate these two words? Don't bureaucrats respect lines of authority?"

For the rest of the session de Vega kept going through the list of sixteen items, pairing one trait with another and trying to get the group to divide itself as to whether the trait was desirable. De Vega paired Traits 1 and 11; 2 and 4; 3 and 12; 5 and 8; 6 and 9; 7 and 14; 10 and 16; and 13 and 15.

Questions

1. In the list of traits, consider the following pairings: 7 and 14, and 10 and 16. Which of these are good traits for a line manager, which are bad, and which are irrelevant? Explain.
2. What point is de Vega trying to make with this list? How is it of value to line managers? Be specific in your answer.

28 A Question of Opportunity

Jack Gilbert had worked for the Acme Insurance Company for five years. During that time period, he had proved himself an outstanding salesman, as evidenced by his earnings record. When Gilbert started with the firm, he was paid $12,000 a year. By the end of five years, his annual income was $24,000.

It was then that Gilbert learned the office manager, George Stephenson, was going to be promoted to a position in the home office. Since it was common practice to fill the office manager position on the basis of seniority, Gilbert assumed that he was going to be the new office manager. When Stephenson called him in a week later, Gilbert felt that the topic of conversation would be his impending promotion.

"Jack, I've asked you to drop by because, as you know, I'm being promoted to a position in the home office. For many years now it has been common practice to fill the office manager's position from within. However, I've been looking over your earnings record, and to be quite frank, you are making $4,000 more than I am. If you were to take this job as office manager, you would have to do so at a cut in salary. For this reason, I've been thinking about recommending Pat Hanson for the job. It would be an increase in salary for her, and it would prevent you from having to take a cut."

"I don't know, George. There are a lot of advantages to being office manager. First, your $20,000 is secure. You don't have to worry about whether the client is going to buy a policy or not. Also, your job entails a lot more responsibility than mine. It's really quite challenging."

"Well, Jack, think it over. I hate to see you take this job and then regret it later. You'd find it lacks both the glamour and financial reward of your current job."

During the next three weeks Gilbert was quite busy and was unable to get back to see Stephenson regarding the office manager's job. However, he felt certain that Stephenson would not make a decision without checking with him. It therefore came as quite a shock when he entered the office on Monday morning and saw all the workers milling around Pat Hanson. "Have you heard?" remarked one of the secretaries. "Pat has been promoted to office manager."

Gilbert didn't know how to take the news. He decided that the best thing to do would be to go in and talk with Stephenson.

"George, I just heard that Pat is to become the new office manager."

"That's right, Jack. After giving the matter serious thought, I felt that this would be the best move."

"To be frank, George, I didn't think you would make a decision without consulting me first."

"Believe me, I thought about it. But when I considered your present position, I just didn't think that this was the right move for you. You know I wouldn't deliberately overlook you for a promotion if I thought it would be good for your career, don't you?"

"Yes, I know that. However, I'm still pretty miffed that I wasn't told about it before I heard this way."

"I wanted to, Jack, but you always seemed so busy that I figured you weren't interested in the job. I thought you'd have gotten back to me if you were."

"Well, I thought you'd be getting back with me."

"Look, Jack, this is all water under the bridge. You've proved your ability to sell, and your future with this firm is sound. You have nothing to worry about. Besides, you salespeople in the field make a lot more money than we do in the office."

Three months later George learned that Jack had resigned from Acme to go to work for a competitor—as an office manager with a starting annual salary of $19,000.

Questions

1. Why did Gilbert take a job with the competition?
2. What job factors motivated him? Make a list, putting them in an order of priority.

Controlling

29 A Productivity Bonus

Jack Canton would have liked to go to college immediately after graduating from high school. However, he had no illusions. The family didn't have the money, and Canton was unable to get a scholarship. The only way he was going to obtain this goal was by working days and going to night classes. Canton knew that one of the major universities in the city offered an extensive night program through which an individual could earn a bachelor's degree in six years. The program was fully accredited and seemed to be just what he wanted. Only the tuition rate, $60 per credit hour, worried him. Nevertheless, he decided this was the right road.

Thanks to an uncle, Canton was able to get a job in a large machine shop. The pay was $6.00 an hour, and if he saved his money, the tuition would not be a problem. Furthermore, in addition to the hourly wage rate, Canton learned that there was an incentive productivity plan in the shop. Employees who did more work than expected received a bonus. The plan operated in this way. Canton would receive $6.00 an hour for all units he produced on his machine up to thirty. For each unit over thirty, he would receive an additional fifteen cents.

In the beginning Canton was unable to earn any bonus. It was difficult enough to turn out thirty units an hour. However, after a couple of months he found his salary averaging $6.30 an hour. The next month it went to $6.60 an hour, and the following month it was $7.00 an hour. That was when Canton was stopped by Erica Rundquist, the shop steward in the plant.

"Jack, I'd like to talk to you during your coffee break. Can you take one now?"

"Sure thing, Erica, what's on your mind?"

As the two walked toward the cafeteria, the shop steward began spelling out the problem.

"You've been working for the company how long now, five months?"

"Right."

"How are you making out on that productivity bonus?"

"Pretty well. I'm averaging close to $7.00 an hour, but I think I can go higher."

"That's what I want to talk to you about. The other people on the line have been watching your progress. Everyone is aware that you are going to night school, and the last thing anyone wants to do is stifle your chances. On the other hand, we don't want to ruin a good thing. If you get up past $7.00 an hour, the management is going to start wondering why you were able to become so efficient so quickly. Everyone else here is holding to an average hourly rate of $7.00. Why don't you do the same?"

Canton promised to consider the matter.

Questions

1. Why are all the workers able to produce more than thirty units? Should management raise the amount required before allowing the workers to qualify for the productivity bonus?
2. What does this case tell you about informal organization structures? Explain.
3. What should Canton do? Why?

30 Managerial Tool

"Bob, this is my first day on the job, so I may be speaking prematurely. But I am a little concerned about my new responsibilities because my accounting background is limited. You know what we had in college—basic accounting and cost accounting, and that was it. Do you think I have enough accounting for the job? I would hate to fail."

"Ted, you're just too upset. You always worry. Remember how everyone else did freshman themes? Remember how you sweated? And we all turned out about the same. Sure, the company expects you to know something about accounting, but only as a managerial tool."

"What do you mean?"

"Well, what I'm trying to say is that the firm expects you to be able to make decisions on the basis of what you see in the financial statements you are given."

"You mean I don't have to know how to compute all the financial ratios?"

"Well, of course not. Remember when you saw your first computer? They're still working. You have to know what the ratios mean, naturally, so that you can make intelligent decisions; but the computations themselves will be attached to the financial statement you receive."

"Wow, that sure makes it easier. I thought managers had to be able to work out all those data from scratch."

"A lot of people think that, Ted. But you just need to realize that accounting is not a bunch of numbers that, if analyzed in a special way, reveal hidden secrets. Accounting is a managerial tool. It is a method whereby we are able to see changes in our financial and asset structure. It tells us what has been going on. Using accounting information as a starting point, the manager makes decisions regarding future action. Too many people view accounting as a static tool. Take, for example, the current ratio. A lot of people claim that a firm's current assets must be twice its current liabilities, which is pure nonsense. The correct current ratio can only be determined by the firm itself. What's good for one firm may be bad for another."

"I never really thought of accounting in that light. I always assumed that set percentages or relationships had to exist among assets and liabilities, costs, and revenues. However, your idea makes a lot of sense. Managers should use the financial statements as assistance in determining where their units are financially strong and weak. Then they're more able to decide how the situation can be improved."

"That's it."

"You know, going back again to college memories, I think the profs who said we'd understand better what they were talking about after we got on the job were onto a lot."

Questions

1. Explain in your own words what Bob means when he says accounting is a managerial tool.

2. Would Bob accept or reject this statement? "There is no universal agreement regarding the interpretation of accounting principles."
3. What role do financial statements play in the control process? How does the concept of feedback enter into the picture? How does accounting serve as a communication tool for the manager?
4. Do you think it surprising that many schools now offer a course in managerial accounting? Explain. What content might such a course have?

31 LIFO and FIFO

"Barb, I'm still confused about how we value inventory around here. I know this is my third week with the firm, and believe me, I'm trying to pick up all the information I need to do a good job. However, there are some things I just don't understand, and this is one of them."

As trainee Jim Blake talked, he shifted from one foot to the other. It was evident that he was nervous about his failure to fully understand everything being explained to him. His line manager, Barb Phillips, empathized.

"Sit down, Jim, and let's talk about it. But before we do, remember something for me, will you? No trainee in the firm will ever understand all we have to tell you all at once. The important thing to remember is that if you don't understand, you should ask about it. That's the only way you'll find out. Now, what's the specific problem you seem to be having?"

"Well, it has to do with the ways to value inventory. When I was over in accounting today, the manager kept talking about LIFO and FIFO. About all I got was that one means last-in-first-out, while the other stands for first-in-first-out."

"Right. Now what are you having difficulty understanding?"

"Why do we use these methods at all? I mean, it seems pretty silly. Suppose I come in and buy a machine from the company. In determining the cost of that machine, all we have to do is check our production cost records. Then we can subtract that amount from revenue to determine our profit on the machine."

"You're right. We could do it that way. But why not follow the approach we use in the firm, last-in-first-out?"

"I'm glad you asked that because I have an answer."

"You seem so anxious, I can hardly wait."

"Really, I'm not kidding. My idea makes a lost of sense. If we use LIFO, we assume that the machine we sell is the last one we produced. Therefore, the cost we subtract from the selling price is based upon the assumption that this is correct. However, what if the machine we sell is really the very first one we manufactured? We are not allocating costs properly."

"You're right. However, accountants maintain that it is not necessary to match the physical movement of goods with the cost assigned to them. If we have 100 machines in the warehouse and we intend to sell them all, sooner or later we are going to get around to that last machine. Why not just assume that the first one we sell is the last one we manufactured and start working down the line to the last one?"

"Well, I think maybe I'm getting somewhere. LIFO may not match goods with their respective costs, but it does provide a consistent and perhaps easy-to-understand approach to valuing inventory."

"That certainly is one answer. Now, do you have any problems with the concept?"

"Just one. If we assume that the last machine being produced is the first one being sold, aren't we going to make less profit than if we used first-in-first-out?"

"We sure are. If a machine sells for $100 and because of our increasing costs of raw materials, the first machine cost $50 to manufacture, while the one hundredth cost $65, we are only going to make $35 when we sell the last one."

"Then, why do it? Why not reverse the approach and use FIFO? This way we can make $50 on the first machine and have a higher profit on the sale."

Questions

1. What is the answer to Blake's last question? Why will some companies favor LIFO over FIFO?
2. When might a firm choose FIFO in valuing its inventory? Explain.
3. Are not FIFO and LIFO fictitious ways of valuing inventory? How can a manager control expenses if such fictitious kinds of entries are used? Also, if it is necessary to match the physical movement of goods with the cost assigned to them, does this not indicate lack of control?

32 Progress Reporting

Arnie Boden was confused. For the better part of an hour, he had been trying to fill out the monthly progress report for his department. Fortunately for Boden, he was faced with this task only once every three months. Although it was never easy, he somehow had always managed to stumble through. This time, however, he decided to go talk to his boss, Sam Chernik, about the matter.

"Mr. Chernik, it's time to fill out the quarterly progress report. However, before I go any farther on it, I thought I'd come in and talk to you. I'm having trouble with it."

"You've filled it out before, Arnie."

"Yes, but this time it's posing a bigger problem than before."

"Why don't you dig out what you submitted last time and let that serve as a guide for you?"

"Well, it's just not that easy. The reporting system has changed over the past three months. The data we're receiving from the operating units now are in different forms. It's tough to translate exactly what's going on and put it into the report."

"Well, just do the best you can."

"Okay, but I'm having trouble determining what to include in the report and what to leave out."

"Put in whatever you think is necessary and just leave out the rest."

"Why is it necessary to fill it out at all? I've frankly never understood the value of this report. We fill them out, send the original to the home office, and keep two copies on file. However, no one ever questions the report. In fact, I don't even know if anyone would miss it if we failed to send it in. Tell me, why is this report necessary?"

"Why, Arnie, how would management know what's going on without it?"

"Well, the home office could rely on any of the other four progress reports it gets. I think this particular report is extraneous. Why do we fill it out anyway?"

"That's a very important report, Arnie. I've been here thirty years, and we've always had to fill it out; so you can bet top management feels it's a key report."

Realizing that Chernik did not wish to pursue the matter any further, Boden excused himself, went back to his desk, and began to write the report.

Questions

1. What are Chernik's reasons for believing the report is important?
2. What do you think would happen if Boden filed the two office copies and then threw away the original (the home office copy) without sending it on for top management?
3. What is the point of this case? What would you recommend be done?

33 Mr. Close Control

Tina Aaron could remember the days when she would get up in the morning and literally run over to the plant. Her job was so exciting that she couldn't wait to get there. "Now I'm not saying it was an easy job, Bob; it wasn't. But it sure was challenging." Bob Merrill nodded his understanding. "Are you saying that the challenge is no longer there?" Aaron pondered for a moment.

"Let me put it this way. The job still calls for the same basic decisions. However, it's not the same. Now I know my job coming and going. Before, I was lucky to get done with my work by 7 PM. Now I can wrap it up by 2 PM."

"Well, why don't you start taking on more responsibility? Surely there are other things you can do in addition to your present duties."

"That's just it. Mr. Martin won't give me anything else."

"Why not?"

"Well, I think it all goes back to when I first started working here. Mr. Martin told me that I should come and see him if I had problems. You can imagine how lost I was. I'll bet I went in to his office three times a day. Without him, I never would have made it. Gradually, of course, things got better and I found myself calling him less and less."

"I'd think that this would indicate to Mr. Martin that you don't need to rely on him as much any more."

"Unfortunately, that isn't how it worked. In the beginning, every time I'd finish an assignment, he'd want to check it. That was fine with me. However, he's still following the same procedure. He won't let go."

"Why don't you tell him?"

"Two reasons. First, I feel I owe him something for all that help he gave me. Second, he thinks he's helping me out and doing the right thing."

Questions

1. Why do you think Martin continues to exercise close control?
2. How does a manager know that close control is no longer required? Explain.

34 The Breakeven Point

One of the key control concepts a manager should understand is the breakeven point. In graphic form, a breakeven chart looks like Figure 1.

Figure 1
A Breakeven Chart

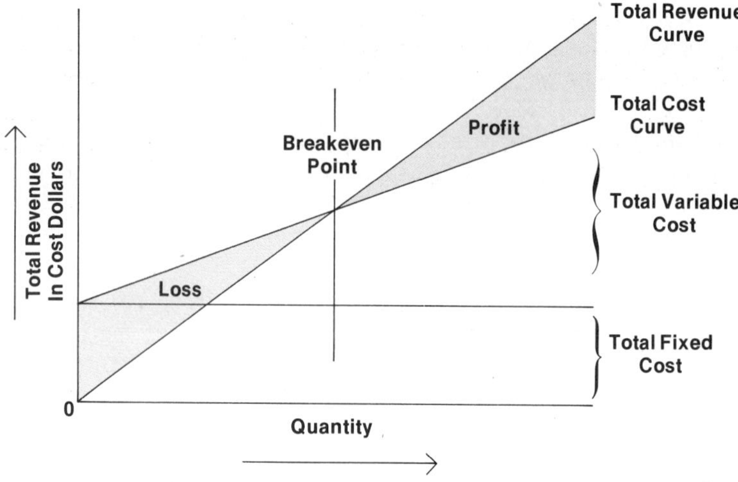

Several factors make up a breakeven chart. First, there are fixed costs. The firm must meet these even if it produces nothing. Local property taxes are an example. Whether the plant is in operation or not, the company must pay these taxes. A second would be payments due on the building or machinery. If the company has borrowed money to buy plant or equipment, payments on the principal and interest must be forthcoming, regardless of the amount of production. Second are the variable costs. These are costs associated with the day-to-day operations of the business. Wages and materials are examples. These costs are variable because they depend on how many items the firm is going to produce. If the company produces 1 million items, the materials bill is probably going to be twice as large as if it produced only half a million items. The sum of fixed and variable costs is equal to total cost. Whenever the company manufactures and sells a product above variable cost, it makes some money, which can go to cover the fixed cost. If it sells enough of the product, the firm will soon be able to cover all the fixed cost. The point at which this occurs is called the breakeven point. From there on, the firm moves into the profit column.

In a very large manufacturing enterprise, it would be difficult to determine the breakeven point without some mathematical assistance. For example, the number of units that must be sold if a company is to reach the breakeven point can be determined as follows:

$$\text{Breakeven point (in units)} = \frac{\text{Total fixed cost}}{\text{Selling price per unit} - \text{variable cost per unit}}$$

The following can be used for determining the breakeven point in dollars.

$$\text{Breakeven point (in dollars)} = \frac{\text{Total fixed cost}}{1 - \dfrac{\text{variable cost per unit}}{\text{selling price per unit}}}$$

John Person, vice-president of marketing for Lazin, Inc., was delighted to have these control tools at his disposal because he had just received a request from the manufacturing department asking him how many units he thought should be produced during the upcoming fiscal year. Fortunately, on the basis of current market research relating price and demand (see Table 1), Person had some indication as to the demand of various price levels.

Table 1
Price-Demand Table

Selling Price per Unit	Units Demanded
$ 90	65,000
120	50,000
150	40,000
200	20,000

In addition to these data, Person knew that the total fixed cost for the manufacturing department was $1,500,000, and the variable cost per unit would be $80 at all levels of production.

Questions

1. What is the breakeven point, in terms of units, if the firm prices its product at $90? $120? $150? $200?
2. What is the breakeven point, in terms of dollars, at each of the four price levels?
3. Which of the four alternatives is most profitable for the firm? How many units, then, should be scheduled for production? How much profit will result?

35 A Broken Promise?

When the Aubrey Company's financial statements came out, return on investment proved to be 6 percent, down from the previous year's 11 percent. Aubrey's president, James Rockner, decided to call in a team of management consultants to find out how the situation could be improved. After analyzing the company's operations, the consultants recommended that it adopt a management by objectives approach. Nancy Logan, spokesman for the team, put it this way:

> Mr. Aubrey, the problem we find with your company is lack of direction. Many of your people appear unclear as to what they should be doing and how their performance will be measured. We recommend that you adopt a management by objectives approach. MBO, as it is generally called, is really quite simple. Both managers and subordinates agree on the objectives that the latter will attempt to attain within a given time period, say, six months. Then, at the end of that time, the two sit down and review the progress. Since the subordinates know what is expected and how performance will be measured, MBO removes a lot of the doubt and insecurity which subordinates would otherwise feel.

Logan then went on to explain the system in greater detail, pointing out that it was necessary for top management to support an MBO approach if it was to work. Rockner agreed.

Over the next six months, the system was installed at Aubrey, starting at the top. As each group began to work with MBO, it had nothing but good remarks about the system.

Helen Werner, one of the company's sales managers, looked forward to implementing the program with her staff, because she felt that salespeople in general are just too unstructured. In talking to one of the other managers about MBO, she said, "I'm really looking forward to using it. My people do whatever they please. With a system for structuring their selling activities, I think I can really improve their performance."

Werner was thinking specifically about Kara Penfield. Penfield had been a pain in the neck from the day she was hired. Not only was her selling record poor, but she often abandoned the sales pitch she was taught and tried to use her own. The result was usually catastrophic. Penfield's sales were only half the average of the rest of the sales staff. Thus, when Werner called Penfield in to talk about MBO, she was extra careful in ensuring that the saleswoman understood what was going to be expected of her.

"Kara, sit down. I want to talk to you about our new MBO program. Are you familiar with MBO?"

"Yes, I am."

"Fine. Then I'll get right to the point. What goals do you think we should set for you for the next six months?"

"Well, I'd like to do what everyone else is doing."

"Okay. That calls for 260 calls on potential buyers, or two a day for six months."

"Sounds fair to me."

"All right. But this time, Kara, I want you to stick solely to the company sales pitch. Don't start going off on your own."

"I agree."

"Good. Then let's set a quota for you. For the last year, you've been selling half the amount of the average salesperson in our firm. That means 15 percent of all your calls resulted in sales. What do you say we raise you to the average? Do you think you can do it?"

"I do. I'm really going to try. I promise."

"Okay. That means seventy-eight sales in the next six months. You agree?"

"Right."

Six months later Werner and Penfield met to review performance. Penfield had sold 52 units by that time.

"Well, Kara, your performance is only 67 percent of what we set. How about that?"

"Look, Helen, you don't have to tell me that I haven't come up to the goal we set. I know that. The question is, what can be done about it? Now, I agree that MBO is a great management tool for controlling and evaluating performance, but it only accentuates the obvious. How can MBO help me sell better? If we are going to improve performance, we have to do better than point out that it's below par. We're going to have to come up with some ways to improve it."

Questions

1. What response should Werner give?
2. Is MBO a good control technique? How can it help a salesperson such as Penfield?
3. What goals should the two women set for Penfield for the next six months? Explain.

Glossary

The following are definitions of many of the concepts and terms used in this book. They correspond to those given in the text and represent the commonest meanings you are likely to encounter in modern organizations.

Acceptance. The third step in the communication process. It involves getting the receiver to agree to, comply with, or accept the directive. The term also refers to willingness to go along with a change because one sees more to be gained from the new conditions than to be lost by them.

Achievement Test. A test which measures proficiency in a given area, such as knowledge of a particular subject, or the ability to do a sample of actual work.

Action. The last step in the communication process. It involves a duty on the part of both the receiver and the sender to follow up and do what was expected, or to see that it is done.

Adaptive Mode. A type of strategic behavior used by organizations that have matured. It is characterized by a short-run time horizon, reactive decision making, and a desire to work under conditions of certainty.

Ad Hoc Committee. A committee that is appointed for a specific purpose and, once the job is completed, is disbanded.

Adhocracy. A term that refers to temporary organization structures, as found in the case of matrix designs used by project managers. *(See* **Matrix Structure.**)

Adult Ego State. A psychological state in which a person deals objectively with reality. Problem solving and rational thinking are products of the adult ego state.

Aptitude Test. A test which measures a person's capacity to learn a particular job or type of work.

Assets. Those things that a company owns, such as cash, inventory, land, buildings, and equipment.

Attention. The first step in the communication process. It involves getting the listener to screen out all disturbances or other distractions that can interrupt concentration.

Authoritarian Leadership. A leadership style that tends to be heavily work centered, with major emphasis given to task accomplishment and little concern to the human element.

Authority. The right to command.

Balance Sheet. A financial statement that provides the organization with a picture of its assets, liabilities, and owners' equity at a particular moment in time.

Basic Mission. The primary business the organization is in.

Behaviorally Anchored Rating Scales (BARS). An appraisal method in which behavioral scales are constructed and evaluations are tied directly to specific job behaviors.

Breakeven Point (BEP). The volume of sales sufficient to cover all fixed and variable expenses but providing no profit.

Budget. A type of plan that specifies anticipated results in numerical terms and serves as a control device for feedback, evaluation, and follow-up.

Career Patterns. Work-stimulated behavior patterns that people tend to follow during their careers. There are six in all: breaking away, initial adulthood, the transition period, becoming one's own person, mid-life crisis, and the reestablishment of equilibrium.

Career Strategies. Techniques or tactics that can be used for improving one's chances for promotion. Illustrations include: being a high achiever, helping your boss succeed, finding a sponsor, documenting your accomplishments, giving and getting loyalty, considering swimming against the tide, and being mobile.

Case Method. A widely used training technique. It involves using a written case in which a real decision is required. Trainees are required to read and analyze the case and then offer their recommendations for action.

Causal Variable. A variable that determines the results that will be achieved. Management decisions, business strategies, and leadership behavior are all illustrations. (*See also* **Intervening Variable** and **End-Result Variable.**)

Central Tendency. A response tendency in which a rater gives out neither very good nor very bad ratings. Everyone tends to be rated average.

Certainty. Decision situations in which the manager knows all the alternatives and the outcomes of each.

Change Agent. A term used to describe an individual who helps bring about organizational changes. It is commonly employed in referring to outside consultants who are brought in to carry out OD interventions.

Child Ego State. A state in which the individual does things the way he or she did when a child. Common facial expressions, for example, include twinkling eyes, mischievous winks, and broad grins.

Civil Rights Act of 1964. Federal legislation which seeks to ensure equal opportunity for all and forbids discrimination on the basis of race, color, religion, sex, or national origin.

Coaching and Counseling. A widely used training and development method employed among both workers and managers. It involves answering questions and providing advice to the subordinates.

Coercive Power. Power based on fear.

Commanding. Directing workers toward the accomplishment of organizational objectives through the use of effective leadership.

Communication. The conveying of meaning from sender to receiver.

Complementary Transaction. A transaction between two people that progresses along expected lines. For example, when one individual assumes the child ego state and talks to the other's parent and the latter assumes the parent ego state in responding to the individual's child, this is a complementary transaction. (*See* **Crossed Transaction.**)

Conceptual Skills. Those skills that help the manager see the enterprise as a whole, realizing that what affects one particular part of the organization can have effects in other parts as well.

Consumerism. One of the primary social responsibilities facing business. It includes the obligations firms have in areas such as advertising claims, pricing policies, product safety, product and service warranties, and service activities.

Contingency Management. The drawing together by the manager of all the things he or she has learned in all the management-related areas of business and applying it to the problem at hand.

Contingency Organization Design. A term that describes the current organizational design phenomenon in which companies abandon strict adherence to classic organizational design principles and use whatever works best for them.

Controlling. The process of determining that everything is going according to plan. In essence, controlling consists of three steps: (a) the establishment of standards, (b) the comparison of performance against standards, and (c) the correction of deviations that have occurred.

Coordinating. Achieving cooperation and harmony among all levels and units of the organization.

Counterbalancing Approach. A technique used in the selection process. It involves weighing all of the candidate's qualifications and seeing whether any deficiencies are counterbalanced by strengths before dropping the person from further consideration. (For a contrast, *see* **Multiple Cutoff Technique.**)

Crossed Transaction. A transaction between two people that does not progress along expected lines. One of the parties is not choosing the right ego state. For example, when one individual talks to another by assuming the adult ego state and addressing the other person's adult, but the latter responds with a parent to child transaction, this is crossed transaction. (For comparison, *see* **Complementary Transaction.**)

Current Ratio. A financial ratio that is computed by dividing current assets by current liabilities, it measures a firm's ability to meet its current obligations.

Debt/Equity Ratio. A financial ratio that measures the percentage of the business's assets that are a result of debt financing and the percentage that are contributed by equity financing.

Decentralization. A system of management in which a great deal of decision-making authority rests at the lower levels of the hierarchy.

Decisional Roles. Those roles the manager performs when acting as an entrepreneur or owner-manager seeking to improve the unit and adapt it to changing conditions, handle disturbances, and/or allocate resources.

Decision Making. The process of choosing among alternatives.

Decision Tree. An operations research tool that permits (a) the identification of alternative courses of action in solving a problem, (b) the assignment of probability estimates to the events associated with these alternatives, and (c) the calculation of the payoffs corresponding to each act-event combination.

Decode. To interpret the message that one has received from a sender. *(See* **Encode.**)

Development. The process by which managers obtain the skills, experiences, and attitudes necessary to become and/or remain successful leaders.

Diagonal Communication. Communication that occurs between people who are neither in the same department nor on the same level of the hierarchy. The basic purpose of such communications is to increase organizational efficiency by cutting across departmental lines and minimizing red tape.

Differential Piece Rate. An incentive wage system formulated by Frederick W. Taylor that paid a fixed rate per piece for all production up to standard and a higher rate for all pieces if the standard was met.

Downward Communication. Communication that a superior initiates and directs to a subordinate.

Eclectic Manager. A manager who chooses those ideas and concepts in management theory that can help him or her get things done through other people and discards the rest.

Ecology. One of the primary social responsibilities facing business. It relates to the firm's obligation to protect the environment from damage or harm.

Empathy. Putting oneself, figuratively speaking, into another person's shoes. In so doing, the individual begins to see things from this other person's point of view.

Encode. To put a message into a form that is understandable to the receiver.

End-Result Variable. A variable which reflects the result of a causal variable. Some common illustrations are profit, productivity, and output. (*See also* **Causal Variable.**)

Entrepreneurial Mode. A type of behavior used by owner-managers. It is typified by such attitudes and actions as an emphasis on growth, an attempt to mold the environment to the individual's own personal tastes, and willingness to work in an environment of uncertainty.

Equal Opportunity. One of the major social responsibilities of business. It entails providing job opportunities for people and giving equal pay for equal work.

Equal Pay Act. Federal legislation which seeks to correct wage differentials that are based on sex. It forbids discrimination on the basis of sex for jobs that require equal skills, effort, and responsibility and that are performed under similar working conditions.

Equity Theory. A motivation theory which holds that, in order to be motivated, individuals must believe the rewards they are receiving are fair. This results in people comparing their work/reward ratio to that of others.

Esteem Needs. Motives that include the need to feel important and to receive recognition from others which supports such feelings. They are satisfied through feelings of self-confidence and prestige.

Ethics. The observation, evaluation, and conduct of right and wrong thinking or behavior.

Expectancy. A term used in expectancy/valence theory, it refers to the perceived probability of attaining a first-level outcome.

Expected Value. The net result that is obtained when a conditional return is multiplied by the probability of its occurrence. Expected value is of particular importance in the use of decision trees.

Expert Power. Power based on competence.

Extrapolation. The simplest form of economic forecast. It consists of merely projecting current trends into the future.

Extrinsic Rewards. External types of reinforcement, such as money, working conditions, and job security.

Fiedler's Theory. A leadership theory developed by Fred Fiedler which postulates that a leader's effectiveness is determined by three variables: (a) how well the leader is accepted by the subordinates; (b) the degree to which the subordinates' jobs are routine and spelled out in contrast to being vague and undefined; and (c) the formal authority provided for in the position the leader occupies.

First-Line Manager. A manager who supervises operating employees. The individual is often called a foreman or supervisor.

5,5 Managerial Style. Often referred to as a middle-of-the-road management style. The 5,5 individual assumes that there is an inherent conflict between the concerns for production and people. This manager tries to compromise and balance these two dimensions.

Flat Structure. An organization structure in which there is a wide span of control with only a small number of levels in the hierarchy.

Flexible Budget. A budget that is set up to adjust to changing conditions so that if sales are higher than anticipated, the production and marketing budgets can be easily raised to accommodate this demand.

Free-Form Structure. *(See* **Organic Structure.**)

Functional Authority. Authority in a department other than one's own, as seen in the case of the comptroller who can order production personnel to provide him or her with cost per unit data.

Functional Departmentalization. A department organized along the lines of major activities. In a manufacturing firm so organized, it is not uncommon to find marketing, production, and finance departments reporting directly to the president.

Functional Game. A management simulation in which the trainees make decisions in particular areas, such as production scheduling, advertising, or materials purchasing.

Functional Manager. A manager who is responsible for a particular organizational activity such as marketing, production, or finance.

General Management Simulation. A management simulation in which the trainees operate their own businesses and compete with the other members of the training group. Usually there are three to five people per team in such a simulation.

General Manager. A manager who is in charge of a company, an independent operating division, or a subsidiary.

Graphic Rating Scale. The simplest type of rating technique. It consists of evaluating people along a series of continua which measure such things as work quality and performance.

Grid Organizational Development. A total organizational development intervention based on the concepts of the managerial grid. It consists of six phases designed to examine and improve organizational performance at all levels of the hierarchy.

Halo Effect. A rater response tendency in which a rater allows his or her overall assessment of an individual to influence the evaluation of that person on all the factors being rated.

Hawthorne Studies. Studies by Elton Mayo and others that provided the impetus for the human relations movement. Conducted at the Western Electric plant in Chicago, Illinois, they had four major phases: (a) illumination experiments; (b) relay assembly test room experiments; (c) massive interviewing programs; and (d) the bank wiring observation room study.

High Achievers. Individuals with a strong need to succeed. They tend to (a) like situations in which they take personal responsibility for finding solutions to problems; (b) take moderate, rather than high or low, risks; and, (c) want concrete feedback on their performance.

Human Resource Forecasting. The process of determining how many people the organization will need during the next fiscal year, how many it currently has on board, and how many new recruits will be required.

Human Skills. Skills that help an individual interact with other people. These skills are very important for middle-level managers who must lead other managers.

Hygiene Factors. As identified by Frederick Herzberg in his two-factor theory of motivation, factors that will not motivate people by their presence but will cause dissatisfaction by their absence. Some of the hygiene factors Herzberg identified include money, security, and working conditions.

Illumination. That stage of the creative thinking process when the solution to the problem is discovered.

In-Basket Technique. A management training technique. It involves giving the trainee a box which contains typical items that might be found in his or her mailbox and a telephone list and asking the individual to make decisions on what should be done. All of this has to be accomplished in a limited time period, after which the person is evaluated and critiqued on the number of decisions made in the allotted time.

Income Statement. A financial statement which shows the company's revenues and expenses over a particular period of time.

Incubation. A stage of the creative thinking process. It is marked by the unconscious mind working on the problem.

Inference. An assumption made by the receiver of a message.

Informational Roles. Those roles the manager performs when acting as a monitor of information, a disseminator, or a spokesperson.

Intelligence Test. A test which measures intellectual capacity.

Intergroup Team Building. An OD intervention that involves two groups coming together, determining what they dislike about each other and what they feel the other dislikes about them, followed by a sharing of these feelings and the development of an action plan for working out their differences and becoming more cooperative in their work relationships.

Internal Audit. An audit conducted by the organization's own staff. It involves an examination and evaluation of the firm's operations and a determination of where things have gone well and where they have gone poorly.

Interpersonal Roles. Those roles the manager performs when acting as a figurehead, a leader, or a liaison person.

Intervening Variable. A variable which reflects an individual's internal state. Loyalty, attitude, and motivation are all illustrations. *(See* **Causal Variable** and **End-Result Variable.**)

Intrinsic Rewards. Internal types of reinforcement, such as challenge, feelings of accomplishment, and recognition for a job well done.

Inventory Turnover. A financial ratio that is computed by dividing cost of goods sold by ending inventory. It measures how fast the organization is selling its inventory.

Job Analysis. An evaluation of a job. It consists of studying work activities, machines, tools, equipment, job-related knowledge, and work experience.

Job Definition. Description of the authority and responsibilities that accompany a job.

Job Design. Job content, the methods to be used on the job, and the manner in which the particular job will relate to others in the organization.

Job Enlargement. Increasing the range of a job by giving the individual more to do.

Job Enrichment. Building into a job psychological motivators, such as increased responsibility and a feeling of accomplishment, by giving the person increased authority to (a) plan the work by organizing and scheduling the tasks, and (b) control the job by taking care of follow-up functions, such as inspecting, testing, and repairing.

Job Rotation. Moving an individual from one job to another for the purpose of reducing boredom.

Job Specifications. The general requirements an applicant for a job must have. These include such things as experience, education, and job skills.

Johari Window. A method of examining the four aspects of communication relationships: open, hidden, blind, and unknown.

Key Area Control. A control technique by which a firm measures its performance in a number of vital areas. At General Electric, for example, these areas include profitability, market position, productivity, product leadership, personnel development, employee attitudes, public responsibility, and integration of short- and long-range objectives.

Lag Indicators. Series of economic indicators which often follow changes in the economic cycle.

Language. Defined as one of the common communication barriers. It involves the fact that people often use different meanings for the same word.

Lateral Communication. Communication that takes place between people on the same level of the hierarchy. The most common reason for this communication flow is to promote coordination and teamwork.

Leadership. The process of influencing people to direct their efforts toward the achievement of some particular goal(s).

Leadership Characteristics. Characteristics possessed by effective leaders. Some of the most commonly cited include drive, originality, persistence, and tolerance of stress.

Lead from Strength. A strategy formulation rule which holds that an organization should build a strategy around those things which it does best.

Lead Indicators. Series of economic indicators which often precede changes in the economic cycle.

Learning. The acquisition of skills, knowledge, and abilities that result in a relatively permanent change in behavior.

Least Preferred Co-Worker Scale. A questionnaire which asks the leader to describe the person with whom he or she can work least well. The instrument is used by Fiedler in his contingency model.

Legitimate Power. Power vested in the manager's position or role in the hierarchy.

Leniency. The tendency to give good performance ratings to everyone, even the poorest workers.

Liabilities. The debts of an organization ranging from current liabilities to long-term liabilities.

Life and Career Planning Intervention. An OD intervention that tries to draw together a group's past, present, and future by getting individuals to concentrate on (1) what they have done thus far in their career, (2) where they currently are in the career, and (3) where they hope to go in the future. This type of intervention is very helpful for those individuals who feel unsure of how to manage the remainder of their careers.

Line Authority. Direct authority, as in the case of a superior who can give orders directly to a subordinate.

Loyalty Dilemma. A problem faced by young people in their career. It entails the fact that bosses often see loyalty in different ways. Some believe it means being totally honest, others see it as meaning that the subordinate should help the unit by never saying anything bad about it, and still others believe it means that the subordinate should help the superior out in any way possible, whether the required conduct is ethical or not.

Management. The process of getting things done through people.

Management Audit. A detailed evaluation of an organization's performance is often carried out by outside experts every three to five years. The best known is that conducted by the American Institute of Management, which assigns points for various operational categories, evaluates each, and then comes up with a total score.

Management by Objectives (MBO). An appraisal method in which superior and subordinate identify the latter's major areas of responsibility and use these measures as guides for assessing the contribution of the individual.

Management Game. A training technique used with management trainees, it involves having the individuals make decisions in a simulated environment. There are numerous types of games from functional (advertising, product development) to general management simulations.

Managerial Grid. An organizational development technique used for helping managers identify their leadership styles and determine how they can develop more effective styles.

Manager Replacement Chart. A chart that allows one to determine the current performance and promotion potential of organizational employees.

Matrix Structure. A hybrid combination of both project and functional structures; project managers operating within this form of departmentalization are forced to rely on the functional managers for support and assistance, since project managers have no line authority.

Mechanistic Structure. An organization structure that is often effective in a stable environment in which external factors have little impact on organization performance.

Message Competition. One of the primary problems in getting people's attention. It involves the fact that a listener is likely to have many things on his or her mind, all of them vying with the speaker for the listener's attention.

Middle Manager. A manager who is located between first-line managers and top managers. This individual often carries the title of unit manager or department manager.

Mid-Life Crisis. A term used to describe a life adjustment phase in which managers evaluate their career progress and feel that they are not doing well. A period of emotional disequilibrium follows.

Motivational Force. One's drive toward a given objective. In expectancy theory terms it is defined as valence times expectancy.

Motivators. As identified by Frederick Herzberg in his two-factor theory of motivation, those factors that will build high levels of motivation and job satisfaction. Some of the motivational factors Herzberg identified include recognition, advancement, and achievement.

Motive. A "why" of behavior. It can consist of needs, drives, wants, and/or impulses within the individual.

Multiple Cut-off Technique. An approach used in the selection process. It involves eliminating candidates from further consideration if they fail to pass any one of the specific screening devices, such as the application blank, interview, tests, or physical exams. The persons are eliminated immediately from any further consideration. (For a contrast *see* **Counterbalancing Approach.**)

Narrow Span of Control. A span of control that is very small—for example, two to three. These are typical of tall organization structures.

Need for Achievement. An inner drive found among high achievers. It is a motivational drive to accomplish things.

Need for Affiliation. An inner drive found among people who are interested in warm, friendly relationships.

Need for Power. An inner drive often found among successful managers. It is a motivational drive to control or influence situations.

9,9 Managerial Style. A managerial style that is referred to as team management. Regarded by many as the ideal management style, it calls for a manager who has high concern for work and high concern for people.

9,1 Managerial Style. A managerial style that is highly concerned with production but has low concern for people. The individual plans the work and pushes to get it out. The manager shows little interest in the workers. If they cannot keep up, they are replaced by others who can.

Off-the-Job Training. Training that is carried out away from the work setting, as in the case of individuals who are sent to vocational schools or institutes where they can learn necessary job-related skills.

1,9 Managerial Style. A managerial style in which the manager tends to have a high concern for people's feelings, comfort, and needs, but low concern for getting the work out.

1,1 Managerial Style. A managerial style in which the manager tends to put people on the job and leave them alone. The individual does not check up on their work nor try to interact with them by offering praise and/or encouraging them to keep up good work. There is low concern for both work and people.

On-the-Job Training. The most widely used method of employee training. It involves placing the individual in the work situation and having an experienced individual show the trainee how the job is done.

Operational Objectives. Quantified, specific short-range objectives which the organization hopes to attain during the next year. Illustrations include increased productivity, lower costs, and reduced absenteeism.

Operational Planning. The setting of short-run goals and targets that are in accord with the subobjectives and substrategies of the intermediate-range plan.

Operations Research. The application of mathematical tools and techniques to the decision-making process.

Organic Functions. Activities that must be carried out if an organization wishes to remain in existence. In a manufacturing firm, for example, these would include marketing, production, and finance.

Organic Structure. An organization structure that is often effective in a dynamic environment in which external factors have a significant impact on organization performance.

Organizational Climate. A set of properties of the work environment perceived by individuals who work there and which serve as a major force in influencing their job behavior.

Organizational Development (OD). A long-range effort to improve an organization's problem-solving and renewal processes. It relies on the assistance of a change agent and the use of applied behavioral science, including action research.

Organizational System. A term which describes how the various units and departments are interrelated.

Organizing. The assignment of duties and the coordination of efforts among all organizational personnel to ensure maximum efficiency in the attainment of predetermined objectives.

Orientation. An approach to introducing a new employee to the job. It involves telling the person how things are done and creating the basis for interpersonal relations between the new individual and the regular work team.

Owner's Equity. The difference between total assets and total liabilities. This figure represents the real value the owner holds in the business.

Paired Comparison. An appraisal method in which the rater compares every employee in the work group with every other employee. The final ranking of each is determined by the number of times he or she is judged superior to the others.

Parent Ego State. A psychological state in which individuals act as they perceived their parents to act. The parents serve as role models for the individual's behavior.

Participative Leadership. A leadership style that is characterized by a high concern for both people and work.

Paternalistic Leadership. A leadership style that tends to be heavily work-centered but which shows some consideration for the personnel as well.

Path-Goal Theory of Leadership. A leadership theory which holds that the manager's job is to (a) clarify the tasks to be performed by subordinates, (b) clear away any roadblocks to goal attainment, and (c) increase the opportunity for subordinates to obtain personal satisfaction.

Perception. A person's view of reality.

Performance Appraisal. A four-step process used in appraising individuals. It consists of (a) establishing performance standards, (b) determining individual performance, (c) comparing performance against standards, and (d) evaluating individual performance.

Personal Characteristics. Personal factors that are often possessed by effective leaders. Some of the most commonly cited include superior intellectual ability, emotional maturity, and problem-solving skills.

Personality Test. A controversial type of test, it is designed to provide insights to the individual's personality.

Personal Need. The first step in the creative thinking process, it refers to the inner drive of the individual to be creative.

Physiological Needs. Basic physical needs, such as food, clothing, and shelter.

Planning. The formulation of objectives and steps that will be employed in attaining them.

Planning Mode. A type of strategic behavior used by organizations which employ formal planning. It is characterized by an emphasis on efficiency and growth, long-run time horizons, and a desire to work in an environment of risk.

Plural Executive Committee. A committee that has the authority to order its recommendations implemented.

Policy. A guideline to thinking and action.

Preparation. The first work stage of the creative thinking process. It involves getting ready to be creative.

Process Approach. An approach to studying management. It consists of identifying the major functions performed by the manager and then systematically studying each in depth.

Product Departmentalization. A department that is organized along product lines. General Electric, for example, uses this approach, as seen by its consumer product group. So, too, do General Motors, Ford Motor, Chrysler, and a host of other large organizations.

Project Structure. An ad hoc organization form that is used for attaining a particular objective. It is abandoned once the objective is achieved.

Rationalization. The behavioral process during which a person justifies a decision. Often this justification is a defense of the action rather than a mere explanation of it.

Reality Shock. A term used to describe what happens to people when they take their first job and find that things are not at all as they expected them to be.

Referent Power. Power based on the follower's identification with the leader.

Reliability. A term used to describe an evaluation instrument that has consistency (alternative methods of gathering the same information yield substantially similar results) and stability (the same measuring instrument will give the same results several times in a row if the characteristic it is supposed to be assessing has not changed).

Return on Equity. A financial ratio that is computed by dividing profit by stockholders' equity. This tells the firm the return it is attaining on the monies invested by the stockholders and retained from previous years' profits.

Return on Investment (ROI). A control technique used to determine how well a firm is managing its assets. In essence, the ROI computation is:

$$\frac{\text{Earnings}}{\text{Sales}} \times \frac{\text{Sales}}{\text{Total Investment}}$$

Reward Power. Power based on the ability to offer rewards in exchange for compliance.

Risk. Decision situations in which the manager has some information on the outcomes of each alternative and can formulate probability estimates based on this knowledge.

Role Analysis Technique (RAT). An OD intervention designed to clarify both role expectations and the obligations of team members.

Role Playing. A common form of training used in organizational development. It consists of the spontaneous acting out of a realistic situation involving two or more people. The purpose of the training is to acquaint one or more of the participants with the proper way of handling a given situation.

Rule. An inflexible guide to action.

Safety Needs. Needs for security, stability, and the absence of pain. These are often satisfied in organizational settings by such things as medical insurance, retirement programs, and other fringe benefits.

Scientific Management. A system of management, popularized by Frederick W. Taylor and others in the early twentieth century, that sought to develop (a) ways of increasing productivity by making work easier to perform and (b) methods for motivating workers to take advantage of these labor-saving devices and techniques.

Scientific Method. A logical problem-solving process used in identifying the problem, diagnosing the situation, gathering preliminary data, classifying the information, stating a tentative answer to the problem, and testing the answer.

Self-Actualization Needs. The desire to become more and more what one is, to become everything one is capable of becoming.

Social Needs. Needs for affiliation and interaction in which people give and receive friendship and affection. These needs are often satisfied on the job by joining informal groups.

Social Responsibility. Those social obligations that business has toward society, including equal opportunity to work and consumer and ecological considerations.

Span of Control. The number of subordinates who report to a given superior.

Staff Authority. Auxiliary authority as seen in the case of individuals who advise, assist, recommend, or facilitate organizational activities. An example is the company lawyer who advises the president on the legality of contract matters.

Strategic Objectives. Long-range objectives which the organization hopes to attain over a three- to five-year period. Illustrations include share of the market, growth, and return on investment.

Strategic Planning. The determination of an organization's major objectives, policies, and strategies that will govern the acquisition, use, and disposition of resources in achieving these objectives.

Strategy Formulation. The setting of long-range objectives and the construction of a plan to meet these objectives.

Strategy Implementation. The pursuing of the objectives which have been set in the strategy formulation stage. (*See* **Strategy Formulation.**)

Structured Interview. An interview in which specific questions are asked in a predetermined manner.

System. A combination of parts forming a complex or unitary whole.

System I. An exploitive autocratic management style in which management has little confidence in the subordinates and makes wide use of threats and punishment in getting things done.

System II. A benevolent autocratic leadership style in which management acts in a condescending manner toward the subordinates and has little trust in the latter.

System III. A consultative democratic leadership style in which management has quite a bit of confidence and trust in the subordinates; decision making tends to be delegated to some degree; and there is some confidence and trust between superior and subordinates.

System IV. A participative democratic leadership style in which management has complete confidence and trust in the subordinates; decision making is highly decentralized; communication flows up and down the hierarchy; and formal and informal organization are often one and the same.

Tall Structure. An organization structure in which there is a narrow span of control with a large number of levels in the hierarchy. (For a contrast, *see* **Flat Structure.**)

Task Concept. Planning the work of every individual at least one day in advance so that the individual receives complete written instructions describing what he or she is to accomplish as well as how the work is to be done.

Technical Skills. Skills that help an individual determine how things work. These are very important for lower-level managers such as first-line managers.

Territorial Departmentalization. The organization of a department along the lines of geographical location. An example is found in the company with four major divisions: eastern, midwestern, western, and foreign.

Theory X. A set of managerial assumptions described by Douglas McGregor which hold that people (a) dislike work, (b) have little ambition, (c) want security above all else, and (d) must be coerced, controlled, and threatened with punishment in order to attain organizational objectives through them.

Theory Y. McGregor's set of managerial assumptions which hold that (a) people working under favorable conditions will not only accept, but seek, responsibility; (b) people who are committed to organizational objectives will exercise self-control and self-direction; and (c) commitment is a function of rewards associated with goal attainment.

Top Manager. A member of the small group of executives who determine the organization's major operating decisions.

Training. The process of systematically changing behavior and/or attitudes of employees in order to increase organizational effectiveness.

Transactional Analysis (TA). A technique designed to help managers communicate with and understand their people through an analysis of their own and subordinates' behavior through transactions among them in various ego states.

Ulterior Transaction. A disguised transaction in which one message is spoken but another is actually sent.

Uncertainty. Decision situations in which managers feel they cannot develop probability estimates because they have no way of gauging the likelihood of the various alternatives.

Understanding. The second step in the communication process. It involves getting the receiver to comprehend the meaning of the transmission.

Unstructured Interview. An interview in which the interviewer may have a general direction or objective but in which the questions are not predetermined, and the interview is allowed to develop spontaneously.

Upward Communication. Communication that takes place from subordinate to superior.

Valence. A term used in expectancy/valence theory. It refers to a person's preference for a particular outcome.

Validity. A term used to describe the degree to which an instrument measures what it is supposed to measure.

Values. Those things which are important to people. Illustrations include money, power, and status.

Verification. The last step in the creative thinking process. It involves testing the solution to see if it will work or if some modification is needed.

Vertical Loading. A job enrichment principle. It involves closing the gap between the "doing" and "controlling" aspects of the job.

Vestibule Training. Training that takes place in an environment that simulates the actual work place but is often located in another area of the building or plant.

Vocational Interest Test. A test which attempts to determine an individual's preferences among different types of work.

Wide Span of Control. A span of control that is quite large, such as eight to twelve. These are typical of flat organizational structures.

Zero-Based Budgeting (ZBB). A budgeting approach in which each year is viewed as a new beginning and every manager is required to justify his or her entire budget request for the year.

Name Index

Subject Index

U

V

W

Z